"Information through Innovation"

Working with Lotus 1-2-3 for Windows

Don Barker
Gonzaga University
School of Business Administration

Jan Weingarten
Training Coordinator
Corporate Office of the Sisters of Providence

John Weingarten
Perfect Training
Spokane, Washington

Kenneth Avery
Spokane Falls Community College
Spokane, Washington

boyd & fraser publishing company

CREDITS:

Publisher: Tom Walker
Acquisitions Editor: James H. Edwards
Production Coordinator: Pat Stephan
Marketing Manager: Christopher Will
Interior Design and Composition: Custom Editorial Productions, Inc.
Cover Design: Ken Russo

 © 1993 by boyd & fraser publishing company
A Divison of South-Western Publishing Company
Danvers, MA 01923

All rights reserved. No part of this work may be reproduced or used in any form or by any means—graphic, electronic, or mechanical, including photocopying, recording, taping, or information and retrieval systems—without written permission from the publisher.

Manufactured in the United States of America

Names of all products mentioned herein are used for identification purposes only and may be trademarks and/or registered trademarks of their respective owners. South-Western Publishing Company and boyd & fraser publishing company disclaim any affiliation, association, or connection with, or sponsorship or endorsement by such owners.

Cover slide courtesy of Lotus Development Corporation

Library of Congress Cataloging-in-Publication Data

Barker, Donald, 1953–
    Working with Lotus 1-2-3 for Windows/Don Barker . . . [et al.].
       p.   cm.
    Includes index.
    ISBN 0-87835-796-3
   1. 1-2-3 for Windows. 2. Business—Computer programs. 3. Electronic spreadsheets. 4. Windows (Computer programs)
I. Title
HF5548.4.L67B375 1992
650'.0285'5369—dc20   92-7267
                                                                                                                CIP

123456MT432

PREFACE

Lotus 1-2-3 for Windows is part of a new generation of software designed to take advantage of the graphical and integrated environment of Microsoft Windows. As a result, this best-selling software is now easier to learn and easier to use, making it an even more powerful and productive tool.

Working with Lotus 1-2-3 for Windows requires little or no computer experience to learn the fundamentals of 1-2-3 for Windows. It is intended for use in a one-credit computer lab course or as a supplement to a software application class. In addition, corporate trainers will find it especially well suited for seminars or self-paced study for business users. Finally, this book should benefit anyone who wants a comprehensive introduction to Lotus 1-2-3 for Windows, the electronic spreadsheet of the 1990s.

Self-paced, hands-on tutorials help you quickly become proficient with the program's key features. Step-by-step instructions provide a smooth and enjoyable learning experience.

ABOUT THE BOOK

Working with Lotus 1-2-3 for Windows is a cumulative learning experience. It is based on the incremental development of "real-world" applications. These applications provide consistent threads throughout the book that enable the key features of 1-2-3 to be explained in a natural and logical fashion.

Instead of being exposed to a laundry list of software commands, you'll learn about the capabilities of Lotus within the context of actual projects. Thus, you'll not only discover how each command works, but, more important, how they can work together to solve problems and perform critical tasks.

The book is divided into eight chapters. The first chapter explains the concepts and skills necessary to work in the Windows environment. In Chapter 2, you'll learn to create a simple worksheet. Chapters 3 and 4 will extend your expertise by having you modify and enhance the worksheet.

Chapter 5 shows you when and how to build persuasive and dazzling graphs. Chapter 6 illustrates 1-2-3's database capabilities. Chapter 7 explores the possibilities afforded by automating 1-2-3 commands and keystrokes with macros. Macros provide a convenient and powerful way of "storing" commands that can be repeatedly issued. The final chapter teaches you how to work with multiple worksheets and worksheet files.

DISTINCTIVE FEATURES

Working with Lotus 1-2-3 for Windows has a number of attributes that clearly distinguish it from other Lotus for Windows books. The most important ones are listed below.

- *Working with Lotus 1-2-3 for Windows* is a hands-on text, designed to be used in front of a computer, at your own pace. Step-by-step tutorials let you teach yourself the power and elegance of the most popular electronic spreadsheet.
- Over 150 illustrations minimize frustration, with ample points of reference for comparing your work with the book. This visual reinforcement provides a constant reassurance that you are progressing correctly.
- "Real-world" applications incrementally build your awareness and mastery of the software. They provide an ideal medium for learning the capabilities of 1-2-3 for Windows in the context of actual projects.
- Each lesson has been extensively tested and refined to ensure clarity and reliability.
- Self-paced, hands-on lab exercises take advantage of Windows' uniform and intuitive nature, allowing you to rapidly and "painlessly" become a productive 1-2-3 user.
- You can work through this text with little or no previous computer experience. All the necessary fundamentals are skillfully demonstrated at the appropriate times.
- Every chapter begins with an overview of the material to be presented and ends with a *Coming Attractions* . . . section to prepare you for upcoming topics.

- Learning objectives spell out what you should be able to accomplish after completing each subject.
- Exercises provide reinforcement of the information introduced in the chapter tutorials. These practice problems offer a convenient way to assess your progress.
- Each chapter concludes with a set of review questions (true/false and multiple choice) to test for comprehension of important concepts.
- Three types of "signposts" alert you to potential opportunities, dangers, and points of interest. For easy recognition, they are set off by boxes and titled Hints, Hazards, and Notes.
- Key terms are defined at the end of every chapter in a glossary for quick and easy reference.
- An Instructor's Manual is available with a sample syllabus and answers to all the labs, review questions, and practice exercises.

ABOUT THE AUTHORS

Don Barker is a co-author of three popular textbooks from boyd & fraser: *Working with Windows 3*, *Working with WordPerfect for Windows*, and *Using Harvard Graphics for Business Presentations*. His credits also include *Developing Business Expert Systems with LEVEL5* and *Lotus 1-2-3, dBase III Plus, and WordPerfect: Exercises and Applications*, published by Merrill Publishing. Don is a contributing editor for the computer magazine *PCAI: Intelligent Solutions for Desktop Computers*. His other publications include an impressive list of both academic and trade articles that deal with the innovative uses of computer technology.

As Coordinator of the Computer-Assisted Learning Center in the School of Business Administration at Gonzaga University, Don is able to develop and test his textbook tutorials thoroughly before publication, ensuring a reliable and effective learning experience for the student. He holds a Masters degree in Business Administration from Eastern Washington University and has worked as a Business Development Specialist and computer consultant.

Jan Weingarten is currently Training Coordinator for the Corporate Office of the Sisters of Providence health care systems. She has been an independent WordPerfect consultant and trainer, working with corporations and law offices to adapt WordPerfect to the needs of each company. She has set up document management and training systems for large law firms in Seattle. As a result of her experience as an on-site WordPerfect troubleshooter for a major Seattle law firm, she has an in-depth perspective on the daily needs and concerns of end users. Jan is also a Certified WordPerfect Resource and is a co-author of *Working with WordPerfect for Windows*.

John Weingarten has trained hundreds of people to use WordPerfect and Lotus 1-2-3 over the past five years. John is the owner of Perfect Training, a computer training company in Spokane, Washington, specializing in WordPerfect Corporation products, as well as Lotus 1-2-3. John has written customized training materials for many of Spokane's largest companies. As a former manager of the network systems division for Computer Factory, a 50-store retail organization, and as a former general manager with PacTel Infosystems, a Fortune 500 company, John has an exceptional perspective on the personal computer industry. John is a Certified WordPerfect Resource and a co-author of *Working with WordPerfect for Windows*.

Kenneth Avery is a computer instructor at Spokane Falls Community College, where he teaches a variety of software applications courses. He is also an independent computer consultant.

ACKNOWLEDGMENTS

Don wishes to thank his wife, Chia-Ling, for her countless hours of help in editing and testing this manuscript. She was nothing short of a life saver.

Jan would like to thank Mary Suhm for her support and Sisters of Providence for their encouragement during this project.

John wishes to thank his wife, Pam, and his children, Sarah and Joshua, for putting up with him while he spent hours substituting grunts for real communication.

We also want to extend our gratitude to Bob Toshack and David Stewart for their valuable contributions. Bob's fanatical dedication to testing and checking this manuscript was instrumental in the quality of the final product.

Our thanks to Halcyon Software for their DoDot software, which helped us capture the screens for the illustrations.

Preface

Finally, without the enthusiastic encouragement of the dean, faculty, staff, and students of the School of Business Administration at Gonzaga University, this book would never have been written.

Don Barker
Jan Weingarten
John Weingarten
Kenneth Avery
March 1992

CONTENTS

CHAPTER 1   *Getting Started*   *1*

OBJECTIVES   *1*
OVERVIEW   *1*
LAB 1-1 GETTING AROUND   *2*
LAB 1-2 CONTROLLING A WINDOW   *12*
LAB 1-3 GETTING HELP   *30*
COMING ATTRACTIONS . . .   *38*

CHAPTER 2   *Creating a Worksheet*   *47*

OBJECTIVES   *47*
OVERVIEW   *47*
SPREADSHEET BASICS   *47*
LAB 2-1 GETTING AROUND IN A WORKSHEET   *50*
LAB 2-2 USING LABELS, COLUMN WIDTHS, AND RANGES   *53*
LAB 2-3 ENTERING VALUES, FORMULAS, AND @FUNCTIONS   *67*
LAB 2-4 PRINTING THE RESULTS   *78*
COMING ATTRACTIONS . . .   *85*

CHAPTER 3   *Modifying a Worksheet*   *92*

OBJECTIVES   *92*
OVERVIEW   *92*
LAB 3-1 USING SMARTICONS   *92*
LAB 3-2 EDITING DATA   *96*
LAB 3-3 MOVING DATA   *113*
LAB 3-4 COPYING DATA   *118*
LAB 3-5 PROOFING A WORKSHEET   *129*
COMING ATTRACTIONS . . .   *132*

CHAPTER 4   *Enhancing a Worksheet*   *138*

OBJECTIVES   *138*
OVERVIEW   *138*

xi

LAB 4-1 FORMATTING RANGES *138*
LAB 4-2 CHANGING CELL STYLES *143*
LAB 4-3 USING GLOBAL FORMATS AND TITLES *159*
LAB 4-4 NAMING CELL RANGES *169*
COMING ATTRACTIONS . . . *174*

CHAPTER 5 *Graphing Your Data* **180**

OBJECTIVES *180*
OVERVIEW *180*
LAB 5-1 CREATING A GRAPH *181*
LAB 5-2 ENHANCING A GRAPH *194*
COMING ATTRACTIONS . . . *204*

CHAPTER 6 *Database Applications* **211**

OBJECTIVES *211*
OVERVIEW *211*
DATABASE BASICS *211*
LAB 6-1 CREATING, EDITING,
  AND SORTING A DATABASE *212*
LAB 6-2 SEARCHING A DATABASE *218*
LAB 6-3 EXTRACTING AND DELETING RECORDS *226*
COMING ATTRACTIONS . . . *230*

CHAPTER 7 *Creating a Macro* **237**

OBJECTIVES *237*
OVERVIEW *237*
WHAT ARE MACROS? *237*
LAB 7-1 WRITING A SIMPLE MACRO *238*
LAB 7-2 ASSIGNING A MACRO TO A SMARTICON *249*
LAB 7-3 PAUSING A MACRO FOR INPUT *255*
COMING ATTRACTIONS . . . *258*

CHAPTER 8 *Working with Multiple Worksheets and Files* **263**

OBJECTIVES *263*
OVERVIEW *263*
UNDERSTANDING THREE-DIMENSIONAL
  WORKSHEETS *263*
LAB 8-1 USING MULTIPLE WORKSHEETS *264*
LAB 8-2 USING MULTIPLE WORKSHEET FILES *279*

INDEX *297*

CHAPTER 1

Getting Started

• *Objectives*

Upon completing this chapter, you'll be able to:
1. Start Windows and Lotus 1-2-3 for Windows.
2. Use the mouse to select menus, commands, and icons.
3. Control the size and placement of a window.
4. Obtain help on using Lotus 1-2-3 for Windows.
5. Quit Lotus 1-2-3 and Windows.

OVERVIEW

The tutorial labs in this chapter will teach you the fundamental concepts and skills necessary to work with Lotus 1-2-3 for Windows. Along the way, you'll also learn to use Microsoft Windows.

Lotus 1-2-3 for Windows is an electronic spreadsheet program that uses a worksheet of columns and rows to let you quickly enter and manipulate labels, numbers, and formulas. It replaces the manual operations normally done on paper with pencil, eraser, and calculator. For example, you can use Lotus 1-2-3 for Windows to prepare budgets, forecast sales, reconcile a checking account, plan investments, and estimate mortgage payments. Because Lotus 1-2-3 takes advantage of Microsoft Windows' intuitive graphical environment, you are able to create impressive top-quality documents quickly and easily.

Microsoft Windows is a **graphical user interface** (GUI) that lets you communicate with your computer by pointing at easy-to-understand menus and icons (pictures) instead of typing difficult-to-remember text commands. To master Lotus 1-2-3 for Windows, you'll need to become familiar with operations of Windows. The following material will teach you to work with the windows, icons, menus, and dialog boxes used in Lotus 1-2-3.

LAB 1-1 GETTING AROUND

In this lab, you'll begin by using a window and an icon to launch 1-2-3 for Windows. Next, you'll get a chance to select commands from a menu and pick options in a dialog box. You'll create a new worksheet, close it, and end the lab by practicing the steps in exiting Lotus 1-2-3 and Windows safely. As you perform these operations, your adeptness with the mouse will gradually improve.

Starting Windows

Your computer system may be set up to start Windows automatically when it is switched on. If this is not the case, you'll need to perform the following instructions.

1. At the DOS prompt, type: **WIN**
2. Now press the Enter key.

The first time Windows is started, it displays a screen like the one shown in Figure 1-1. Think of this screen as a **desktop**. Like the surface of an ordinary desk, it can hold a variety of objects. You can add, remove, and manipulate these items in much the same way that you handle the stuff on a real desk.

Figure 1-1. The opening screen of Windows 3.

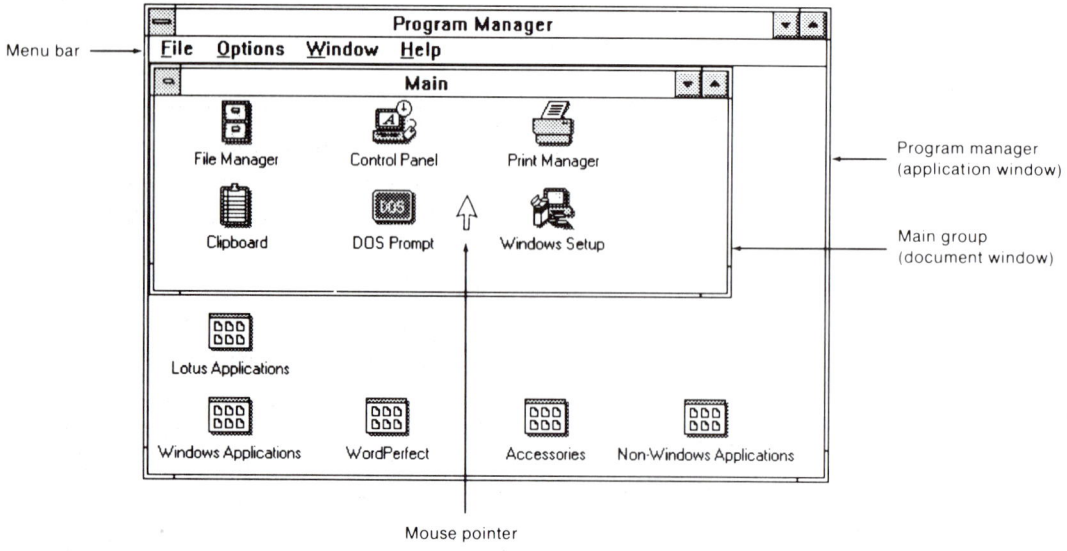

Chapter 1 Getting Started

At present, your imaginary desktop should contain the Program Manager window with the Main work group open inside it. **Program Manager** is the central staging area for all the work you'll do in Windows. It enables you to organize and launch your applications.

The Main **group window** displays the icons (small graphics with titles) for File Manager, Control Panel, Print Manager, Clipboard, DOS Prompt, and Windows Setup. These programs help you manage your computer system and the Windows environment. Other groups of applications are represented by the icons shown at the bottom of the Program Manager window.

Don't worry if your screen doesn't exactly match Figure 1-1. One of the best qualities of Windows is its ability to be customized. Previous sessions with Windows may have left different items on the desktop.

The number of icons may also vary depending on the applications currently installed on your machine. Regardless of these differences, the same basic elements are always present and you'll soon discover how to manipulate them to your own tastes.

Using the Pointer

Find the arrow-shaped **pointer** (⇨) on your screen. This mouse pointer is your means of communicating with Windows. It will change shape to indicate its current capabilities. For instance, when sizing a window, the pointer assumes the shape of a double arrow (⇔). The single arrow shape allows you to choose a command, move a window, or activate a program. Table 1-1 illustrates the various pointer shapes and their functions.

Table 1-1. Pointer shapes.

Shape	Description	Allows You to
⇨	Arrow	Select a command from the menu bar, move a window, or activate an application (program).
I	I-Beam	Enter text.
⇔	White two-headed arrow	Adjust the size of a window by "dragging" the side or corner of a window.
⧖	Hourglass	Do nothing while this shape is visible. Windows is occupied with a task requiring its full attention. You must wait until the pointer changes shape before continuing.

Table 1-1 continues on next page

Shape	Description	Allows You to
☝	Pointing hand	Jump between Help topics.
↕	Two-headed vertical arrow	Split a worksheet window vertically and resize a row.
↔	Two-headed horizontal arrow	Split a worksheet window horizontally and resize a column.
✏	Pencil	Draw freehand in a graph.
✋	Hand	Move an item in a graph.
☝	Pointing finger	Select one or more items in a graph.
+	Thin black cross	Place an item in a graph.

Your mouse controls the movements of the pointer. For instance, if you slide the mouse to the right, the pointer moves to the right. Likewise, maneuvering it to the left moves the pointer left. If you run out of room, just pick the mouse up and set it down where there is more room. Lifting the mouse has no effect on the pointer.

NOTE

The tutorial exercises in the book are designed to be completed with a mouse. For those desperate or fanatical enough, the keyboard equivalents can be found in the original Windows documentation. However, we strongly urge that you use a mouse because much of the grace and elegance of Windows is lost without it.

It's time to gain some experience in navigating around your imaginary desktop. The instructions below will take you on a brief tour. Be sure to observe how the pointer changes shape when it passes over certain objects on your screen.

1. Slide your mouse forward until the pointer rests at the top of the screen.
2. Move the pointer to the upper right corner.
3. Pull the mouse down and to the left so that the pointer moves diagonally from the upper right corner to the lower left corner of your desktop.
4. Repeat step 3, except this time start in the upper left corner and move to the lower right.
5. Now practice moving the pointer around until you feel comfortable with the mouse.

Learning to move the pointer is only half the story. To select objects on the screen, you'll also have to become familiar with the use of the left mouse button. It can be used in one of three ways: clicking, double-clicking, and dragging. **Clicking** is a single press and release, **double-clicking** is two rapid presses, and **dragging** consists of pressing and holding down the button while moving the mouse. These mouse actions can be combined with the keys on your keyboard to perform special functions such as selecting more than one item.

You can use these motions to select menus and commands to perform other interesting operations. In the next section, you'll get a chance to put these mouse actions to work.

> **NOTE**
>
> If Program Manager has been reduced to an icon in the lower portion of your screen, position your pointer on it and double-click with the left mouse button. This will restore Program Manager to a window.

Recognizing Window Types

There are two basic kinds of windows: application and document. An **application window** holds a program that is currently running. For example, Program Manager is running in an application window. A **document window** is a framed work area inside an application window. The Main group window in Figure 1-1 is a document window belonging to Program Manager. An application, such as Program Manager or Lotus 1-2-3 for Windows, can have multiple document windows. Document windows are easy to spot because, unlike application windows, they have no visible menu options.

Recognizing Icons

Icons are graphic symbols that represent collapsed windows or programs stored on disk. They are made up of a graphic and a title. The graphic and title let you easily identify the purpose of an icon.

For example, the **document icons** across the bottom of Program Manager depict windows that have been collapsed to save space. You can expand a document icon into a window by placing the mouse pointer on it and pressing the left mouse button twice rapidly.

The Main group window shown in Figure 1-1 displays the **program item icons** for starting various applications. The same double-clicking motion used to expand a document icon will load and start a program. Once an application is launched, you can reduce it to an application icon at any time.

Application icons depict programs running in the background. They can be expanded back into windows when desired. (We'll talk more about manipulating icons in Lab 1-2, *Controlling a Window*.)

Starting 1-2-3 for Windows

To start 1-2-3 for Windows from Program Manager, expand the Lotus Applications group icon into a window by double-clicking on it. Then double-click on the 1-2-3 for Windows program item icon. The pointer will change momentarily into an hourglass while Windows launches the application.

● HINT

Whenever an hourglass symbol appears on the screen, that means the computer is currently processing a command. The hourglass tells you to wait until the present action is finished before any other action can be taken.

1. Position the pointer on the document icon labeled "Lotus Applications" at the bottom of Program Manager and double-click the left mouse button.

   The group window shown in Figure 1-2 will appear.

Figure 1-2. The Application work group window.

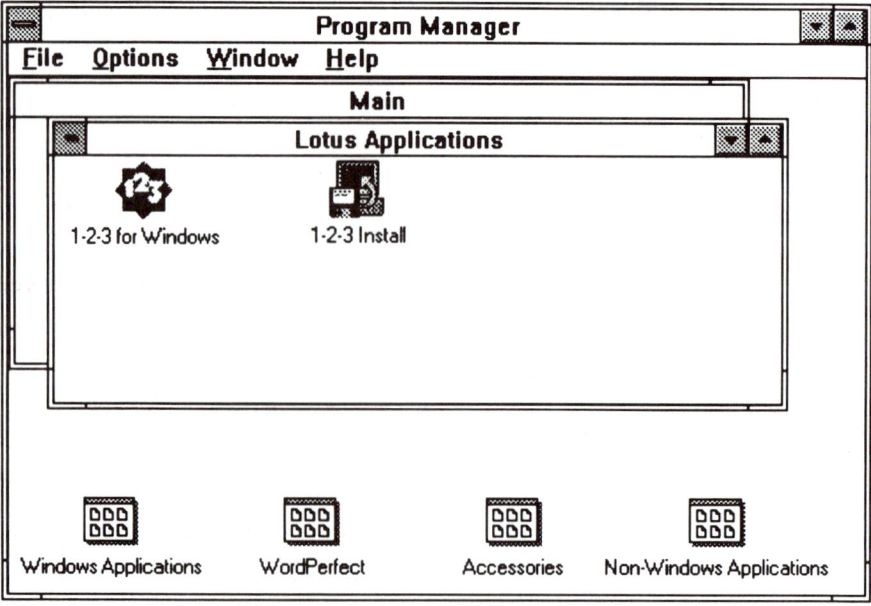

Chapter 1 Getting Started   7

2. Place the mouse pointer on the program item icon titled "1-2-3 for Windows" and double-click.

This action will cause the 1-2-3 application window to appear, as shown in Figure 1–3. Notice the document window in the workspace. It uses a series of rows and columns to form a **worksheet**. As you'll see in Chapter 2, a 1-2-3 worksheet (document window) provides a convenient means for storing and manipulating data.

Figure 1–3. The 1-2-3 application window.

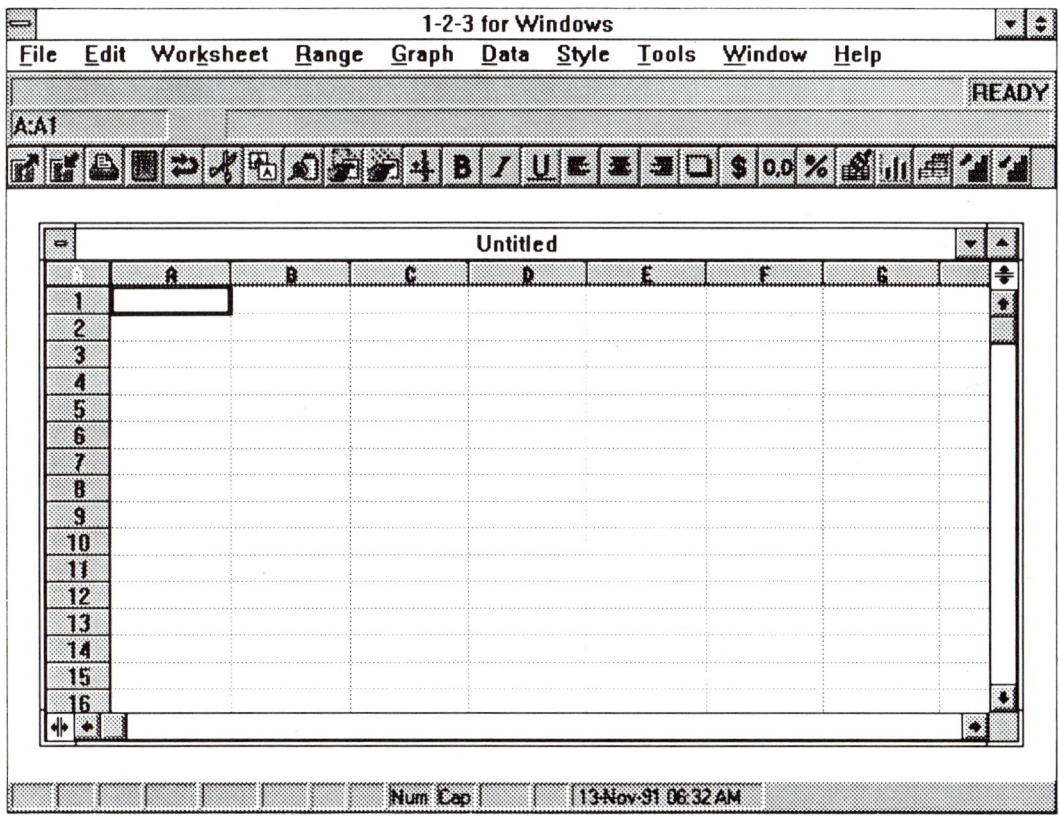

Working with Menus

A **command** is a word or phrase that instructs your computer to carry out a specific activity. Commands that are designed to achieve some collective purpose are grouped into a **menu** for convenient access. In Windows, the **menu bar,** located at the top of the application, lists the menus available for the application. The menu bar in 1-2-3 for Windows includes File, Edit, Worksheet, Range, Graph, Data, Style, Tools, Window, and Help menus.

To select a menu from the menu bar, position your pointer over the name and click. Clicking on a menu name will cause a box that contains a list of commands to drop down. To cancel the selection of a menu, simply click on the name again or click anywhere outside the drop-down menu.

You'll see how these procedures work as you perform the following steps.

1. Move the mouse so the tip of the pointer rests on the Help option in the menu bar.
2. Click the left mouse button once to trigger the drop-down menu. (If the menu doesn't appear, move the pointer so that more of the tip rests on the word "Help," and click again).
3. Move the pointer outside the menu box.
4. Click to cancel the menu.
5. Repeat steps 1 and 2 to reopen the Help menu.

Figure 1–4 displays the Help menu. **Drop-down menus** like this one observe several conventions. First, horizontal lines are used to group related options together. Second, commands are dimmed when they are unavailable. Third, checkmarks are used with toggle commands to signal they're switched on. Fourth, an ellipsis (...) after a name tells you that additional information is needed to carry out the command (e.g., *About 1-2-3...*).

To select a command from a drop-down menu, simply click on it.

6. Point at the *About 1-2-3...* option in the Help menu.
7. Click the left mouse button.

● **HINT**

A faster one-step method for selecting a command is to position the pointer on the menu name, hold the left mouse button down, drag the pointer to the desired option, and release. When you release the button, the command is executed.

Understanding Dialog Boxes

When you select a command with an ellipsis (...) following it, 1-2-3 will display a **dialog box**. A dialog box lists the options available for the

Chapter 1 Getting Started 9

command. Issuing the *About 1-2-3...* command from the Help menu caused the About 1-2-3 dialog box shown in Figure 1-5 to appear.

Figure 1-4. The menu bar in 1-2-3 contains ten drop-down menus.

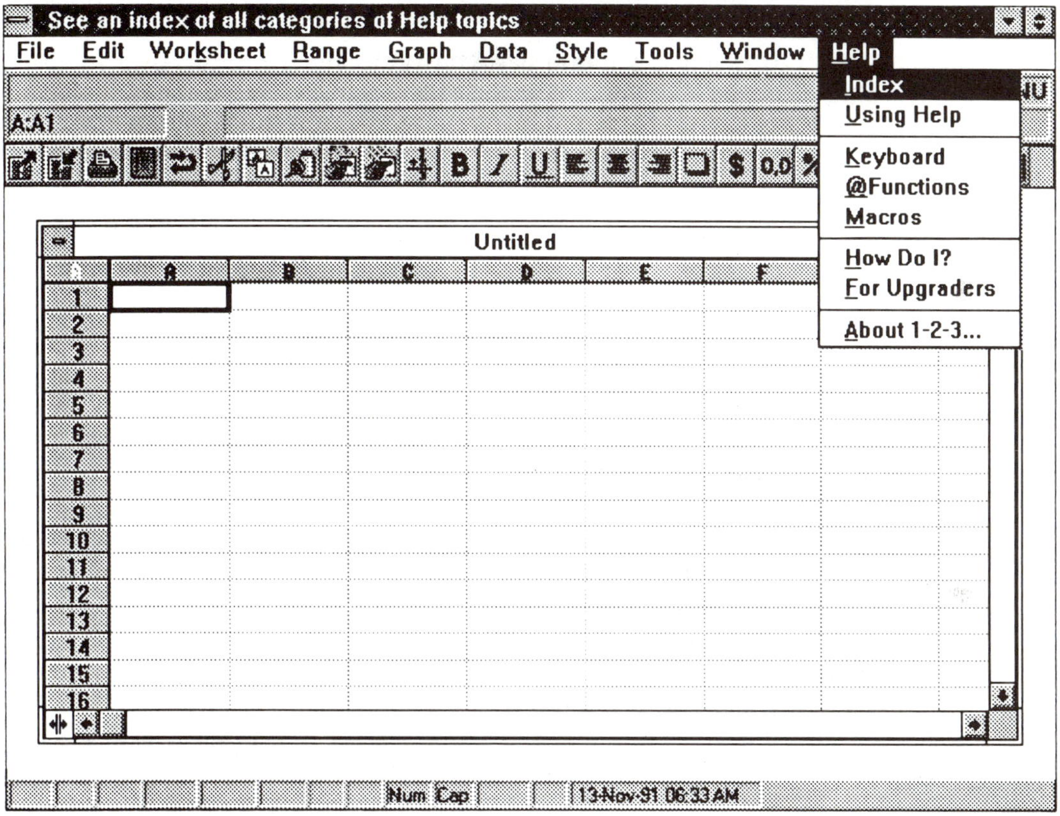

Figure 1-5. The About 1-2-3 dialog box displays the license number and release date of the program.

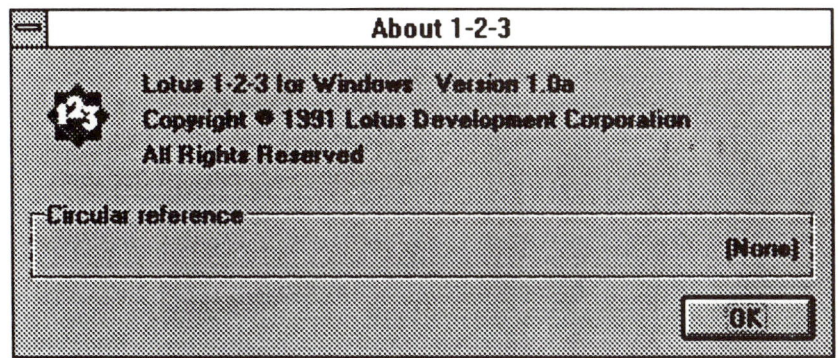

Every dialog box will contain one or more of the options described below.

- *Command buttons* carry out the command, cancel the command, or display additional options. A command button is selected by clicking on it. For example, clicking the *OK* button in the 1-2-3 dialog box will return you to Lotus 1-2-3.
- *Radio buttons* let you choose a single option from a group of options. A dot will appear in the circle of an option presently switched on. Clicking on the circle will remove the dot and toggle the option off. Clicking on an option with an empty circle places a dot in it and switches the option on.
- *Text boxes* provide an area for typing information into a dialog box.
- *List boxes* allow you to pick a single item from a list. A scroll bar will appear if the list is longer than the space available for displaying (you'll learn how to use a scroll bar in Lab 1-2). To select an item from a list box, click on it.
- *Drop-down list boxes* serve the same function as a standard list box, except they don't display a list until instructed to. Initially, a drop-down list box shows only the current default selection in a text box. Clicking the down arrow button on the text box will cause the list box to fold down. You can then select a different item from the list by clicking on it.
- *Check boxes* let you turn the options on or off. An × will appear in the box of an option currently toggled on. Clicking on the box will remove the mark and switch the option off. Clicking it again will toggle the option back on.

Since the About 1-2-3 dialog box is meant only to display, not gather, information, it makes use of only one of these options. Once you have finished examining the dialog box, click the *OK* button to return to 1-2-3 for Windows.

1. Position the pointer over the *OK* command button in the About 1-2-3 dialog box.
2. Click the left mouse button once.

Quitting 1-2-3 for Windows

You quit 1-2-3 by choosing the *Exit* command from the File menu.

Chapter 1 Getting Started 11

1. Open the File menu.
2. Now click on the *Exit* command near the bottom of the drop-down menu.

Ending a Windows Session

Always quit Windows from Program Manager. This will guarantee you an opportunity to save any work you neglected to store on disk earlier.

To end a Windows session, first choose the *Exit Windows...* command from the File menu in Program Manager.

1. Click on *File* in the menu bar of Program Manager.
2. Click on the command *Exit Windows....*

Figure 1-6.

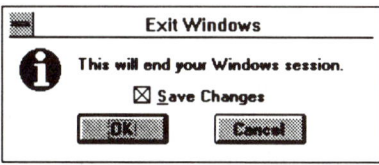

The dialog box shown in Figure 1-6 will appear. Windows is making sure you really want to quit. Clicking on the *OK* button in the dialog box will end the Windows session and return you to the DOS prompt. Selecting the *Cancel* button will nullify the *Exit Windows...* command and return you to Program Manager.

By default, Windows will save the changes you have made to its environment (e.g., showing the Accessory group window open). However, you can tell Windows to "forget" these alterations by removing the X from the *Save Changes* check box in the Exit Windows dialog box. To switch off the *Save Changes* check box, simply click on it and the check mark will disappear.

During this course, you should always make sure this setting is disabled before ending a Windows session. Switching this option off causes Windows to retain its original look and feel for the next user, thus lessening the possibility of confusion by leaving a "fresh" and familiar environment to come back to.

3. If the *Save Changes* check box is toggled on (contains an X), then click on the check box to switch it off.
4. Click on the *OK* button to end the session.

When the DOS prompt appears, you can safely shut your computer system down.

⊘ **HAZARD**

Never turn off your computer before exiting Windows. This will cause the changes you've made to Windows, plus any other work not yet saved, to be lost.

LAB 1-2 CONTROLLING A WINDOW

In this lab, you'll be formally introduced to the elements of a window. You'll learn to use these elements to collapse, expand, restore, move, size, and close a window. These techniques will assist you in controlling, organizing, and using 1-2-3 for Windows.

Recognizing the Elements of a Window

Although we've casually peeked through a window or two, it's now time to take a closer look inside. As you have seen, a window is a boxed area where applications run, worksheets display, and other activities occur. Figure 1-7 illustrates the common components of a window. Some of these parts may be familiar, while others, no doubt, are new to you. Take a moment to study the following descriptions.

- The **frame** is the border around the outside of a window.
- The **control-menu box**, in the upper left corner of a window, closes a window. (It also provides keyboard users with a menu for moving, sizing, minimizing, maximizing, closing, and switching between windows.)
- The **title bar** displays the name of the application or worksheet. It is positioned at the top of a window. When more than one window is open on the desktop, the title bar of the active window (the one you're working with) will have a different color or intensity from the others.
- The **menu bar** lists the menus available for a particular window. You'll find it just below the title bar. Most menu bars contain a File menu, Edit menu, and Help menu.
- The **maximize box**, in the upper right corner of a window, expands a window to its maximum size. Windows applications enlarge to cover the entire desktop, while worksheet windows can only grow to the borders of an application. After a window is expanded, the maximize box becomes a restore box. You can use it to return the window to its previous dimensions.

Figure 1-7. The common parts of a window.

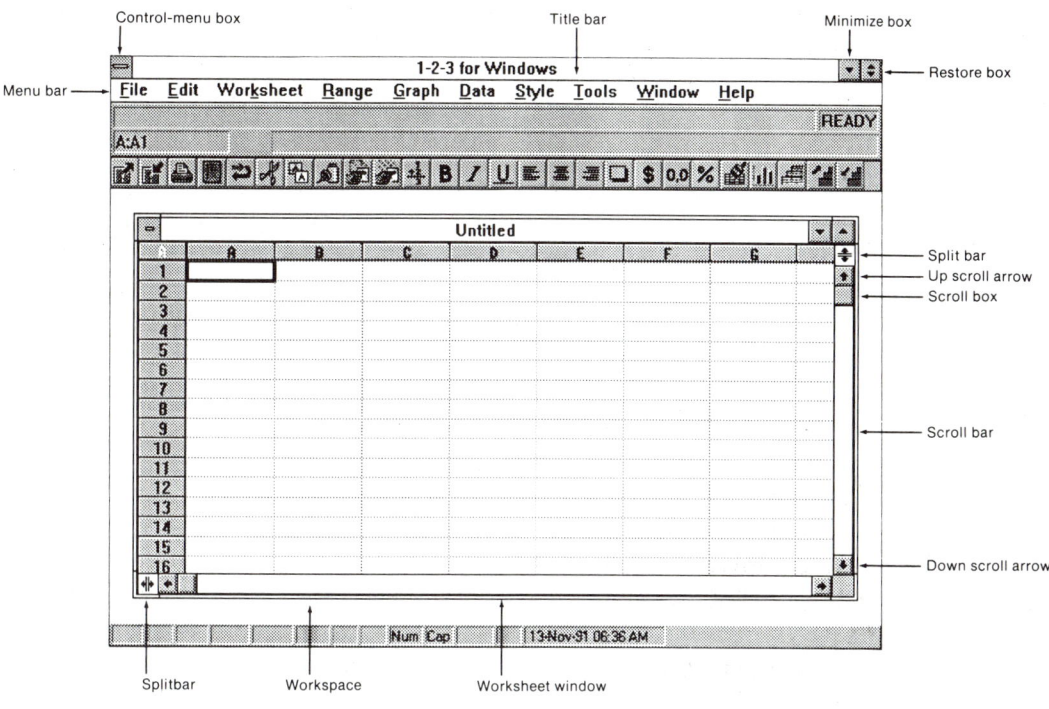

- The **minimize box**, just left of the maximize box, reduces a window to an icon.
- **Scroll bars**, located along the bottom and right side of a window, allow you to view parts of a worksheet too large to fit in a window.
- The **split box**, positioned just above and below the vertical scroll bar, lets you split a window into two separate panes for simultaneously viewing different portions of the same worksheet.
- The **workspace**, in the center area of a window, is where most of the work on an application is carried out.

These elements of a window provide you with a great deal of control over your desktop environment. They let you organize and arrange the way things are displayed. The following exercises will give you an opportunity to practice manipulating them.

Scrolling the Contents of a Window

To scroll a window, drag the scroll box along the scroll bar to a position that corresponds approximately with the location you want to view (e.g., top, middle, or bottom). Let's use this technique for viewing various portions of your worksheet.

1. Start Windows.
2. If Program Manager has been reduced to an icon, double-click on it.
3. Launch 1-2-3 for Windows from the Lotus Applications group.
4. Point at the down arrow button on the vertical scroll bar and click once.

Notice the worksheet scrolls up one row.

5. To scroll up one more row, click on the same down arrow again.
6. Point at the same scroll arrow, but this time hold down the mouse button until you reach row 32.

Rows 17 through 32 in your worksheet should be visible, as shown in Figure 1-8. This method of scrolling works well for moving around a small area of your worksheet. However, you can move rapidly through a worksheet by simply dragging a scroll box in the direction you want to travel.

7. To see the top of your worksheet again, point at the scroll box, press and hold down the left mouse button, slide the scroll box to the top of the bar, and release the button.
8. To move quickly down your worksheet, press and hold down the left mouse button, slide the scroll box to the bottom of the scroll bar, and release the button.
9. Now, point at the scroll box in the scroll bar located along the bottom of your worksheet, press and hold down the left mouse button, slide the scroll box all the way to the right, and release the mouse button.

Your worksheet will come to rest against column AP row 121. Your worksheet actually extends much farther in both directions. (We'll talk more about the size and layout of worksheets in Chapter 2.) Another useful technique for viewing a large worksheet is to "page" through its contents. The scroll bar will let you jump one screen at a time.

Chapter 1 Getting Started **15**

Figure 1-8. The scroll bars let you move quickly around your worksheet.

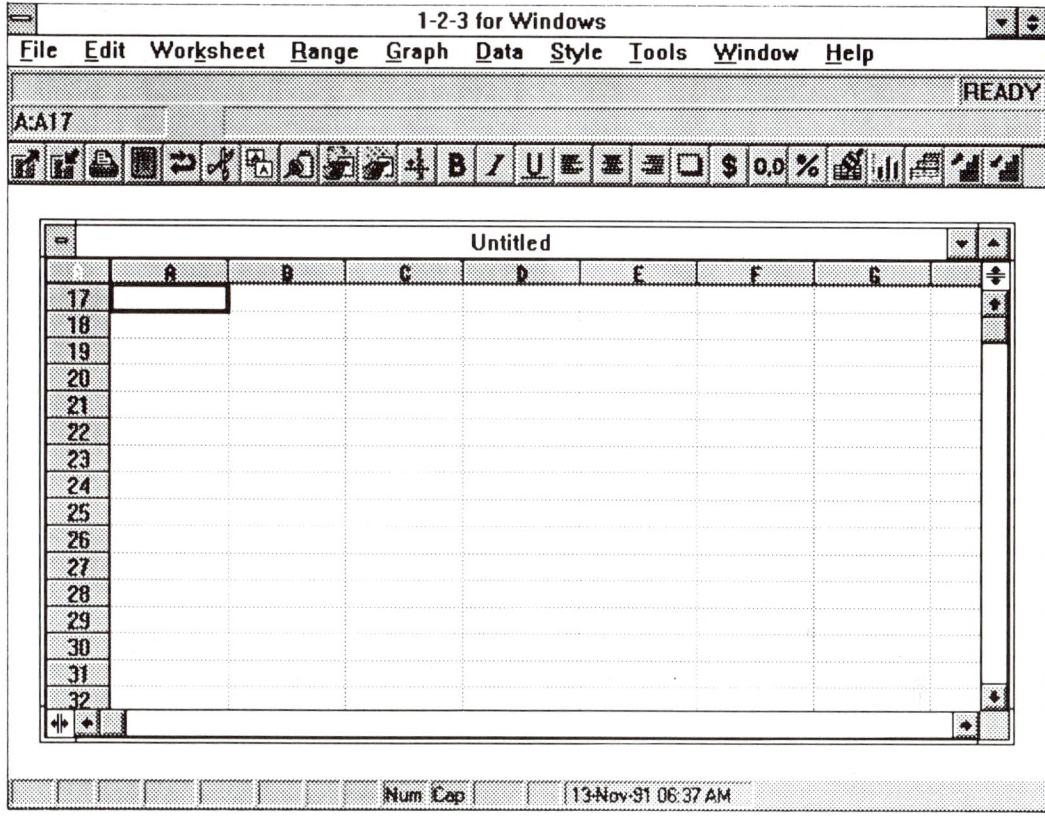

10. Position the pointer above the scroll box in the vertical scroll bar and click twice.

    Observe that the scroll box jumps position twice, causing the worksheet to scroll up two pages.

11. To view the top left portion of your worksheet again, drag the scroll box in the vertical scroll bar to the top and release it. Then drag the scroll box in the horizontal scroll bar all the way to the left and release it.

    You can use the same actions to scroll through any other window or list box that contains a scroll bar. The table below summarizes the scroll bar actions.

TO SCROLL	ACTION
One row at a time	Click one of the scroll arrow buttons.
Multiple rows or columns	Point at one of the scroll arrows and hold down the left mouse button.
One screen at a time	Click on one side or the other of the scroll box.
To a variable location	Drag the scroll box in the direction you want to view.

Splitting a Worksheet Window

You can simultaneously view different sections of a worksheet by splitting its window into two panes. A worksheet can be split either vertically or horizontally. The two resulting panes are separated by a split bar. Since each window pane will have scroll bars, you can individually adjust the panes to provide different views of the same worksheet. This is a handy feature when you need to compare or update one portion of a worksheet with another.

To split a worksheet into top and bottom panes, position the pointer on the split box, located just above the vertical scroll bar, press and hold down the left mouse button, drag the split box down to where you want the split, and release it.

1. Move the mouse pointer over the split box at the top of the vertical scroll bar. (It will assume the black two-headed vertical arrow shape.)
2. Press and hold down the left mouse button.

    A split bar will appear.

3. Drag the split bar down to roughly the center of your worksheet window and release it.

You should now have two approximately equal window panes, as illustrated in Figure 1-9. To adjust the location of the split bar, position the pointer anywhere on the split bar, drag it to where you want the split, and release it.

4. Place the pointer over the split bar (the black two-headed vertical arrow shape will appear when it is in the correct position).
5. Drag the split bar to within approximately 1 inch of the button of the worksheet window and release it.

Chapter 1 Getting Started

Figure 1-9. The split bar lets you divide a document window into two separate window panes.

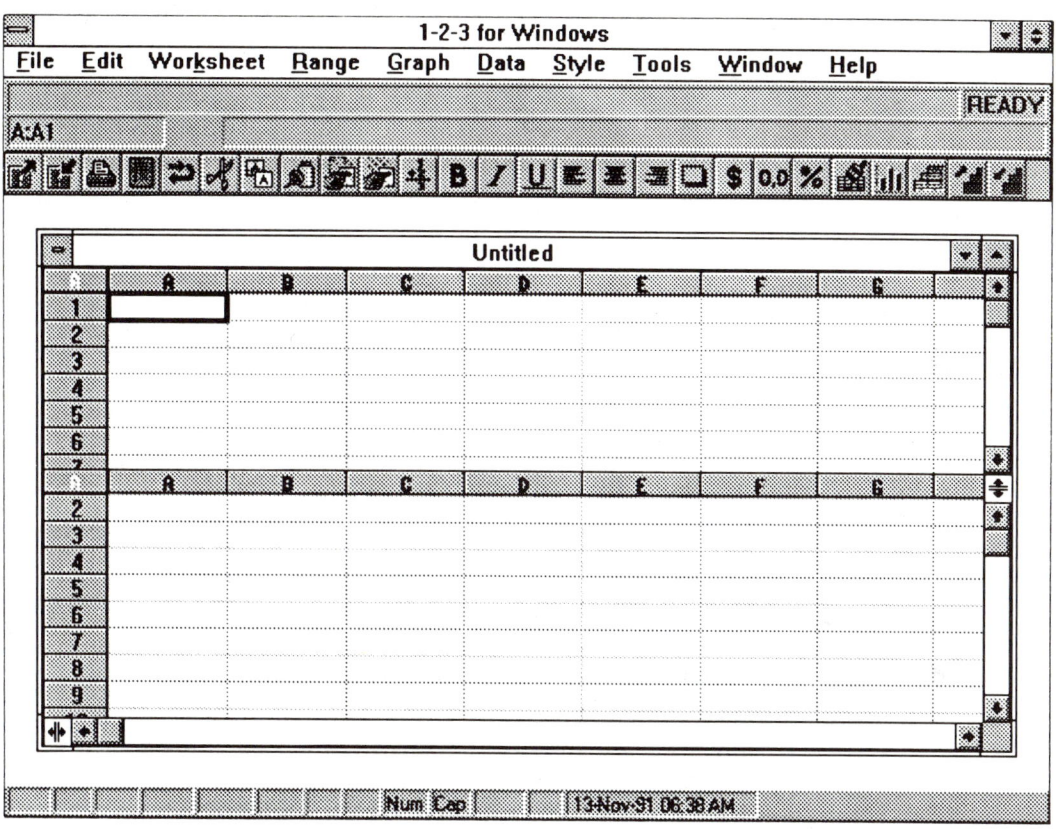

You close the extra pane by moving the split bar all the way to either the top or bottom of the worksheet window.

6. Drag the split bar to the bottom of the worksheet and release it.

To split the worksheet into a left and right pane, grab the split box located to the far left of the horizontal scroll bar, drag the split bar to the spot where you want the window split, and release it.

7. Move the mouse pointer over the split box at the far left of the horizontal scroll bar. (It will assume the black two-headed horizontal arrow shape.)
8. Press and hold down the left mouse button.

The split bar will appear.

9. Drag the split bar right to roughly the middle of your worksheet window and release it.

Feel free to experiment with using the scroll bars in either window pane to scroll to a different position in your worksheet.

10. When you are done exploring, close the extra pane by dragging the split bar all the way left or right and releasing it.

Creating a New Worksheet Window

When you create a new worksheet window in 1-2-3, it will appear in the foreground of your workspace, partially (or entirely) obscuring any existing worksheets. However, the worksheets created earlier will remain open and available for use. This allows you to have multiple worksheets open at the same time. To create a new worksheet window, select the *New* command from File menu.

1. Open the File menu.
2. Click on the command *New*.

After completing the command, a second worksheet window will appear with the title bar displaying the name "FILE0001.WK3." Lotus 1-2-3 automatically assigns each new worksheet the default name "FILE" and the file extension .WK3. The number following the assigned name reveals the order in which the worksheet was created (e.g., 0001, 0002, 0003, etc.).

Arranging Worksheet Windows

When you need to work with two or more worksheet windows at the same time, you can use the *Tile* and *Cascade* commands in the Window menu (see Figure 1-10) to arrange them. The *Tile* command will organize all open worksheet windows so they occupy an equal area of the workspace. This arrangement is convenient for transferring information from one worksheet to another or comparing the contents of several worksheets.

The *Cascade* command will layer all open worksheet windows so that their title bars are visible. This stacked approach makes it easy to switch between worksheet windows quickly.

At present, you have two worksheet windows open—Untitled and FILE0001.WK3. The Untitled window, however, is hidden behind

Chapter 1 Getting Started **19**

Figure 1-10.

FILE0001.WK3. Let's use the *Tile* command to display both windows fully.

1. Select the *Tile* command from the Window menu.

Issuing this command will cause the two worksheet windows to appear, sharing equally the available workspace, as shown in Figure 1-11. FILE0001.WK3 occupies the left half, while the Untitled worksheet window is displayed in the right half.

2. To see the two windows in a stacked formation, issue the *Cascade* command from the Window menu.

Figure 1-11. The *Tile* command in the Window menu arranges document windows so that each shares an equal portion of the workspace.

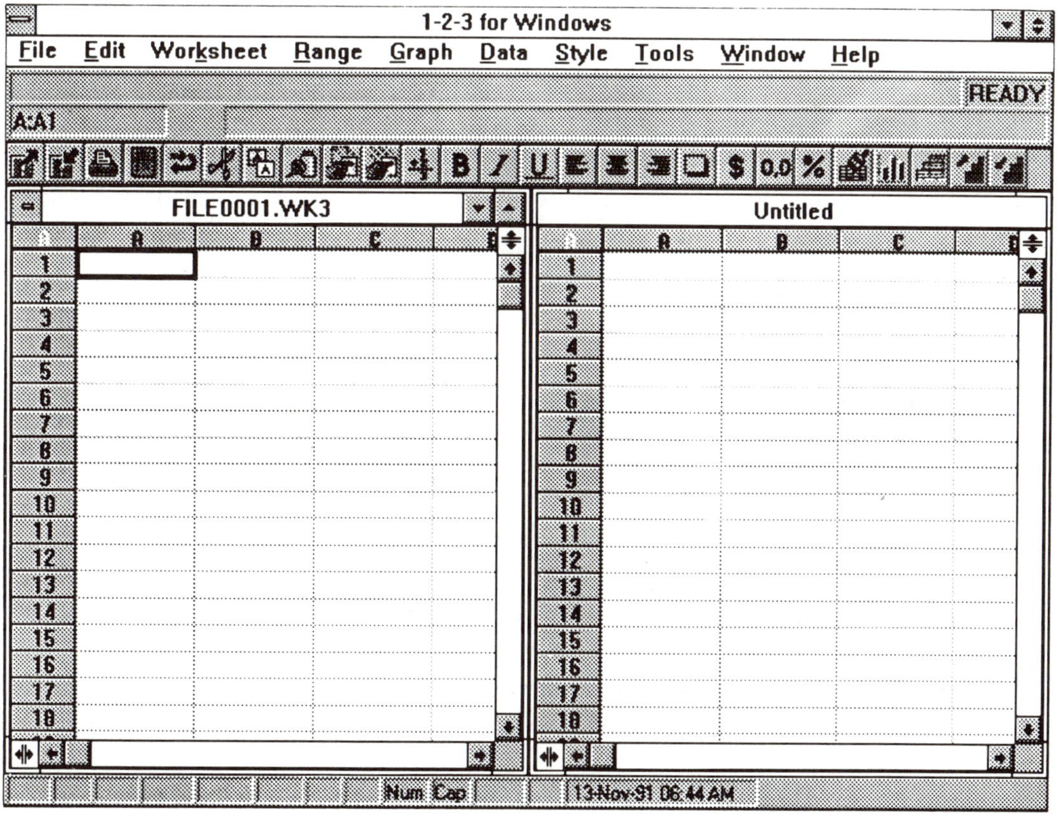

Compare your screen with the one pictured in Figure 1-12. The two worksheet windows are now layered. Observe that only the title bar for the Untitled worksheet is exposed.

Figure 1-12. The *Cascade* command in the Window menu stacks document windows so the title bar of each is visible.

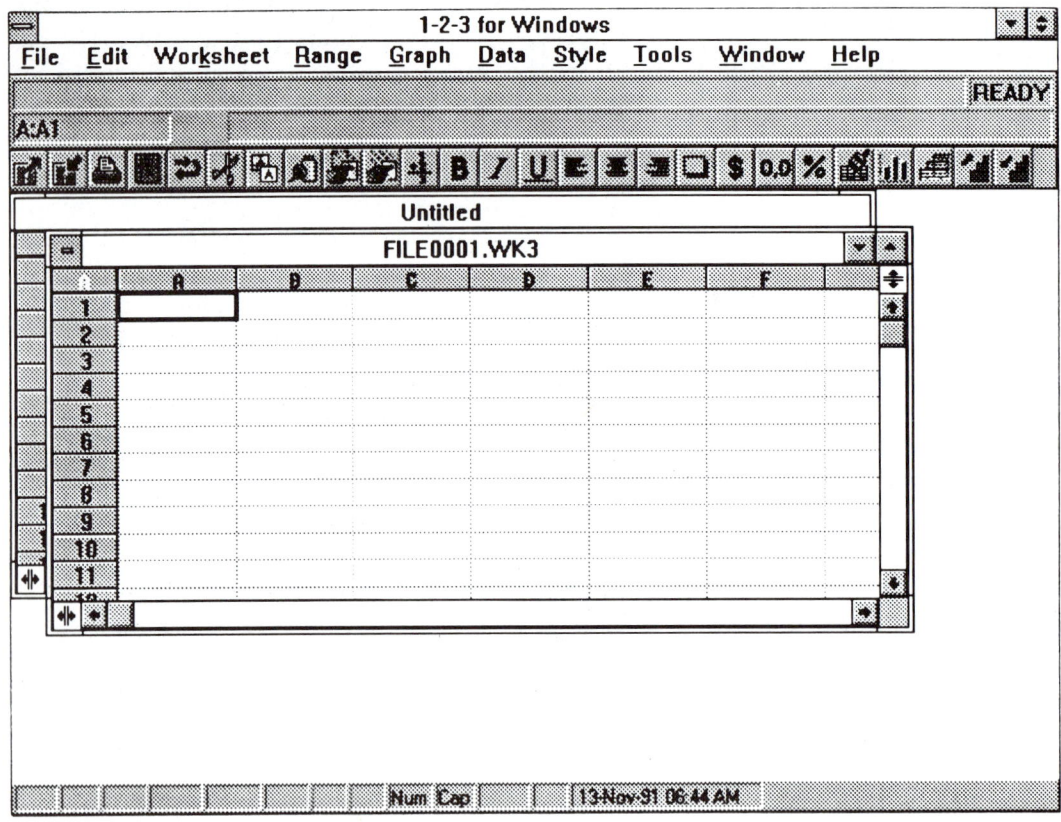

NOTE

The Windows' utility Task List offers the same commands for arranging application windows. You can summon Task List by double-clicking any empty area of the desktop.

Selecting a Window

In Windows, the window you are currently working with is called the **active window**. Only one worksheet or application window can be active at a time. The active window will typically display a title bar with a color different from the other windows.

To make a different window active, you simply select it. You select a window by either clicking on it or picking it from a menu. Let's practice both of these procedures by using your two worksheet windows.

1. To make the Untitled window active, click on its exposed title bar.

The Untitled worksheet will come to the foreground, partially obscuring the FILE0001.WK3 window. Its title bar will change color to signify it is the active window.

2. Click on the exposed lower portion of the FILE0001.WK3 window.

This worksheet again becomes the active window and comes into clear view. Sometimes a window you want to work with is totally hidden by other windows. In 1-2-3, you can use the Window menu to select any open worksheet window even if it's not currently visible.

3. To select the Untitled worksheet, open the Window menu.

Notice that FILE0001.WK3 has a check mark in front of it. This indicates it is the active window. You make the Untitled worksheet the active or current window by clicking on that menu option.

4. Now, click on the Untitled option in the Window menu to make it the current worksheet.

Once this command is completed, the Untitled window again comes into the foreground. If you open the Window menu, you'll see that the check mark in front of FILE0001.WK3 has been removed and placed in front of the Untitled worksheet.

NOTE

You can also use the Windows' utility Task List to select an application window. Just issue the *Switch To...* command from the control-menu box of any application window and then choose the desired program from the list box in Task List.

Collapsing a Window to an Icon

Just like the surface of a real desk, your Windows desktop and 1-2-3 workspace can become cluttered. As you open more windows, the available space diminishes.

Fortunately, Windows provides a convenient way to shrink applications and worksheets without closing them. If you click on the minimize box of a window, it will be reduced to an icon. As icons, applications continue to run in the background without consuming as much space on your desktop. Worksheets reduced to icons also remain in memory and are available for immediate use.

To gain experience in minimizing windows, follow these steps.

1. Move the pointer so it's over the minimize box in the upper right corner of the Untitled worksheet window.
2. Click once to reduce the window to an icon.
3. To shrink FILE0001.WK3 to an icon, click on its minimize box.

Your screen will resemble the one portrayed in Figure 1-13. Both worksheet windows now reside as icons in the lower left corner of your workspace. In their reduced state, they take up little room.

Figure 1-13. Worksheet windows can be reduced to icons to conserve on workspace.

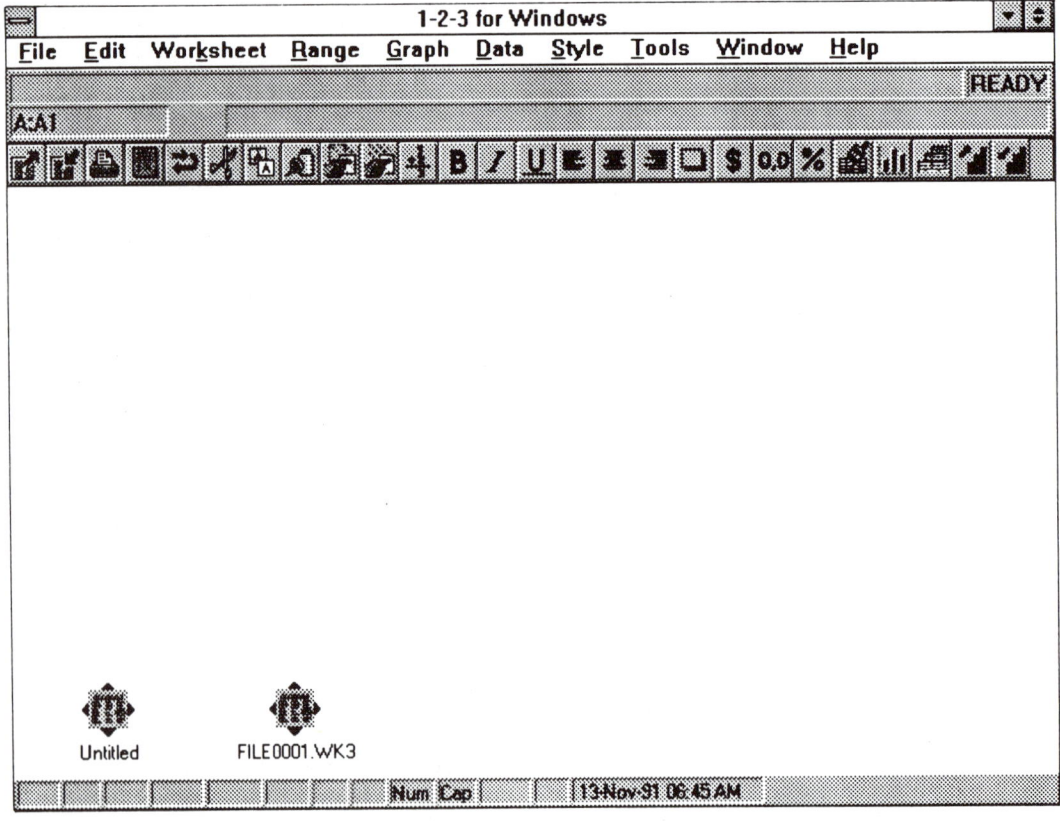

Chapter 1 Getting Started

4. To reduce 1-2-3 to an application icon, click on its minimize box in the far upper right corner of your screen.

Figure 1-14 displays the Program Manager window and the 1-2-3 application icon in the lower left corner.

Figure 1-14. Application windows can also be shrunk to application icons to save room on your desktop.

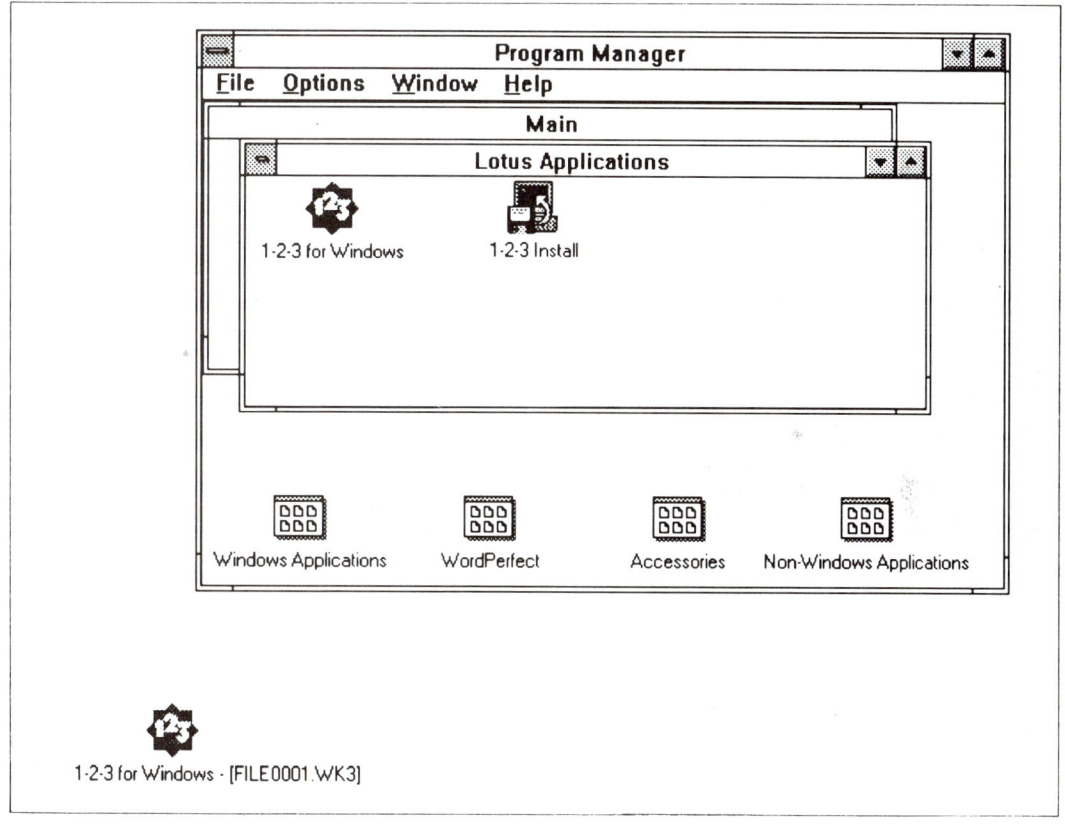

Expanding an Icon to a Window

To expand an icon into a window, simply double-click on it. If you click too slowly, the control-menu will pop up. Then to complete the expansion process, you must either double-click on the icon again or select the *Restore* command from the control-menu.

1. Point at the 1-2-3 application icon in the lower left corner of your desktop.
2. Double-click to expand the icon to a window.

3. Point at the Untitled document icon in the lower left corner of 1-2-3.
4. Double-click to expand it to a window.
5. Double-click on the FILE0001.WK3 icon.

1-2-3 will expand to cover the desktop again, and the two worksheet windows will enlarge to their original size and location.

⊘ HAZARD

If you accidentally double-click on the 1-2-3 program item icon in the Lotus Applications group window, you'll receive a warning that you cannot start more than one copy of the specified program. Just click *OK* to acknowledge the message and perform step 1 above.

Enlarging a Window

When you are working with a single application or a program such as 1-2-3, you'll want it to display as much detail as possible. By default, 1-2-3 occupies your entire desktop. A worksheet window can be expanded to fill the entire workspace of an application. You enlarge a window by clicking on its maximize box.

1. Place your pointer over the maximize box in the upper right corner of the FILE0001.WK3 worksheet window.
2. Click once to enlarge the window.

The FILE0001.WK3 window will expand to fill the entire workspace while the Untitled window disappears. However, the Untitled worksheet remains in your workspace, hidden behind the full-blown FILE0001.WK3.

Reducing a Window

When you expand a window to cover the whole screen, the maximize box becomes a restore box. Clicking on the restore box will cause a window to return to its previous size and location.

1. Move the pointer so that it rests on the restore box (the one with a double arrow in the far upper right corner) of the 1-2-3 window.
2. Click once.

1-2-3 will assume a medium size on your desktop, as shown in Figure 1–15. Notice that the application window now possesses four borders. Its title bar also displays the name of the enlarged worksheet window because the title bar of the worksheet is no longer visible.

Figure 1–15. The restore box reduces a window to its previous size.

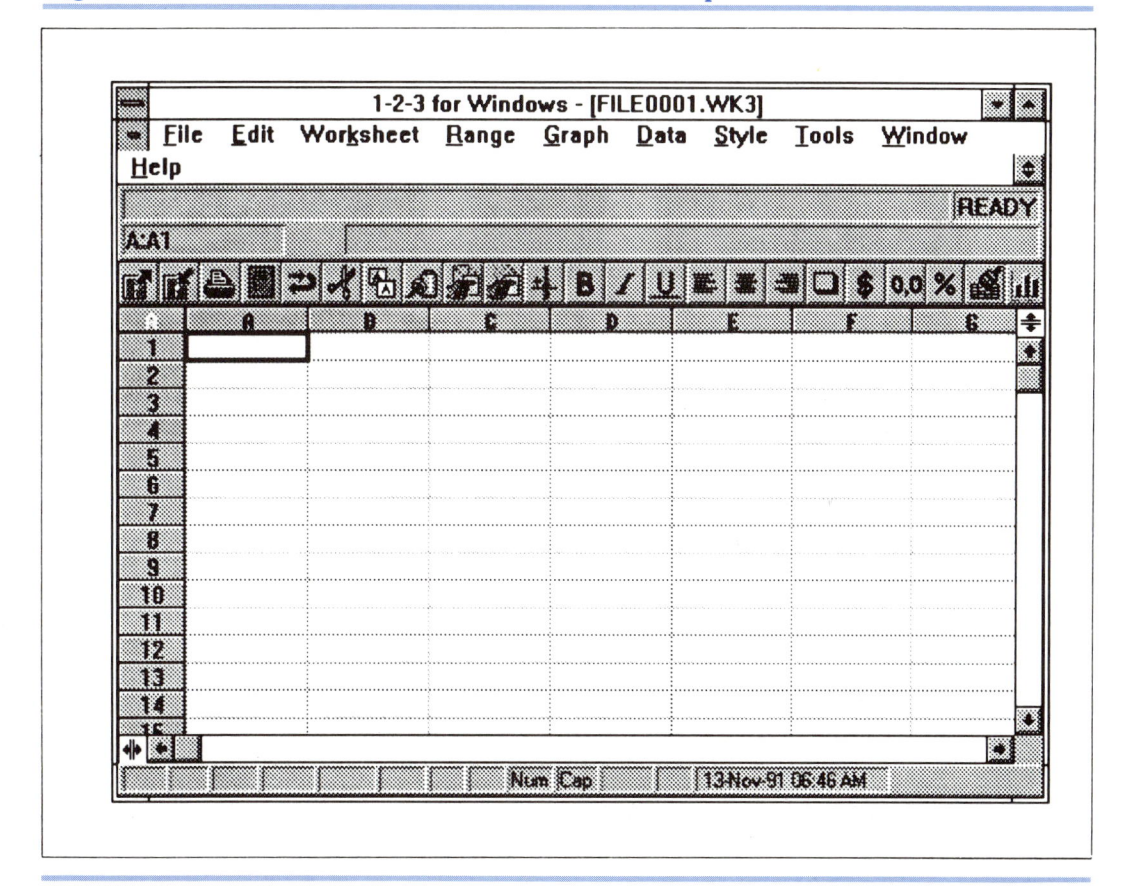

Moving a Window

When you want to view more than one window at a time, you'll need to rearrange your desktop. Windows makes this task easy by allowing you to move both application and worksheet windows manually. An application window can be repositioned anywhere on your desktop, while the movement of a worksheet window is restricted to the borders of 1-2-3.

To move a window, you just drag it to a new location by pointing at the title bar and holding down the left mouse button, then releasing the mouse button when you reach the desired spot. As you drag it, an outline will appear to help you determine the space it will occupy when released. Let's see if we can move the 1-2-3 and Program Manager windows so that both are visible (see Figure 1-16).

Figure 1-16. Windows are easy to move with the mouse.

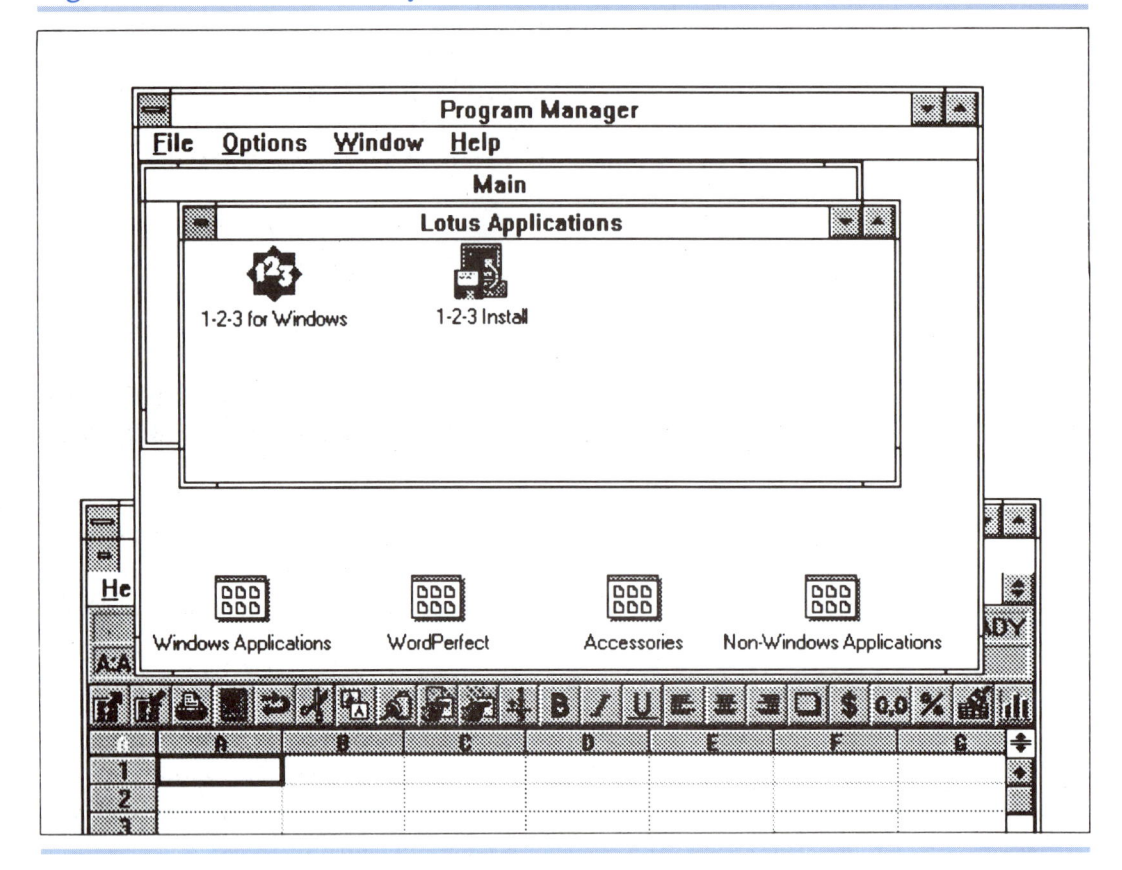

1. Position the pointer on the title bar of the 1-2-3 application window.
2. Press and hold down the left mouse button and drag the window outline down toward the bottom of your desktop so that only about half the window remains visible.
3. Release the left mouse button to fix the window in the new position.
4. Now move the Program Manager window to the top of your desktop.

Your screen should loosely resemble the one shown in Figure 1-16. 1-2-3 and Program Manager may be arranged differently, but notice there is simply insufficient room to display both of the applications.

Sizing a Window

Resizing a window offers another means to make more room on your desktop or within a workspace of an application window. You can resize a window by using your mouse to grab a side or corner and drag it. The first step in this process (and the most tricky) is to place the pointer so it exactly straddles a side or corner of a window. You'll know the pointer is in the correct position when it changes shape.

If you are adjusting the sides, the pointer will look like this: ⇔ When you are moving the top or bottom borders, the pointer looks like this: ↕ Positioning the pointer on the corner of a window lets you change its height and width simultaneously.

Let's see how this works by sizing the 1-2-3 and Program Manager windows so they both fit on your desktop.

1. Click on 1-2-3 to make it the active window and bring it to the foreground.
2. Move it to the center of the desktop by pointing at the title bar, holding down the left mouse button, and dragging the window to the desired position.
3. Position the pointer in the lower right corner of the 1-2-3 window. (You'll know the pointer is in the right location when it changes to a slanted double arrow.)
4. Press and hold down the left mouse button. Move the mouse so the 1-2-3 window shrinks in size.
5. When the window is roughly 3 inches wide and 3 inches high, release the mouse button.
6. Move the 1-2-3 window to the lower right corner of the desktop (or to a place where it doesn't overlap the Program Manager window).
7. Now repeat the same process to resize the Program Manager and reposition both application windows to match Figure 1-17.

Both 1-2-3 and Program Manager should be in clear view. Moving and sizing windows offer a powerful combination for customizing your desktop or workspace. To see how these techniques can be used to organize your workspace, complete the following steps.

8. Expand the 1-2-3 window to cover the entire desktop by clicking its maximize button.
9. To expose the border of the FILE0001.WK3 window, click its restore button in the upper right corner of the window.

FILE0001.WK3 will return to its previous size.

Figure 1-17. Sizing and moving windows provide a powerful combination to organize your desktop.

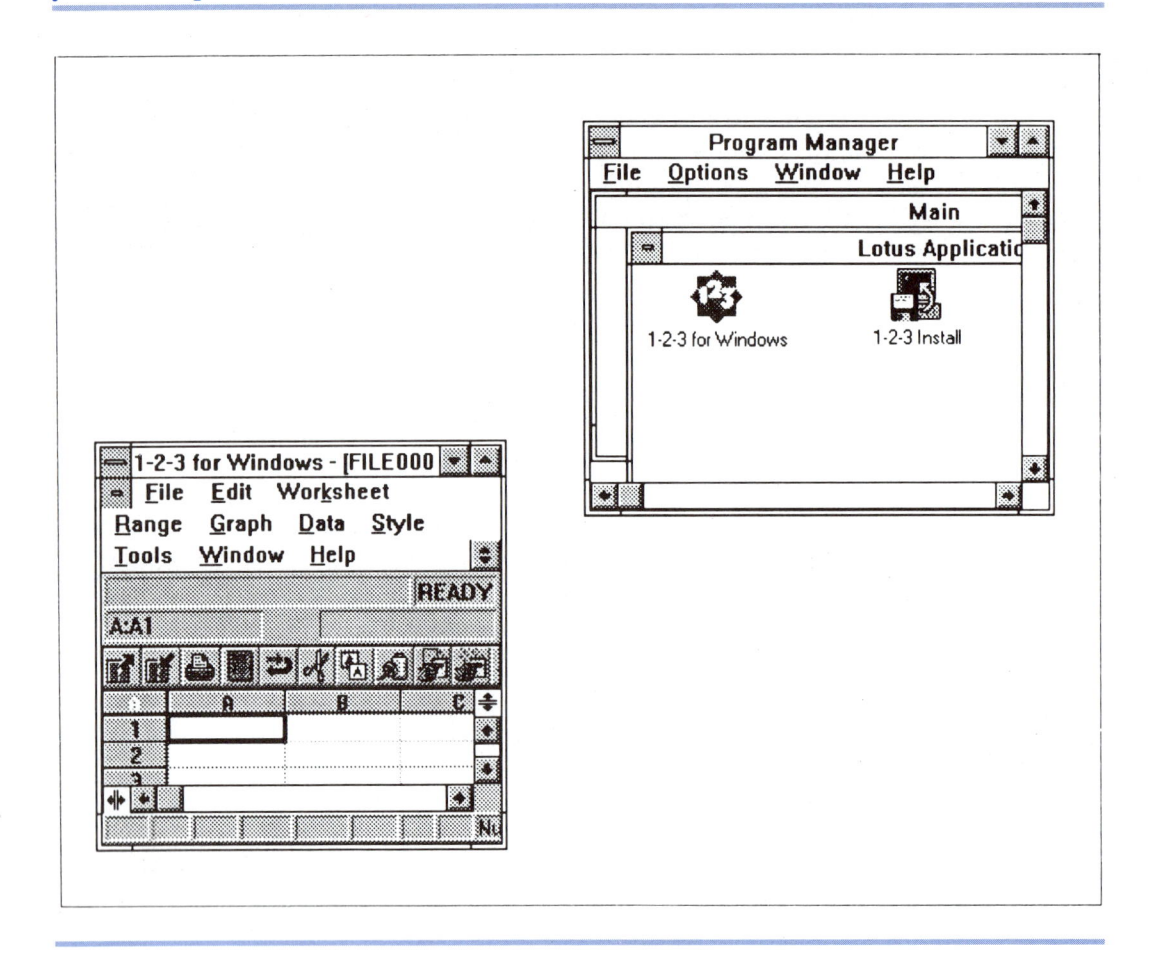

10. Grab the left border of the FILE0001.WK3 window and drag it to the left until the window is only about 2 inches wide.
11. Click on the Untitled worksheet to make it the active window and resize it to match the FILE0001.WK3 window.
12. Finally, reposition both worksheets to match those pictured in Figure 1-18.

As you learn to use more applications and worksheets, you'll find that these procedures will be extremely helpful in managing your work.

Closing a Window

Double-clicking on the control-menu box of a window will close it. However, in the case of an application window, it is always better to

Chapter 1 Getting Started **29**

Figure 1-18. You can also size and move worksheet windows to organize your workspace.

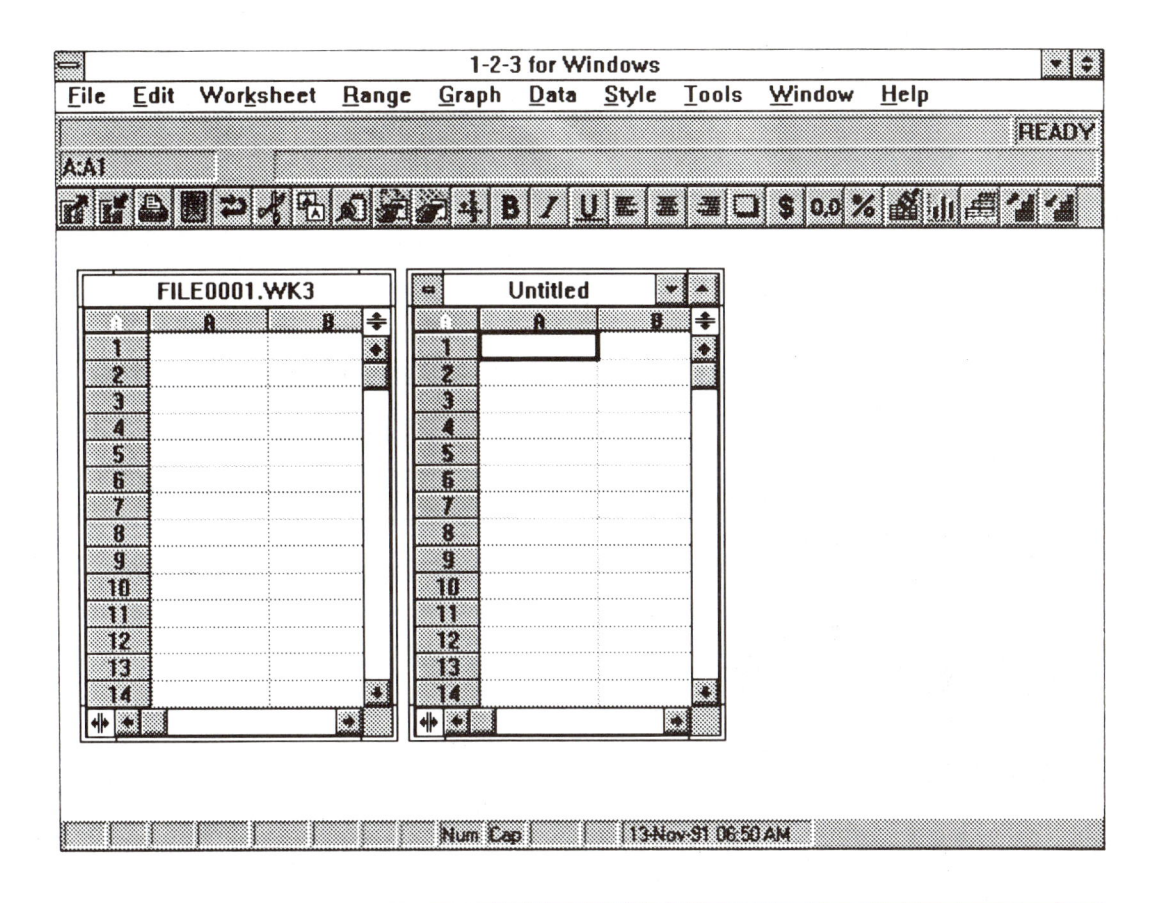

quit by selecting the *Exit* command from the File menu. Closing an application clears it from your desktop, but the program may continue to occupy space in memory. Worse yet, some applications close without saving your work!

Closing is a fast and convenient way to clear away windows when you're sure there is nothing to be lost. The worksheet windows in 1-2-3 are safely closed by double-clicking on their control-menu boxes.

1. To close the FILE0001.WK3 window, double-click on its control-menu box.

You can also close the active Untitled window by choosing the *Close* command from the File menu. If you've made changes in the worksheet since the last time you saved it, 1-2-3 will ask if you want to save before closing.

2. To close the current worksheet window, open the File menu and click on the *Close* command.

Since 1-2-3 assumes you want to work on a fresh worksheet, another Untitled window will appear to replace the closed one.

3. To end your Windows sessions, select the *Exit Windows...* command from the File menu in Program Manager, toggle off the *Save Changes* check box, and click the *OK* button.

LAB 1-3 GETTING HELP

Getting help when you encounter a problem can save you both frustration and time. In this lab, you'll learn to use Windows' **Help** facility to locate the information you need to solve problems and explore new options. You'll experiment with the Index, Browse, Back, and Search features of Help.

Starting Help

You can receive assistance in using Lotus 1-2-3 by selecting Help from the menu bar and then using the options in Help to locate information on the desired topic.

> **• HINT**
>
> If you are working with a version of Windows higher than 3.0, you may find that some of the following Help features are arranged differently. However, the same basic components will be present, and with a little ingenuity you should be able to work through the lab.

Suppose you are using 1-2-3 and want to know more about the procedure for quitting the application. You can use the Help facility to find this information. Let's try it.

1. Start Windows.
2. If Program Manager has been reduced to an icon, double-click on it.
3. Launch 1-2-3 for Windows from the Lotus Applications group.
4. Click on *Help* in 1-2-3's menu bar.

Chapter 1 Getting Started

The drop-down menu, portrayed in Figure 1-19, displays the categories of Help available for 1-2-3. These items are typical of what you'll find in the Help menus of most Windows applications. Below is a brief explanation of each category.

- *Index* is a list of the Help topics available for 1-2-3.
- *Using Help* is a brief tutorial on how the Windows Help facility works.
- *Keyboard* is a table of keystrokes for using a keyboard with 1-2-3.
- *@Functions* is a list of the predefined formulas in 1-2-3 along with explanations.
- *Macros* is a brief tutorial on creating and using automatic command sequences.

Figure 1-19. The drop-down Help menu displays the categories of Help available for 1-2-3.

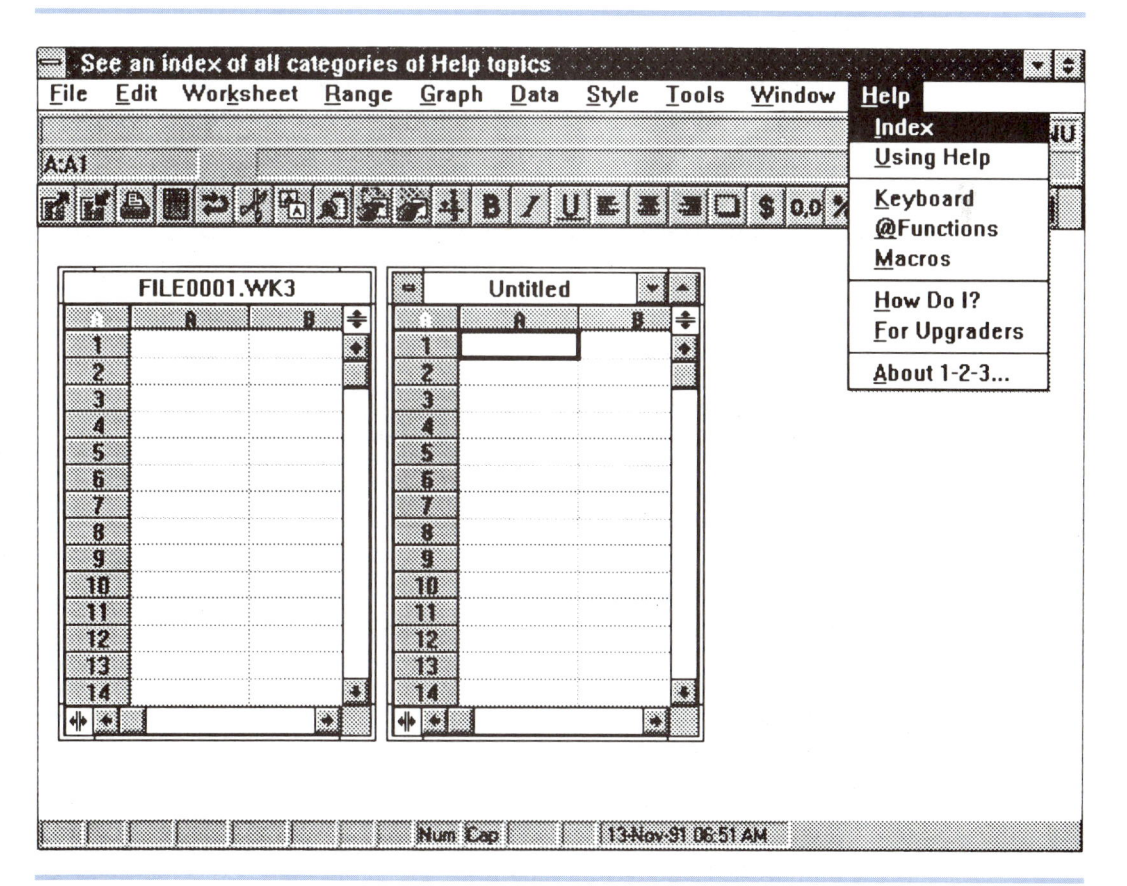

- *How Do I?* is an alphabetical list of specific tasks in 1-2-3.
- *For Upgraders* is a brief tutorial describing the 1-2-3 classic (character-based) menu.
- *About 1-2-3...* shows the copyright, version, and name of the current application.

When you select one of these items, a window will appear with detailed information on the chosen topic.

Checking the Index

To see an alphabetized index of all the topics available for 1-2-3, just click on the *Index* command in the Help menu.

1. With the Help menu displayed, point at the *Index* command.
2. Click once to produce the window pictured in Figure 1-20.

Figure 1-20.
The Help Index for 1-2-3 for Windows.

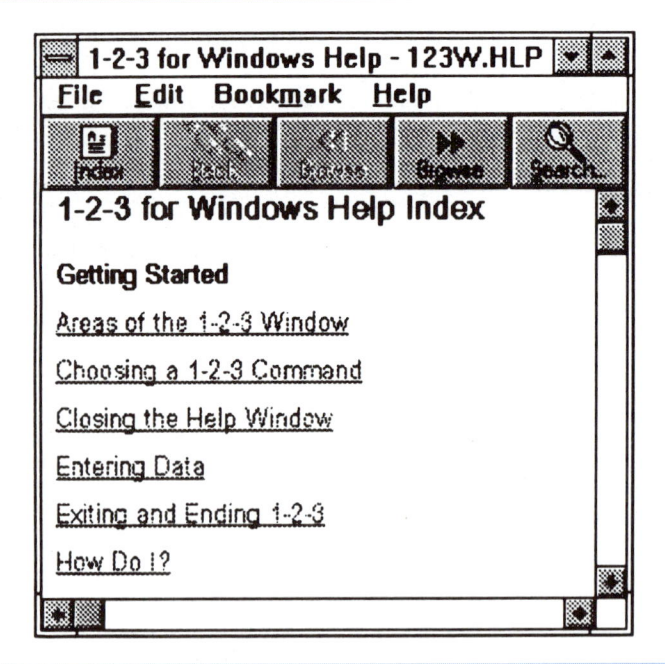

The Help Index lists the topics available for 1-2-3 by category. You can get help on a particular topic by pointing at it and clicking the left mouse button.

3. Point at the topic *Exiting and Ending 1-2-3*.

Observe that the mouse pointer changes to the shape of a pointing hand. This indicates that additional information is available.

4. Click once to display the topic.

Your Help window should resemble the one shown in Figure 1–21. As you scroll through this topic, you'll notice the phrase "Control menu" is displayed in green and underlined. This highlighting signifies it is a key term. If you click on a key phrase or word, additional information on the term will appear. For instance, to get additional details on the control-menu, do the following.

5. Once you finish reading the current topic, point at the key term *Control menu*.
6. When the pointer assumes the shape of a hand, press the left mouse button.

Figure 1–21. The Help topic *Exiting and Ending 1-2-3 for Windows*.

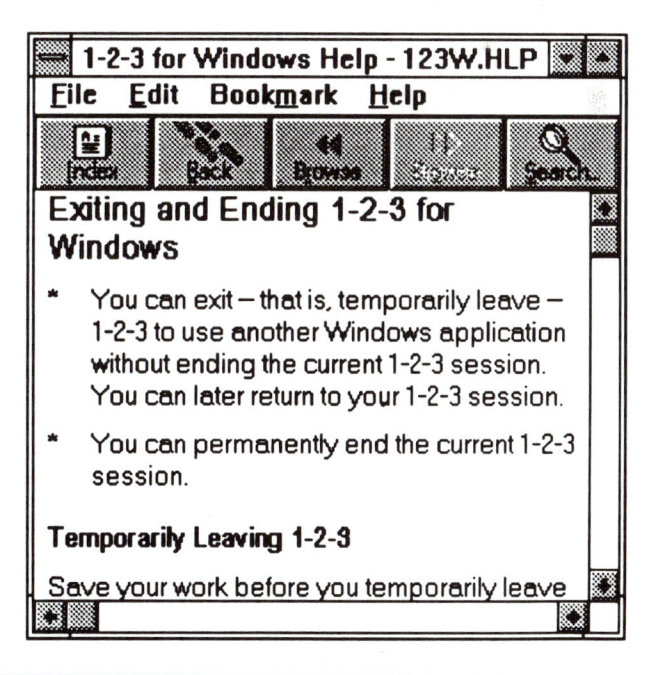

A Help window explaining the key term will appear, as shown in Figure 1–22.

Figure 1-22.
A highlighted key term lets you view a topic with additional information.

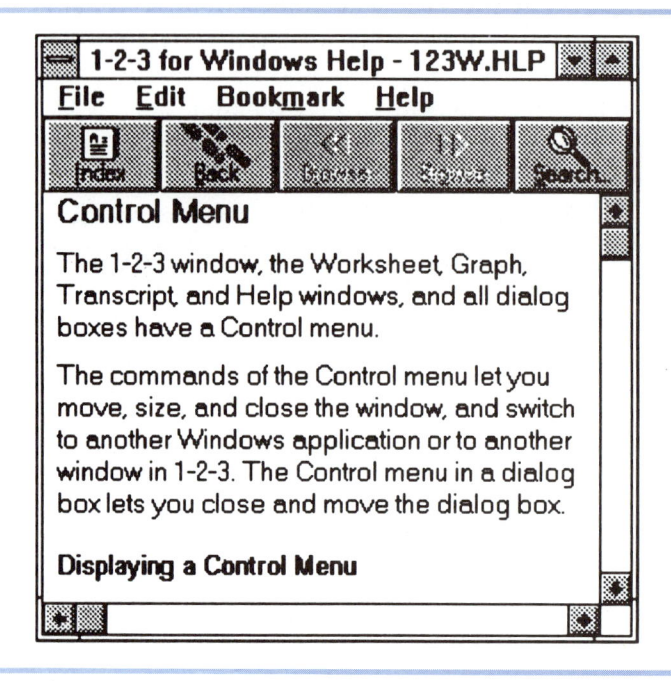

• HINT

On occasion, you might want to move and resize the Help window so you can refer to it while working with 1-2-3. A Help window can also be maximized for easier reading.

Until now we've ignored the function buttons across the top of the Help window. These buttons enable you to find topics quickly. For instance, the *Index* button sends you to the list of topics available for 1-2-3. In our case, this happens to be the window where we began our journey.

7. Point at the *Index* button.
8. Click once to bring up the original Help Index window.

Going Back

Clicking on the **Back** button sends you to the previous Help window. If you keep clicking on this button, it will eventually retrace your steps through all the topics you've seen.

1. Position the pointer on the *Back* button.
2. Click once to go to the previous topic, *Control menu*.

Chapter 1 Getting Started

3. Select *Back* once more to view the topic *Exiting and Ending 1-2-3 for Windows*.
4. Click *Back* one final time to see the original Index window.

The *Back* function button is now dimmed, signaling that it's no longer available. You have arrived at the entry point into the Help system.

5. Close the Help window by double-clicking on its control-menu box.

Browsing

You can use the forward **Browse** button (▶▶) to move through a series of related topics. When you reach the last topic, the forward Browse button will dim, indicating it's no longer active.

1. To view more details on how to use the Help facility, select the *Using Help* command from the Help menu in the Help window.
2. After studying the first topic, place the pointer over the forward *Browse* button (▶▶).
3. Continue to click this button until you reach the last topic and the button dims.

The backward *Browse* button (◀◀) takes you to the previous topic in a series. It will dim when you reach the first topic in the chain.

4. Point at the backward *Browse* button (◀◀).
5. Click it until you arrive at the beginning topic and the button dims.

Searching

The **Search** button is the fastest way to locate a particular topic. You use it by selecting or typing in a key word or phrase and letting Help find the information for you.

1. Click on the *Search* button.

Help displays the dialog box shown in Figure 1-23. You can either type a phrase in the *Search For* text box or select one from the list box just below. Let's use the search facility to see how rapidly we can locate the *Exiting and Ending 1-2-3* topic.

2. In the *Search For* text box, type: **exit**

Figure 1-23. The Search dialog box locates topics that match the key term you enter or select.

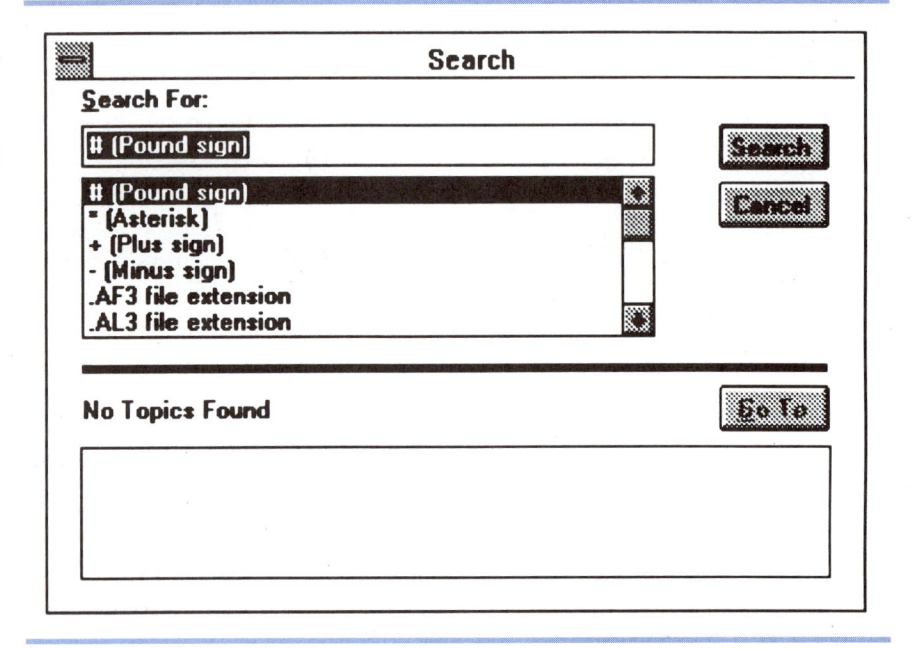

Notice that Help has already located the topic before you can finish typing the word "exit." It is highlighted in the list box just below where you were typing. To see a list of related topics, select the *Search* button.

3. Click on the *Search* button in the Search dialog box.

A list of topics that closely relate to or match the key word or phrase is displayed in the list box located at the bottom of the Search dialog box. In this case, four topics were found, as illustrated in Figure 1-24. The first topic in this list box is always highlighted. When multiple topics are present, you can choose another by simply clicking on it.

To view the highlighted topic, click the *Go To* button. To cancel the whole search procedure at any time, click the *Cancel* button.

4. Select the *Go To* button.

The *Search* facility quickly displays the same information that took numerous steps to locate with the *Index* button. It should be obvious from this example that, if you know the word or phrase you want help on, *Search* is a far more efficient way to get where you're going.

Figure 1-24.
A list box displays the topic(s) found that relate to your key word or phrase.

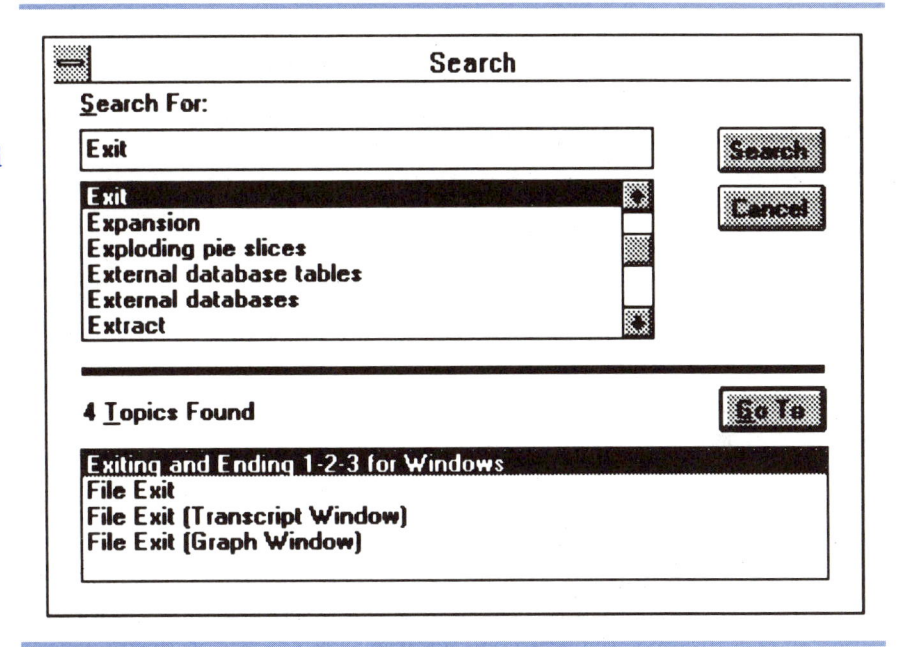

> **NOTE**
>
> *Search* is not case-sensitive. This means that the key words or phrases you enter can either be in lowercase or uppercase. Also, it's unnecessary to type in the entire word. Windows will search for topics that come as close as possible to matching a partial term.

Printing Help

You can get a printout of any topic in Help. First, find the item you want to print, then select the **Print Topic** command from the File menu in Help. As the topic is being printed, a dialog box displaying a *Cancel* button will appear. You can stop printing by clicking the *Cancel* button.

1. Make sure your printer is turned on and ready to print.
2. To print a copy of the current topic, select the *Print Topic* command from the File menu in Help.
3. When the topic is finished printing, quit Help by selecting the *Exit* command from the File menu.
4. Exit Windows from Program Manager after verifying that the *Save Changes* check box is switched off.

> **NOTE**
>
> The menu bar in the Help window contains two other items not mentioned above: Edit and Bookmark. The *Copy* command in the Edit menu lets you place a topic in Clipboard for printing or pasting to another application. The *Annotate...* command in Edit makes it possible to add your own comments to a particular topic, thereby customizing the help screens. The *Define...* command in the Bookmark menu allows you to mark the topics you use often for quick reference. For more information on using these commands, press the F1 function key while in the Help window and choose the Help commands option.

COMING ATTRACTIONS...

Congratulations. You've mastered the primary concepts and skills necessary for using 1-2-3 and Windows. To quickly recap, you began by working with icons to start 1-2-3, briefly explored using menus, proceeded from there to organize and manipulate the items on your desktop and in your workspace, and ended by using Help to find information on a variety of topics.

In Chapter 2, you'll learn to create and print a worksheet. Chapter 3 explains how to edit, move, and copy data in a worksheet, while Chapter 4 discusses ways to further enhance a worksheet's appearance.

KEY TERMS

Active window The window you are currently working with.

Application icon A graphical representation (picture) of a running application that has been minimized. Application icons are visible on the desktop (Windows background).

Application window A framed area that contains a running program.

Back Help button that sends you to the previous Help window.

Browse Help buttons that let you move forward or backward through a series of related topics.

Clicking A term referring to a single press of the left mouse button.

Command A word or phrase that instructs Windows to carry out some specific activity.

Control-menu box Double-clicking on this window element (a small box located in the upper left corner of a window) closes the window.

Desktop The background screen for Windows. The Windows desktop is similar to the surface of the desk you use at work or home. Many of the same tasks you perform on your real desk can be performed on the Windows desktop.

Dialog boxes Rectangular boxes that appear any time a command with an ellipsis (...) is executed. Dialog boxes request and/or provide information.

Document icons Graphic symbols that represent documents (worksheets) which can be expanded into document (worksheet) windows. Document icons all look the same; only their titles serve to distinguish them.

Document windows A type of window found inside an application window (e.g., 1-2-3's worksheets). Multiple document (worksheet) windows permit you to work with more than one project at a time.

Double-clicking Two rapid presses and releases of the left mouse button.

Dragging A procedure for relocating an object on the Windows desktop. It involves pointing at the item, pressing and holding the left mouse button, sliding the mouse in the direction you want it to move, and releasing the button when the item is positioned in the new location.

Drop-down menus A submenu that appears when an option is selected from the menu bar.

Frame The border surrounding all windows.

Graphical user interface (GUI) A means of communicating with your computer by pointing at easy-to-understand menus and icons (pictures) instead of typing difficult-to-remember text commands.

Group windows Document windows exclusively found in Program Manager. They help you to organize and access your applications.

Help A menu bar option, appearing in many application windows, that provides on-line assistance for users.

Icons Graphic symbols that represent programs on disk, worksheets, or running applications.

Index Help button that displays the index of topics available for the current application.

Maximize box Clicking on this window element (a small box with an up arrow in the upper right corner of a window) expands the window to fill the entire desktop.

Menu A means of grouping together commands designed to achieve some collective purpose.

Menu bar Bar located at the top of an application window that lists the options available for the current application.

Microsoft Windows A graphical user interface (GUI) that lets you communicate with your computer by pointing at easy-to-understand menus and icons (pictures) instead of typing difficult-to-remember text commands.

Minimize box Clicking on this window element, the box just left of the maximize box, will reduce a window to an icon.

Pointer A small graphic image that floats on the screen and moves correspondingly with the motions of your mouse. The pointer will assume a different shape to indicate its present capabilities.

Print Topic File menu command in the Help window that lets you print the current topic.

Program item icons Icons that start applications and appear only in the group windows of Program Manager.

Program Manager The central staging area for launching and managing applications from Windows.

Scroll bars Window elements, along the right and bottom of a window, that let you view parts of a worksheet too large to fit in the window.

Search Help button that provides the fastest method for finding a particular Help topic.

Split bar The element that splits a worksheet window into two separate panes for simultaneously viewing different sections of the same worksheet.

Title bar Window element, at the top of a window, that displays the name of the application or worksheet. When there is more than one window on the desktop, the title bar of the active window (the one you're working with) changes color or intensity.

WIN The command entered at the DOS prompt to activate the Windows environment.

Worksheet A document window that uses cells formed by rows and columns to perform calculations.

Workspace The area in the center of a window where most of the work on an application is carried out.

EXERCISES

The practice exercises in this and the ensuing chapters will provide a review of the concepts and techniques covered in the lab tutorials.

1-1. The instructions below will furnish you with the opportunity to review the material presented in Lab 1-1.

a. Start Windows if it is not already active.
b. Click on the menu name Window in the menu bar of Program Manager.
c. Choose the Lotus Applications group by selecting the Lotus Applications option in the drop-down Window menu.
d. Load 1-2-3 for Windows by double-clicking on its icon in the Lotus Applications group window.
e. Open the File menu and click on the *Exit* command to leave 1-2-3.
f. Open the Accessories group window in Program Manager, as shown in Figure 1-25.

Figure 1-25. The Accessories group window in Program Manager.

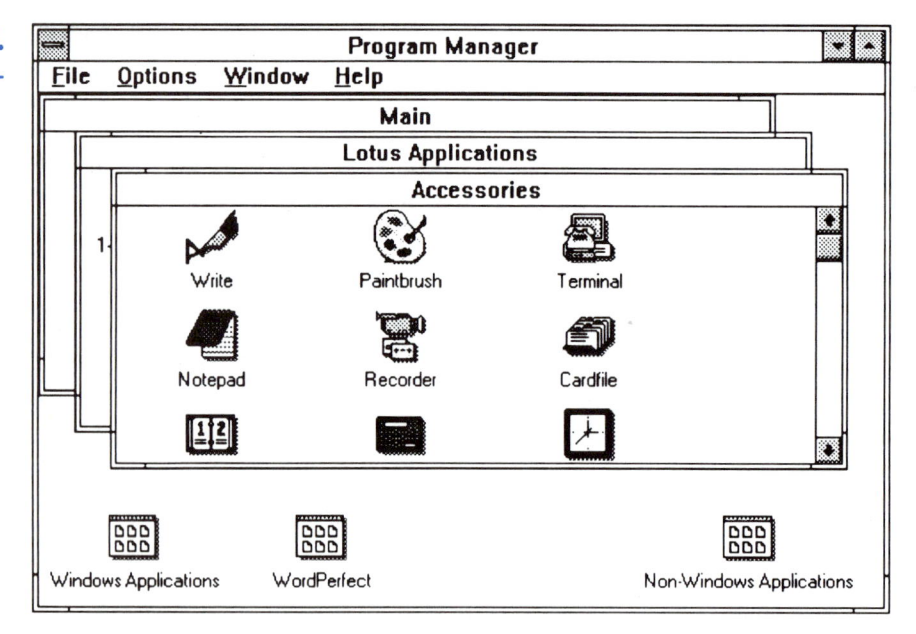

g. Launch the Clock application by double-clicking the program item icon titled "Clock."

The Clock application will appear, as pictured in Figure 1-26. Clock is a Windows' accessory program that displays the time of day.

h. Quit Clock by selecting the *Close* command from its Control-menu box.
i. You may end your Windows session after confirming that the *Save Changes* check box in the Exit Windows dialog box is switched off.

Chapter 1 Getting Started 41

Figure 1-26.

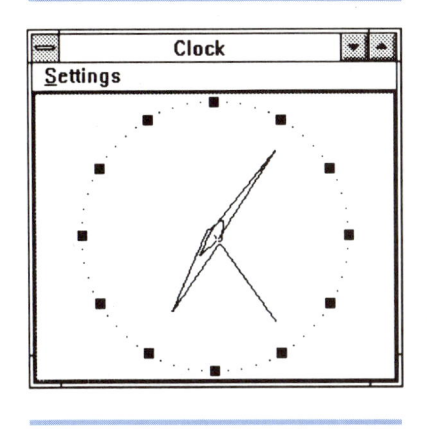

1-2. In this exercise, you'll review the concepts and procedures covered in Lab 1-2. We'll focus on the techniques for manipulating windows and icons.

    a. If necessary, launch Windows.
    b. Double-click on the Lotus Applications document icon located at the bottom of Program Manager.
    c. Start 1-2-3 for Windows by double-clicking on its icon in the Lotus Applications group window.
    d. Click the restore box in the 1-2-3 application window to reduce it to a medium size.
    e. To resize the 1-2-3 window, place your pointer on the right border of the window. When it assumes the shape of the sizing pointer, press and hold the left mouse button.
    f. Drag the frame of the window all the way to the right edge of your desktop and release the button.

Note that this action makes the window wider but not taller.

    g. Next, place the pointer in the upper left corner of the window. The pointer will change to the shape of the sizing pointer angled at approximately 45°. Drag the frame to the left and down. When the frame is approximately one-half the width and height of the original 1-2-3 window, release the mouse button.
    h. Make the Program Manager window active by clicking on it.
    i. Reduce Program Manager to an application icon by clicking on its minimize box.

Program Manager will shrink to an icon in the lower portion of your desktop.

    j. Expand the 1-2-3 window to fill your entire desktop by clicking on its maximize box.
    k. Shrink the Untitled window to a document icon.
    l. Expand it back to a window by double-clicking on the document icon.
    m. Move the Untitled worksheet to the center of the workspace in 1-2-3 by grabbing and dragging its title bar.
    n. Resize the worksheet window to approximately one-quarter of its current width and height.

o. Move the smaller worksheet window to the lower right corner of the workspace.

Your screen should resemble the one shown in Figure 1-27.

Figure 1-27. The Untitled worksheet window resized and moved.

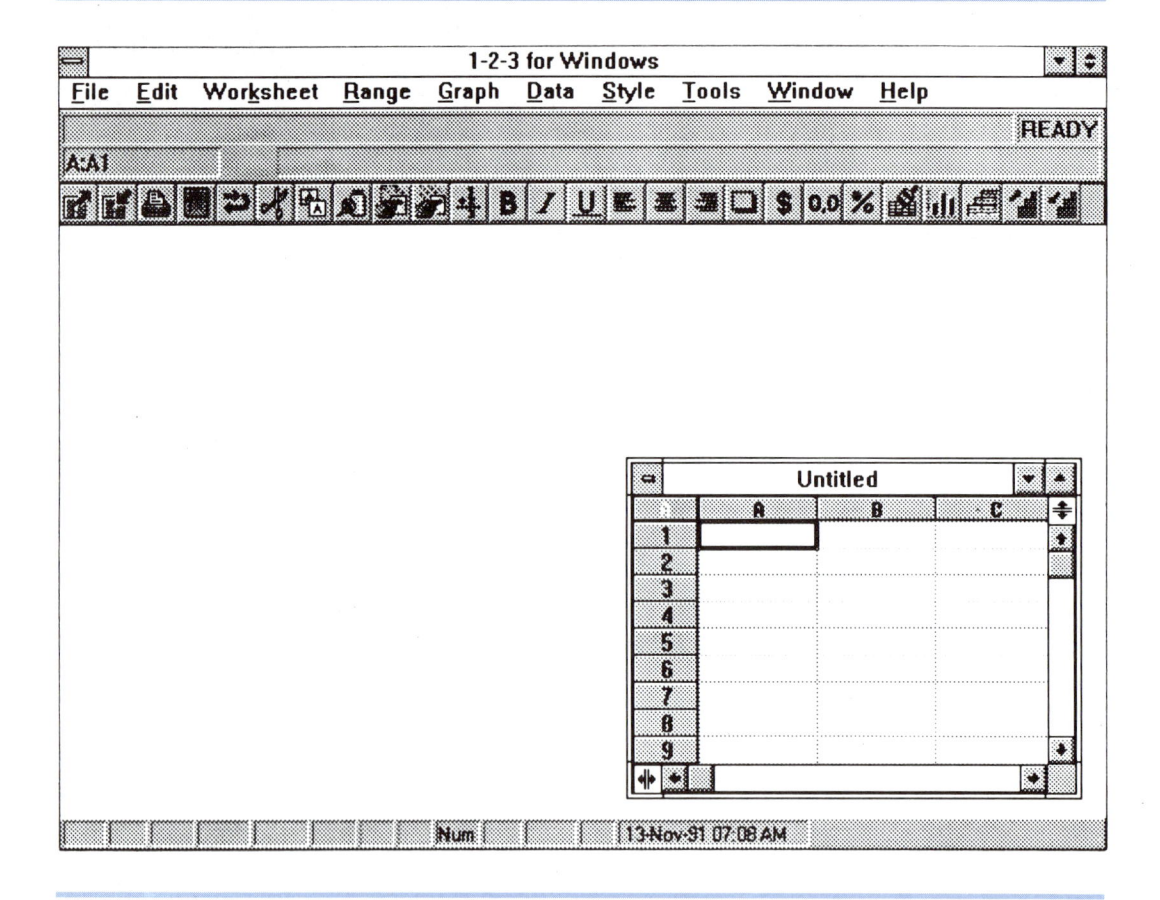

---

p. Issue the *New* command from File menu to create a second worksheet window.
q. Make the Untitled worksheet window active by clicking on it.
r. Choose the *Tile* command from the Window menu to organize the two worksheet windows.

Check your screen against the one shown in Figure 1-28.

Chapter 1 Getting Started 43

Figure 1-28. Each worksheet window shares an equal portion of the available workspace in 1-2-3.

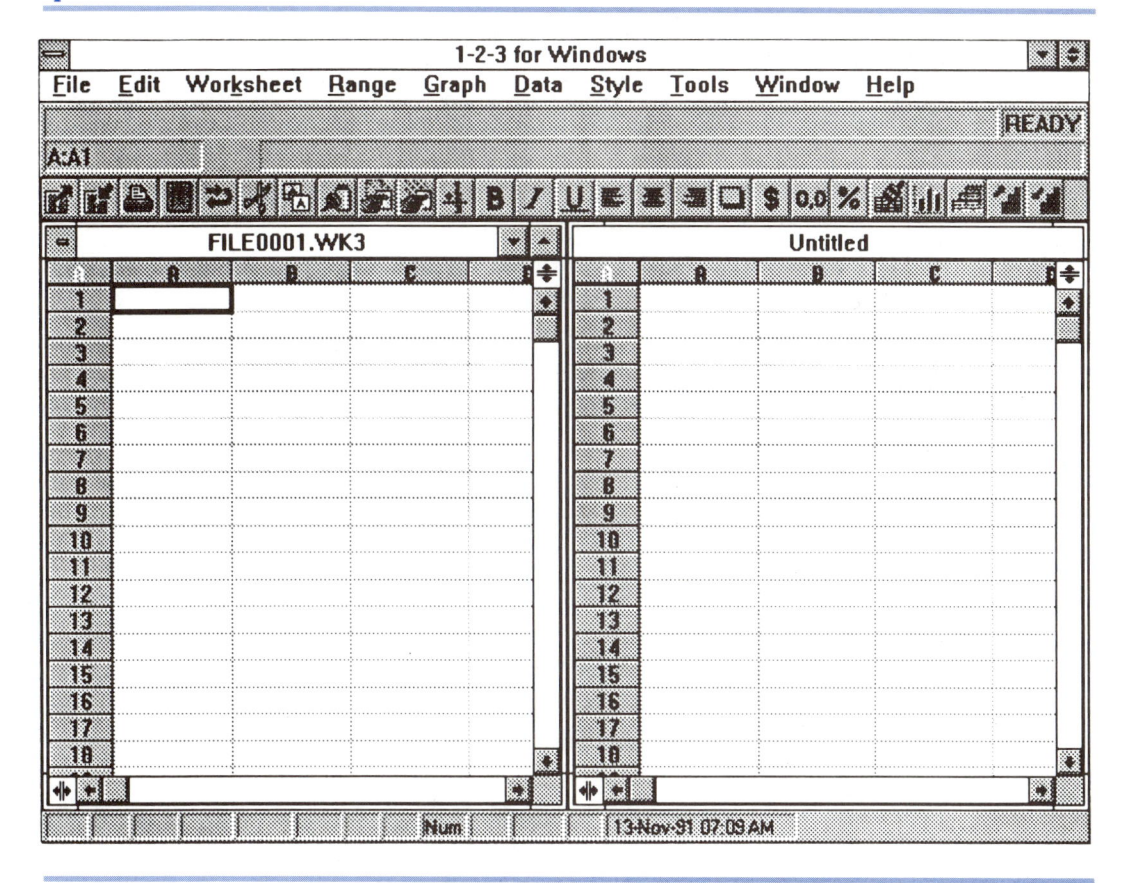

[Figure: Screenshot of 1-2-3 for Windows showing two worksheet windows side by side - FILE0001.WK3 and Untitled]

> **s.** Close the FILE0001.WK3 window and expand the Untitled worksheet to fill all of the workspace area.
> **t.** Quit 1-2-3 by selecting the *Exit* command from the File menu.
> **u.** Exit Windows after verifying that the *Save Changes* check box is switched off.

1-3. The following directions review the concepts and procedures demonstrated in Lab 1-3. You'll practice using the most interesting features in the Windows Help facility.

> **a.** If it is not already active, start Windows.
> **b.** Launch 1-2-3 for Windows.
> **c.** Select the *Index* command from the Help menu in 1-2-3.

    d. Maximize the Help window.
    e. Scroll to the topic *Help Window* and select it.
    f. When the next help screen appears, select the related topic *Print Topic*.
    g. Since the term "Help Window Commands" is displayed in green, you can view additional information about the Window menu by pointing at it and pressing the left mouse button.
    h. Click on the *Back* button three times to return to the original list of topics in the Help Index.
    i. Click on the *Search* button to display the Search dialog box, and enter the following term in the *Search For* text box: **menu bar**

As you enter the text, notice the search begins as you type. You don't have to enter an entire word before Help starts working on your request. This speeds up the search process.

    j. Click the *Search* button in the Search dialog box to display the results of the search.
    k. Click the *Go To* button to see the topic found.

Your dialog box should now match the one shown in Figure 1–29.

    l. Select the *Print Topic* command from the File menu to produce a hard copy of it.
    m. Close the Help window and exit Windows after verifying that the *Save Settings on Exit* command in the Option menu of Program Manager is switched off.

REVIEW QUESTIONS

True or False Questions

1. **T**   **F**   Using the *Search* feature of Help is slower and less efficient than the *Index* button.
2. **T**   **F**   Index is a list of the Help topics available for 1-2-3.
3. **T**   **F**   Application windows cannot be moved across the Windows desktop.
4. **T**   **F**   To start 1-2-3 for Windows, simply type GO 123W at the DOS prompt.
5. **T**   **F**   1-2-3 for Windows can be used without a mouse, but it's very difficult.

Figure 1-29.
The Help topic Control Panel.

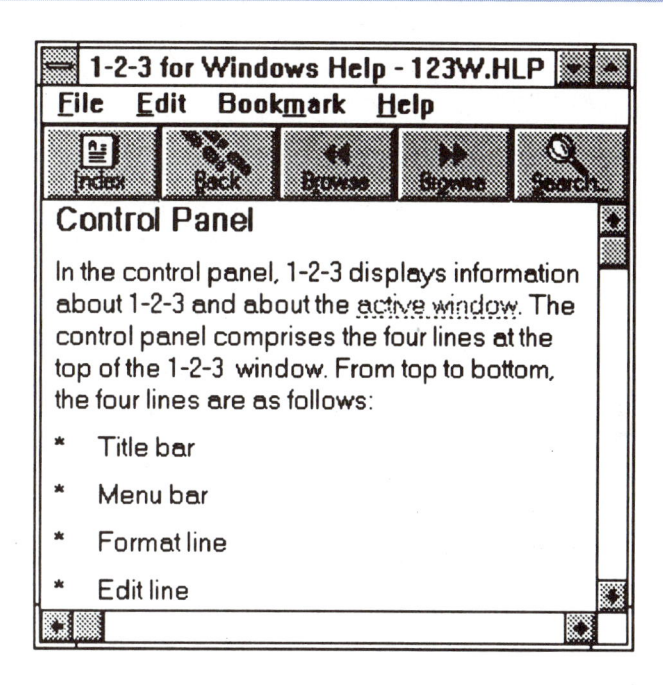

6. T F Double-clicking means to click both the right and left mouse buttons simultaneously.

7. T F Double-clicking the control-menu box of a window closes the window.

8. T F Scroll bars are used to make the active window larger or smaller.

9. T F Maximizing a window expands the window to fill the entire desktop (screen).

10. T F Clicking the *Back* button in the Help window sends you to the previous Help window.

Multiple Choice Questions

1. Which of these Help features is a brief tutorial of how to use the Help facility in Lotus 1-2-3 for Windows?

   a. *Index*
   b. *Using Help*
   c. *How Do I?*
   d. *About 1-2-3*
   e. None of the above

2. Which of the following are examples of a basic window type?

   a. Text window
   b. Document window
   c. Application window
   d. b and c
   e. a and c

3. The basic skills of mouse navigation include all but one of these techniques.

   a. Clicking
   b. Double-clicking
   c. Triple-clicking
   d. Dragging

4. Which pointer shape indicates that you can enter text?

   a. Hand pointer
   b. Hourglass pointer
   c. Arrow pointer
   d. I-beam pointer

5. Which window command shrinks an application window down to an icon?

   a. Maximize
   b. Restore
   c. Neutralize
   d. Iconize
   e. None of the above

6. Which icon type represents a program running in the background?

   a. Program item icons
   b. Application icons
   c. Document icons
   d. Graphic icons

7. Which is NOT a characteristic of the *Search* option?

   a. Accessed from the Help window
   b. Faster than *Index*
   c. Efficient
   d. b and c
   e. None of the above

8. In order to move a window, you place the mouse pointer on which part of it?

   a. Scroll bar
   b. Title bar
   c. Menu bar
   d. Movement guidance bar
   e. None of the above

9. Which of the following is used to request and provide additional information?

   a. Help boxes
   b. Control boxes
   c. Dialog boxes
   d. Exit boxes

10. Which window element displays the name of the application?

    a. Title bar
    b. Menu bar
    c. Workspace
    d. Frame
    e. None of the above

CHAPTER 2

Creating a Worksheet

• Objectives

Upon completing this chapter, you'll be able to:
1. Navigate within a worksheet.
2. Enter and align labels.
3. Change column widths individually (using ranges) and globally.
4. Save and open a worksheet.
5. Enter values, formulas, and @functions.
6. Print your worksheet.

OVERVIEW

In this chapter, you will create your first worksheet, save it, and exit 1-2-3 for Windows. You will be using many of the basic Windows skills you learned in the first chapter. One of the advantages of using Windows programs is that the basic techniques you learn can be used in many different programs.

The worksheets you'll be creating in this book will be kept relatively short. We want to guide you through the many wonderful features of 1-2-3 without making you enter unnecessarily large amounts of data. You are about to begin a relationship with the most popular spreadsheet software on the market today. Enjoy the journey.

SPREADSHEET BASICS

The electronic spreadsheet is credited with ushering in the age of personal computing. It earned this recognition by giving people an easy way to interact with computers. Previously, users had to be sophisticated enough to write massive lines of obscure and often complex code to produce even the simplest calculations. However, the electronic spreadsheet introduced a user interface so straightforward and friendly that practically anyone can use it to build a diverse and powerful computational model.

What Is an Electronic Spreadsheet?

An **electronic spreadsheet** is a computer program that uses a *worksheet* of columns and rows to let you quickly enter and manipulate labels, numbers, and formulas. It replaces the manual operations normally done on paper with pencil, eraser, and calculator. You can easily change and update the figures in an electronic worksheet.

But the real power of this software comes from its ability to perform automatic calculations based on the formulas you enter. These computations range from basic addition and subtraction to highly sophisticated financial and statistical computations.

This built-in calculator lets you play "what-if" games with the numbers in a worksheet. When you change a value, all the formulas in the worksheet can be automatically recalculated to display the results of your revision. As a consequence, you can test various assumptions and immediately see the impact of the changes. This "sensitivity analysis" makes it possible to examine many different scenarios quickly and, thus, plan much more effectively and efficiently for the future.

The worksheets you create with an electronic spreadsheet can be altered and enhanced in a variety of ways. For instance, you can delete, insert, and adjust the columns (vertical strips) and rows (horizontal strips) in a worksheet to produce a custom layout. You can also specify the appearance and format of numbers (e.g., dollars, percentages, dates, etc.).

Many spreadsheet programs offer facilities for sorting, searching, and graphically displaying data. They are invaluable for creating professional-looking reports and presentations.

An electronic spreadsheet can be used for almost any job requiring the manipulation and analysis of numbers. Typical tasks include budgeting, forecasting sales, reconciling a checking account, investment planning, and estimating mortgage payments.

A worksheet is composed of a grid of columns and rows. The intersection of a column and a row is called a **cell**, as shown in Figure 2-1. A cell is where you enter a label, number, or formula.

The top and left side of a worksheet display the **worksheet frame**. The worksheet frame holds the *column letters* and *row numbers* for locating a particular cell. For example, cell B3 is located at the intersection of column B, row 3. This is called the **cell address**.

Figure 2–1. The opening screen of 1-2-3 for Windows.

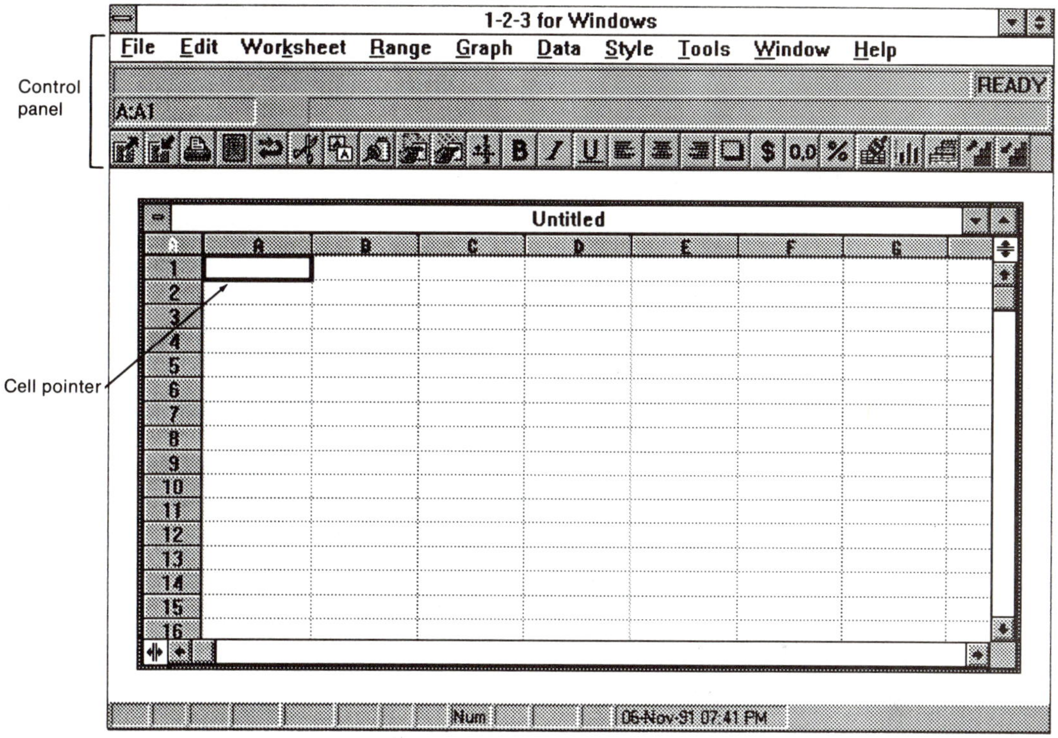
1-2-3 for Windows
File Edit Worksheet Range Graph Data Style Tools Window Help
Control panel
READY
A:A1
Untitled
A B C D E F G
1 2 3 4 5 6 7 8 9 10 11 12 13 14 15 16
Cell pointer
Num
06-Nov-91 07:41 PM

The highlighted box in Figure 2–1 is called a **cell pointer**. When you move around in a worksheet, the cell pointer indicates the cell you are working with. The cell holding the cell pointer is referred to as the **current cell**.

Although not part of the worksheet, the control panel plays an essential part in your interaction with the worksheet. The **control panel** consists of the top four rows of the 1-2-3 window, as depicted in Figure 2–1. The first two rows of the control panel include the title and menu bars, as described in Chapter 1. Row three is the **format line**. The left side of the format line will display the format of the current cell when the cell has been altered from the normal 1-2-3 settings. The **mode indicator** is displayed on the right side of the format line. This indicator displays 1-2-3's current mode or state. (Table 2–3, in the *Key Terms* at the end of this chapter, summarizes the modes 1-2-3 utilizes.) The final line of the control panel is the **edit line**. It consists of the **address box**, which displays the current cell, and the **contents box**, which reveals the contents of the current cell.

The address box shows the full cell address including the worksheet letter. The cell address A:A1 designates worksheet A, column A, row 1. This position (cell A1) on each worksheet is called the *home position*.

A worksheet has 256 columns and 8,192 rows. The columns are labeled A through IV (e.g., A–Z, AA–AZ, etc.). The rows are labeled consecutively from 1 to 8,192. This immense grid provides an astounding 2,097,152 cells!

1-2-3 processes information in a cell based only on its contents, not its format. Remember, the purpose of the 1-2-3 program is to manipulate data. It makes no difference if a value appears red or green, has borders, or is displayed in a different font. 1-2-3 ignores these formatting niceties and concentrates on the actual contents of the cell. This is also true for formulas. When you enter a formula, the formula itself is displayed in the control panel, while the results of the formula are displayed in the cell. The only way to view the actual contents of a cell is to look at the control panel. This will be more evident in the tutorial labs. Be sure to pay particular attention to this concept.

NOTE

The size of your worksheet is limited by the amount of memory your computer is equipped with. If you need to work with larger worksheets than your computer's current configuration can accommodate, extra memory can be added.

It's time for you to begin discovering 1-2-3's potential as a powerful business tool. Let's start exploring.

LAB 2-1 GETTING AROUND IN A WORKSHEET

This lab will teach you the essentials of finding and selecting a cell in a worksheet. Since a worksheet is composed of over 2 million cells, you must sometimes travel vast distances to locate and select a particular cell. We'll discuss a number of features in 1-2-3 that make this process both convenient and easy.

Selecting a Cell

Selecting a cell enables you to place data in the worksheet at a specific location. To choose a cell, simply place the mouse pointer over the desired cell and click once. The cell pointer will mark the chosen spot. If the desired cell is out of view, you can use the scroll bars to find it.

Let's practice this technique by selecting several random cells.

1. To launch 1-2-3 for Windows, open the Lotus Applications work group and then double-click on the 1-2-3 for Windows program icon.

When 1-2-3 first appears, its worksheet window is scaled to medium size. In order to provide the best view possible, always expand it to fill the entire workspace. This is done by clicking on its maximize box in the upper right corner of the worksheet window.

2. Place the mouse pointer over the maximize box in the upper right corner of the worksheet window and click.

The worksheet will expand to fill the entire workspace area, as shown in Figure 2-2. Now you can see more cells in the worksheet. Notice that the cell pointer resides in cell A1 (the "home position"). Let's move it to the cell located at the intersection of column B and row 5.

3. Position the pointer over cell B5 and click.

The cell pointer immediately moves to cell B5, and the address box changes to display the new cell address. Let's try another move.

4. Select cell C3 by pointing at it and clicking.
5. Now choose cell D8.

The position of the cell pointer and the coordinates displayed in the address box always let you know which cell is currently selected. This eliminates confusion about your exact location in the worksheet.

Navigating in a Worksheet

In Chapter 1, you learned to use the scroll bars to view different portions of your worksheet. The scroll bars let you rapidly move to the area of the worksheet containing the cell (or cells) you want to select. Since a worksheet is quite large, we'll show you some techniques for moving to more distant spots.

Clicking on the right side of the scroll box on the horizontal bar will take you one screen to the right, while clicking below the scroll box on the vertical scroll bar will move you down one screen.

Figure 2-2. The worksheet expanded to utilize the entire workspace.

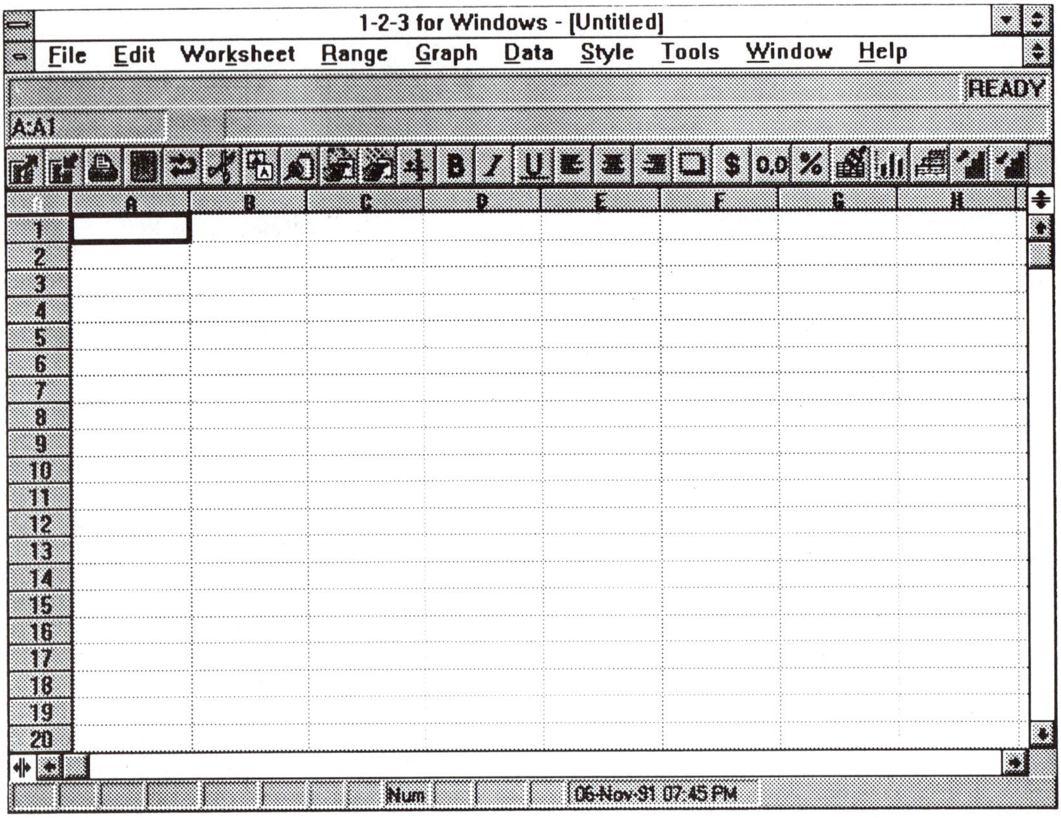

Let's move to cell AA70.

1. Click the horizontal scroll bar, just to the right of the scroll box, once.

   Notice that the column letter now starts with I and the scroll box moved about 1 inch to the right on the horizontal scroll bar.

2. Click just to the right of the scroll box again, and wait for the scroll box to move.

   The worksheet will move one screen to the right.

3. Repeat step 2.

   At this point, you should be able to see column AA on your screen.

4. Click just below the scroll box on the vertical scroll bar.

Chapter 2 Creating a Worksheet 53

The row visible at the top of your screen will change, and the scroll box will move about 1 inch down on the vertical scroll bar.

5. Repeat step 4 twice.
6. Click on cell AA70.

Next, we'll move to BG16.

7. Click on the right side of the scroll box once and wait for it to move.
8. Repeat step 7.

At this point, the scroll box is at the far right side of the scroll bar. To move any farther to the right, you'll need to use the right scroll arrow. Since the right scroll arrow only moves you to the right one column at a time, you'll have to click on it repeatedly or hold down the left mouse button to get to column BG.

9. Point at the right scroll arrow and hold down the left mouse button until column BG appears.
10. Drag the vertical scroll box all the way to the top of the scroll bar.
11. Select cell BG16.
12. Using the scroll bars, select cell Z100.

You can instantaneously return to the original or "home" address of a worksheet by clicking the upper left corner of the worksheet frame (where the letter "A" is displayed). This action will place the cell pointer in cell A1.

13. Click the upper left corner of your worksheet frame.
14. If you're not continuing with the next lab right now, you may end your 1-2-3 for Windows session by selecting the *Exit* command from the File menu.

NOTE

If you accidentally entered any data in your practice worksheet, 1-2-3 will ask if you want to save the worksheet. Select the *No* button in the File Exit dialog box to quit without saving.

LAB 2-2 USING LABELS, COLUMN WIDTHS, AND RANGES

In this lab, you'll begin creating a Cash Flow Budget for Going Native, a growing horticultural consulting service specializing in native plants.

The owner, Rosalind Planter (nicknamed "Wild Rose"), provides customers with a CAD (computer-aided design) blueprint of their landscape. She uses drought-tolerant, wildlife-supporting native plants.

Wild Rose wants you to develop a cash flow budget to help her predict future cash needs and surpluses. We'll start by entering the labels necessary to organize Rose's financial data.

A **label** is any cell entry that begins with a letter or label-prefix character. A **label-prefix character** determines the placement of a label in the cell. For example, when you type a letter (e.g., a, b, or c) in a cell, 1-2-3 automatically inserts an apostrophe (') in front of the entry. This label-prefix character causes the label to be left aligned. However, you can manually enter a different label-prefix character to change the placement of a label in a cell. Table 2-1 summarizes the most common label-prefix characters.

Table 2-1. Label-prefix characters.

Label Prefix	Effect on Label Position in the Cell
'	Left justifies a label (aligns to the left side of the cell)
"	Right justifies a label
^	Center justifies a label
\	Fills the entire cell with the characters in the label

Entering Labels

Labels let you organize the values that appear in a worksheet. In other words, they act as identifiers of numeric data. For instance, cash flow budget labels can serve as headings to identify the source of cash receipts (e.g., consulting fees) and to classify the types of cash disbursements (e.g., rent, office supplies, and utilities), as illustrated in Figure 2-8.

You enter a label by simply selecting the desired cell and typing in the characters. The following instructions will step you through creating the labels necessary for identifying the various rows and columns of our cash flow budget. These headings will help clarify the sources and uses of the cash generated by Going Native.

1. If necessary, start 1-2-3 for Windows.
2. Expand the worksheet to its full size by clicking the maximize box.
3. Move the cell pointer to cell C1.
4. Type only the letter **C**. This is the first character of the title "Cash Flow Budget."

Chapter 2   Creating a Worksheet 55

Take a moment to observe the mode indicator in the upper right corner of the control panel. It has changed from the READY mode to the LABEL mode. 1-2-3 assumes the data you have started to enter is text because the first character you typed was a letter. Anything you enter in this cell from now on will be treated as part of that label.

Now look at the contents box of the control panel. It displays a *Cancel* button (red X), a *Confirm* button (green check), and the character "C," shown in Figure 2-3. Anything you do from the keyboard will now take place in the contents box. The only editing key that works in the LABEL mode is the Backspace key.

Figure 2-3. The contents box showing the *Cancel* and *Confirm* buttons.

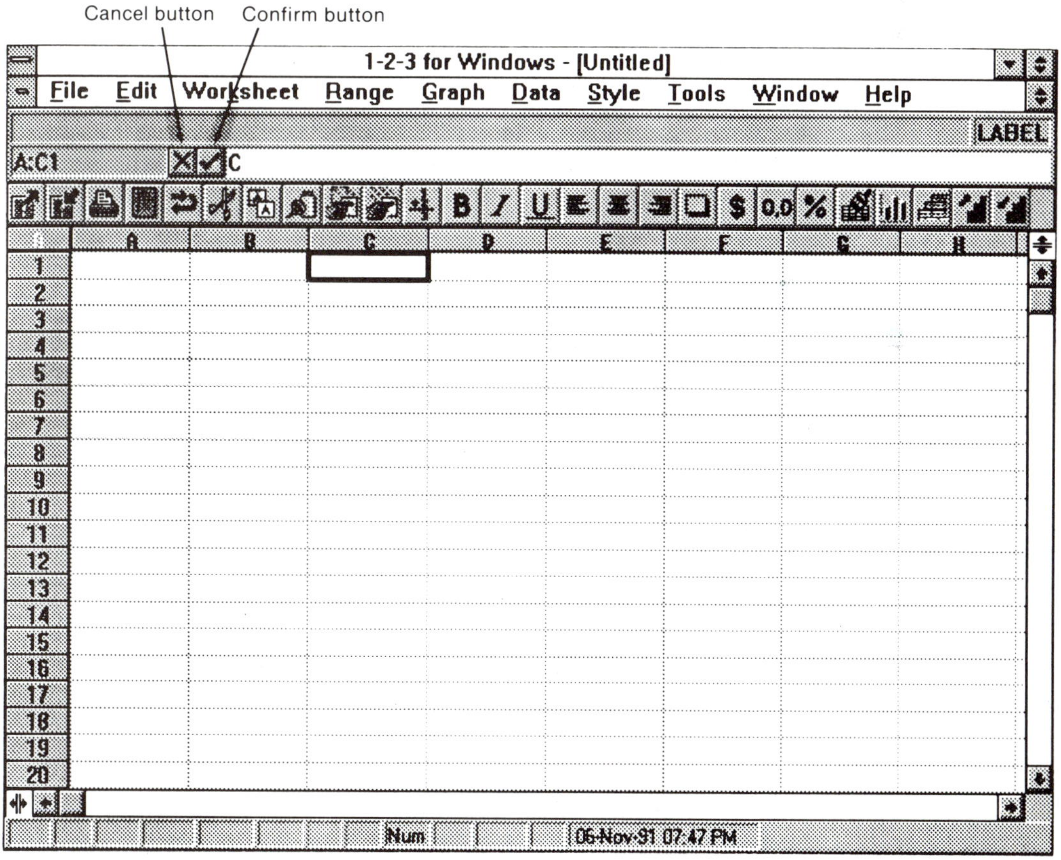

Let's experiment with the Backspace key by typing a few incorrect letters and then backspacing to remove them.

5. Type: **sdj**
6. To erase these characters, tap the Backspace key 3 times.

Although you have entered and removed several characters, nothing has yet appeared in your worksheet. To place the entry in a cell, you must either click on the *Confirm* button or press the Enter key. You can abort the entry by backspacing over all the characters in the contents box, or by clicking the *Cancel* button.

> **NOTE**
>
> Pressing an arrow key will also confirm a cell entry and, at the same time, move the cell pointer in the indicated direction.

To complete our title, perform the following steps.

7. Type the balance of the label: **ash Flow Budget**
8. Click the *Confirm* button to enter the label into the current cell.

The label will appear in cell C1, and the *Confirm* and *Cancel* buttons will vanish. The contents box now shows the contents of the cell preceded by a label-prefix character. The cell pointer remains in C1.

9. To enter the next heading, select cell C2, type **Going Native**, and then click the *Confirm* button.
10. Choose C3, type **1993 - First Quarter**, and click the *Confirm* button.

What's this?! 1-2-3 signals that an error (ERR) has occurred. What caused the error? Entering the number "1" told 1-2-3 to expect a value when you actually intended to type a label. The error resulted from attempting to enter the number "1993" followed by the characters "First Quarter." To avoid this problem, you can place a label-prefix character in front of any number you want to use as a label. This will signal that a label is forthcoming.

11. While still in cell C3 enter **'1993 - First Quarter** (be sure to type the apostrophe first) and click the *Confirm* button.

In addition to the letters of the alphabet, you can also use other characters as labels. For example, to separate different kinds of data, you might want to create borders using a hyphen, "-." By filling a cell with hyphens, you can produce a line or border look. The backslash "\" label-prefix character offers you a shortcut method for repeating a character within a cell.

Chapter 2   Creating a Worksheet

12. Select cell C4, type \- (the backslash and a hyphen), and select the *Confirm* button.

   Just a few simple keystrokes filled the entire cell. Later in this book, you will learn a more elegant method for creating borders, but for now add one more cell to your border and resume entering labels.

13. In cell D4, enter: \-

   If a label contains more characters than the cell will allow, it will "spill" over into an adjacent empty cell. The next label you enter will demonstrate this.

14. In A5, enter: **CASH RECEIPTS**

   Although the label appears to be in both A5 and B5, it is actually in cell A5. 1-2-3 is allowing a portion of the label in A5 to overflow in B5. You can confirm this by viewing cell B5.

15. Select B5.

   The contents box is presently empty. Try entering a label in B5 to see what happens to the text that's currently overflowed from A5. We'll use the caret (^) symbol to center the label in B5. The caret is produced by holding down the Shift key and typing the number 6.

16. Enter: **^Jan**

   Notice that only the portion of "CASH RECEIPTS" that fits in A5 is visible. By placing data in cell B5, 1-2-3 has shortened the label displayed in A5.

17. Move the cell pointer to A5.

   Even though the displayed portion has been shortened, you can see from the contents box that the cell still contains the full label.

Changing Column Width

The labels you enter in a worksheet will often require more space to display than provided by a standard column width. Fortunately, 1-2-3 makes it easy to alter the width of any column.

Column width is the number of characters that 1-2-3 can display in a column. The default column width is 9 characters, but you can assign a column width from 1 to 240 characters. (A **default** is an initial setting that 1-2-3 uses until you specify something different.) The column width you choose must be the same for the entire length of a column.

To adjust the width of a column, you simply move to the top of the desired column, grab one of its border lines on the worksheet frame, and drag it either closer or farther away from the other border line. Dragging it closer causes the column to narrow, while dragging it away from the other side widens the column.

1. On the worksheet frame, position the pointer on the line separating columns A and B.

The pointer will change to a double-headed arrow, as shown in Figure 2-4. In Lab 1-2, you used the double-headed arrows to split worksheets and resize windows. You use the same dragging method to change the width of a column.

Figure 2-4. Using the double-headed arrow to change the width of a column.

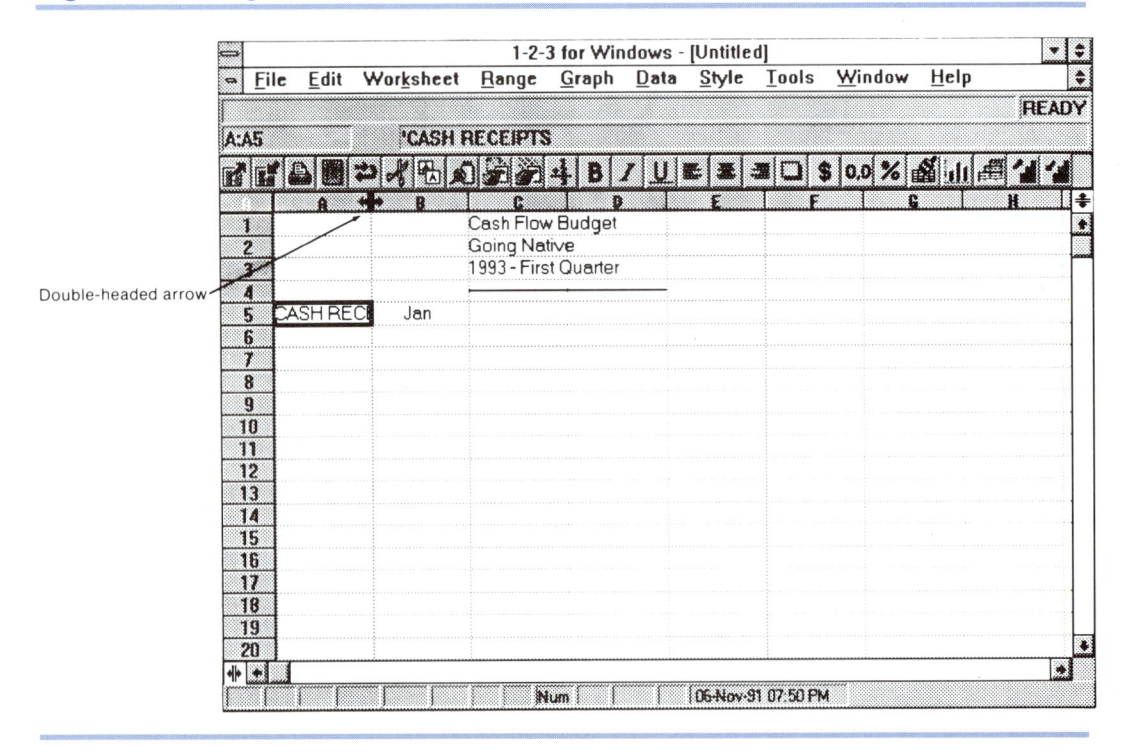

Chapter 2 Creating a Worksheet 59

2. Hold down the left mouse button, and drag the pointer to the right until you are about even with the grid line separating columns B and C. Release the mouse button to complete the operation.

The width of the entire column will change as you drag the pointer to the right. The format line will show the new column width, as pictured in Figure 2-5. The format line reveals only formatting changes that are different from default settings. We'll experiment with this technique again.

Figure 2-5. The column is now wide enough to display the entire label.

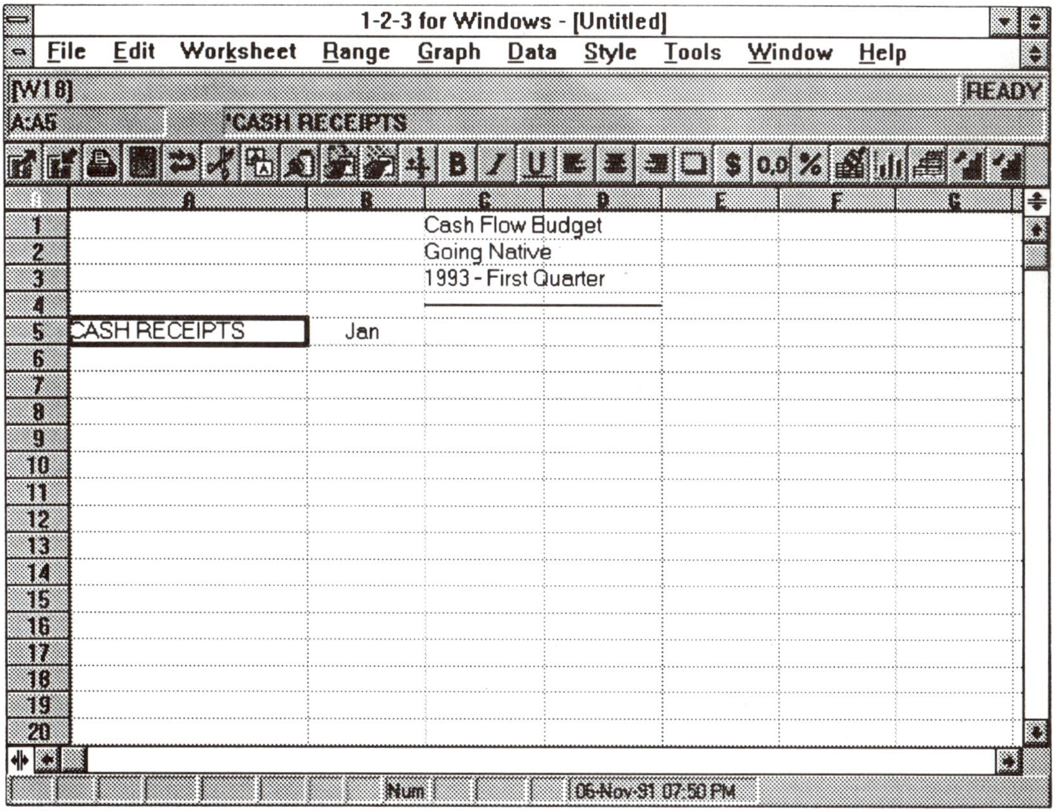

3. Using the same method, make column C approximately twice as large.
4. Next, adjust column A to only 1 or 2 characters wide (don't worry about the label in column A, we'll fix it in a moment).

This is a quick method for changing column widths. In addition to being fast, it doesn't require the cell pointer to be located in the column being adjusted. However, this technique can only alter one column at a time. It is also difficult to set a column to a specific width (e.g., 10, 20, 25, etc.) using this method.

Fortunately, 1-2-3 provides you with alternatives that overcome these disadvantages. One such command is *Column Width...* from the Worksheet menu. By using the *Column Width...* command, you can open a dialog box that lets you precisely adjust the width of a column.

5. Select cell A3.
6. Choose *Column Width...* from the Worksheet menu.

Figure 2-6.

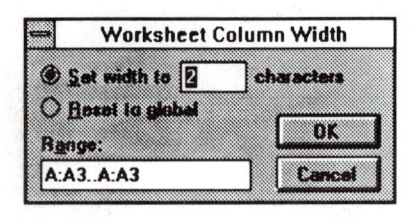

The Worksheet Column Width dialog box will open, as illustrated in Figure 2-6. This dialog box contains two radio buttons and a text box. The first button is always selected when the dialog box is first opened. It allows you to set a column width by entering a number in the *Set width to* text box. The second radio button permits you to return a column to the global column width. The *Range* text box enables you to enter a range (you will use this feature later in the lab).

Some text boxes allow you to type an entry without deleting the current contents first. In these text boxes, the contents are highlighted, as pictured in Figure 2-6. If the contents of the text box are not highlighted, you'll be required to edit or delete the contents first.

By entering the exact width in the *Set width to* text box, you can accurately set the width of a column.

7. Type: **20** (click the *OK* button to accept your entry).

The column will now assume the desired width. The easiest way to use this method is to make sure the cell pointer is located in the column you want to change. Practice this method a few more times.

8. Select B5.
9. Using the same method, change the width to **10**.
10. Move to C8 and change the width to **4**.

Selecting a Range

The methods we've used so far for adjusting column widths work well for single columns. However, these techniques become quite tedious when you need to change multiple columns. 1-2-3 offers a convenient way of altering more than one column at a time.

You can perform actions on groups of columns or cells by first selecting the desired range. A **range** can consist of a single cell, a block of adjoining cells, or even an entire worksheet. A range must always be rectangular and is identified by a range address. The **range address** consists of the cell addresses of any two diagonally opposite corner cells of the range. These cell addresses are always separated by two periods (e.g., B4..E20, or C3..A20). A range can be designated by either typing the cell addresses or using the cell pointer to highlight the desired range.

Using range commands is a very convenient way to interact with 1-2-3, and you will find yourself using them frequently. Let's create your first range.

1. Point at cell B1, and press and hold down the left mouse button.
2. Drag the cell pointer to E1.

The range address will appear in the contents box as you drag the cell pointer to the right. The mode indicator changes from the READY mode to the POINT mode. Releasing the mouse button will leave the cell pointer surrounding the desired range.

3. Release the mouse button.

The cell pointer now encloses the range, and 1-2-3 returns to the READY mode. The range you have selected includes columns B to E. Now you can change several columns at one time.

4. Pick *Column Width...* from the Worksheet menu.

The range address you identified with the cell pointer is displayed in the *Range* text box. By entering a value in the *Set width to* text box, you can affect the entire range.

5. Change the column width to 5.

The whole range is immediately set to a column width of 5 characters. You can also adjust multiple columns by manually entering a range address in the Worksheet dialog box.

6. Choose *Column Width...* from the Worksheet menu.
7. Click on the *Range* text box in the Worksheet Column Width dialog box.
8. Use editing keys to delete the current range and then type: **a1..d1**
9. Click on the *Set width to* text box.

The contents of this text box are not highlighted. Thus, you must use the editing keys to modify or delete its contents before making an entry.

10. Delete the contents of the text box, enter a column width of **6**, and click *OK*.

Ranges let you adjust multiple columns quickly. But you may, on occasion, want to change settings that affect your entire worksheet. 1-2-3 has a set of options that makes this task easy. They are called **global commands** because they apply to the whole worksheet. Global commands are found in the Worksheet menu.

You can use the *Global Settings...* command in the Worksheet menu to alter the column width setting for your entire worksheet. Just select the command, and when the Worksheet Global Settings dialog box appears, type in the new default column width.

To understand how global commands work, let's use one to change column widths for the entire worksheet.

11. Select the *Global Settings...* command from the Worksheet menu.

The Worksheet Global Settings dialog box will appear, as portrayed in Figure 2-7. This dialog box contains radio buttons and check boxes to control the Zero display, Align labels, Group mode, and Protection options. There is also a *Format...* button along with the standard *OK* and *Cancel* buttons. You will be using some of these features in Lab 4-3. The final item in the dialog box is the *Column width* text box. This is where you will enter the global column width setting.

12. Click on the *Column width* text box.
13. If necessary, use the editing keys to erase unwanted characters. Type **2** and click the *OK* button.

Notice that the columns altered earlier are not affected by this global command. When a range command is used to change a default

Chapter 2 Creating a Worksheet 63

setting such as column width, the range command takes precedence over any global commands. To see how 1-2-3 handles global changes, let's look at a cell that was unaltered prior to the global change.

Figure 2-7. The Worksheet Global Settings dialog box will make changes that affect the entire worksheet.

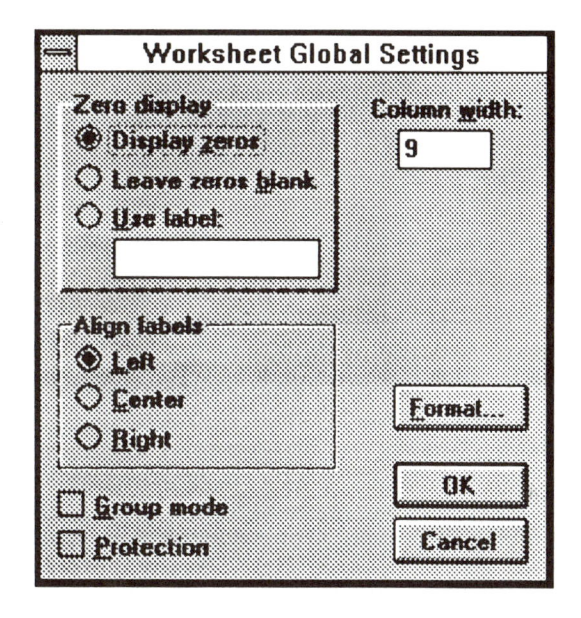

14. Select G1.

The format line remains blank for this cell because it was changed globally. Global changes are considered to be the new defaults. The format line reveals only the format changes that are neither default nor global settings. Default settings will stay in place until they are changed by another method, such as a *Range* command.

Let's finish adjusting the column widths for our worksheet.

15. Change the global column width to **9**.
16. Widen Column A to **20**.
17. Using the range method, make columns B to F **8** characters wide.
18. Enter the rest of the labels shown in Figure 2-8, with the proper label alignment.

Figure 2-8. The remainder of the worksheet labels.

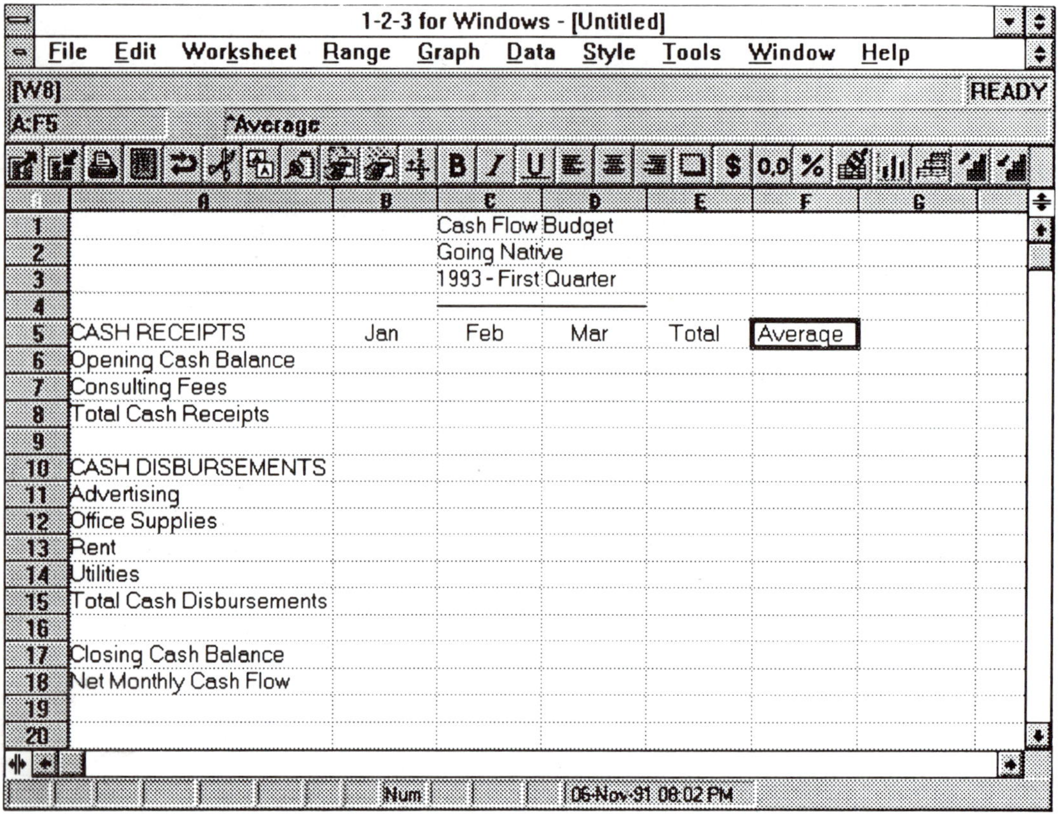

NOTE

The height of a row can also be altered in 1-2-3. **Row height** is the height of the largest character that can be fully displayed in a row. The unit of measurement for row height is points. A **point** is a typesetting measurement that divides each inch into 72 parts. When you start 1-2-3, it has a default row height of 12 points. As with column width, row height is the same for the entire row. The height of every cell in a row is always the same.

The techniques for changing column width and row height are very similar. A row can be made taller or shorter by dragging the border that separates rows. Creating a range and selecting *Row Height...* from the Worksheet menu will open a dialog box comparable to the Worksheet Column Width box. There isn't a global setting for changing row height as there is for columns.

Saving a Worksheet File

You've just spent at least several minutes of your valuable time entering data into your computer's memory. Are you feeling pretty secure? DON'T! Until you save your work, your worksheet is vulnerable to a huge variety of misfortunes that can render it useless. You should save your work in progress every 10 to 20 minutes so that, no matter what happens, you'll never lose more than a small portion of your effort.

The *Save As...* command allows you to name your worksheet file and determine the location where the file is to be stored.

For the labs and exercises in this book, we'll assume you are storing your worksheets on a floppy disk in drive A.

1. Insert a formatted disk in drive A.
2. Click on the *Save As...* command from the File menu.

This action will open the dialog box shown in Figure 2-9. It contains a *File name* text box that lets you name your worksheet. *Files, Directories,* and *Drives* list boxes enable you to indicate where you want your file kept. A check box for adding password protection and a *Save All* button for storing multiple worksheets are also available.

Figure 2-9. The File Save As dialog box appears when you want to save a file.

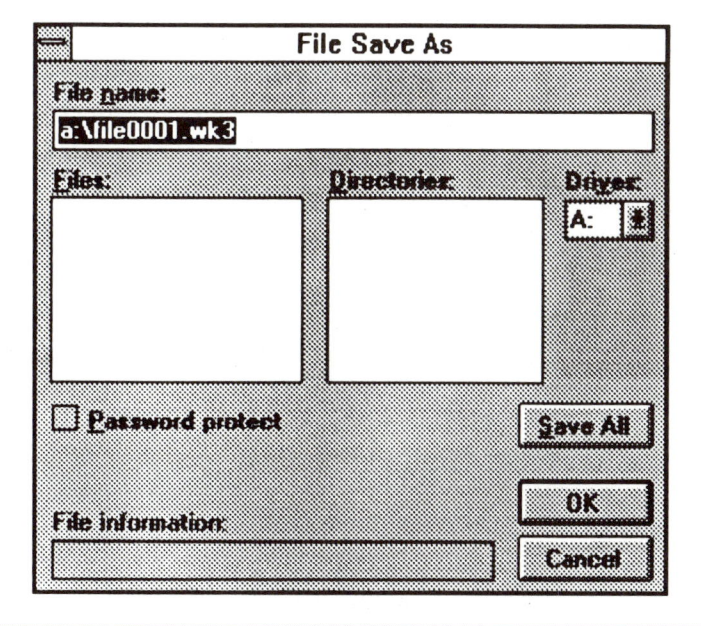

The *File name* text box lets you name your document. You can use any legal file name (eight characters or less with no spaces). It is not necessary to include an extension as part of your file name. 1-2-3 will automatically add the extension .WK3 as it saves your file to disk. This allows 1-2-3 to later display your file in various file lists. By choosing your own extension, you override this capability, thus making it more difficult to identify the file as a 1-2-3 worksheet.

When picking a file name, try to stay with something that will help identify the type of information contained in the worksheet. Since this is a cash flow budget, let's name the worksheet "budget".

3. To save the worksheet to drive A, type the file name: **A:\BUDGET**.WK3

NOTE

You can also use the *Directories* and *Drives* list boxes to choose the directory and/or drive where you want to store your document. To select a directory, simply double-click the directory in the *Directories* list box. If the directory you want is not on the current drive, you can click on the down arrow in the *Drives* list box to display a list of drive choices. Just click on the one you want to use.

4. Click the *OK* button.

The mode indicator will change to the WAIT mode while 1-2-3 writes your file to the disk. When the process is complete, it will return to the READY mode.

HAZARD

If you use a file name that already exists, you will get a warning message, as displayed in Figure 2-10. You can replace the file on the disk by selecting the *Replace* button. This will overwrite the file with the current worksheet. Selecting the *Backup* button will cause the file on the disk to be renamed. It will have the same file name with the extension BAK. The current worksheet will then be written to the disk. The backup feature allows you to keep a previous version of your worksheet, but increases the amount of disk space used.

Chapter 2 Creating a Worksheet

Figure 2-10.

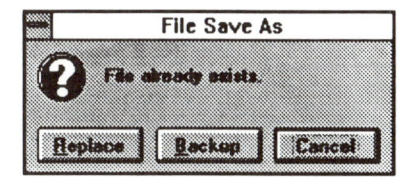

Your worksheet is now saved on the disk. You are ready to exit 1-2-3 and return to Program Manager. From Program Manager, you can end your Windows session.

5. Select the *Exit* command from the File menu on the 1-2-3 menu bar.

LAB 2-3   ENTERING VALUES, FORMULAS, AND @FUNCTIONS

Labels are an important component of a worksheet. But labels reveal only a fraction of an electronic spreadsheet's potential. Once you start using values and formulas, you begin to realize the true power of 1-2-3.

Wild Rose wants to predict future cash needs and surpluses. To do this, you will need to enter some financial data in the form of values. Those values will be used to perform calculations based on the formulas you create. 1-2-3 has many built-in formulas (@functions) to simplify this process.

This lab will guide you through the steps necessary to retrieve your worksheet from your disk. You will then use it to practice entering values. Finally, you will discover how to have 1-2-3 perform calculations using formulas.

Opening a Worksheet

Before you begin your investigation of values, you must retrieve the file currently stored on your disk. To open a 1-2-3 for Windows file, choose the *Open...* command from the File menu, select the filename from the Open File dialog box, and click *OK*.

For the labs and exercises in this book, we'll assume you are retrieving your worksheets from a floppy disk in drive A.

1. Place your data disk in drive A.
2. If it is not already active, start Windows.
3. Then launch 1-2-3 for Windows.
4. Select the *Open...* command from the File menu.

After issuing the *Open...* command, the File Open dialog box, as shown in Figure 2-11, will materialize. This dialog box is very similar in appearance to the Save As dialog box you used to save your worksheet.

Figure 2-11.
The File Open dialog box allows you to select a file from a list box.

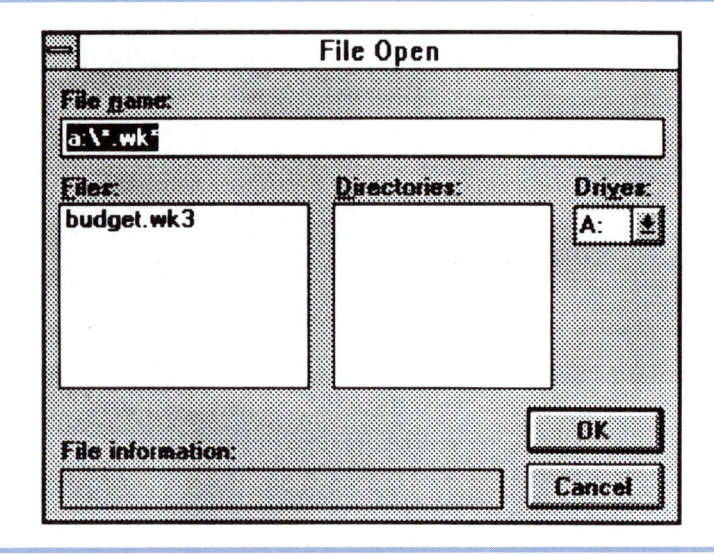

[File Open dialog box shown with File name "a:*.wk*", Files list containing "budget.wk3", empty Directories list, Drives showing "A:", File information field, and OK/Cancel buttons.]

If your worksheet is displayed in the *Files* list box, you can click on it and then choose the *OK* button to open it. A faster method of opening a file is to simply double-click on its name.

Use the *Directories* list box and the *Drives* drop-down list box to change the drive or directory when your worksheet is not displayed. Clicking the down arrow on the *Drives* list box will cause the list box to drop down.

5. Click the down arrow on the *Drives* list box.

The list box will drop down, showing you the available drives. To select a drive, you will need to click on the one you want.

6. Locate drive A and click on it.

Your file will be displayed in the *Files* list box.

7. To load your worksheet, click on BUDGET.WK3 in the *Files* list box, and then click the *OK* button.

1-2-3 replaces the Untitled worksheet with BUDGET.WK3 from the previous lab. Before you continue, maximize the worksheet to take advantage of all the available workspace.

8. Click the worksheet's maximize box.

Entering Values

A **value** is simply a number, or the results of a formula. Numbers provide the basis for most spreadsheet work. To enter a value into a worksheet, move the cell pointer to the desired cell, type the number, and click the *Confirm* button.

The values in a 1-2-3 worksheet can be formatted in a variety of ways. They can be made to appear as dollars, percentages, and dates—to mention just a few formats. For now, we'll stick with the general format initially used by 1-2-3.

Just as with labels, a cell can contain a larger number than it can display. Unlike labels, values will not overlap into adjacent cells. The way a number is shown is determined by the size of the number and the width of the cell. Table 2-2 shows some examples of how certain numbers are displayed at various column widths.

Table 2-2. Samples of values using the general format.

Value	Cell Width	Value Displayed
199763	<6	****
199763	=6	2E+05
199763	>6	199763
2.00395	=1	*
2.00395	2 to 5	2
2.00395	6 to 7	2.004
2.00395	>7	2.00395

When a cell is not wide enough to allow a value to be fully shown, 1-2-3 will round decimals down, change integer values to scientific notation, or fill the cell with asterisks (stars). You must widen the column in order to display these values properly, much as you did with oversized labels.

⊘ HAZARD

Values are always right justified (aligned on the right side of the cell). If you use a label-prefix character to change the placement of a number, the number will become a label rather than a value. While this may appear to work, 1-2-3 is no longer able to use that data in a calculation.

You are now familiar with entering labels on a worksheet. Values are entered in the same manner. Place the cell pointer on the desired cell and type the value using the number keys.

1. Select B6, and then type: **2**

This action will cause 1-2-3 to enter the VALUE mode because the first character entered is a number. The number will appear in the contents box, and the *Confirm* and *Cancel* buttons will become visible.

2. Type **000** to complete the entry.

After you complete the entry, click the *Confirm* button to accept it.

3. Select the *Confirm* button.

The value will appear in both the cell and the contents box, and 1-2-3 will return to the READY mode. Now let's try entering a larger number to see how 1-2-3 reacts.

4. Choose B7 and enter: **1,234,567,890** (use the *Confirm* button to confirm the selection).

Because the number is too large for the cell, 1-2-3 displays it in scientific notation. The contents box confirms that the cell actually contains the correct value. (Notice that the number in the contents box lacks commas because 1-2-3 ignores commas when you use them in a number.)

Next we'll see what happens when you enter a large decimal number.

5. Go to C6 and type: **443954.76** (always use the *Confirm* button or press Enter to complete your entry).

This time 1-2-3 will round the value up to a larger number. The contents box, however, shows the full amount.

By making the column width smaller for columns B and C, you will be able to see what happens when scientific notation and rounding fail to solve the problem.

6. Select B6.
7. While pressing the left mouse button, drag the cell pointer to C6.
8. Release the mouse button.

Chapter 2   Creating a Worksheet　　　　　　　　　　　　　　　　　　　　71

This action will select a cell range that incorporates both columns containing numbers. By using the *Column width...* command, you can now change the width of both columns simultaneously.

9. Choose the *Column width...* command from the Worksheet menu.

The Worksheet Column Width dialog box will open. The contents of the *Set width to* text box will be highlighted. You can use this text box to type in a narrower width for the columns indicated by the current range selection.

10. Type **4** and click the *OK* button.

The values in columns B and C will change to asterisks, as pictured in Figure 2-12. The asterisks indicate the cell is not wide enough to show its contents. By widening the column, you can correct the problem and replace the asterisks with the hidden values.

Figure 2-12. A cell will display asterisks when it is not wide enough to display the value it contains.

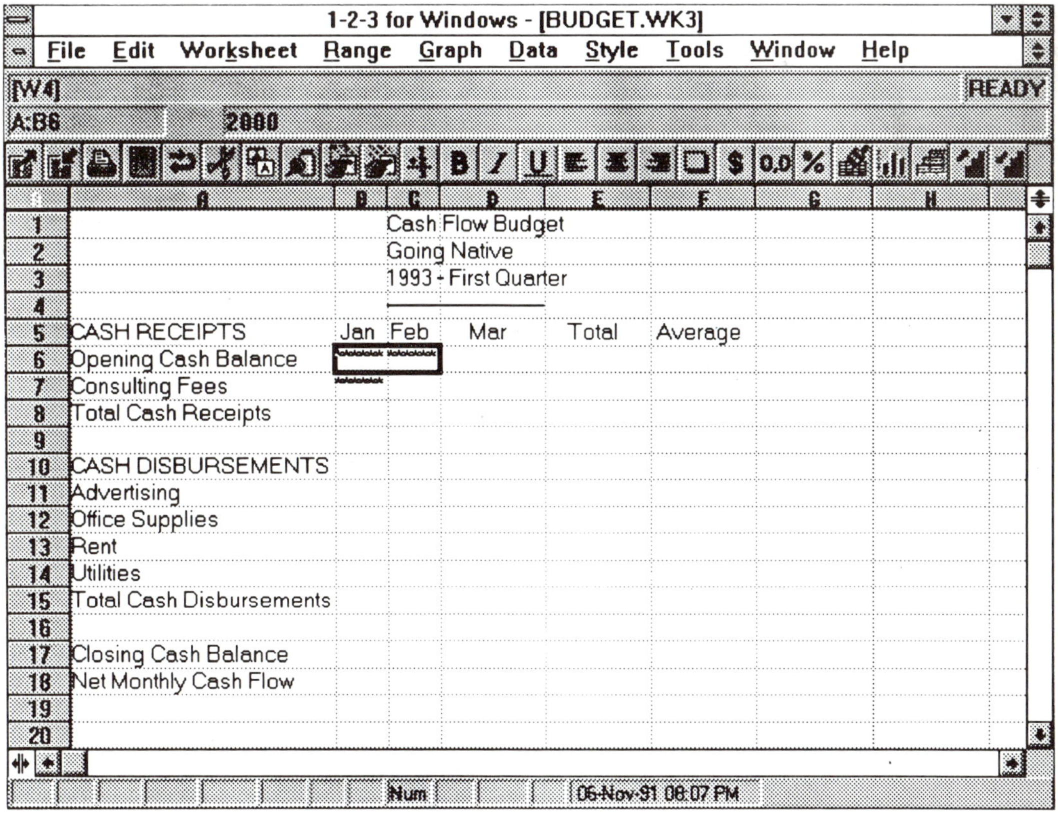

11. Issue the *Column width...* command from the Worksheet menu.
12. Click on the *Set width to* text box and type: **8**
13. Click the *OK* button.

The values replace the asterisks.

You can replace an existing value with a new one by selecting the cell and typing in the new value. Let's put more meaningful values into the worksheet.

14. Choose C6, type **2315** and press Enter.

The new number will replace the value previously displayed in C6.

15. Select B7 and enter: **1345**
16. Enter the rest of the values shown in Figure 2-13.

Figure 2-13. The values you will need to enter on your worksheet.

	A	B	C	D	E	F
1			Cash Flow Budget			
2			Going Native			
3			1993 - First Quarter			
4						
5	CASH RECEIPTS	Jan	Feb	Mar	Total	Average
6	Opening Cash Balance	2000	2315			
7	Consulting Fees	1345				
8	Total Cash Receipts	3345				
9						
10	CASH DISBURSEMENTS					
11	Advertising	100				
12	Office Supplies	90				
13	Rent	700				
14	Utilities	150				
15	Total Cash Disbursements	1040				
16						
17	Closing Cash Balance	2305				
18	Net Monthly Cash Flow	305				

Remember, it is wise to save your work periodically. This prevents accidental loss from power failures or other catastrophes. By using the *Save* command from the File menu, you can save the current version of your worksheet both quickly and easily.

17. Choose the *Save* command from the File menu.

1-2-3 replaces the file on your disk with the current contents of your worksheet.

⊘ HAZARD

If you are experimenting with a worksheet, you may not want to use this feature. When you use the *Save* command, you always replace your original worksheet. Instead, use the *Save As...* command and give the worksheet a new, unique name. This way, you prevent the earlier version from being lost.

Constructing Formulas

Your worksheet presently contains an assortment of labels and values. However, up to this point, you have done all the work. Fortunately, once data are entered in an electronic spreadsheet, you can use formulas to put the spreadsheet to work!

1-2-3 automatically performs calculations on the data in a worksheet based on the formulas you enter. A **formula** uses values, labels, operators, cell and range addresses, and @functions to calculate. While most formulas result in values, some formulas can produce labels. For now, we'll concentrate on those that result in values.

A formula uses an **operator** (e.g., +, −, or *) to indicate the relationship between two values. The type of operators used in this lab will be arithmetic operators. **Arithmetic operators**, as the name implies, perform arithmetic operations such as addition (+), subtraction (−), multiplication (*), division (/), and exponentiation (^).

Let's start by creating a formula to compute the Total Cash Receipts for January. This formula will add the Opening Cash Balance and the Consulting Fees together. Currently, the total shown in cell B8 is a fixed value, not a formula. Although the data are correct, we'll run into problems if any of the relevant values are changed. We'll demonstrate this problem and then show you how a formula can correct it.

1. Click on B8.

The value contained in this cell is a fixed value. It represents the sum of the current values shown in cells B6 and B7.

2. Select B6 and enter: **2500**

Cell B6 will change to reflect the new entry. Nevertheless, B8 will continue to display the original value. It no longer accurately reports the total of the two cells. To rectify the situation, you will need to base the value in cell B8 on the relationship between cells B6 and B7.

You can do this by entering the formula B6+B7 in cell B8. The addition operator (+) will automatically sum the contents of B6 and B7. This way, B8 no longer contains a static or fixed value but a dynamic formula that will change based on the entries made to the referenced cells.

The following steps show you how to enter your first formula.

3. Choose B8 and type: **B** (don't use the *Confirm* button yet).

Since the first character typed is a letter, 1-2-3 changes to the LABEL mode. However, we need to enter a formula that will result in a value. To do this, the first character we enter must cause 1-2-3 to change to the VALUE mode.

This is done by first typing an operator in front of the cell address. The operator causes 1-2-3 to assume you are entering a value. You can then successfully enter the cell address.

NOTE

In addition to operators, you can also use special characters such as the "at" symbol [@], period [.], parenthesis [(], pound sign [#], and dollar sign [$] to cause 1-2-3 to enter the VALUE mode.

The most typical operator used for entering a formula is the plus sign. Let's use it to invoke the VALUE mode.

4. Press the Backspace key to remove the letter "b."
5. Type **+B6+B7** and click the *Confirm* button.

The results of the formula will appear in cell B8. The actual formula will be displayed in the contents box. To see how the formula works, we'll alter the contents of a cell referenced by it and watch what happens.

6. Select B6 and enter: **2000**

The value in B6 changes to 2000. Simultaneously, B8 also changes to reflect this alteration. The flexibility and power of formulas are the real reasons for the popularity of electronic spreadsheets. They automate many of the operations that normally require a calculator. What's more, formulas instantly recalculate changes without the need to re-enter data!

There are other locations in your worksheet where formulas can prove beneficial. For example, we can use formulas to compute dynamic values for the Total Cash Disbursements, Closing Cash Balance, and the Net Monthly Cash Flow.

7. Select B15.

The value in this cell should display the results of totaling cells B11 through B14. To accomplish this, we'll replace the fixed value in B15 with the formula below.

8. Type: **+B11+B12+B13+B14** (click *Confirm*).

Again, the results of the formula will be shown in the cell, while the actual formula will appear in the contents box. If any of the values in B11 to B14 change, the new total will instantly be calculated and displayed in B15.

Now we'll try a formula that involves subtraction. The cash balance for the month results from deducting cash disbursements from cash receipts.

9. Select B17.

Don't forget to start your formula with a character that tells 1-2-3 to enter the VALUE mode.

10. Enter: **+B8−B15**

To calculate the cash flow, subtract the opening balance from the closing balance.

11. Select B18 and enter: **+B17−B6**

A relationship now exists between all the values for January. Altering any single value will cause all the formulas to be updated, and new values will be displayed. This will keep all the totals current. Let's change a value to see this happen.

12. Choose B7 and enter: **1445**

The new total in B8 is 3445, the closing balance in B17 shows 2405, and the cash flow in B18 becomes 405. With the formulas in place, you can now change a fixed value to see its impact on the totals.
Suppose you want to see what happens if rent increases.

13. Go to B13 and enter: **800**

The total disbursements will change, as will the closing balance and cash flow based on your assumption about a rent increase. This type of "what-if" analysis lets you anticipate various possibilities. It also helps you to prepare contingency plans to make the best of a changing world.
One other item in your worksheet needs some attention. Cell C6 contains the results of the closing balance from the previous month. Using a technique called *cell referencing*, you can link related information.

14. Select C6 and enter: **+B17**

This formula will cause the closing balance in January to be the opening balance in February. If anything changes in January, it will automatically alter the value in February.

Using @Functions

Using simple arithmetic operators alone would make it impractical for 1-2-3 to add several hundred values together. Lotus 1-2-3 for Windows comes with a large set of built-in formulas (over 200) to overcome this problem. @Functions also allow users to perform complex calculations very simply.
An **@function** is a built-in formula that performs specialized calculations automatically. Some @functions are as simple as @SUM. @SUM(C3..C9) will instruct 1-2-3 to add the values in the range C3..C9. This is much easier and quicker than typing out the entire formula +C3+C4+C5+C6+C7+C8+C9.

Other @functions replace complex formulas. For example, @STD calculates the standard deviation of a list of values. Standard deviation is a frequently used method of statistical analysis. This would normally involve several complex calculations. 1-2-3 automates these calculations with just a few simple keystrokes. An indexed list of the @functions is accessible from the Help menu.

Using @functions is very much like using formulas. Place the @function in the cell where you want the results displayed. Type the @function name followed by the range it will act upon. When you click the confirm button the results of the @function will then be displayed. Use the @SUM function to replace the formula contained in B15.

1. Move the cell pointer to B15.

Using the "at" symbol will automatically cause 1-2-3 to enter the VALUE mode. @Functions act upon a range of cells. Following the @function name will be the range address surrounded by parentheses.

2. Type **@SUM(B11..B14)** and click the *Confirm* button.

The sum of the values in the range B11 to B14 is displayed in cell B15. The contents box will show that the @SUM function has replaced the previously entered formula. However, the displayed results will remain the same.

Let's change the value of cell B14 and find out how it affects the @SUM function.

3. Select B14 and enter: **175**

The @SUM function will automatically recalculate the sum of the range B11 through B14. This is exactly what the previous formula accomplished. But using a built-in formula makes it a much simpler task.

There is another method for entering ranges into an @function. It is necessary to enter some additional data before trying this alternative method.

4. Place the value **1500** in C7.
5. In C8 enter the formula: **+C6+C7**
6. Type **150** in C11.
7. Select C12 and enter: **90**
8. Enter **700** in C13.
9. Go to C14 and type: **175**

You will now need to total the Cash Disbursements for February. Instead of manually typing the range in the contents box, point to it.

Start by moving the cell pointer to where the total will appear. Type the @SUM function and the left parenthesis. Click the pointer in the beginning cell of the range to be summed. Hold the mouse button down and drag the pointer to the ending cell of the range. Release the mouse button and type the right parenthesis to complete the @SUM function. Clicking the *Confirm* button will prompt the worksheet to automatically perform the calculation.

10. Select C15 and type: **@SUM(**
11. In C11 click and hold the left mouse button down.
12. Continue to hold the button down and move the pointer to C14.
13. Release the button, type **)** and click the *Confirm* button.

The sum of the range C11 to C14 will automatically be calculated. Your worksheet should resemble Figure 2-14.

Congratulations! You have now completed this lab. Don't forget to save your work before you begin celebrating.

14. Choose the *Save* command from the File menu.

1-2-3 will replace the file on your disk with the current worksheet. Now exit 1-2-3 and Windows.

15. Select the *Exit* command from the File menu.

LAB 2-4 PRINTING THE RESULTS

Many times you will need to have a printed copy of your worksheet. You may want to include the data in a report or business presentation. Printed copies are also a convenient way to review, analyze, and share your worksheet. In this lab, you will explore the techniques to produce a printed copy of your worksheet.

There are three components to printing your worksheet. First, you will want to lay out, or set up, your printed page. Selecting *Page Setup...* from the File menu will allow you to include information on each printed page that is not part of your worksheet. Textual information that is placed at the top of each printed page is called a **header**. A **footer** is information that is placed at the bottom of each page. You can also include things that 1-2-3 does not normally print, such as grid lines and worksheet frames.

Chapter 2   Creating a Worksheet

Figure 2-14. The completed worksheet.

```
┌─────────────────────────────────────────────────────────────┐
│              1-2-3 for Windows - [BUDGET.WK3]               │
│  File  Edit  Worksheet  Range  Graph  Data  Style  Tools  Window  Help │
│ [W8]                                                  READY │
│ A:C15         @SUM[C11..C14]                                │
├─────────────────────────────────────────────────────────────┤
│         A              B         C         D      E      F       G    │
│  1                          Cash Flow Budget                           │
│  2                          Going Native                               │
│  3                          1993 - First Quarter                       │
│  4                                                                     │
│  5  CASH RECEIPTS        Jan       Feb       Mar    Total  Average     │
│  6  Opening Cash Balance 2000      2280                                │
│  7  Consulting Fees      1445      1500                                │
│  8  Total Cash Receipts  3445      3780                                │
│  9                                                                     │
│ 10  CASH DISBURSEMENTS                                                 │
│ 11  Advertising           100       150                                │
│ 12  Office Supplies        90        90                                │
│ 13  Rent                  800       700                                │
│ 14  Utilities             175       175                                │
│ 15  Total Cash Disbursements 1165  1115                                │
│ 16                                                                     │
│ 17  Closing Cash Balance 2280                                          │
│ 18  Net Monthly Cash Flow 280                                          │
│ 19                                                                     │
│ 20                                                                     │
│                    Num            09-Dec-91 01:58 PM                   │
└─────────────────────────────────────────────────────────────┘
```

After setting up your page, you will want to preview it by choosing *Preview...* from the File menu. This permits you to see on the monitor how each page will appear when printed. By using this feature, you will avoid delays caused by printing pages that aren't quite right. Finally, you will print your worksheet by picking the *Print...* option from the File menu.

Setting up a Page

The *Page Setup...* command in the File menu lets you add a header and a footer to each printed page. For example, a descriptive header, at the top of each page, provides quick identification of a particular printout. A footer, on the other hand, typically offers supplemental information for the contents of a page.

To see how these features work, we'll add both a header and a footer to your document. If your worksheet is not currently open, you will need to retrieve it from the disk.

1. Place your data disk in drive A.
2. If it is not already active, start Windows.
3. Then launch 1-2-3 for Windows.
4. Select the *Open...* command from the File menu.
5. If necessary, click the down arrow on the *Drives* list box and select drive A.
6. To open BUDGET.WK3, double-click on it in the *Files* list box.
7. Click the worksheet's maximize box.

You are now ready to enter header and footer information you want to include on every page.

8. From the File menu select *Page Setup....*

This will cause the File Page Setup dialog box to materialize, as portrayed in Figure 2-15. This dialog box has several features that control the layout of your printed page. Besides the *Header* and *Footer* text boxes, there are several other boxes containing buttons or check boxes.

The Margins box contains text boxes to change the top, bottom, left, and right margins. By simply clicking in the appropriate box, you can edit the default values 1-2-3 uses. Let's continue to use the initial settings for now.

To identify data properly from page to page, you may want to have headings for certain rows or columns. These are called borders. **Borders** are ranges from your worksheet you want included on every page. Since you have a small worksheet, you will not need to include borders at this time.

The Compression box includes radio buttons to enlarge or reduce your worksheet to fit on a page. If you select the *Automatically fit to page* button, 1-2-3 will shrink or expand your worksheet for you. This feature can be used in combination with the Landscape mode (described below) to print extra wide reports.

The initial settings for 1-2-3 will print a worksheet without grid lines or a worksheet frame. You can change these defaults by checking the suitable boxes in the Options area.

The direction of the printing relative to the paper is controlled by the radio buttons in the Orientation box. The *Portrait* orientation prints

Chapter 2   Creating a Worksheet **81**

Figure 2-15. The File Page Setup dialog box lets you control how your page will look when it is printed.

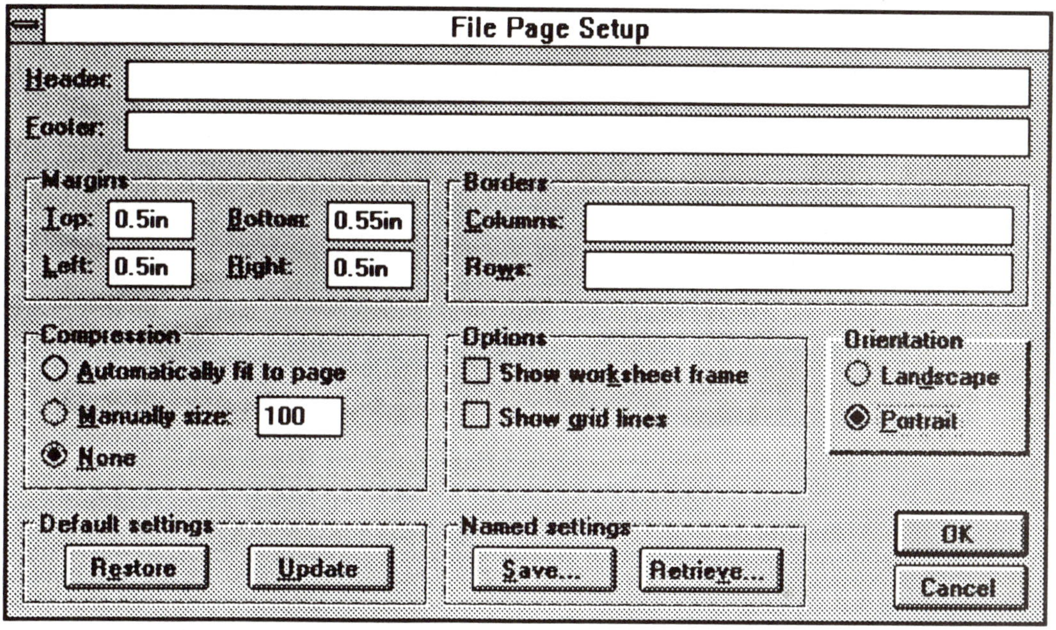

---

across the width of the paper. *Landscape* prints lengthwise and is sometimes called sideways printing. Portrait orientation is the default because it is the most commonly used.

By clicking in the *Header* text box, you will be able to create a header that will appear at the top of every page.

9. Click the *Header* text box (if the insertion point is not already in the *Header* text box).
10. Type: **Lab 2-4**

Next create a footer that contains your name and the course title to identify your printed page.

11. Click in the *Footer* text box.
12. Enter your name and the course title (e.g., Rosalind Planter, 1-2-3 for Windows).
13. Click the *OK* button.

Previewing the Page

The File Page Setup dialog box provides many different options for laying out the appearance of the printed worksheet. The *Preview...* feature will allow you to view and fine-tune these options prior to printing. There is one final step you will need to complete before previewing your worksheet.

A worksheet might be as large as 256 columns by 8192 rows. Most of your worksheet is actually blank. It would be a tremendous waste of time and paper to print these blank areas. By defining a print range, you will be able to print just the portion you desire.

The print range is selected using the same method you used to select a range for changing column width. Place the cell pointer at the beginning of the range and hold the left mouse button down. Drag the cell pointer to the end of your range and release the button.

1. Select A1 and continue to press the left mouse button.
2. Drag the cell pointer to F18 and release the button.

You are now ready to see how the worksheet will appear on the printed page.

3. Choose the *Preview...* command from the File menu.

As shown in Figure 2-16, a File Preview dialog box opens. Selecting the *Page Setup...* button is equivalent to selecting it from the File menu. Notice there are also some text boxes to control which pages are previewed in a large worksheet.

Figure 2-16. The File Preview dialog box.

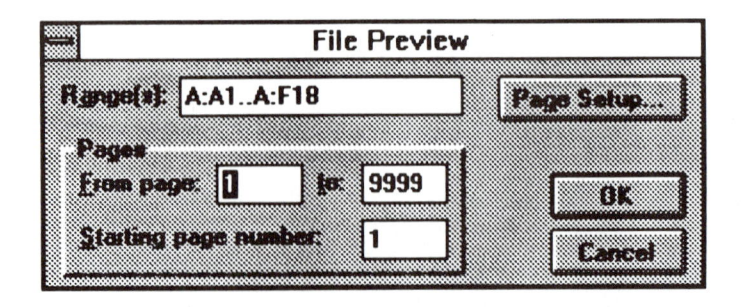

The range you selected prior to opening the dialog box is shown in the *Range(s)* text box. You can manually enter a range by clicking in the box. Clicking the *OK* button will allow you to preview how your printed copy will appear.

4. Click the *OK* button.

The Print Preview window appears, as seen in Figure 2-17. The window represents a sheet of paper. A line on the sheet outlines the margins that were set during the page setup. The header and footer also appear in the Print Preview window. Although it is difficult to read the text, it serves the purpose of showing the page layout. Clicking anywhere on the window will return you to your worksheet.

5. Click anywhere on the page.

Figure 2-17. The preview page shows you a representation of how your printout will appear.

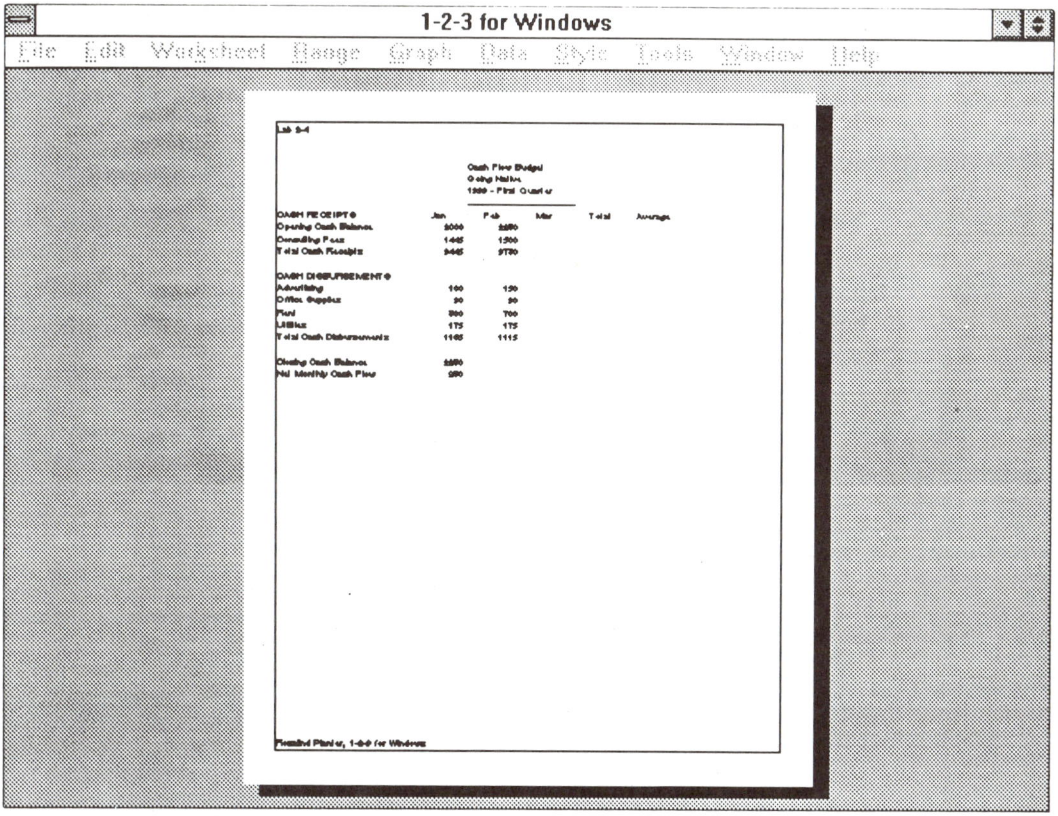

There is something different about the appearance of your worksheet. The area that was selected as the print range is now surrounded by a gray dashed line. This line represents the current print range. Until the print range is redefined, this range will stay in effect.

Printing Your Worksheet

You are now ready to print your worksheet. By selecting *Print...* from the File menu, you will be able to produce your first "hard copy" printout.

It is a good practice to save your work before printing. This will prevent accidental loss resulting from problems with the print device.

1. Choose *Save* from the File menu.

1-2-3 will replace the file on the disk with a copy of the current worksheet.

Make sure your printer is ready. If you are using a dot-matrix printer, you will need to check the position of the paper in the printer.

2. Select *Print...* from the File menu.

The File Print dialog box will appear, as portrayed in Figure 2-18. This box includes buttons to *Preview* your page and to perform *Page Setup*. As in the File Preview dialog box, you can choose which pages to print by using text boxes. The current print range is displayed and can be manually changed if necessary. Also shown is the current print device. Generally, these settings will be the same as the ones from the File Preview dialog box. Clicking the *OK* button starts the printing process.

Figure 2-18. The File Print dialog box shows you the device on which 1-2-3 will print your worksheet.

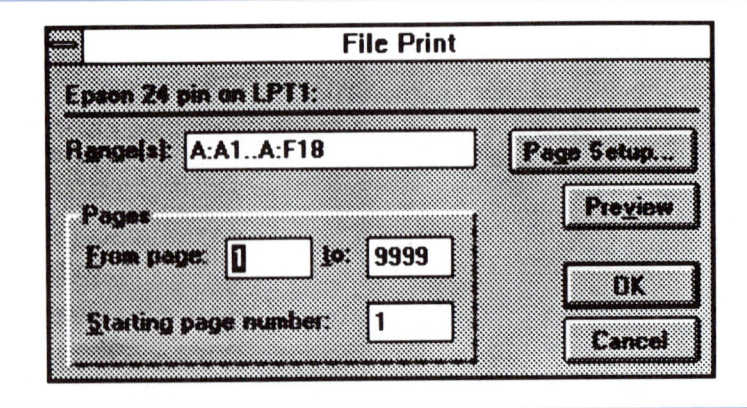

Chapter 2   Creating a Worksheet

> ⊘ **HAZARD**
>
> If the printer shown is different than the printer you intend to use, you will need to change the printer selection. This can be done from the File menu by selecting the *Printer Setup...* command. The labs and exercises in this book will assume your default printer is the printer you want to use.

   3. Click the *OK* button.

Figure 2-19.

There will be a short delay while 1-2-3 builds the data to send to the printer. During this time, you will see a message box as illustrated in Figure 2-19, which shows the destination of the information 1-2-3 is sending. It is possible to abort the printing by clicking on the *Cancel* button. When 1-2-3 is finished sending the data to the printer, it will return to the READY mode.

Congratulations! You have now produced your first printed worksheet.

   4. To exit 1-2-3 for Windows, double-click on the 1-2-3 control-menu box.

Figure 2-20.

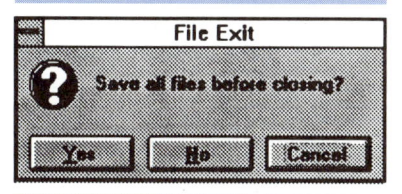

As shown in Figure 2-20, the File Exit warning message will appear. If you select the *Yes* button, 1-2-3 will attempt to save your worksheet to disk. If a worksheet with the same name already exists on the disk, the buttons in the File Exit box will change to *Replace* or *Backup*. Using the backup feature preserves the older version on the disk.

Choosing the *No* button will cause 1-2-3 to close. The contents of the worksheet will not be saved to the disk. This allows you to open a functional worksheet and experiment with making changes to it. Since the good copy is on the disk, there is no need to save the experimental version.

   5. Click the *No* button.

COMING ATTRACTIONS...

You've explored a lot of new territory in this chapter. Not only can you now navigate; enter labels, values, and formulas; use @functions; alter column width; and store and retrieve your worksheet, you can also print it.

Chapters 3 and 4 will show you how to make changes and enhance your worksheet. In Chapter 5, you will learn to display data from your worksheet in graphs and charts.

KEY TERMS

@Function Built-in formula that performs specialized calculations automatically.

Address box Displays the current cell address.

Arithmetic operators Perform arithmetic operations such as addition (+), subtraction (−), multiplication (*), division (/), and exponentiation (^).

Borders Ranges of column or row headings from the worksheet that are included on every printed page.

Cell The intersection of a column and a row. A cell is where you enter a label, number, or formula.

Cell address The column letter and row number of a cell. The cell address B3 is the cell located at the intersection of column B and row 3.

Cell pointer The highlighted box surrounding a cell that indicates the active cell on the worksheet.

Column width The number of characters that 1-2-3 can display in a column.

Contents box The contents box reveals the contents of the current cell, allowing the actual contents to be viewed or edited. In the EDIT mode, it will contain a *Confirm* and *Cancel* button.

Control panel The top four rows of the 1-2-3 window, as shown in Figure 2-1.

Current cell The cell holding the cell pointer.

Default An initial setting that 1-2-3 uses until you specify a different setting.

Edit line The final line of the control panel. It consists of the address box and the contents box.

Electronic spreadsheet A computer program that uses a worksheet of columns and rows to let you quickly enter and manipulate labels, numbers, and formulas.

Footer Textual information that is placed at the bottom of each printed page.

Format line The third row of the control panel. The left side of the format line will display the format of the current cell when the cell has been altered from the normal 1-2-3 settings.

Formula Uses values, labels, operators, cell and range addresses, and @functions to perform calculations.

Global commands Commands that apply to the whole worksheet.

Header Textual information that is placed at the top of each printed page.

Label Any cell entry that begins with a letter or label-prefix character.

Label-prefix character Special characters that determine the placement of a label in the cell.

Mode indicator The right side of the format line. This indicator displays the mode or state 1-2-3 is presently in. Table 2-3 provides a summary of these modes.

Operator Used to indicate the relationship between two values (e.g., +, −, or *).

Point A typesetting measurement that divides each inch into 72 parts.

Range An area on the worksheet consisting of a single cell, a block of adjoining cells, or even an entire worksheet. A range must always be rectangular and is identified by a range address.

Range address The cell addresses of any two diagonally opposite corner cells of the range separated by periods (e.g., A1..B10).

Row height The height of the largest character that can be fully displayed in a row. Characters are measured in points. A point is 1/72nd of an inch.

Value A number, formula, or an @function.

Worksheet frame The top and left side of a worksheet where the row numbers and column letters are displayed.

Table 2-3. Summary of 1-2-3 modes.

EDIT	You are entering or editing text in a text box, or you made an incorrect entry.
ERROR	1-2-3 is displaying an error message.
FILES	You are in 1-2-3 Classic and 1-2-3 is displaying a list of file names.
FIND	You selected *Data Query Find* or pressed F7 (QUERY) during a *Data Query Find* command.
LABEL	You are entering a label.
MENU	You clicked the menu bar, or pressed Alt+F10.
POINT	You are specifying a range before choosing a command, while working in a dialog box, or while entering a formula.
READY	1-2-3 is ready for you to enter data or choose a command.
VALUE	You are entering a value.
WAIT	1-2-3 is completing a command or process, such as saving a file.

EXERCISES

2-1. This exercise will allow you to practice moving around on your worksheet.

   a. Start Windows and launch 1-2-3, if necessary.
   b. To move three screens to the right, click the horizontal scroll bar three times to the right of the scroll box.
   c. Move one screen down by clicking once on the vertical scroll bar.
   d. Select cell Z26.
   e. Drag the horizontal scroll box to the left until it is below column Z.
   f. Point at the up scroll arrow, in the vertical scroll bar, and hold the mouse button down until the cell pointer is in row 1.
   g. Select K10.
   h. Move the cell pointer to A1 by clicking the worksheet letter in the upper left corner of the worksheet frame.
   i. You may end 1-2-3 for Windows without saving your worksheet.

2-2. You can review your skills at entering labels, changing column widths, and selecting ranges by completing this exercise.

   a. Launch 1-2-3 and maximize your worksheet.
   b. In A1 enter the label: **Normal**
   c. Move to A2 and use the caret (^) label-prefix to enter the label: **^Center**

       d. Use the quote (") label-prefix character to right justify the label **"Right** in cell A3.
       e. Fill A4 with asterisks by using the backslash (\) label-prefix: *****
       f. Type the following label into A5: **This is a really long label**
       g. Move the pointer to the line separating columns A and B on the worksheet frame.

The pointer will change to the double-headed arrow.

       h. Drag the border of column A to the right until the column is wide enough to include the entire label in A5.
       i. In B5 enter the label: **Oops!**
       j. Select A5 and use the *Column Width...* command from the Worksheet menu to change the width of column A to 10 characters.

Note that this will cause the cell to display only the part of the long label that can fit in column A. Did you also notice that, as the width of column A changed, the centered, right-justified, and filled labels changed accordingly?

       k. Use the *Global Settings...* command from the Worksheet menu to change the column width of the entire worksheet to 4 characters.

All the columns will change width except for column A, because it was previously altered.

       l. Select the range K5..Z5 by clicking on K5 and holding down the mouse while moving the cell pointer to the right. Release the button when the pointer is in column Z.
       m. Change the column width of the range to 6 characters using the *Column Width...* command.
       n. You may exit 1-2-3 for Windows without saving your file.

2-3. This exercise will give you an opportunity to practice your skills in entering values, formulas, and @functions.

       a. Begin by starting Windows and 1-2-3 and maximizing your worksheet.
       b. In A1 enter the value: **1234567890**
       c. Place the value **1.098765432** in A2.
       d. Enter **654321** in cell A3.

1-2-3 will display A1 in scientific notation, A2 will be rounded to the number of digits that will fully display in the cell, and A3 will show the actual cell contents.

Chapter 2 Creating a Worksheet **89**

    e. Drag the border of column A to make it half its original size.

Cell A1 and A3 will no longer be able to display their contents. The value in A2 is rounded to even fewer digits.

    f. In cell B1 enter **1**, in B2 place the value **2**, and in B3 the value **3**
    g. Add the contents of A1 and B1 into cell C1, using the formula: **+A1+B1**

Do you remember the reason for starting the formula with a plus? (Hint: If you started with the character "a," what mode would 1-2-3 be in: LABEL or VALUE?)

    h. In C2 enter the formula: **+A2−B2**
    i. Place the formula **+A3/B3** in cell C3.
    j. To make all the values display properly, select the range A1..C1 and use the *Column Width...* command to change the column width to 12.
    k. Move to B4 and enter the @function: **@SUM(B1..B3)**
    l. Select B3 and enter: **10**

The values in C3 and B4 will instantly change to reflect the results of the formulas.

    m. Use the *Save As...* command from the File menu to save your worksheet as **A:\EXER2-3**
    n. You may exit 1-2-3 for Windows.

2-4. This final exercise will review the printing techniques you learned in Lab 2-4. (To complete this exercise, you must have done exercise 2-3.)

    a. Start Windows and 1-2-3.
    b. Use the *Open...* command from the File menu to retrieve your worksheet, EXER2-3.WK3, from drive A.
    c. Use the *Page Setup...* command to include the header **Exercise 2-4**, and a footer that contains your name.
    d. Click the *Portrait* orientation button and *OK*.
    e. Save your worksheet.
    f. Select the range A1..C4.
    g. Choose the *Preview...* command to preview your worksheet before printing. Clicking anywhere on the preview page will return you to your worksheet.
    h. Make sure your printer is ready, and print your worksheet using the *Print...* command.
    i. Close 1-2-3 for Windows without saving your worksheet.

REVIEW QUESTIONS

True or False Questions

1. T F Electronic spreadsheets are one of the reasons for the popularity of the personal computer.
2. T F A worksheet may contain over 2 million cells.
3. T F Clicking the upper left corner of the worksheet frame, where the worksheet letter is displayed, will move the cell pointer to the upper left corner of your worksheet.
4. T F 1-2-3 will warn you if you try to exit a worksheet in which you have made changes and not saved.
5. T F A label-prefix character can be used to position a value in a cell.
6. T F A label can only be as wide as the cell that contains it.
7. T F It is possible to change the width of nonadjacent columns all at one time.
8. T F A range must be rectangular.
9. T F Global commands only affect the part of the worksheet showing on the screen.
10. T F 1-2-3 for Windows allows you to print your worksheet sideways.

Multiple Choice Questions

1. What does an electronic spreadsheet allow you to do?
   a. Manipulate labels, numbers, and formulas
   b. Store and retrieve worksheets on a disk
   c. Perform automatic calculations as data are entered or changed
   d. All of the above

2. The intersection of a row and column on a worksheet is the
   a. Range
   b. Cell
   c. Address box
   d. Contents box

3. The initial or default setting for label placement in a cell is
   a. Left justified
   b. Center justified
   c. Right justified
   d. It depends on the length of the label

4. Which of the following can be used to change the width of a column?

   a. Dragging the column border to the right or left
   b. Using the *Column Width...* command from the Worksheet menu
   c. Changing the setting in the *Column width* text box in the Global Settings dialog box
   d. All of the above

5. What does it mean when asterisks are displayed after you enter a value into a cell?

   a. You were actually in the LABEL mode, and the value is being displayed as a label
   b. The number you entered is too big or small for 1-2-3 to process
   c. The column is not wide enough to display the value
   d. You forgot to use commas when entering a large value

6. What is the purpose of the plus (+) when the first character of a formula is a cell reference?

   a. 1-2-3 must always start with addition
   b. To cause 1-2-3 to enter the VALUE mode rather than the LABEL mode
   c. To indicate you are "positive" that this is the correct cell
   d. There is no purpose, the plus is not necessary

7. Which of the following describes @functions?

   a. Extremely complex formulas, only used by experienced programmers
   b. Built-in formulas that automate calculations easily
   c. Only capable of doing simple arithmetic calculations
   d. All of the above

8. Which of the following can be included on a printed copy of your worksheet?

   a. Header
   b. Grid lines
   c. The portion of your worksheet designated by the print range
   d. All of the above

9. What will 1-2-3 do if you try to exit a worksheet you have just edited?

   a. Warn you with a dialog box
   b. Automatically save it and close 1-2-3
   c. Close 1-2-3 and discard your editing changes
   d. Automatically save your work and create a backup file of your previous worksheet

10. What is the advantage of formulas compared to fixed numbers?

    a. Formulas are dynamic and can be recalculated automatically
    b. Since formulas are labels, they can overflow into empty cells if they are too wide for a column
    c. Formulas always require fewer keystrokes to enter than numbers
    d. All of the above

CHAPTER 3

Modifying a Worksheet

• *Objectives*

Upon completing this chapter, you'll be able to:
1. **Use SmartIcons.**
2. **Edit data in a worksheet.**
3. **Move data in a worksheet.**
4. **Copy data in a worksheet.**

OVERVIEW

This chapter will introduce the use of SmartIcons for selecting 1-2-3 commands. SmartIcons provide a faster and "friendlier" way to access many of the drop-down menu commands. They combine numerous mouse actions and keystrokes into a single action. We'll use SmartIcons to edit, move, and copy the data in your worksheet.

LAB 3-1 USING SMARTICONS

One of the advantages of using Windows is the ability to direct actions through the use of icons. For example, without knowing the operating system commands, you can launch 1-2-3 for Windows by double-clicking on its icon. 1-2-3 takes icons one step further with the addition of SmartIcons.

SmartIcons provide immediate and easy access to commonly used 1-2-3 commands. SmartIcons are located in the row below the control panel, as shown in Figure 3–1. This row or group of icons is called the **Icon Palette**. The graphic on each icon represents the action it performs. Since there aren't any official names for the SmartIcons, we'll use the name of the command associated with the icon.

To use most SmartIcons, you will need to select a range first. For example, when you choose a range and click the *Cut* SmartIcon (the

Chapter 3   Modifying a Worksheet   **93**

Figure 3-1. The Icon Palette containing the SmartIcons.

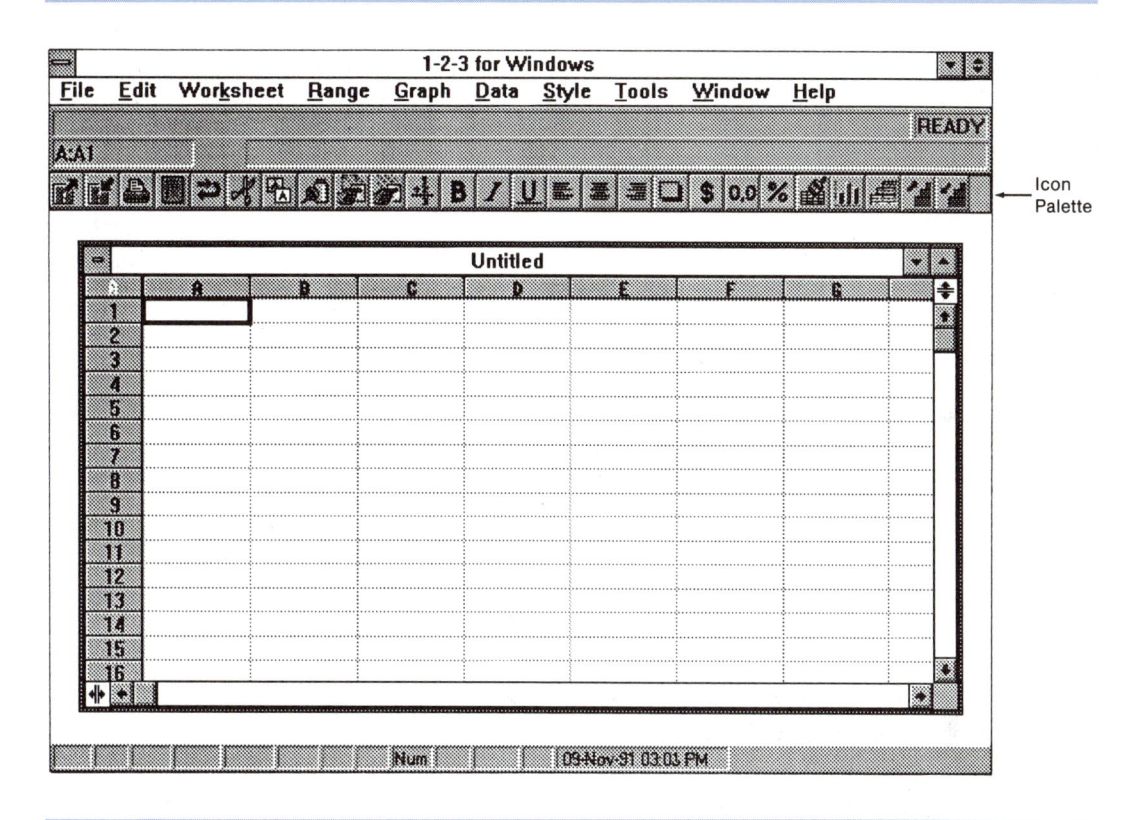

one showing a picture of scissors), the selected range will be cut from the worksheet and placed in Clipboard. **Clipboard** is a temporary storage area for text and graphics that allows you to transfer data within and between application packages.

Some SmartIcons perform direct actions by bypassing dialog boxes altogether. For instance, the *Print* icon will print your worksheet without pausing to display the File Print dialog box. This has the advantage of saving time but eliminates some options.

⊘ HAZARD

Since many SmartIcons perform actions without opening a dialog box, you are afforded less control of some operations. Be careful using the SmartIcons. You should only use them when instructed to do so, or after you have become familiar with their functions.

It's possible to relocate the Icon Palette and customize its contents. However, the labs and exercises in this book assume that you are using the default Icon Palette. This is the original palette created when 1-2-3 for Windows is first installed.

Let's explore the Icon Palette by looking at a few SmartIcon descriptions. (We'll talk about the other SmartIcons as we encounter situations where they can be useful.)

1. Start Windows.
2. Launch 1-2-3 for Windows.
3. Locate the Icon Palette.

If you look at the first SmartIcon on the far left side of the palette, you'll notice that it has a picture of an arrow pointing away from a disk. This picture is meant to depict information moving "from" the disk to your computer.

This is the *Open...* icon. It lets you quickly retrieve a worksheet from your disk. You can receive further information about it or any other SmartIcon by pointing at it and holding down the right mouse button.

4. Place the pointer over the *Open...* icon (the first SmartIcon on the left end of the palette).
5. Press the *right* mouse button and hold it down.

The description of the icon's function will appear in the title bar, as pictured in Figure 3-2.

6. Release the right mouse button when you finish reading the description.

Let's display the description of the *Save* icon. Can you find it? Here is a hint: Look for a disk with an arrow pointing toward it. This graphic represents information moving from your computer to your disk.

7. Point at the second icon from the left (a diskette with an arrow pointing toward it).
8. Click the *right* mouse button and hold it down.

Again, an explanation of the chosen SmartIcon will become visible in the title bar.

9. Release the button and point at the third SmartIcon from the left.

Chapter 3 Modifying a Worksheet

Figure 3-2. A description of the icon's function can be displayed using the *right* mouse button.

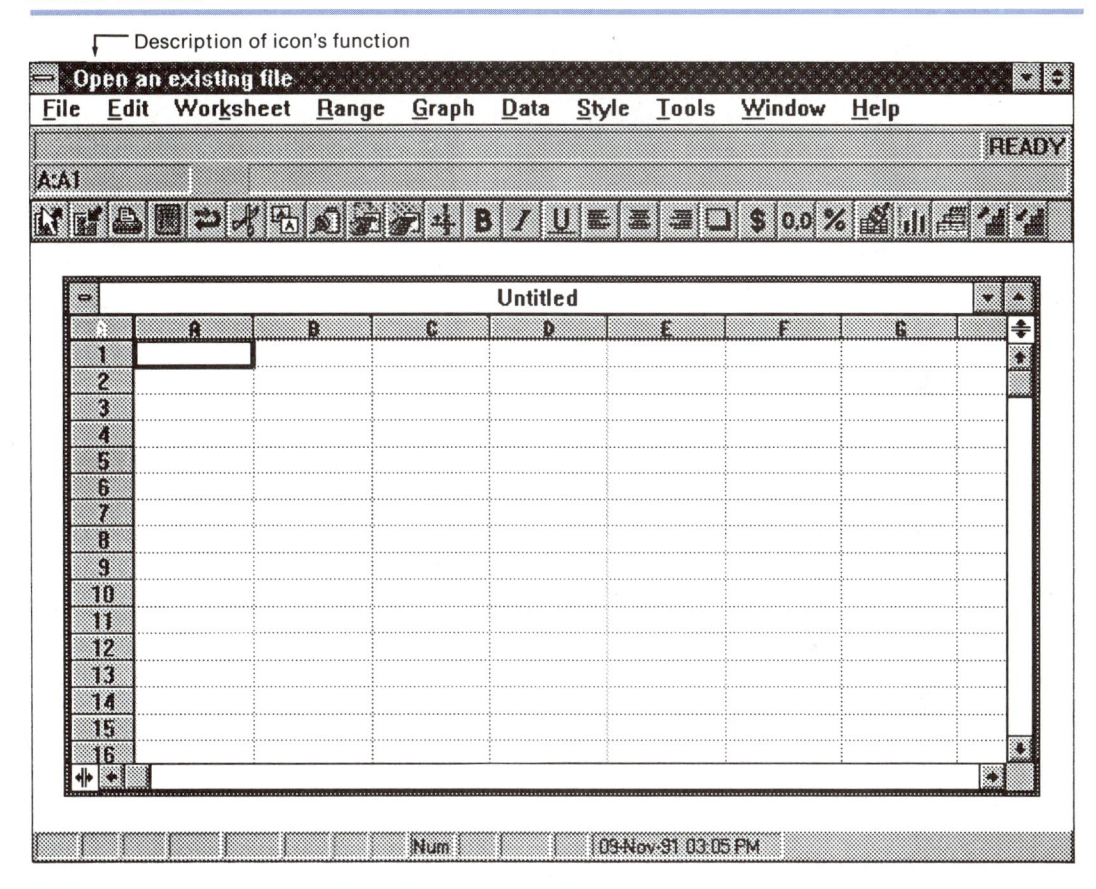

Any guesses what this icon does? The picture of a printer should be a dead giveaway.

10. To confirm your hunch, hold down the right mouse button and read the icon's description in the title bar.

If you've guessed which one is the *Print* icon, then congratulations are in order. If not, don't worry. As you begin working with 1-2-3, recognizing the SmartIcon graphics will quickly become second nature.

To gain some actual experience in using a SmartIcon, we'll use the *Open...* icon to retrieve the worksheet BUDGET.WK3. To do this, you simply click on the *Open...* icon located at the far left end of the Icon Palette. When the File Open dialog box appears, choose the worksheet you want, and click *OK* to load it.

11. Click on the *Open...* icon with the *left* mouse button.

The File Open dialog box will appear, just as if you had selected the *Open...* command from the File menu.

12. If necessary, change to the drive containing your data disk.
13. To retrieve BUDGET.WK3, double-click on it in the *Files* list box.

Your worksheet will replace the Untitled worksheet. As you can see, SmartIcons can be much simpler and easier to work with than drop-down menus.

14. Close the worksheet and continue to the next lab, or quit 1-2-3 if you're leaving us for a while.

> **NOTE**
>
> You can easily add an icon to the Icon Palette. Choose the *SmartIcon...* command from the Tools menu, then select the *Customize...* button. When the Tools SmartIcon Customize dialog box appears, choose the icon you want, click the *Add* button, and select *OK*. To remove a SmartIcon from the palette, simply select the icon and click the *Remove* button in the Tools SmartIcon Customize dialog box.

LAB 3-2 EDITING DATA

In the previous chapter, you created your first worksheet. As your understanding of Lotus 1-2-3 for Windows grows, so will the complexity of your worksheets. You'll find it necessary to change, add, and delete data to incorporate new techniques and features.

Changing a Cell Entry

Many times you will find it necessary to change the contents of a cell. This may involve changing a label, updating a formula, or replacing a value.

There are two methods of modifying the data in a cell. The first one involves replacing the entire contents of a cell with new data. The second technique utilizes the EDIT mode so you can change just a portion of the cell contents.

Chapter 3 *Modifying a Worksheet*

We'll begin by using the first method to change the contents of several cells.

1. If necessary, start Windows and launch 1-2-3 for Windows.
2. Click the *Open...* SmartIcon.

The File Open dialog box will appear.

3. Click the arrow on the *Drives* drop-down list box.
4. Select drive A.
5. Choose the BUDGET.WK3 worksheet by double-clicking on it in the *Files* list box.
6. Maximize the worksheet window.

Suppose you mistakenly entered the rent as 800 when it should have been 750. Since it is a short entry, you can easily correct this oversight by replacing the old value with a new one. To do this, you first select the cell you want to change and then simply type in the correct value.

7. Select the cell holding the rent value for January, B13.
8. Then type: **750**

Remember to always click the *Confirm* button to complete the entry.

9. Click the *Confirm* button.

NOTE

From here on, you'll no longer be reminded to confirm your data entries. When you are asked to enter data in a cell, use the *Confirm* button, Enter key, or an arrow key to complete the action.

Once you complete these actions, the original value in cell B13 of 800 will be replaced with the new figure of 750. Since the rent remains constant throughout the year, it makes more sense to make February's rent dependent on what's entered in January. This way, any changes to rent in January are automatically reflected in February.

To accomplish this, you must alter the contents of the cell containing February's rent to reference the value in January.

10. Choose C13.

The entire contents of the cell require replacement. Again, it's most easily done by entering a new value.

Don't forget to start your cell reference with a plus (+) so that 1-2-3 enters the VALUE mode!

11. Type: **+B13**

Rose has negotiated the rent down to 725 per month for the entire year. We'll change the amount for January.

12. Select B13.
13. Enter: **725**

The value 725 will appear in place of the old value of 750, and the value in February will be updated simultaneously.

Rose decides the title of this worksheet should be Quarterly Cash Flow Budget, instead of Cash Flow Budget. This alteration will involve retyping the existing label. Since the title is rather long, it will be much easier to insert the new word, "Quarterly," at the beginning of the existing label.

Fortunately, 1-2-3 provides an EDIT mode that allows you to alter the contents of a cell selectively.

To enter the EDIT mode, first select the cell you want to change and click in the contents box where you want the editing to occur. Use the Delete and Backspace keys to remove the unwanted portions of the data, and then type in the new data. Selecting the *Confirm* button accepts the new data, and the contents of the cell will change.

14. Choose C1.

The label "Cash Flow Budget" will appear in the contents box. To insert the word "Quarterly," you will need to place the pointer at the beginning of the contents box, between the word "Cash" and the apostrophe ('). Whenever the pointer is in the contents box, it will assume the I-beam shape.

15. Place the I-beam between the apostrophe and the word "Cash" in the contents box.
16. Click the mouse.

The I-beam will change to a vertical bar as shown in Figure 3-3. The position of the vertical bar determines where characters will be inserted or deleted. As you type, any existing characters to the right of the insertion point will automatically be shifted over.

Chapter 3 Modifying a Worksheet

Figure 3-3. The I-beam changes to a vertical bar after you click the mouse.

```
                    1-2-3 for Windows - [BUDGET.WK3]
           File  Edit  Worksheet  Range  Graph  Data  Style  Tools  Window  Help
           [Page] [W8]                                                          EDIT
           A:C1         X √ Cash Flow Budget

                         A              B         C          D        E         F         G
Vertical →  1
bar         2                                  Cash Flow Budget
            3                                  Going Native
            4                                  1993 - First Quarter
            5          CASH RECEIPTS         Jan        Feb        Mar      Total    Average
            6          Opening Cash Balance  2000       2355
            7          Consulting Fees       1445       1500
            8          Total Cash Receipts   3445       3855
            9
           10          CASH DISBURSEMENTS
           11          Advertising            100        150
           12          Office Supplies         90         90
           13          Rent                   725        725
           14          Utilities              175        175
           15          Total Cash Disbursements 1090    1140
           16
           17          Closing Cash Balance  2355
           18          Net Monthly Cash Flow  355
           19
           20
                                             Num            09-Nov-91 03:12 PM
```

Now you will be able to insert the word "Quarterly" without retyping the balance of the label.

● **HINT**

If the vertical bar is not in the position you desire, you can reposition it with the mouse. Place the I-beam in the correct position and click. The vertical bar will move to the new position. The right and left arrow keys will also reposition the vertical bar.

17. Type: **Quarterly** (include a space at the end of the word).
18. Click the *Confirm* button.

Your worksheet title will now include the word "Quarterly." This alteration was made without retyping the whole label. As you can see, the EDIT mode offers a more efficient approach for working with long cell entries.

When reviewing the worksheet, Rose finds another label she would like revised. Her services occasionally include more than just consulting. She would like to change the label "Consulting Fees" to "Professional Fees."

19. Select the label in A7.

To change this label, we'll erase the word "Consulting" and replace it with "Professional." To backspace over a word or sentence, you must first position the I-beam at the end of the word or sentence.

20. Position the I-beam in the contents box so it is to the right of the letter "g" in the word "Consulting."
21. Click the mouse.

This will cause 1-2-3 to enter the EDIT mode. The vertical bar will be next to the letter "g." If the vertical bar is not in the correct position, use the mouse or arrow keys to reposition it.

22. To erase the word "Consulting," tap the Backspace key until the word has been removed.

The vertical bar will end up next to the apostrophe. You are now ready to type in the replacement text.

23. Type **Professional** and click the *Confirm* button.

The new label will appear in the cell. Your worksheet should resemble the one pictured in Figure 3–4.

It is a good idea to save your worksheet routinely to prevent accidental loss. Instead of using the *Save* command from the File menu, use the *Save* icon from the Icon Palette.

24. Click the *Save* icon (the second from the left).

Your worksheet will instantly be saved to the disk.

Clearing a Cell

Often, you will find it necessary to delete, or clear, the contents of a cell. 1-2-3 does not allow you to remove all the contents of a cell by

Chapter 3   Modifying a Worksheet   **101**

Figure 3-4. Your worksheet after changing some of the cells.

```
┌─────────────────────────────────────────────────────────────────┐
│                  1-2-3 for Windows - [BUDGET.WK3]               │
│  File  Edit  Worksheet  Range  Graph  Data  Style  Tools  Window  Help │
│ [Page] [W20]                                              READY │
│ A:A7              'Professional Fees                            │
├─────────────────────────────────────────────────────────────────┤
│           A              B        C        D       E       F   │
│  1                           Quarterly Cash Flow Budget         │
│  2                           Going Native                       │
│  3                           1993 - First Quarter               │
│  4                                                              │
│  5   CASH RECEIPTS       Jan      Feb      Mar    Total  Average│
│  6   Opening Cash Balance 2000    2355                          │
│  7   Professional Fees   1445     1500                          │
│  8   Total Cash Receipts 3445     3855                          │
│  9                                                              │
│ 10   CASH DISBURSEMENTS                                         │
│ 11   Advertising          100      150                          │
│ 12   Office Supplies       90       90                          │
│ 13   Rent                 725      725                          │
│ 14   Utilities            175      175                          │
│ 15   Total Cash Disbursements 1090 1140                         │
│ 16                                                              │
│ 17   Closing Cash Balance 2355                                  │
│ 18   Net Monthly Cash Flow 355                                  │
│ 19                                                              │
│ 20                                                              │
│                    Num        09-Nov-91 03:31 PM                │
└─────────────────────────────────────────────────────────────────┘
```

using the Backspace or Delete keys. Once data is entered into a cell, you must use the *Clear* command to remove it.

To clear the contents of a cell or cells, select the desired range and issue the *Clear* command from the Edit menu. The contents of the cells in the current range will be erased. Remember, a cell range can consist of one or more cells. So if the cell pointer surrounds just one cell, the range is that cell.

You will now clear some of the cells on your worksheet. Don't worry about losing data; your original worksheet has been saved to disk and can be recalled later.

1. Select B6.
2. Choose the *Clear* command from the Edit menu.

The contents of the cell will disappear. Notice there is no warning or dialog box.

An optional feature of 1-2-3 allows you to undo an editing change. This feature requires extra memory and is not a default option during the normal 1-2-3 installation. However, since it can save you a great deal of work, we'll show you how to activate the Undo feature.

To activate Undo, issue the *User Setup...* command from the Tools menu. When the Tools User Setup dialog box appears, place a check mark in the *Enable Edit Undo* check box and click the *OK* button.

3. Select the *User Setup...* command from the Tools menu.
4. When the Tools User Setup dialog box appears, look in the Options area to see if the *Enable Edit Undo* check box contains an ×. If so, skip the next instruction and go to step 7.
5. If the check box is empty, click on it.
6. Click the *Update* button in the Tools User Setup dialog box to make the change permanent.
7. Select *OK* to close the dialog box.

Once Undo is active, you can reverse most 1-2-3 operations. However, it only works on the last operation performed. For example, if you accidentally clear a range of cells, you can bring back the cell contents either by selecting the *Undo* SmartIcon or issuing the *Undo* command from the Edit menu.

Defining a range prior to using the *Clear* command will allow you to clear the entire range.

8. Click in C6 and hold the mouse button down.
9. Drag the cell pointer to C14 and release the button.
10. Select *Clear* from the Edit menu.

The entire range will be deleted. By removing the values in C6..C14, the formula in C15 will automatically become a zero.

Let's use the Undo feature to reverse the results of the *Clear* command. The *Undo* SmartIcon is depicted by the two arrows and is located next to the *Cut* icon.

11. Click the *Undo* icon.

Instantly the values in C6..C14 are returned to the worksheet. Most command actions can be reversed using this technique.

Sometimes you will want to clear a cell of numbers and leave format changes intact. You will learn to format values in Lab 4-2. Even though you have not practiced formatting, let's look at how you would clear a cell if it did contain any format changes.

Chapter 3 Modifying a Worksheet **103**

To avoid clearing the format, you can use the *Clear Special...* command from the Edit menu. This command will open a dialog box that allows you to control what is cleared from a cell range.

Let's try this command.

12. Select the range A10..B14.
13. Choose the *Clear Special...* command from the Edit menu.

Figure 3-5.

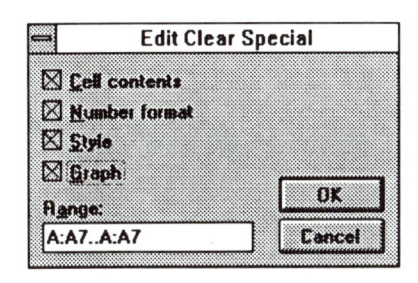

The Edit Clear Special dialog box appears, as shown in Figure 3-5. Check boxes are included for clearing the *Cell contents*, *Number format*, *Style*, and *Graph* options. There is also a *Range* text box that lets you manually enter a cell range. The *Cell contents* and the *Number format* boxes are checked by default. After you pick the items you want to clear, simply click the *OK* button.

Since we haven't created any special formatting yet, we'll accept the default settings.

14. Click the *OK* button.

The dialog box will disappear and the range will be cleared. Let's use the Undo option to reverse the results of the *Clear Special...* command.

15. Click on the *Undo* icon.

The cell contents will reappear.

● HINT

It is possible to clear the contents of a cell or a range by "cutting" the data out of the worksheet and moving it to Clipboard. There is even a SmartIcon that makes this easy to accomplish. We'll explore this technique in Lab 3-3, *Moving Data*.

Before continuing with the next part of this lab, you will need to retrieve the intact copy of your worksheet stored on disk. However, 1-2-3 does not allow two copies of the same file to be in the memory at the same time. Thus, it will be necessary to close the current worksheet before trying to retrieve the original.

16. Issue the *Close* command from the File menu to close the current worksheet.

   Because changes have been made to the worksheet since it was last saved, 1-2-3 will display a dialog box to inquire if you want to save the current worksheet. Clicking the *Yes* button will cause 1-2-3 to replace the file on the disk with the current worksheet. Selecting the *No* button will discard the worksheet, and you will again have the default Untitled worksheet on the screen.

17. Since we don't want to save this worksheet, click the *No* button to discard it.

   The worksheet will be discarded and you will now have the Untitled worksheet.

18. To retrieve the original worksheet, click the *Open...* icon from the Icon Palette.
19. Locate the file BUDGET.WK3, and open it.

   The intact copy of your worksheet will appear.

Deleting Columns and Rows

There will come a time when you'll find it necessary to remove entire columns and/or rows from a worksheet. Although the *Clear* command works fine for erasing data, it can't actually delete a row or a column.

To remove a row or column, select it and issue the *Delete...* command from the Worksheet menu. This will cause the Worksheet Delete dialog box to appear. This dialog box lets you delete the selected columns or rows. It also provides an option for deleting an entire worksheet. You merely select the radio button for the type of action you desire, and then click the *OK* button to complete it.

Earlier, when we explored clearing cells, you discarded the practice worksheet and retrieved the original from disk. We'll use this worksheet to practice the skills needed for deleting rows and columns. Nevertheless, rest assured we still have an intact copy stored on disk.

1. Select C4.
2. Pick the *Delete...* command from the Worksheet menu.

Chapter 3 Modifying a Worksheet

Figure 3–6.

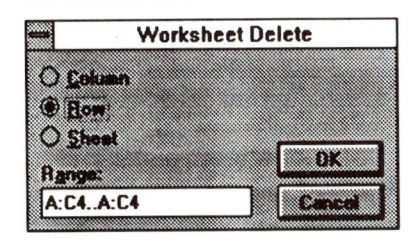

The Worksheet Delete dialog box will appear, as portrayed in Figure 3–6. Radio buttons control the type of deletion that will occur: *Column*, *Row*, or *Sheet*. A *Range* text box is included that allows you to enter a range manually.

3. Click the *Column* radio button to tell 1-2-3 that you want to remove a column.
4. Use the *OK* button to activate the command.

Column C will be deleted. The contents of all the columns to the right of the deleted column will shift to the left to fill the void. Your worksheet should now resemble the one shown in Figure 3–7.

Figure 3–7. Your worksheet after deleting a column.

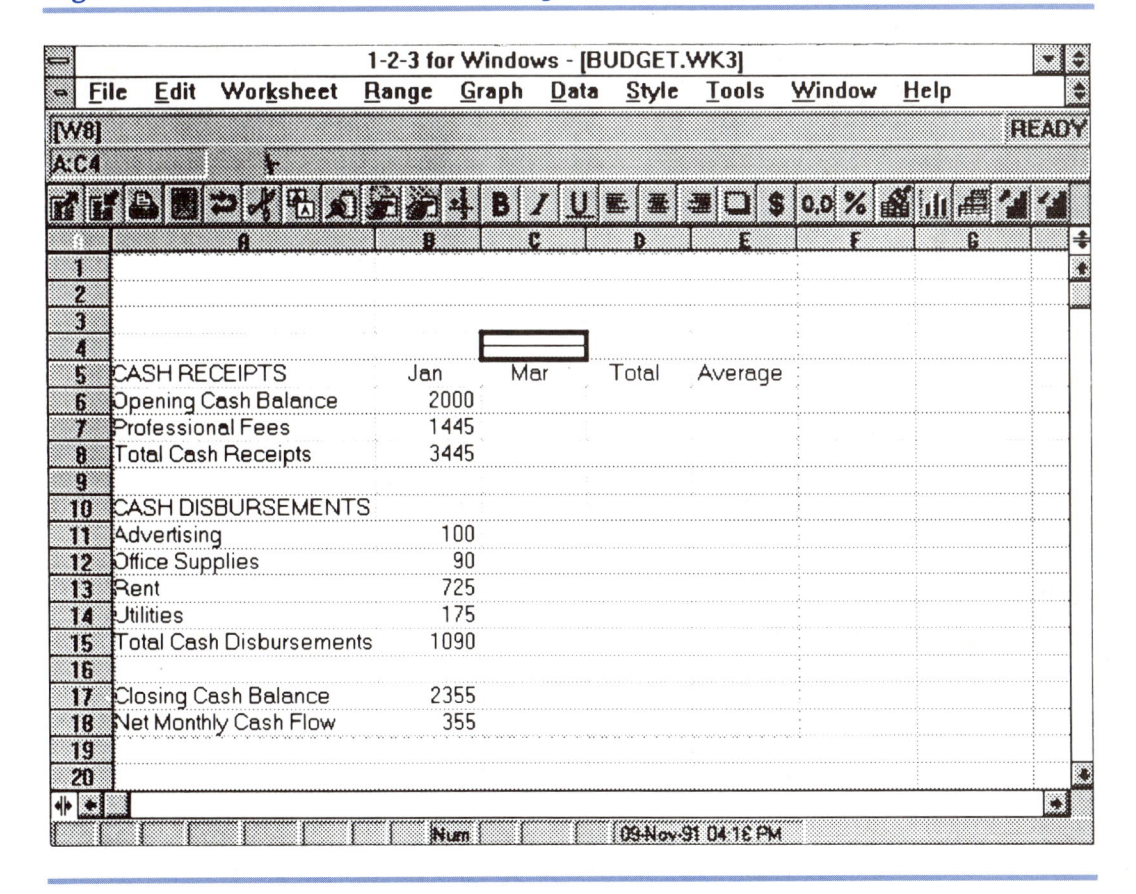

It is possible to delete more than one adjacent column at a time. You must first select a range that includes at least one cell from every column you want to remove. The same process used to delete a single column can then be employed to delete the selected range of columns.

5. Choose the range C4..D4.
6. Issue the *Delete...* command from the Worksheet menu.
7. Click the *Column* radio button.
8. Select the *OK* button to delete the selected columns.

The only column to the right of the deleted columns was the one containing the label "Average." It will shift to the left and appear next to the January column, as illustrated in Figure 3-8.

Figure 3-8. The columns will disappear and everything shifts to the left to fill in the vacant area.

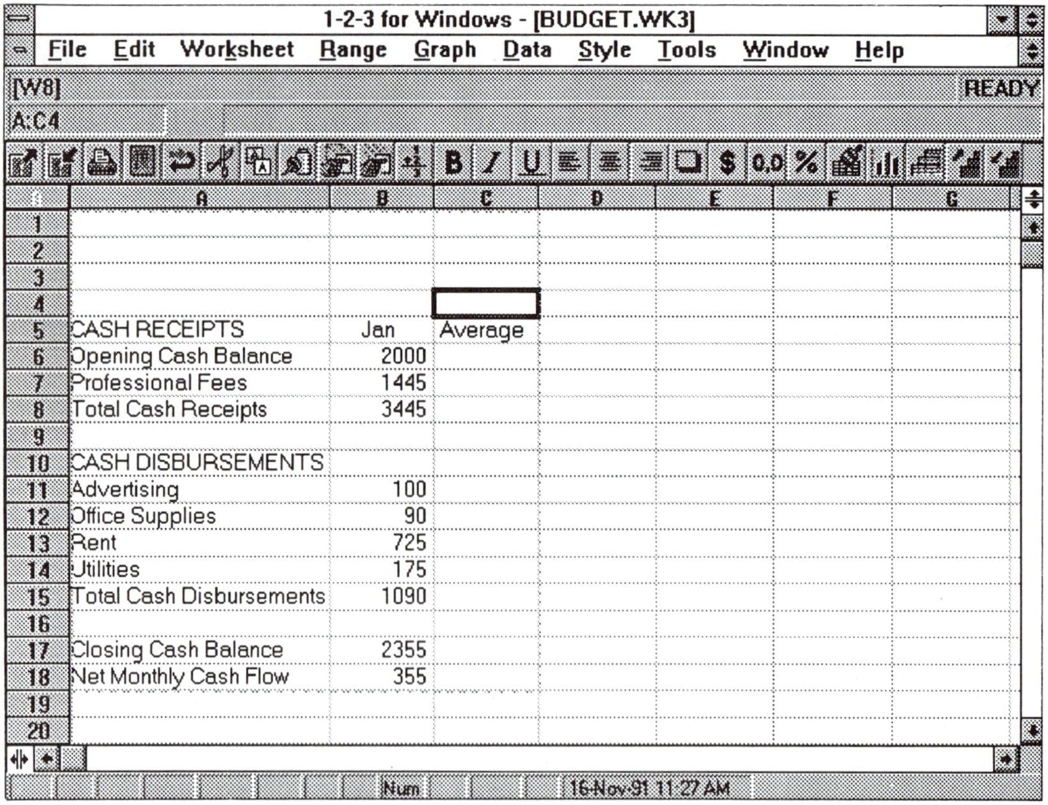

	A	B	C
5	CASH RECEIPTS	Jan	Average
6	Opening Cash Balance	2000	
7	Professional Fees	1445	
8	Total Cash Receipts	3445	
9			
10	CASH DISBURSEMENTS		
11	Advertising	100	
12	Office Supplies	90	
13	Rent	725	
14	Utilities	175	
15	Total Cash Disbursements	1090	
16			
17	Closing Cash Balance	2355	
18	Net Monthly Cash Flow	355	

Chapter 3 Modifying a Worksheet   **107**

You can use the same technique to delete a single row or a range of rows. The only difference is which radio button you check in the Worksheet Delete dialog box. Because the *Row* radio button is the default, you don't have to specify it.

9. Move the cell pointer to A12.
10. From the Worksheet menu pick the *Delete...* command.
11. After the Worksheet Delete dialog box appears, click *OK*.

Row 12 will vanish, and the rows below that point will shift upward to fill in the missing space.

To delete multiple rows, select a range that contains at least one cell in all the adjacent rows you want to remove. Next, issue the *Delete...* command from the Worksheet menu and click the *Rows* radio button. Finally, click *OK* to invoke the command.

Let's use this technique to delete the remaining cash disbursements.

12. Select the range A11..A13.
13. Open the Worksheet Delete dialog box by selecting the *Delete...* command from the Worksheet menu.
14. Choose *OK*.

Instantly, the selected row will vanish, and the data below that point will shift upward, as shown in Figure 3–9.

Not only have the rows vanished, but formulas that used the data in those rows now display an ERRor message. When you delete a row or column that 1-2-3 relies on to perform a calculation, the formula or function will change to display the ERRor message.

The Undo feature can also be used to recover entire rows or columns that have been deleted.

15. Choose the *Undo* icon.

The last action of the *Delete...* command will be undone. Now that you have mastered deleting columns and rows, let's try inserting some columns and rows. First, however, we'll need a fresh worksheet to practice on. Let's close this worksheet without saving the changes and retrieve your unaltered copy from the disk.

16. Choose the *Close* command from the File menu.
17. Select the *No* button to discard the worksheet.

108 Chapter 3 Modifying a Worksheet

Figure 3-9. The data below the deleted row shift upward.

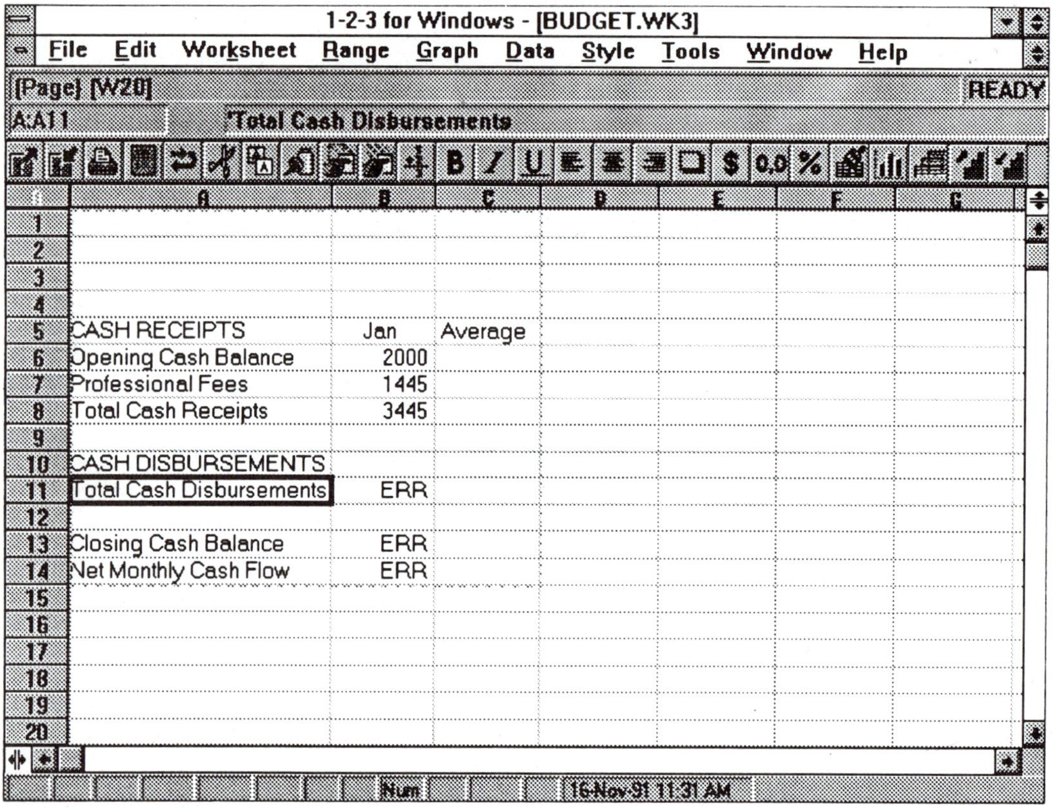

18. Click the *Open...* icon from the Icon Palette to retrieve your original worksheet from drive A.
19. Retrieve BUDGET.WK3.

The original copy of your worksheet should be visible.

Inserting Columns and Rows

The techniques for inserting columns and rows in a worksheet are quite similar to those used to delete columns and rows. You can insert a column or row by placing the cell pointer at the desired insertion point and selecting the *Insert...* command from the Worksheet menu.

Chapter 3 Modifying a Worksheet

To see how this works, we'll insert a column between the Average and Total Column in your worksheet.

Figure 3-10.

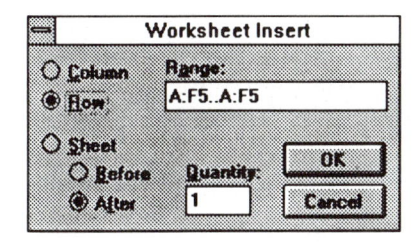

1. Position the cell pointer in F5.
2. Select the *Insert...* command from the Worksheet menu.

The Worksheet Insert dialog box will appear, as pictured in Figure 3-10. It is very similar to the Worksheet Delete dialog box. Radio buttons control the type of operation: inserting columns, rows, or additional worksheets. The *Range* text box lets you specify a range by typing the coordinates.

__NOTE__

The *Before* and *After* radio buttons and the *Quantity* text box are used to insert additional worksheets. Refer to the 1-2-3 Help facility for further information on these options.

3. To insert a column at the current location of the cell pointer, click the *Column* radio button.
4. Then choose the *OK* button.

The new column will materialize at the location of the cell pointer, as illustrated in Figure 3-11. Everything to the right of the cell pointer has moved one column over. Notice that the column width for the new column is different from the column widths on both sides. This is because new columns (and rows) always use the default settings for the worksheet.

Inserting more than one column is just as simple. Place the cell pointer where you want the first new column inserted. Select a range that includes the position of the last column you want inserted. Then issue the *Insert...* command from the Worksheet menu. When the Worksheet Insert dialog box appears, select the *Column* radio button and click *OK*.

Let's expand the worksheet to include three more months. By selecting a range that is three columns wide, you will be able to insert three new columns.

5. Locate the cell pointer in E5.
6. Select the range E5..G5.

Figure 3-11. Everything shifts to the right to make room for the new column.

```
                      1-2-3 for Windows - [BUDGET.WK3]
  File   Edit   Worksheet   Range   Graph   Data   Style   Tools   Window   Help
                                                                            READY
A:F5

              A                B         C         D         E         F         G
  1                               Quarterly Cash Flow Budget
  2                               Going Native
  3                               1993 - First Quarter
  4
  5   CASH RECEIPTS             Jan       Feb       Mar       Total              Average
  6   Opening Cash Balance      2000      2355
  7   Professional Fees         1445      1500
  8   Total Cash Receipts       3445      3855
  9
 10   CASH DISBURSEMENTS
 11   Advertising                100       150
 12   Office Supplies             90        90
 13   Rent                       725       725
 14   Utilities                  175       175
 15   Total Cash Disbursements  1090      1140
 16
 17   Closing Cash Balance      2355
 18   Net Monthly Cash Flow      355
 19
 20
                              Num              16-Nov-91 11:34 AM
```

7. Issue the *Insert...* command from the Worksheet menu to open the Worksheet Insert dialog box.
8. Choose the *Column* radio button and click the *OK* button.

The three new columns will be inserted. What happened to the Total and Average columns? They have been shifted to the right and are on a portion of the worksheet not currently visible. To confirm this, let's scroll the screen to the right.

9. Click the right scroll arrow (in the lower right corner of your worksheet) until the Average label comes into view.

As you can see, the Total and Average columns are there. We inserted these new columns just for practice, so let's Undo this action before continuing.

Chapter 3 *Modifying a Worksheet* 111

10. Select the *Undo* icon.

   Notice that only the last deletion will be undone. To get rid of the other extra column, use the *Delete...* command from the Worksheet menu.

11. Click on F5 and issue the *Delete...* command from the Worksheet menu.
12. Choose the *Column* radio button and click the *OK* button.

   Rose has decided to split the utility expenses into Phone and Utilities, instead of just Utilities. To accomplish this, you will need to insert a new row. The steps are very similar to the ones used to insert columns.

13. Move the cell pointer to A14.
14. Open the Worksheet Insert dialog box by picking the *Insert...* command from the Worksheet menu.
15. Click the *OK* button.

   Everything below the cell pointer will shift down and the new row will appear. You can now enter a heading and data for this new row.

16. While in A14, type **Phone** and *Confirm* the entry.
17. Move to B14 and enter: **100**
18. In C14 place the value: **75**

   An interesting thing happened as you entered the data. The Total Cash Disbursements automatically changed to include the new values. Recall that the @SUM function was used to calculate this value.

   When you inserted the new row, 1-2-3 automatically adjusted the range in the @SUM function to include it. This powerful feature lets you add new data to your worksheet without the need to edit the calculations performed by the @functions.

   Let's reduce the figures in the Utilities category to reflect the removal of the phone expenses.

19. Select B15.
20. Enter the value: **75**
21. Move to C15 and change its value to 75.

   Your worksheet should resemble Figure 3–12.

   It's a good practice to save and print your worksheet before making any drastic changes such as deleting or inserting multiple rows or columns.

Figure 3–12. The Total Cash Disbursements figure reverts back to its previous value.

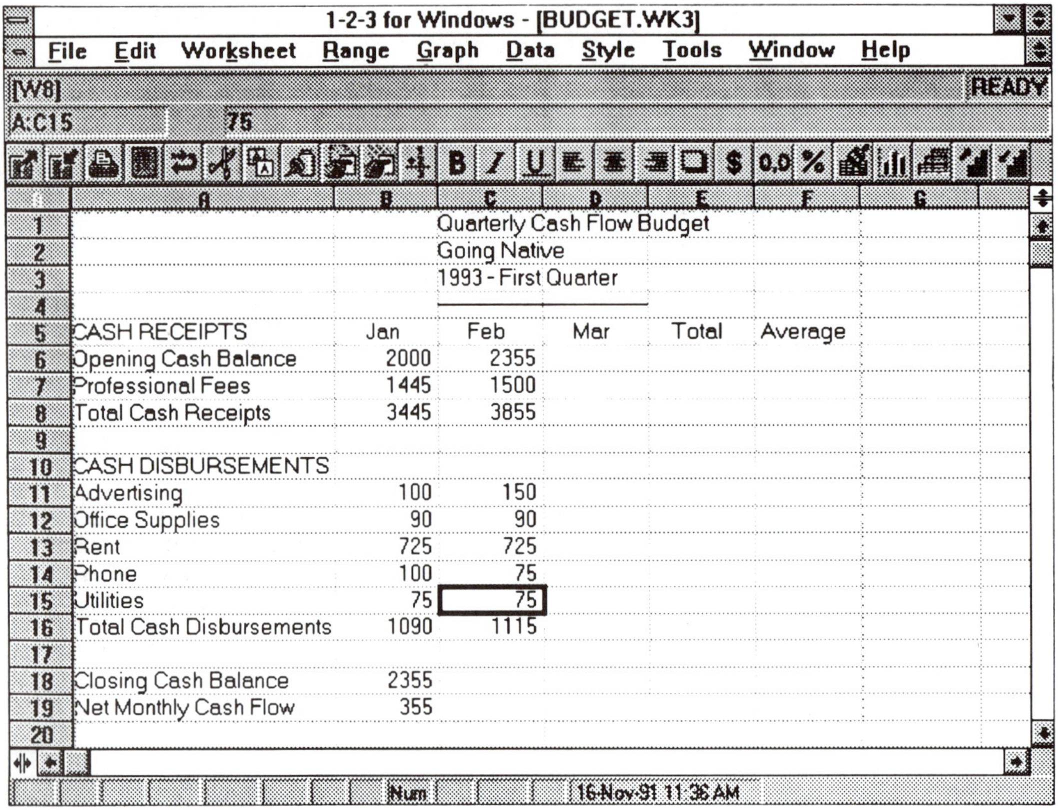

	A	B	C	D	E	F
1			Quarterly Cash Flow Budget			
2			Going Native			
3			1993 - First Quarter			
4						
5	CASH RECEIPTS	Jan	Feb	Mar	Total	Average
6	Opening Cash Balance	2000	2355			
7	Professional Fees	1445	1500			
8	Total Cash Receipts	3445	3855			
9						
10	CASH DISBURSEMENTS					
11	Advertising	100	150			
12	Office Supplies	90	90			
13	Rent	725	725			
14	Phone	100	75			
15	Utilities	75	75			
16	Total Cash Disbursements	1090	1115			
17						
18	Closing Cash Balance	2355				
19	Net Monthly Cash Flow	355				
20						

22. Highlight the range A1..F19.
23. Issue the *Page Setup...* command from the File menu.

The Page Setup dialog box will appear. Use this dialog box to change the header on your printout. You will also want to confirm that the paper orientation radio button is selected for *Portrait*.

Let's add an additional feature to this printout. In the Options area, you can check the boxes that will add the worksheet frame and grid lines to your printout.

24. Change the header to: **Lab 3-2**
25. Confirm that the *Portrait* radio button is selected.
26. Place checks in the *Show worksheet frame* and *Show grid lines* check boxes, and click the *OK* button.

Chapter 3 *Modifying a Worksheet*

To confirm the layout of your worksheet, you can use the *Preview...* feature. This time, however, use the SmartIcon associated with that command. Between the *Print* and *Undo* icons is the *Preview* icon. It contains a graphic showing a page.

27. Select the *Preview* icon.

A preview of your printout will immediately be displayed. Clicking on the page will allow you to return to the READY mode so you can print your worksheet.

28. Click the page to return to your worksheet.
29. Click the *Save* icon on the Icon Palette.
30. Choose the *Print* icon to send your worksheet to the printer.

It will take a few moments for your worksheet to be printed. You can continue when 1-2-3 returns to the READY mode.

Before we end this lab, we'll show you how to insert multiple rows in your worksheet. Start by placing the cell pointer where you want the first row to be inserted. Select a range that includes the number of rows you want inserted. Issue the *Insert...* command from the Worksheet menu to open the Worksheet Insert dialog box, and click the *OK* button.

31. Select the range A5..A11.
32. Choose the *Insert...* command from the Worksheet menu.
33. Click *OK*.

Seven rows will be inserted. All the rows below the original A4 row will shift downward to make room for the new rows.

34. Exit 1-2-3 without saving the worksheet.

LAB 3-3 MOVING DATA

As you become a sophisticated 1-2-3 user, your worksheets will grow in complexity. To manage this complexity, you will find it necessary to move data to different locations. For example, you might want to rearrange a worksheet to add a new section or solve unforeseen problems with the current layout.

Moving labels and values is a straightforward process that consists of two operations. First, you select the range you want to move. Second, you show 1-2-3 the location where you want it relocated.

Moving formulas is slightly more involved. A formula involves a relationship between itself and the cells containing the data it references. If you change the location of either the formula or the data, it will be necessary to redefine the relationships. 1-2-3 can do this automatically using the concepts of relative and absolute cell addressing.

Understanding Relative and Absolute Cell Addressing

A **relative cell address** defines the location of data in a worksheet by the "relative" position of the data to the formula referencing it. For example, let's assume a worksheet contains a formula in cell A1 that references a value in A3. If you move the formula to B1, it will then reference the contents of B3. This is because B3 is in the same "relative" position to B1 as A3 was to A1. When you move or copy a formula, 1-2-3 will automatically adjust the cell references relative to the formula's new location.

An **absolute cell address** is permanent and does not change. To expand the example above, imagine that the formula in cell A1 referenced the absolute cell address of A3. Moving the formula to B1 would not change the cell it references as it would with a relative cell address. The formula would still reference A3. An absolute cell address, in effect, "locks in" the position of data in a worksheet.

You create an absolute cell address by placing a dollar sign ($) in front of either the column letter, row number, or both. Thus, cells can be absolute by column and/or row (e.g., $A1, A$1, or $A$1). You'll want to use absolute cell addressing whenever you move or copy a formula that needs to reference a particular cell.

This lab will explore two different methods for moving data in your worksheet. You'll also use the concepts of relative and absolute addressing. These concepts will also be emphasized in Lab 3-4. So don't panic, you'll have plenty of opportunities to master their use.

Before we begin, you'll need to retrieve your worksheet from disk.

1. Start Windows and launch 1-2-3 for Windows.
2. Click the *Open...* SmartIcon.
3. Open A:\BUDGET.WK3 and maximize the worksheet.

Cutting and Pasting Cell Contents

To move data using the *Cut* and *Paste* commands, first select the range you want to move and click on the *Cut* SmartIcon in the Icon Palette. The data will be transferred to a temporary holding area in Windows

Chapter 3   Modifying a Worksheet **115**

Figure 3-13.

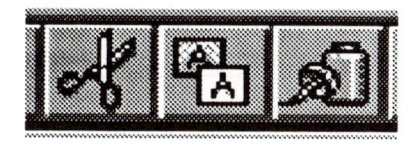

called Clipboard. You then select the range where you want the data to be relocated and click the *Paste* icon from the Icon Palette.

The *Cut* and *Paste* SmartIcons can be identified by their unique graphic symbols, a scissors and a jar of paste, as pictured in Figure 3-13. The same options are also available in the Edit menu. However, since the SmartIcons represent a faster and more efficient method, use them whenever possible.

> **NOTE**
>
> When you use the Menu bar commands instead of the equivalent SmartIcon, you may encounter additional dialog boxes and options.

Let's use this technique to move the worksheet title.

1. Move the cell pointer to C1.

Remember that the labels displayed in the rectangular area C1 to E3 are actually contained in C1 to C3. They spill over into adjacent empty cells. To move the entire heading, including the borders, it will be necessary to specify a range of C1..D4.

2. Drag the cell pointer so it surrounds the range C1..D4.

You are now ready to transfer this range into Clipboard by selecting the *Cut* icon.

3. Click the *Cut* SmartIcon depicted as scissors on the Icon Palette.

Your heading will vanish. It isn't lost forever, it's just being stored in Clipboard until you "paste" it back into your worksheet. To complete the process, move the cell pointer to where you want the heading to reappear and click the *Paste* icon.

4. Move the cell pointer to B1.

It is only necessary to indicate the upper-left corner of the range where you want the heading placed.

5. Click the *Paste* SmartIcon, shown as a jar of paste.

Your heading will be pasted into the new location. Clipboard maintains a copy of the last data that was cut to it. So, your heading is still in Clipboard. One of the advantages of using the cut and paste technique to move data is that it lets you quickly place the same data in several locations in your worksheet.

What will happen if we cut and paste a formula? Let's try it.

6. Select C16.

This cell contains the @SUM function that totals the cash disbursements for February.

7. Click the *Cut* icon.
8. Move the cell pointer to D16 and click the *Paste* icon.

The references in the @SUM range will change from C11..C15 to D11..D15. Since the cell range C11..C15 is relative (contains no dollar signs), it automatically changes to reflect the new location of the @function. This will result in a value of 0 being displayed because the cells in D11..D15 are empty. If the data had been moved with the formula, relative addressing would have provided the correct results using the cut and paste method.

Cut and paste techniques are important to understand because many other Windows applications use this approach to move data. However, there is another method for moving data that avoids some of the pitfalls of the cut and paste method. Before we examine this technique, let's move the formula back to its original position.

9. Click the *Cut* icon.
10. Relocate the cell pointer to C16 and click the *Paste* icon.

The range in the @SUM formula will change back to C11..C15, and the formula will again display the correct results.

Using the *Move Cells...* Icon

The *Move Cells...* command in the Edit menu is especially useful for moving formulas and data separately. It automatically keeps track of the data that belong to a formula and makes the appropriate changes in the formula. As a result, it is a safer and easier way to move data around in your worksheet than cutting and pasting.

Chapter 3 Modifying a Worksheet   **117**

Figure 3-14.

The SmartIcon associated with the *Move Cells...* command is shown in Figure 3-14. The graphic shows a pointing hand and a "moving" worksheet. To use this icon, first select the range you want to move. Then click the *Move Cells* icon to change the pointer to the shape of a pointing hand. Place the pointer in the upper-left corner of the location where your range is to be relocated. Finally, click the left mouse button to complete the move.

To show you how this method differs from cutting and pasting, we'll repeat the same operation you performed earlier, except this time we'll use the *Move Cells* icon.

1. The cell pointer should still be located in C16. Click the *Move Cells* SmartIcon.

   The pointer will change to the pointing hand.

2. Move the pointer to D16 and click the left mouse button.

   Notice the value in D16 is unchanged. To view the contents of D16, move the cell pointer to D16.

3. Move to D16.

   The contents box will confirm that the range in the @SUM function stayed the same: C11..D15. What will happen if the cell containing the formula remains and the data moves? Let's find out. First, let's move the @SUM function back to its original position by simply using the *Undo* command.

4. Click the *Undo* icon.

   The formula will continue to display the correct amount.

5. Select the range C11..C15.
6. Choose the *Move Cells* icon.
7. Move the pointer to E8 and click the mouse.
8. Select C16.

   The range in the @SUM is now E8..E12. The *Move Cells* icon altered the range relative to where the data are located. Using this command avoids the problem you encountered with cutting and pasting.

The *Move Cells* technique also preserves absolute references in formulas when the cell containing the absolute data is moved.

Use the *Undo* command to move the data back to its original position.

9. Click the *Undo* icon.

The data should now appear back in its original location. Print and save your worksheet before exiting 1-2-3.

10. Use the *Page Setup...* command from the File menu, then change the header to: **Lab 3-3**
11. Select the *Preview* icon to confirm the appearance of your worksheet.

● **HINT**

If the preview does not look correct, you may want to re-select the print range of A1..F19 and preview it again.

12. Click the *Save* SmartIcon.
13. Print your worksheet using the *Print* icon.
14. You may exit 1-2-3 or continue.

LAB 3-4   COPYING DATA

Much of the work you do with an electronic spreadsheet will involve duplicating formulas, values, and labels. The ability to copy data in a worksheet greatly reduces the need to perform these repetitive tasks manually. In this lab, we'll show you how to use the copy facilities in 1-2-3 for Windows to replicate formulas, values, and labels both quickly and effectively.

We'll start by adding some additional formulas to your worksheet so you will have something to copy. One of these formulas will involve the use of multiple mathematical operators and introduce the concept of precedence. You will get a chance to use a new @function.

So, let's load your worksheet and explore some new commands that will make your use of 1-2-3 more rewarding.

1. Start Windows and begin 1-2-3 for Windows, if they aren't already running.
2. If necessary, open and maximize your A:\BUDGET.WK3 worksheet.

Chapter 3 Modifying a Worksheet

Overriding the Order of Precedence

All the formulas you've created so far use single arithmetic operators or simple @functions. However, you'll often find it necessary to include more complex expressions and a mixture of operators to create formulas in a worksheet.

Multiple expressions present a problem for 1-2-3. When it encounters a calculation involving multiple steps, it must be told which step to perform first.

For example, the formula 1+10*10 utilizes two operators (+ and *). The result will depend on which operation is performed first.

1-2-3 uses a predetermined order (or precedence numbers) when evaluating the expressions in a formula. **Precedence numbers** represent the sequence 1-2-3 uses to perform calculations. Table 3-1 summarizes the precedence numbers for the arithmetic operators.

Table 3-1. Precedence numbers.

Operator	Operation	Precedence
^	Exponentiation	1
* /	Multiplication	2
+ −	Addition and Subtraction	3

1-2-3 performs operations with the lowest precedence number first. Thus, in the case of 1+10*10, 1-2-3 will perform 10*10 first, then add 1 to the product of 10*10. The answer will be 101.

If two operations have the same precedence, 1-2-3 performs them in the sequence of left to right. However, you can override the order of precedence by enclosing an operation in parentheses. In the case of (1+10)*10, 1-2-3 will perform (1+10) first and then multiply the sum, 11, by 10. The answer will be 110.

Let's create some new formulas that will help Rose predict cash flow. To do this, we'll introduce some assumptions about the anticipated inflation rate and the expected growth rate of her business.

1. Move the cell pointer to A21.
2. Enter the label: **Annual Inflation Rate**
3. In A22 type: **Annual Growth Rate**
4. Select B21 and enter: **6%**

You will notice that 1-2-3 converted the 6% to 0.06 automatically. Later you will learn how to display a value as a percentage.

5. In B22 place the value: **10%**

Rose would like her business to grow at a rate of 10% above the inflation rate each year. Based on the professional fees she plans to earn in January, it is possible to create a formula that will forecast the amount she would have to earn in February and March. Let's examine the steps necessary to construct the formula.

- Step 1. Total of the Annual Inflation Rate and Annual Growth Rate
(B21+B22) $B$21+$B$22
- Step 2. Divide this amount by 12 months
(B21+B22)/12

Notice the formula in step 2 uses parentheses to indicate that the addition must occur before the division. This is because we want to add the Annual Inflation Rate to the Annual Growth Rate before dividing the total by 12 months. Without the parentheses, 1-2-3 would perform the division first because it has a lower precedence number than addition.

- Step 3. Multiply this amount by the January Professional Fees
(B21+B22)/12*b7

Multiplication and division have the same precedence number. When this happens, the operation farthest to the left is performed first. For our present purposes, this order of calculation is proper and requires no parentheses. This formula produces the amount of increase that Rose desires.

- Step 4. Add the January Professional Fees to the amount of increase
(B21+B22)/12*B7+B7

Addition has a higher precedence number than either division or multiplication and will be performed last, which is what we want.

Let's replace the figure in Professional Fees for February with the formula and see what happens.

6. In C7 enter: **(B21+B22)/12*B7+B7**

The results of the formula will be calculated and appear in the cell. The increase from January is very modest. Rose looks at that and says she can do better than a 10% Annual Growth Rate.

7. To increase the Annual Growth Rate to 20%, move to B22 and type: **20%**

Chapter 3   Modifying a Worksheet

The new amount for February is instantly displayed. To create a formula for the Professional Fees in March, you could change the appropriate cell references and type the formula as you did for February. But wait! 1-2-3 has a feature that will duplicate the February formula for you and change the cell references to boot.

Using *Quick Copy*

Copying data is very similar to moving data. The main difference is that the copy commands allow you to duplicate information one or more times without affecting the original data. 1-2-3 uses relative addressing to change formulas when you copy them to new locations. This allows you to reuse formulas and data without recreating them.

Figure 3-15.

From the Edit menu you can access the *Quick Copy...* command. This command is also available as a SmartIcon on the Icon Palette, as shown in Figure 3-15. It is almost identical to the *Move Cells* icon in appearance and use. Look closely at the icon and you will notice the worksheet is shown as a copy instead of a moving worksheet (the pointing hand is also a different color).

Instead of retyping the formula you created for predicting Professional Fees, we'll use the *Quick Copy* icon to duplicate it. First, select the range you want to copy. Then click the *Quick Copy* SmartIcon to change the pointer to the shape of a pointing hand. Finally, move the pointer to the range where the copies will be placed and click the left mouse button.

1. Select C7.
2. Click the *Quick Copy* icon from the Icon Palette.

   The pointer will change to a pointing hand.

3. Move the pointer to D7 and click once.

   The formula will be copied into the new cell.
   There seems to be something wrong. The value for March is the same as February. It should have increased as it did from January to February. Let's look at the formula to see what happened.

4. Reposition the cell pointer to D7.

   The formula displayed in the contents box is not the same as the one you created. Figure 3-16 shows the formula contained in C7, and Figure 3-17 shows the formula from D7.

Figure 3-16. The original formula in cell C7.

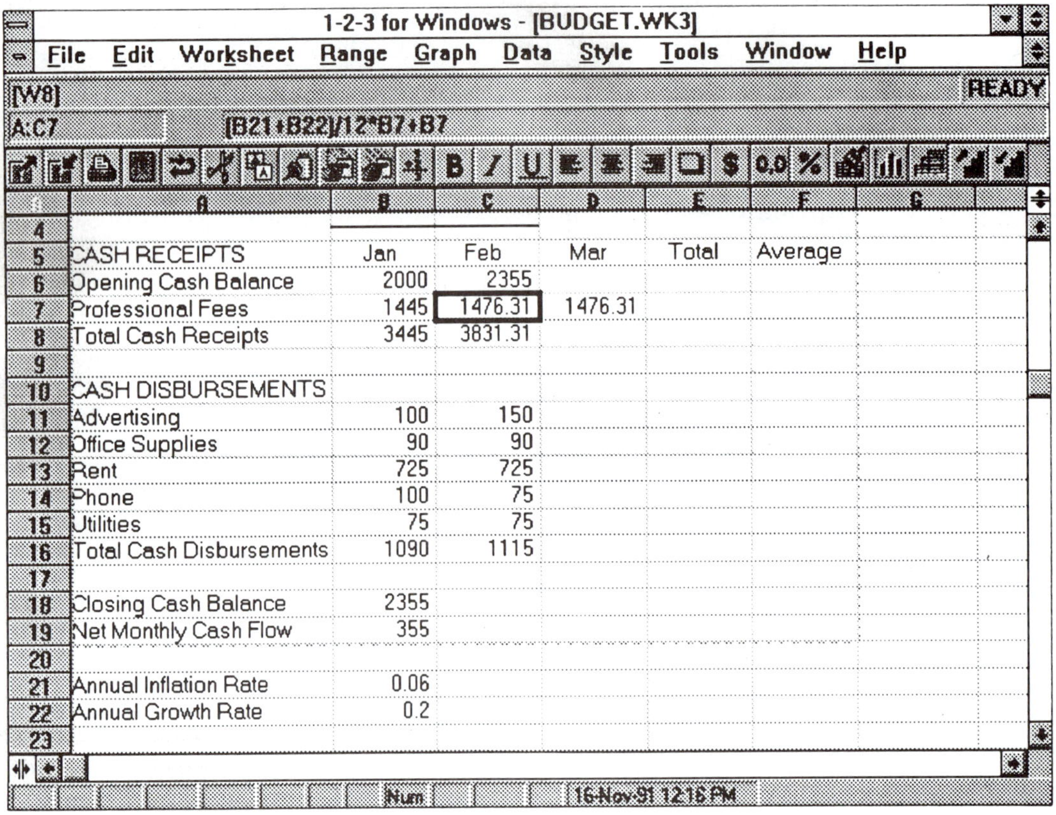

```
1-2-3 for Windows - [BUDGET.WK3]
File  Edit  Worksheet  Range  Graph  Data  Style  Tools  Window  Help
[W8]                                                           READY
A:C7        (B21+B22)/12*B7+B7
```

	A	B	C	D	E	F
4						
5	CASH RECEIPTS	Jan	Feb	Mar	Total	Average
6	Opening Cash Balance	2000	2355			
7	Professional Fees	1445	1476.31	1476.31		
8	Total Cash Receipts	3445	3831.31			
9						
10	CASH DISBURSEMENTS					
11	Advertising	100	150			
12	Office Supplies	90	90			
13	Rent	725	725			
14	Phone	100	75			
15	Utilities	75	75			
16	Total Cash Disbursements	1090	1115			
17						
18	Closing Cash Balance	2355				
19	Net Monthly Cash Flow	355				
20						
21	Annual Inflation Rate	0.06				
22	Annual Growth Rate	0.2				
23						

Handwritten note: $B$22 $B$23 use this formula if you dont want the number to change

All the cell references changed from column B to column C. That is the purpose of relative addressing—it changes cell addresses relative to the new location. When the formula shifted one cell to the right, all the cell references shifted one cell to the right as well. This is fine for the references to C7, because the amount in March is based on the amount in February. The problem is that the references to the Annual Inflation and Growth Rates also shifted to the right. They now refer to empty cells.

To correct this situation, we must use absolute addressing. Recall that absolute addresses will remain unchanged when a formula is moved or copied. Both references contained in the parentheses will need to be changed to absolute. This will require placing a dollar sign ($) in front of the column letter and row number in each address of the original formula.

Figure 3–17. The formula as it was copied from C7 into D7.

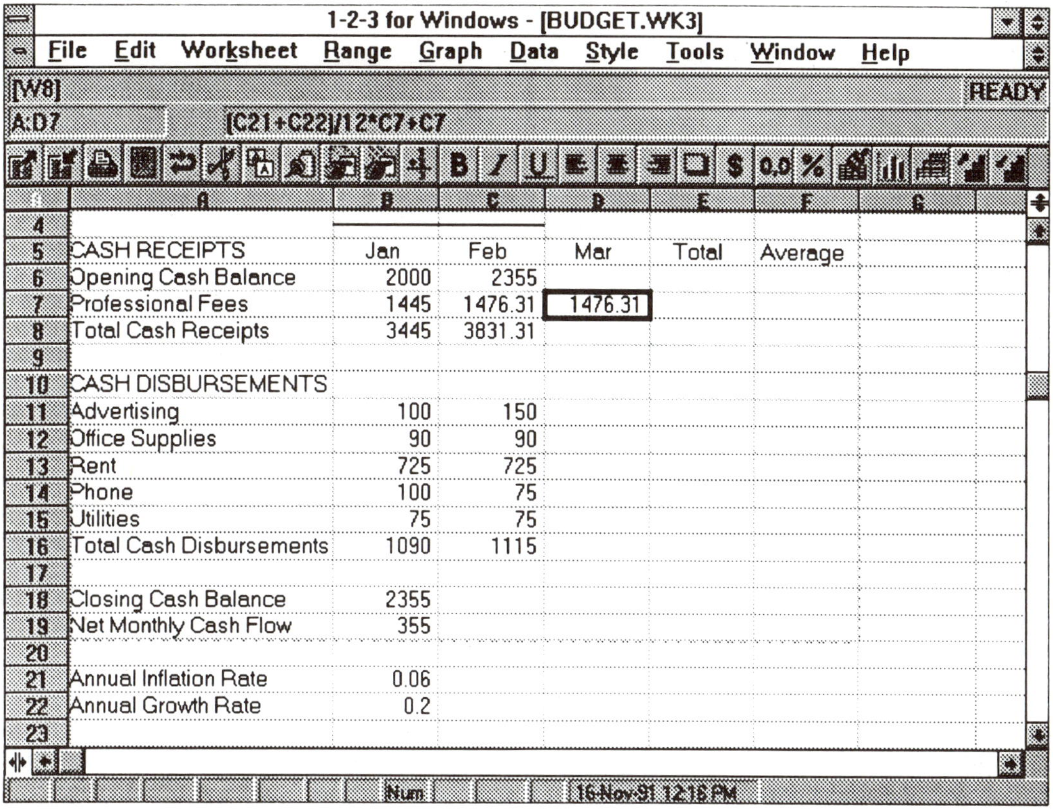

5. Go back to cell C7.
6. Move the pointer to the contents box where the formula is displayed.

The pointer will change to the I-beam.

7. Position the I-beam to the left of the letter "B" in the reference to cell B21.
8. Press the left mouse button.

The I-beam will change to the vertical bar. Anything you type will be inserted where the vertical bar is located. After you insert the dollar sign, move the vertical bar using the right arrow key.

9. To make the column letter B absolute, type: **$**

10. To change the row number 21 to absolute, press the right arrow key once.
11. Then type: **$**

Follow the remaining instructions to make the other cell address absolute.

12. Press the right arrow key three times and type **$**, then move to the right one position, and type **$** again.
13. Click the *Confirm* button.

Nothing will change in C7 because that formula was already correct. When you copy this formula back into D7 you should see a different result.

14. Select the *Quick Copy* icon.
15. Point to D7 and click the mouse.

This time the results will show an increase. Move to D7 and view the formula to see how it was modified.

16. Move to D7.

The references to Annual Inflation and Annual Growth Rates remain absolute, as pictured in Figure 3-18. The original reference to the January Professional Fees changed to February because of relative addressing.

Using a similar formula will allow you to adjust expenses as they increase as a result of inflation. Let's replace the fixed figure for Advertising in February with a formula. This formula will show an increase over the previous month's expense by the Annual Inflation Rate.

17. Select C11.
18. Type: **$B$21/12*B11+B11**

The results of the formula will replace the previous value. We'll use the *Quick Copy* icon to duplicate the formula for the other expenses.

19. Click the *Quick Copy* SmartIcon.

The pointer will become a pointing hand. We'll use the pointer to copy over the top of the existing data.

Figure 3-18. The references to B21 and B22 remain absolute.

```
                1-2-3 for Windows - [BUDGET.WK3]
  File  Edit  Worksheet  Range  Graph  Data  Style  Tools  Window  Help
[W8]                                                              READY
A:D7           [$B$21+$B$22]/12*C7+C7
```

	A	B	C	D	E	F
4						
5	CASH RECEIPTS	Jan	Feb	Mar	Total	Average
6	Opening Cash Balance	2000	2355			
7	Professional Fees	1445	1476.31	1508.3		
8	Total Cash Receipts	3445	3831.31			
9						
10	CASH DISBURSEMENTS					
11	Advertising	100	150			
12	Office Supplies	90	90			
13	Rent	725	725			
14	Phone	100	75			
15	Utilities	75	75			
16	Total Cash Disbursements	1090	1115			
17						
18	Closing Cash Balance	2355				
19	Net Monthly Cash Flow	355				
20						
21	Annual Inflation Rate	0.06				
22	Annual Growth Rate	0.2				
23						

Num   16-Nov-91 12:43 PM

20. Using the pointer, select the range C12..C15.

The contents of the range will be replaced with a formula that is relative to each row. The Annual Inflation Rate will remain the same because of absolute addressing. Let's complete the formulas for February by copying the Closing Cash Balance and Net Monthly Cash Flow formulas from January.

21. Highlight the range B18..B19.
22. Select the *Quick Copy* icon.
23. Point to C18 and click the mouse.

All the values in February are now referenced to values in January. Next, we'll use the *Quick Copy* icon to copy all these formulas to March. Relative addressing will change all references so March will be linked to the values in February, except those using absolute addresses, of course.

24. Select the range C6..C19.
25. Click the *Quick Copy* icon.

It is only necessary to point to the upper-left corner of the range to which you want the copy inserted.

26. Point to D6 and click the mouse.

The formulas will be copied, relative to their new location, and the results will appear as shown in Figure 3-19.

Figure 3-19. The formulas are copied relative to their new location.

	A	B	C	D	E	F
5	CASH RECEIPTS	Jan	Feb	Mar	Total	Average
6	Opening Cash Balance	2000	2355	2735.86		
7	Professional Fees	1445	1476.31	1508.3		
8	Total Cash Receipts	3445	3831.31	4244.15		
9						
10	CASH DISBURSEMENTS					
11	Advertising	100	100.5	101.003		
12	Office Supplies	90	90.45	90.9023		
13	Rent	725	728.625	732.268		
14	Phone	100	100.5	101.003		
15	Utilities	75	75.375	75.7519		
16	Total Cash Disbursements	1090	1095.45	1100.93		
17						
18	Closing Cash Balance	2355	2735.86	3143.23		
19	Net Monthly Cash Flow	355	380.858	407.368		
20						
21	Annual Inflation Rate	0.06				
22	Annual Growth Rate	0.2				

This technique could be used to predict values for several months, or several years, into the future. This model uses only a few simple variables. It is possible to include other factors in the formulas. For

Chapter 3 Modifying a Worksheet

example, increases and decreases in utility expenses caused by weather changes could be added.

Let's complete the worksheet by calculating a total and average value for each row. We'll use a built-in @function and the *Quick Copy* icon to complete this task.

27. Move to E6 and type: **@SUM(B6..D6)**

The sum of the indicated range will appear in E6. There is also an @function that will calculate the average value of a range. It is used just like the @SUM function.

28. Select F6 and enter: **@AVG(B6..D6)**

The cell will display the average value of the specified range. It is a simple task to copy these formulas so that the total and average of each row can be calculated and displayed.

29. Highlight the range E6..F6.
30. Click the *Quick Copy* icon.

You will need to point to the beginning cell throughout the range in which you want the copy placed.

31. Point to the range E7..E19 and click the mouse.

Wow! 1-2-3 copies the formulas, makes the necessary changes relative to the new locations, calculates, and displays the results. This sure beats the old-fashioned way of doing things with paper, pencil, and a calculator.

Unfortunately, Figure 3–20 shows that when you included blank rows in your range, 1-2-3 copied the formulas there too. No problem. With just a few quick "cuts" these can be removed.

32. Select the range E9..F10.
33. Click the *Cut* SmartIcon.
34. Highlight and *Cut* E17..F17.

Your worksheet should now resemble the one shown in Figure 3–21.

In the previous lab, you found the *Move Cells* icon to be more efficient than cutting and pasting data. This is also true of the *Quick Copy* icon. It is faster and easier to use than copying and pasting data in a worksheet.

Figure 3-20. The formulas were also copied into the blank rows.

```
                    1-2-3 for Windows - [BUDGET.WK3]
  File   Edit   Worksheet   Range   Graph   Data   Style   Tools   Window   Help
[W8]                                                                          READY
A:E6              @SUM(B6..D6)
```

	A	B	C	D	E	F
4						
5	CASH RECEIPTS	Jan	Feb	Mar	Total	Average
6	Opening Cash Balance	2000	2355	2735.86	7090.86	2363.62
7	Professional Fees	1445	1476.31	1508.3	4429.6	1476.53
8	Total Cash Receipts	3445	3831.31	4244.15	11520.5	3840.15
9					0	ERR
10	CASH DISBURSEMENTS				0	ERR
11	Advertising	100	100.5	101.003	301.503	100.501
12	Office Supplies	90	90.45	90.9023	271.352	90.4508
13	Rent	725	728.625	732.268	2185.89	728.631
14	Phone	100	100.5	101.003	301.503	100.501
15	Utilities	75	75.375	75.7519	226.127	75.3756
16	Total Cash Disbursements	1090	1095.45	1100.93	3286.38	1095.46
17					0	ERR
18	Closing Cash Balance	2355	2735.86	3143.23	8234.08	2744.69
19	Net Monthly Cash Flow	355	380.858	407.368	1143.23	381.075
20						
21	Annual Inflation Rate	0.06				
22	Annual Growth Rate	0.2				
23						

```
                              Num            16-Nov-91 12:54 PM
```

However, if you prefer, you can use the *Copy* command from the Edit menu or the *Copy* icon from the Icon Palette to send a selected range to Clipboard. The data copied are not removed from the worksheet as with the *Cut* command. Issuing the *Paste* command duplicates the data at the current location of the cell pointer.

• HINT

Copying and pasting data provide a quick way to make multiple copies of a cell or range. Since the data are stored in Clipboard, you're free to paste them repeatedly throughout your worksheet. This option is unavailable with *Quick Copy...* because it bypasses Clipboard.

Let's print and save your worksheet to your disk and exit Windows.

Chapter 3 *Modifying a Worksheet* **129**

Figure 3-21. Your worksheet is ready to print and save.

```
                    1-2-3 for Windows - [BUDGET.WK3]
  File  Edit  Worksheet  Range  Graph  Data  Style  Tools  Window  Help
 [W8]                                                                  READY
 A:E17

           A              B        C         D         E        F        G
   4
   5   CASH RECEIPTS      Jan      Feb       Mar       Total    Average
   6   Opening Cash Balance  2000  2355    2735.86    7090.86   2363.62
   7   Professional Fees     1445  1476.31  1508.3    4429.6    1476.53
   8   Total Cash Receipts   3445  3831.31  4244.15   11520.5   3840.15
   9
  10   CASH DISBURSEMENTS
  11   Advertising           100   100.5    101.003   301.503   100.501
  12   Office Supplies       90    90.45    90.9023   271.352   90.4508
  13   Rent                  725   728.625  732.268   2185.89   728.631
  14   Phone                 100   100.5    101.003   301.503   100.501
  15   Utilities             75    75.375   75.7519   226.127   75.3756
  16   Total Cash Disbursements 1090 1095.45 1100.93  3286.38   1095.46
  17
  18   Closing Cash Balance  2355  2735.86  3143.23   8234.08   2744.69
  19   Net Monthly Cash Flow 355   380.858  407.368   1143.23   381.075
  20
  21   Annual Inflation Rate 0.06
  22   Annual Growth Rate    0.2
  23
                          Num              16-Nov-91 12:55 PM
```

35. Change the header on your printout to **Lab 3-4** and turn off the *Show worksheet frame* and *Show grid lines* options.
36. Click the *Save* SmartIcon.
37. Select the range A1..F22 and print your worksheet.
38. You may exit 1-2-3.

LAB 3-5 PROOFING A WORKSHEET

After creating and editing a worksheet, you should always take time to validate or "proof" the worksheet. This involves checking labels to make sure that they correctly identify data and verifying that your values and formulas are accurate.

It's a good idea to have a "second set of eyes" examine your worksheet for things you might have missed. Another person can often spot problems you have overlooked.

In keeping with this advice, Rose asked her accountant to examine her cash flow worksheet. The accountant suggested several changes. We'll make them now.

1. Launch Windows and 1-2-3, if necessary.
2. Open A:\BUDGET.WK3.

The label "Total Cash Receipts" should actually read "Total Cash Available" because only the professional fees are considered receipts, not the opening cash balance.

3. Select A8 and change the cell contents to read: **Total Cash Available**

The "opening cash balance" for the quarter, summed in E6, should actually be the January opening cash balance. The present formula misrepresents the opening cash balance by summing all three months. These figures are cumulative from month to month; thus, it is inappropriate to total them. The formula in cell E6 should be "+B6."

4. Select E6 and enter: **+B6**

The "total cash receipts (available)" for the quarter, summed in cell E8, should be the sum of the opening cash balance and the total of professional fees. The current formula is incorrect for the same reason given in the item above. The formula in cell E8 should read "+E6+E7."

5. Choose E8 and change the formula to **+E6+E7**

The closing cash balance in cell E18 should be March's closing cash balance. Thus, we should change the formula to "+D18."

6. Click on E18 and enter: **+D18**

The "CASH RECEIPTS" label is on the same row as the column titles (i.e., Jan, Feb, etc.) It would look more professional if the column titles were moved up one row.

7. Highlight B5..F5 and use the *Move Cells* icon to move the range to B4.

Now the worksheet looks a bit crowded. Let's insert a row just below the heading "1993-First Quarter."

8. Move to A4, select the *Insert...* command from the Worksheet menu, and then choose *OK*.

Once all the modifications have been made, your worksheet should resemble the one shown in Figure 3–22. Let's save and print the worksheet.

9. Select the range A1..F20.
10. Preview your worksheet.
11. Change the header to read: **Lab 3-5**
12. Click the *Save* SmartIcon.
13. Print your worksheet.
14. You may exit 1-2-3.

Figure 3–22. The results of using the *Move Cells*, *Copy to Clipboard*, and *Paste* techniques.

	A	B	C	D	E	F
1		Quarterly Cash Flow Budget				
2		Going Native				
3		1993-First Quarter				
4						
5		Jan	Feb	Mar	Total	Average
6	CASH RECEIPTS					
7	Opening Cash Balance	2000	2355	2735.86	2000	2363.62
8	Professional Fees	1445	1476.31	1508.3	4429.6	1476.53
9	Total Cash Available	3445	3831.31	4244.15	6429.6	3840.15
10						
11	CASH DISBURSEMENTS					
12	Advertising	100	100.5	101.003	301.503	100.501
13	Office Supplies	90	90.45	90.9023	271.352	90.4508
14	Rent	725	728.625	732.268	2185.89	728.631
15	Phone	100	100.5	101.003	301.503	100.501
16	Utilities	75	75.375	75.7519	226.127	75.3756
17	Total Cash Disbursements	1090	1095.45	1100.93	3286.38	1095.46
18						
19	Closing Cash Balance	2355	2735.86	3143.23	3143.23	2744.69
20	Net Monthly Cash Flow	355	380.858	407.368	1143.23	381.075

COMING ATTRACTIONS...

Chapter 4 will show you how to enhance and organize your worksheet. You will then explore the means to display your data graphically in Chapter 5. In Chapter 6, you'll find that, in addition to powerful graphic capabilities, 1-2-3 can also function as a database.

KEY TERMS

Absolute cell address Cell references that remain unchanged when copied or moved. To create an absolute cell address, precede the address with a dollar sign (e.g., $A1, $A$1, or A$1).

Clipboard A temporary storage area for text and graphics that allows you to transfer data within and between application packages.

Icon Palette A row or group of SmartIcons. The Icon Palette can be moved and customized according to the needs of the user. The default location is below the edit line.

Precedence numbers The number representing the sequence 1-2-3 uses to perform calculations. The lower the number, the higher the precedence.

Relative cell address A cell address that defines the location of data in a worksheet by the "relative" position of the data to the formula referencing it.

SmartIcons A 1-2-3 feature that provides immediate and easy access to commonly used 1-2-3 commands.

EXERCISES

3-1. This exercise will review the material covered in Lab 3-1.

  a. Start Windows and launch 1-2-3.
  b. Review the description of each SmartIcon by placing the pointer on each and holding the *right* mouse button.

We'll use some of these SmartIcons to build a small worksheet that calculates the hours you study each week. Let's begin by entering some labels and initial values.

  c. Enter the following labels in your worksheet at the locations shown:

  In C1, type: **Study Tracker**

  In B3, type: **Week 1**

  In A3, type: **Nights**

  In A5, type: **Sunday**

  In A6, type: **Monday**

  In A7, type: **Tuesday**

  In A8, type: **Wednesday**

Chapter 3 Modifying a Worksheet

In A9, type: **Thursday**

In A10, type: **Friday**

In A11, type: **Saturday**

In A12, type: **Total**

    d. Enter the values below in the locations shown:

In B5, type: **3**

In B6, type: **3**

In B7, type: **4**

In B8, type: **6**

In B9, type: **5**

In B10, type: **3**

In B11, type: **5**

    e. To total the week's studying time, move the pointer to B12 and click the *Sum* icon (next to the *Move Cells* icon).

The total of the values directly above B12 will instantly appear in the cell. This icon will sum the first range of adjacent values above it (in the column). If there aren't any values above the current cell, it will sum the adjacent range to the left (in the row).

Next, we'll copy column B across your worksheet to create the initial values for three more weeks.

    f. Highlight the range B3..B12.

    g. Click the *Copy to Clipboard* icon (located between the *Cut* and *Paste* icons).

    h. Select the range C3..E12 and click the *Paste* icon.

    i. Change the column titles in cells C3, D3, and E3 so they read Week 2, Week 3, and Week 4, respectively.

    j. Change the values for each week to reflect the approximate hours you studied during the last month (be honest).

    k. Use the *Save As* command to save your worksheet with the name **A:\EXER3-1**

    l. Select the range A1..E12.

    m. Use the *Page Setup...* command to create a header that reads **Exercise 3-1** and a footer with your name and the label **1-2-3 for Windows**

    n. Click the *Print* SmartIcon and click *OK*.

    o. You may exit 1-2-3 if you've had enough for now.

3-2. This exercise will provide you the opportunity to practice changing data, clearing cells, and deleting or inserting rows and columns. (To complete the instructions below you must have done Exercise 3-1.)

    a. Begin your Windows session and launch 1-2-3, if necessary.
    b. Use the *Open...* icon to load EXER3-1.WK3 and maximize it.
    c. Highlight the range A12..A13 and use the *Insert...* command to insert two new rows.
    d. Use the *Insert...* command to insert a new column between the labels in column A and the first week of studying times.
    e. Use the *Cut* icon to clear C14..F13.
    f. Click the *Undo* icon to recover the cleared data.
    g. Use the *Delete...* command to remove row 12.
    h. Highlight the range A1..F14 and use the *Page Setup...* command to change the header to: **Exercise 3-2**
    i. Use the *Save As...* command to save your worksheet as: **A:\EXER3-2**
    j. Click the *Print* icon to print your worksheet.
    k. You may continue with the next exercise or exit 1-2-3.

3-3. In this exercise, you'll practice the techniques for copying and moving data introduced in Lab 3-3. (You must have finished Exercise 3-2 to do this exercise.)

    a. Launch Windows and 1-2-3, if necessary. Open the file A:\EXER3-2.WK3 and maximize your worksheet.
    b. Use the *Cut* icon to remove C13..F13.
    c. Move the pointer to C16 and click the *Paste* icon.

The formulas will be pasted on to your worksheet, but they aren't the correct totals.

    d. *Undo* your last command, move the pointer back to C13, and click the *Undo* icon again.

Nothing happens—have we lost the formulas?

    e. Click the *Paste* icon.

Remember that cut and paste operations are done using Clipboard. Pasted formulas change relative to their new location, regardless of where the original data are located.

Chapter 3 Modifying a Worksheet

      f. Highlight the range C13..F13 and click the *Move Cells* icon.
      g. Place the pointing hand in C16 and click.
      h. Select the range C5..F11.
      i. Click the *Move Cells* icon, move the pointer to C6, and click again.

Using a move operation preserved the formulas in both cases: moving the formula and moving the data.

      j. Print the range A1..F16 with the header **Exercise 3-3**, and select the check boxes to include the grid lines and worksheet frame (from the Page Setup dialog box).
      k. Save this worksheet as **A:\EXER3-3**
      l. You may exit 1-2-3.

3-4. This exercise will give you a chance to work with the two concepts introduced in Lab 3-4: precedence and absolute cell addressing.

      a. Start Windows and 1-2-3, if necessary. Maximize the default Untitled 1-2-3 worksheet.
      b. In A1 enter the following formula: **10*10/2+8−6*10**
      c. In A2 enter a similar formula: **10*(10/2+8)−6*10**
      d. Move to A3 and type this formula: **10*10/(2+8)−6*10**
      e. Enter one last variation of the formula in A4: **10*10/2+(8−6)*10**

You can see that using parentheses to change the order of precedence has a tremendous impact on the results of your formulas.

      f. Move to A6 and enter: **50%**
      g. In B1, type the formula: **+A1*A6**
      h. Use the *Quick Copy* icon to copy B1 to B2..B4.

Do you know why the zeros result? It's because the formulas in cells B2..B4 reference empty cells (i.e., B6, C6, and D6, respectively). We can fix this problem by making the reference to A6 an absolute cell reference.

      i. Edit B1 so the formula reads +A1*$A$6.
      j. *Quick Copy* the formula from B1 to B2..B4.
      k. Save the worksheet as **A:\EXER3-4**
      l. Print the worksheet with the grid lines and worksheet frame turned off, and use the header **Exercise 3-4**
      m. You may exit 1-2-3.

REVIEW QUESTIONS

True or False Questions

1. T F SmartIcons are slower and more difficult to use than menu commands.
2. T F It is not possible to change the location of the Icon Palette.
3. T F It is possible to edit a long label without completely retyping it.
4. T F Using the *Undo* feature, you can reverse up to the last three commands you performed.
5. T F It is possible to insert multiple columns into nonadjacent locations in one action.
6. T F The normal default for 1-2-3 is relative addressing.
7. T F The *Move Cells* feature will change a formula relative to the data when either the formula or the data is moved.
8. T F Addition has a higher precedence than division.
9. T F When using the *Quick Copy* icon, you must define the range you want to copy from after selecting the icon.
10. T F The normal default is for 1-2-3 to print grid lines when you print your worksheet.

Multiple Choice Questions

1. Which of the following is a true statement?
   a. All SmartIcons open a dialog box
   b. You can add and remove SmartIcons from the Icon Palette
   c. It is not possible to get a description of what a SmartIcon can do without consulting the reference manual
   d. All of the above

2. Which of the following is a legitimate editing technique?
   a. Replacing the entire contents of a cell by simply typing a new entry
   b. Replacing part of a label by editing it in the contents box
   c. Adding additional information to an existing label by editing it in the contents box
   d. All of the above

3. Which of the following is correct about inserting rows?
   a. Only one row can be inserted at a time
   b. More than one nonadjacent row can be inserted at one time
   c. Unless you manually enter a range, the row will be inserted at the location of the cell pointer
   d. A row can be inserted at the same time as a column

Chapter 3 Modifying a Worksheet   137

4. What is the correct character to use in a cell address to signify absolute addressing?

   a. @
   b. $
   c. &
   d. %

5. Absolute addresses can be absolute for what?

   a. Row
   b. Column
   c. Row and column
   d. All of the above

6. Which of the following is true about the Undo feature?

   a. Undo will only work with actions done by other SmartIcons
   b. You can Undo the same data to several locations
   c. Undo will only work with commands that were issued from the 1-2-3 menu bar
   d. Only the last action initiated will be affected by the *Undo* command

7. What is the advantage of moving data with Clipboard?

   a. It can be pasted back to several locations
   b. It will change formulas to reflect the location of the data rather than relative to its new location
   c. It is always faster than using the *Quick Copy* icon
   d. All of the above

8. Which of the following operations would be performed first?

   a. Addition
   b. Subtraction
   c. Exponentiation
   d. Multiplication

9. In the calculation 10*(10+10)−10/10, which operation would be done first?

   a. * (multiplication)
   b. + (addition)
   c. − (subtraction)
   d. / (division)

10. The *Quick Copy* icon can be used to copy what type of data?

    a. Labels
    b. Values
    c. Formulas
    d. All of the above

CHAPTER 4

Enhancing a Worksheet

• *Objectives*

Upon completing this chapter, you'll be able to:
1. Change the format of numbers and labels.
2. Add style to your worksheet.
3. Globally change the format and freeze titles.
4. Create and use named ranges.

OVERVIEW

This chapter explores the techniques for enhancing the appearance of your worksheet. You can make your worksheet more appealing and understandable by changing the appearance of numbers and text. You'll learn to alter such things as the color, style, size, and alignment of data to accentuate and group information.

We'll also take a look at features that help you work with large worksheets. You'll see how to format an entire worksheet, "freeze" titles so they don't scroll off the screen, print wide reports, and assign names to cell ranges for easy reference.

LAB 4-1   FORMATTING RANGES

In this lab, you'll examine the options for altering the appearance or format of the numeric data in your worksheet. You'll enhance your worksheet with a variety of formats such as percentages and dollar signs. You'll also explore the options for hiding and converting data.

Let's begin by renaming your worksheet. This will provide an unaltered copy for later use. It will also assure you of a backup in case something goes wrong.

1. Start Windows and launch 1-2-3 for Windows.
2. Open the A:\BUDGET.WK3 worksheet from your data disk.
3. Choose *Save As...* from the File menu.
4. Type **A:\BUDGET2.WK3** and click the *OK* button.

1-2-3 will save a copy of the current worksheet to your disk with the name BUDGET2.WK3. The worksheet window will now display the new file name BUDGET2.WK3. Since we want to work with the original file, we'll close this worksheet and retrieve BUDGET.WK3 again.

5. Select *Close* from the File menu.
6. Use the *Open* icon to retrieve the A:\BUDGET.WK3 worksheet.
7. Maximize the worksheet.

Formatting Numeric Data

Formatting is the process of changing the display characteristics of a cell or range of cells. It is a simple task to alter the format 1-2-3 uses to display numeric data. Just select the range that you want to alter and choose the *Format...* command from the Range menu. A dialog box will open displaying a list of format types to choose from. Once you make a selection and close the dialog box, the new format will be applied to the selected range.

One way to enhance the look of the data in your worksheet is to display any values that represent dollar amounts in currency format.

1. Select the range B7..F20.
2. Choose the *Format...* command from the Range menu.

This causes the Range Format dialog box to appear, as shown in Figure 4-1. From the *Format* list box you can select the type of format you want to display. Table 4-1 summarizes the types of numeric formatting available.

This dialog box also contains two text boxes. The *Decimal places* text box lets you control the number of decimal places your numbers display. The *Range* text box shows the selected range. You can use it to specify a range by selecting the text box and typing in a new range.

Figure 4–1.
The Range Format dialog box lets you format the values in your worksheet.

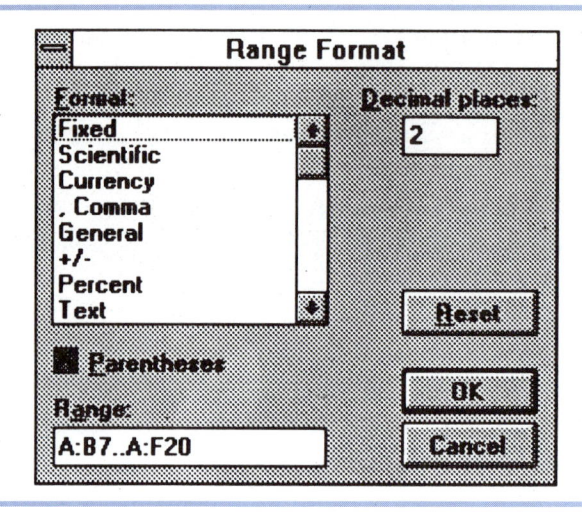

Table 4–1. Numeric formats.

Type	Description
Fixed	Displays numbers with up to 15 decimal places, a — (minus sign) for negatives, and a leading zero for decimal values.
Scientific	Displays numbers in scientific (exponential) notation.
Currency	Displays numbers with a currency symbol and thousands separators.
, Comma	Displays numbers with thousands separators.
General	Displays numbers with no thousands separators.
Percent	Displays numbers as percentages (that is, multiplied by 100) with a percent sign.

If you click the *Parentheses* check box, your values will appear surrounded by parentheses. The Range Format dialog box also has a *Reset* button to return the selected range to the default or global format.

To choose a format, simply click on it with the mouse.

3. Click on the Currency format.

This will cause the Currency format to be highlighted. The *Decimal* text box displays a 2. Although currency is normally displayed with 2 decimal places, we'll change it to 0.

4. Change the value in the *Decimal places* text box to 0 and click the *OK* button.

1-2-3 will change the values to the nearest dollar, as portrayed in Figure 4–2.

Chapter 4   Enhancing a Worksheet   **141**

Figure 4-2. The worksheet displays values rounded to the nearest dollar.

	A	B	C	D	E	F
1		Quarterly Cash Flow Budget				
2		Going Native				
3		1993-First Quarter				
4						
5		Jan	Feb	Mar	Total	Average
6	CASH RECEIPTS					
7	Opening Cash Balance	$2,000	$2,355	$2,736	$2,000	$2,364
8	Professional Fees	$1,445	$1,476	$1,508	$4,430	$1,477
9	Total Cash Available	$3,445	$3,831	$4,244	$6,430	$3,840
10						
11	CASH DISBURSEMENTS					
12	Advertising	$100	$101	$101	$302	$101
13	Office Supplies	$90	$90	$91	$271	$90
14	Rent	$725	$729	$732	$2,186	$729
15	Phone	$100	$101	$101	$302	$101
16	Utilities	$75	$75	$76	$226	$75
17	Total Cash Disbursements	$1,090	$1,095	$1,101	$3,286	$1,095
18						
19	Closing Cash Balance	$2,355	$2,736	$3,143	$3,143	$2,745
20	Net Monthly Cash Flow	$355	$381	$407	$1,143	$381

Figure 4-3.

You can use the same technique to alter the appearance of the percentage values in B21 and B22, but there is a faster way. There are three default SmartIcons you can use to specify the format of numeric data. These icons are shown in Figure 4-3.

The $ icon on the left changes the format to currency with two decimal places. The center icon, *0,0*, formats a range so it displays whole numbers with a thousands separator. The far right % icon formats data as percentages with two decimal places.

To use these SmartIcons, you must first select a range and then click on the desired icon. Formatting will take place immediately without the need to respond to a dialog box.

5. Drag the cell pointer to surround the range B22..B23.
6. Click the % SmartIcon.

The selected values will be instantly displayed as percentages. The numeric formatting on your worksheet should now look like Figure 4-4.

Figure 4-4. Values can be formatted as percentages.

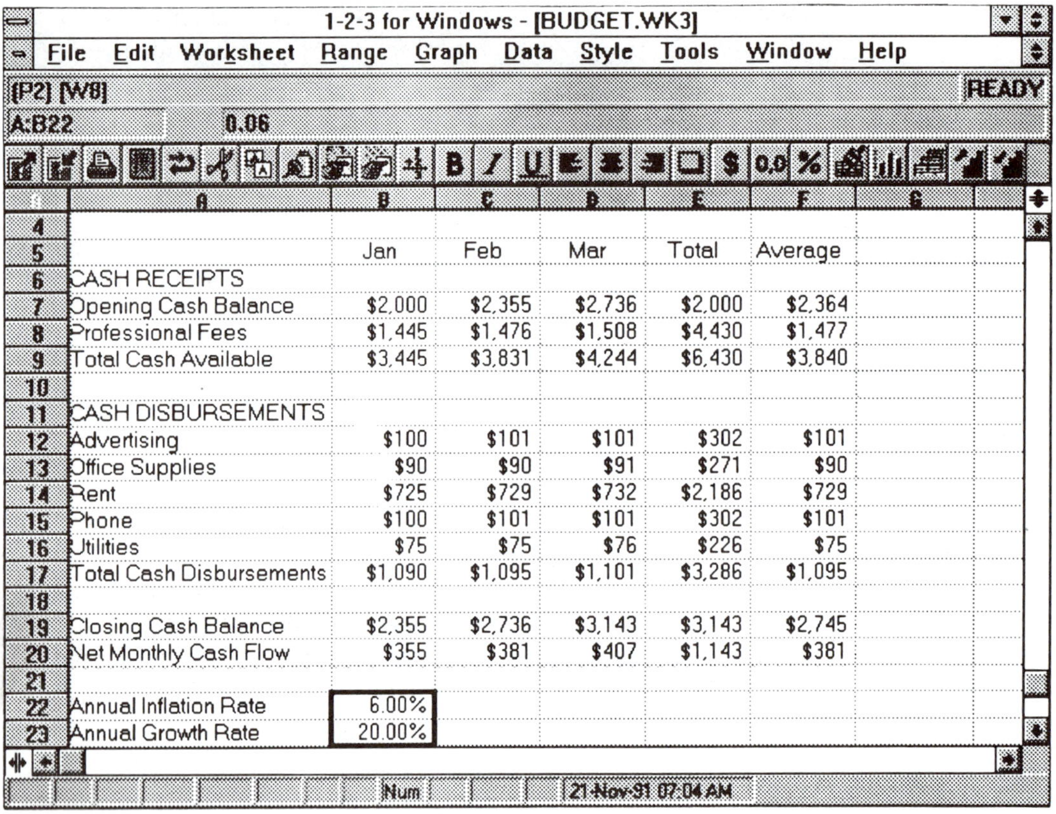

	A	B	C	D	E	F
		Jan	Feb	Mar	Total	Average
6	CASH RECEIPTS					
7	Opening Cash Balance	$2,000	$2,355	$2,736	$2,000	$2,364
8	Professional Fees	$1,445	$1,476	$1,508	$4,430	$1,477
9	Total Cash Available	$3,445	$3,831	$4,244	$6,430	$3,840
10						
11	CASH DISBURSEMENTS					
12	Advertising	$100	$101	$101	$302	$101
13	Office Supplies	$90	$90	$91	$271	$90
14	Rent	$725	$729	$732	$2,186	$729
15	Phone	$100	$101	$101	$302	$101
16	Utilities	$75	$75	$76	$226	$75
17	Total Cash Disbursements	$1,090	$1,095	$1,101	$3,286	$1,095
18						
19	Closing Cash Balance	$2,355	$2,736	$3,143	$3,143	$2,745
20	Net Monthly Cash Flow	$355	$381	$407	$1,143	$381
21						
22	Annual Inflation Rate	6.00%				
23	Annual Growth Rate	20.00%				

Hiding Data

There may be times when you want to conceal some of the data in a worksheet from other users. To hide data, simply select it, choose the *Format...* command from the Range menu, pick Hidden from the *Format* list box, and click *OK*.

The contents of the range will no longer be visible on the worksheet. However, you can still view the contents of a hidden cell by selecting the cell and looking at the contents box. Let's hide the annual inflation rate and annual growth rate.

1. Select the range A22..B23.
2. Choose the *Format...* command from the Range menu.

Chapter 4 Enhancing a Worksheet

The Range Format dialog box will appear.

3. Use the scroll bar to highlight *Hidden* in the *Format* list box, click on *Hidden*, and click the *OK* button.

The range will vanish from the worksheet. Nonetheless, the contents box will continue to display the data in the hidden cells. To unhide the hidden data, simply select the *Reset* button from the *Format* command in the Range menu.

You can now save your worksheet before exiting 1-2-3 and Windows.

4. Select the range A1..F23.
5. Use the *Page Setup...* command from the File menu to change the header to **Lab 4-1**
6. Click the *Save* icon.
7. Print the worksheet.
8. You may exit 1-2-3.

LAB 4-2 CHANGING CELL STYLES

Formatting goes beyond just changing the way numeric data are displayed. You can alter the shape, size, color, and alignment of the characters in a cell. These styles allow you to emphasize important data and make your worksheet both functional and visually appealing.

The Style menu lets you access the commands that control the various elements of style. Let's retrieve your worksheet and enhance its appearance through the use of these commands.

1. Start Windows and open 1-2-3 for Windows.
2. Retrieve A:\BUDGET.WK3 from your disk.
3. Maximize your worksheet.

Changing Fonts

Font is a traditional typesetting term that refers to the size and style of a particular typeface (e.g., 8-point Times Roman Bold or 12-point Helvetica Italic). The term is applied a little more loosely in the computer/desktop publishing world and is generally used interchangeably with "typeface" to refer to the entire family of characters of a particular shape or design. In this book, we will use the term *font* in the way it is used in desktop publishing to mean the actual design or shape shared by a set of characters (such as Times Roman or Helvetica.)

The list of fonts available to you depends on the capabilities of your printer and which version of Windows you are using. For this lab, we will assume you are using the default fonts available when 1-2-3 is installed using Adobe Type Manager (ATM). If your font choices are different, you'll have to select the closest font you have to the one shown.

To change the font, select a range, and issue the *Font...* command from the Style menu. This will cause the Style Font dialog box to appear. Choose the font you want, and click *OK*.

Let's experiment by trying a different font.

1. Select the range A1..F23.
2. Choose the *Font...* command from the Style menu.

As shown in Figure 4-5, the Style Font dialog box will appear. It contains a *Fonts* list box that displays the available choices. It also has check boxes for controlling the attributes *Bold*, *Italics*, and *Underline*. A drop-down list box, just below *Underline*, lets you choose between different line types. The *Range* text box shows the currently selected range and allows you to enter a new range manually.

Figure 4-5.
The Style Font dialog box lets you change to a different font.

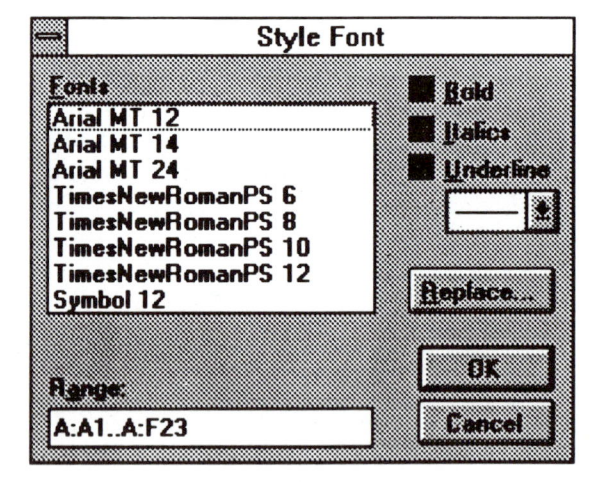

NOTE

You can change the current selection of fonts and sizes in the *Fonts* list box by clicking the *Replace...* button in the Style Font dialog box. This will open a second dialog box with options for changing the current font set and their associated sizes. For further information on using these options, see the topic *Style Font Replace* in the Help facility.

3. Highlight the font *TimesNewRomanPS 8* and click the *OK* button.

The selected range will change to display the new font and size. The smaller font is much more difficult to read. Let's change back to Arial MT 12.

4. Pick the *Font...* command from the Style menu.
5. Select the Arial MT 12 font and click the *OK* button.

Figure 4-6.

This is the font 1-2-3 uses initially. Let's continue to use this font, but change its attributes. The SmartIcons, pictured in Figure 4-6, offer a quick method for altering font attributes. The letters on the icons refer to (B)old, (I)talics, and (U)nderline. Simply select a range from your worksheet, click the icon you want, and the data in the range will change to display the new font attribute.

We'll use these SmartIcons to enhance some labels in your worksheet.

6. Move the cell pointer to B1.

Since the entire label, QUARTERLY CASH FLOW BUDGET, is contained in this one cell, it is unnecessary to specify a larger range. We are now ready to select the *Bold* icon to boldface this label. This will bypass the Style Font dialog box and change the font attribute immediately.

7. Click the *Bold* icon.

The label will be immediately boldfaced. The Style Font dialog box won't appear, so no time will be wasted in responding to prompts.

Next, we'll emphasize the other uppercase headings by boldfacing them too.

8. Select A6 and click the *Bold* icon.
9. Use the *Bold* icon to change A11.

You can also use SmartIcons to change a font to italics, or to underline it. However, the *Underline* SmartIcon defaults to a single underline. If you want a double or thicker underline, use the *Font...* command from the Style menu.

To make the company name stand out, we'll underline it.

10. Select B2 and click the *Underline* icon.

The company name will now appear with a single underline. Suppose you actually wanted italics instead of underlining. To remove an attribute, simply select a range and choose the same attribute again. For example, if you click on the *Underline* icon once more, the company name will return to its earlier state.

11. Click the *Underline* icon.

The underline will vanish.

12. Select the *Italics* icon.

The company name will be displayed in italics, as pictured in Figure 4–7.

Figure 4–7. The company name appears in italics.

		Jan	Feb	Mar	Total	Average
1	Quarterly Cash Flow Budget					
2	Going Native					
3	1993-First Quarter					
4						
5		Jan	Feb	Mar	Total	Average
6	CASH RECEIPTS					
7	Opening Cash Balance	$2,000	$2,355	$2,736	$2,000	$2,364
8	Professional Fees	$1,445	$1,476	$1,508	$4,430	$1,477
9	Total Cash Available	$3,445	$3,831	$4,244	$6,430	$3,840
10						
11	CASH DISBURSEMENTS					
12	Advertising	$100	$101	$101	$302	$101
13	Office Supplies	$90	$90	$91	$271	$90
14	Rent	$725	$729	$732	$2,186	$729
15	Phone	$100	$101	$101	$302	$101
16	Utilities	$75	$75	$76	$226	$75
17	Total Cash Disbursements	$1,090	$1,095	$1,101	$3,286	$1,095
18						
19	Closing Cash Balance	$2,355	$2,736	$3,143	$3,143	$2,745
20	Net Monthly Cash Flow	$355	$381	$407	$1,143	$381

● HINT

You can also use the *Clear Special...* command from the Edit menu to clear the style of a cell. This command is convenient when you have made multiple style changes to a cell or cells and want to clear them all at once.

Aligning Cells

Up until now, you have been manually entering label-prefix characters to alter the alignment (justification) of labels in a cell. A quicker method exists. The *Align Left*, *Center*, and *Align Right* SmartIcons, shown in Figure 4-8, let you change the justification of existing labels without editing the contents of a cell.

To align labels with these icons, select a range and then click on the icon that offers the type of alignment you desire.

Figure 4-8.

Let's use the *Align Right* icon to make your row titles easier to read.

1. Select the range A12..A16.
2. Click the *Align Right* icon.

The alignment of the labels in the cells will change from the left side to the right side of each cell.

The contents box will also confirm that the label-prefix has changed from the apostrophe (') to the double quote (") character.

Let's try one more.

3. Move to A8 and click the *Align Right* icon.

Again, the justification of the cell will immediately change.

● HINT

If you want to align nonadjacent labels in the same column, just select a range that includes all of them. Don't worry if the range also surrounds values or empty cells. The alignment icons will only affect the cells holding labels.

Although these icons offer a rapid means of aligning cells, they have one drawback. You can't use them to align the contents of one cell over more than one column. To align a label spanning several columns, select the range, issue the *Alignment...* command from the Style menu, choose the type of justification, and click *OK*.

We can use this procedure to make the headings in your worksheet easier to read.

4. Highlight the range B1..E3.
5. From the Style menu choose the *Alignment...* command.

Figure 4-9.

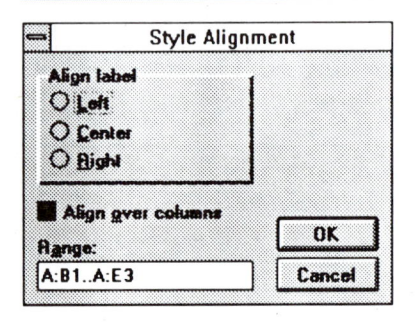

Figure 4-9 shows the Style Alignment dialog box that will appear. It contains radio buttons for *Left*, *Center*, and *Right* justification. These are the counterparts of the alignment SmartIcons covered earlier.

In addition to the standard *Range* text box there is an *Align over columns* check box. This check box allows you to align labels over more than one column.

6. Click the *Align over columns* check box.

Figure 4-10.

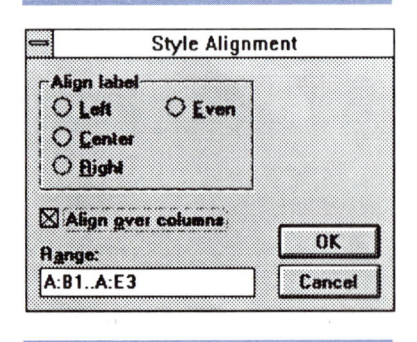

Another radio button will appear in the dialog box, as depicted in Figure 4-10. The *Even* option causes the characters and words in the selected range to expand out and become evenly spaced across the entire range.

7. Choose the *Even* radio button and click *OK*.

Extra spacing will be inserted to spread the labels over the range. In this case, the labels are harder to read. So, let's center align the label instead.

8. Pick the *Alignment...* command from the Style menu.
9. Check the *Align over columns* box.
10. Click the *Center* radio button and *OK*.

The three rows that make up the heading of your worksheet will be centered in columns B to E. Even though the labels are centered across columns, the actual cell contents remain in their original cells.

11. Move to B2.

Your contents box will show that cell B2 contains "Going Native," but the label will actually appear in cells C2 and D2, as portrayed in Figure 4-11 The alignment command centers a label across the columns in the specified range.

Figure 4-11. The label "Going Native" appears to be in cells C2 and D2 of your worksheet, but the contents box reveals it actually resides in B2.

```
                1-2-3 for Windows - [BUDGET.WK3]
  File  Edit  Worksheet  Range  Graph  Data  Style  Tools  Window  Help
[Italics Text] [W8]                                              READY
A:B2        ^Going Native
```

	A	B	C	D	E	F	G
1		Quarterly Cash Flow Budget
2			Going Native
3			1993-First Quarter
4							
5		Jan	Feb	Mar	Total	Average	
6	CASH RECEIPTS						
7	Opening Cash Balance	$2,000	$2,355	$2,736	$2,000	$2,364	
8	Professional Fees	$1,445	$1,476	$1,508	$4,430	$1,477	
9	Total Cash Available	$3,445	$3,831	$4,244	$6,430	$3,840	
10							
11	CASH DISBURSEMENTS						
12	Advertising	$100	$101	$101	$302	$101	
13	Office Supplies	$90	$90	$91	$271	$90	
14	Rent	$725	$729	$732	$2,186	$729	
15	Phone	$100	$101	$101	$302	$101	
16	Utilities	$75	$75	$76	$226	$75	
17	Total Cash Disbursements	$1,090	$1,095	$1,101	$3,286	$1,095	
18							
19	Closing Cash Balance	$2,355	$2,736	$3,143	$3,143	$2,745	
20	Net Monthly Cash Flow	$355	$381	$407	$1,143	$381	

Num   22-Nov-91 08:29 AM

⊘ HAZARD

Never use the *Align over columns* option to justify a range containing adjacent labels. The range should have labels only in the leftmost column. Otherwise, the labels may appear overlapping and truncated.

Don't forget to save your work routinely.

12. Use the *Save* icon to copy your worksheet to your disk.

Adding Borders and Changing the Display Options

You can further emphasize or distinguish the data in your worksheet by surrounding it with a border. A **border** is simply a line that sets off data in your worksheet. 1-2-3 has several options available for the placement and style of borders.

Figure 4-12.

To create a border quickly, simply select a range and click the *Outline and drop shadow* icon shown in Figure 4-12. This will create a nifty looking three-dimensional border around the selected range.

1. Select the range B1..E3.
2. Click the *Outline and drop shadow* icon.

Your heading will be outlined with the three-dimensional effect of the drop shadow, as portrayed in Figure 4-13. To get the full visual impact of this enhancement, we'll insert a row above the border.

Figure 4-13. The heading in the worksheet is set off by a three-dimensional border.

	A	B	C	D	E	F
1		Quarterly Cash Flow Budget			
2		Going Native			
3		1993-First Quarter			
4						
5		Jan	Feb	Mar	Total	Average
6	CASH RECEIPTS					
7	Opening Cash Balance	$2,000	$2,355	$2,736	$2,000	$2,364
8	Professional Fees	$1,445	$1,476	$1,508	$4,430	$1,477
9	Total Cash Available	$3,445	$3,831	$4,244	$6,430	$3,840
10						
11	CASH DISBURSEMENTS					
12	Advertising	$100	$101	$101	$302	$101
13	Office Supplies	$90	$90	$91	$271	$90
14	Rent	$725	$729	$732	$2,186	$729
15	Phone	$100	$101	$101	$302	$101
16	Utilities	$75	$75	$76	$226	$75
17	Total Cash Disbursements	$1,090	$1,095	$1,101	$3,286	$1,095
18						
19	Closing Cash Balance	$2,355	$2,736	$3,143	$3,143	$2,745
20	Net Monthly Cash Flow	$355	$381	$407	$1,143	$381

Chapter 4   Enhancing a Worksheet   151

3. Move the cell pointer to A1.
4. Choose the *Insert...* command from the Worksheet menu.
5. Click *OK*.

This is quite an improvement. However, the appearance of the border would be more impressive if the grid lines were removed from the worksheet. This is easily done with the *Display Options...* command in the Windows menu.

6. From the Windows menu select the *Display Options...* command.

This will cause the Window Display Options dialog box to appear, shown in Figure 4-14. From this dialog box you can control a myriad of display options including color and zoom features. However, for our present purposes, we'll only be discussing the *Grid lines* check box. Feel free to use the Help facility to satisfy your curiosity about any of the other features.

Figure 4-14. The Window Display Options dialog box offers a wide variety of display options to control the appearance of your worksheet.

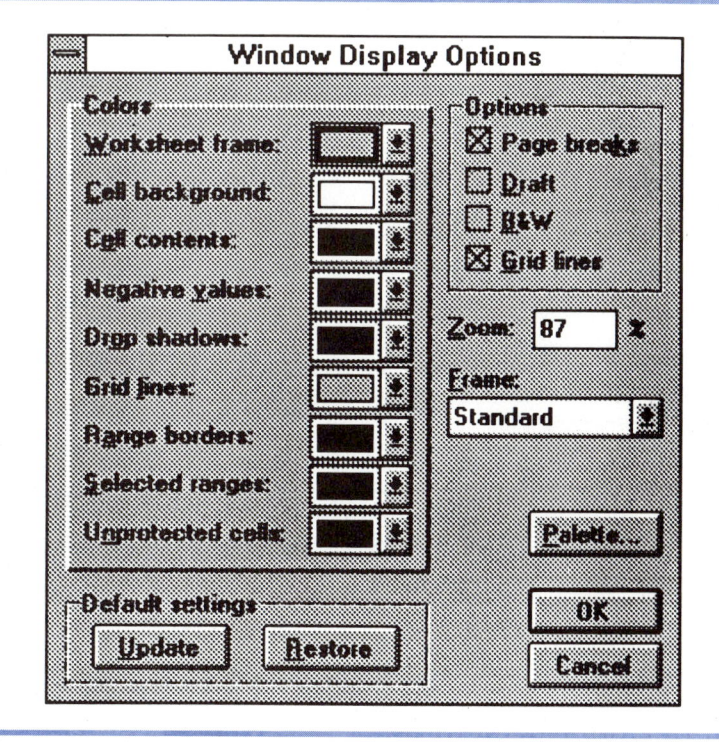

The *Grid lines* check box allows you to control the display of grid lines on your worksheet. The default setting is for 1-2-3 to display them.

To clear the grid lines from your current worksheet, simply toggle the *Grid lines* check box off.

7. Remove the check mark from the *Grid lines* check box by clicking it, then click *OK*.

The worksheet will no longer display grid lines, as shown in Figure 4-15. This makes the heading really stand out from the rest of the worksheet.

Figure 4-15. The worksheet no longer displays grid lines.

	Jan	Feb	Mar	Total	Average
CASH RECEIPTS					
Opening Cash Balance	$2,000	$2,355	$2,736	$2,000	$2,364
Professional Fees	$1,445	$1,476	$1,508	$4,430	$1,477
Total Cash Available	$3,445	$3,831	$4,244	$6,430	$3,840
CASH DISBURSEMENTS					
Advertising	$100	$101	$101	$302	$101
Office Supplies	$90	$90	$91	$271	$90
Rent	$725	$729	$732	$2,186	$729
Phone	$100	$101	$101	$302	$101
Utilities	$75	$75	$76	$226	$75
Total Cash Disbursements	$1,090	$1,095	$1,101	$3,286	$1,095
Closing Cash Balance	$2,355	$2,736	$3,143	$3,143	$2,745

Quarterly Cash Flow Budget
Going Native
1993-First Quarter

Let's use some of your previous skills to prepare the worksheet for other enhancements. First, we'll delete the blank rows that separate data.

8. Move to A11.
9. From the Worksheet menu choose the *Delete...* command.
10. Click *OK*.

This will delete the unnecessary blank row. Use the same technique to remove the other extra rows.

11. Delete row 18.

Insert a column on the left side of the worksheet.

12. Select A1 and insert a column.

Let's next reduce the size of column A to center the data on your screen.

13. Move the pointer to the line separating column A and column B on the worksheet frame.

The pointer will change to the double-headed arrow.

14. Drag the pointer to the left until column A is about two-thirds of its original width and release the mouse button.

Your data should now appear centered on your screen, as illustrated in Figure 4-16.

Removing the grid lines improved the appearance of the heading; however, it made it more difficult to locate data in a particular row or column. We can alleviate this problem by creating a border around each cell. In effect, this will simulate grid lines for a specified range.

15. Select the range B6..G19.
16. From the Style menu choose the *Border...* command.

The Style Border dialog box will appear, as depicted in Figure 4-17. It uses seven check boxes to control the placement of the border around a cell or range. The *All edges, Top, Bottom, Left,* and *Right* boxes determine what borders appear around a cell. For example, selecting the *All edges* check box places a border on all four sides of cell, while the *Top* check box puts a border across the top of a cell.

The *Outline* check box places a border around a range of cells. You can add a drop shadow to any of the above effects by selecting the *Drop shadow* check box. The standard *Range* text box shows the currently selected range and makes it possible to enter a new range, if desired.

Each of the border options has a drop-down list box that lets you pick one of three border types. You can choose from a thin single line, thin double line, or a thick single line. We'll use the default thin single line to surround all the edges of the cells in the range.

Figure 4-16. The data in the worksheet appear centered on the screen.

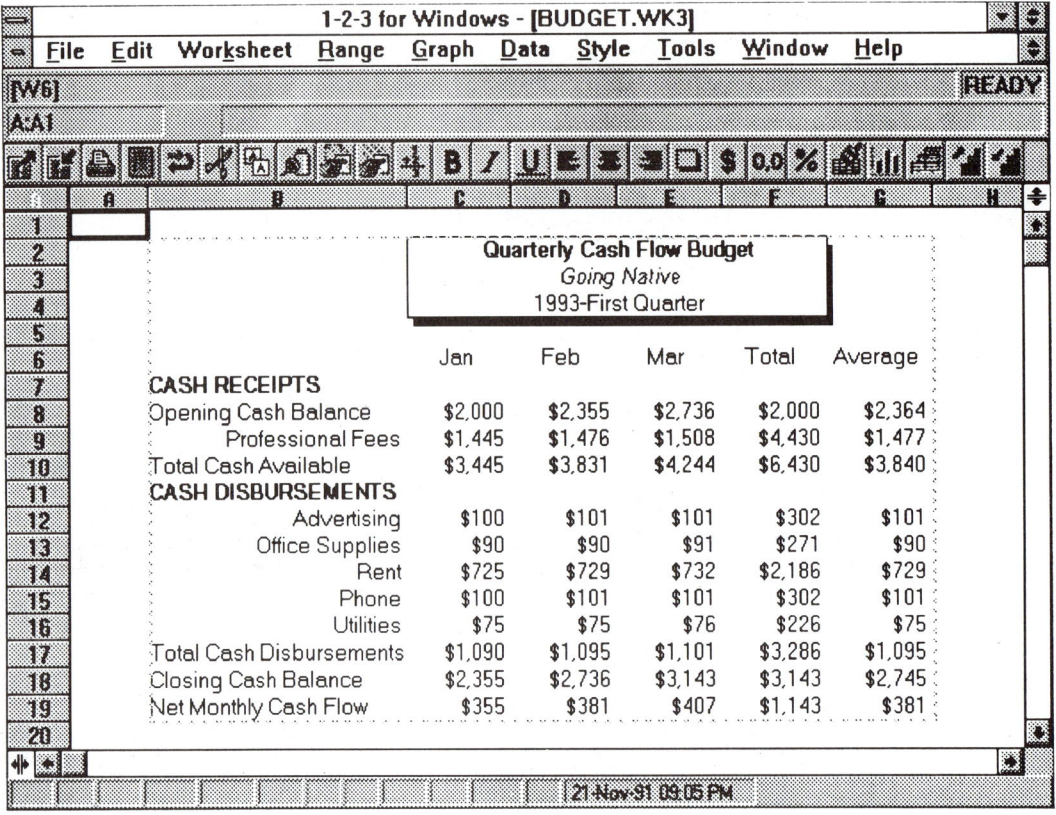

Figure 4-17. The Style Border dialog box determines the location and type of borders you can add to a selected range.

Chapter 4   Enhancing a Worksheet

17. Check the *All edges* box.
18. Add a three-dimensional effect by selecting the *Drop shadow* box.
19. Click on the *OK* button.

All the cell edges in the selected range on your worksheet will be surrounded by the single thin line border, as shown in Figure 4-18. These borders make it easy to identify the values belonging to each heading without the use of grid lines.

20. Click the *Save* icon before continuing.

Figure 4-18. The worksheet displays a variety of borders to enhance and emphasize data.

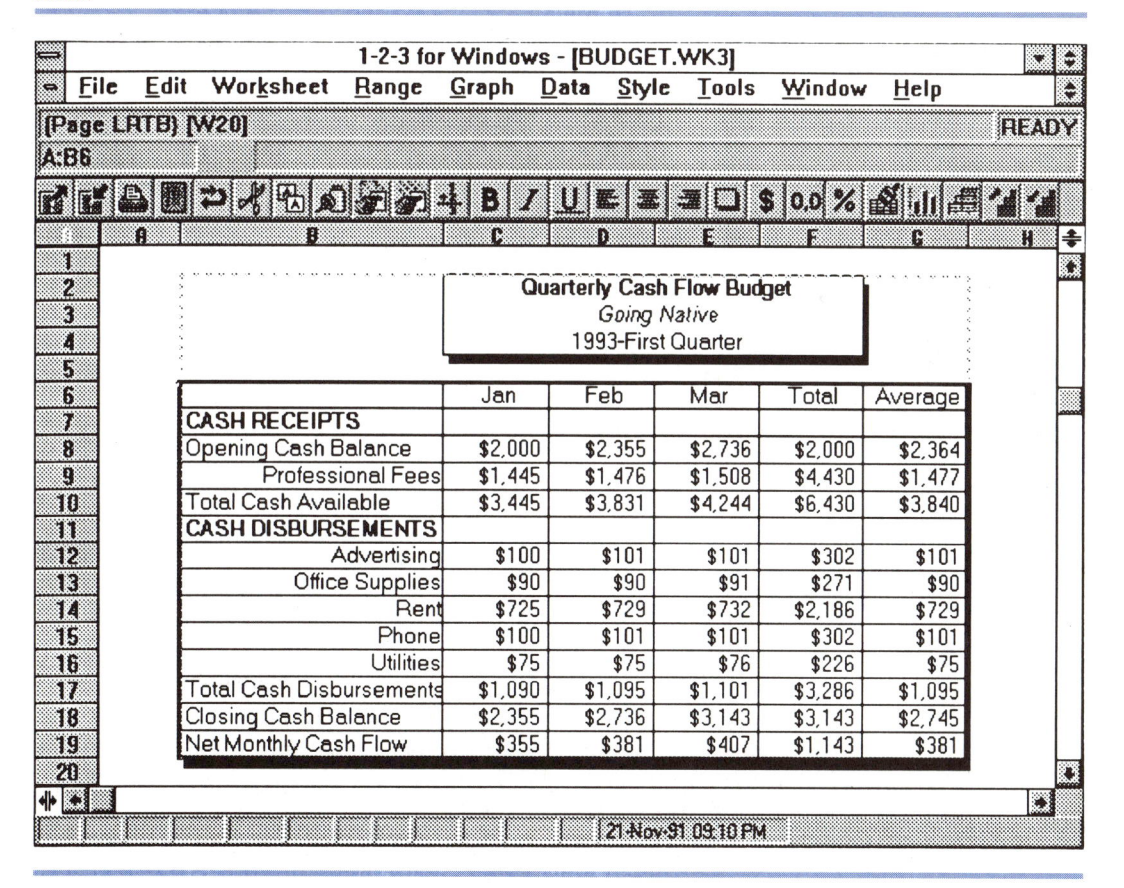

	Jan	Feb	Mar	Total	Average
CASH RECEIPTS					
Opening Cash Balance	$2,000	$2,355	$2,736	$2,000	$2,364
Professional Fees	$1,445	$1,476	$1,508	$4,430	$1,477
Total Cash Available	$3,445	$3,831	$4,244	$6,430	$3,840
CASH DISBURSEMENTS					
Advertising	$100	$101	$101	$302	$101
Office Supplies	$90	$90	$91	$271	$90
Rent	$725	$729	$732	$2,186	$729
Phone	$100	$101	$101	$302	$101
Utilities	$75	$75	$76	$226	$75
Total Cash Disbursements	$1,090	$1,095	$1,101	$3,286	$1,095
Closing Cash Balance	$2,355	$2,736	$3,143	$3,143	$2,745
Net Monthly Cash Flow	$355	$381	$407	$1,143	$381

Altering Colors

The *Color...* command from the Style menu lets you add color to your worksheet. Color can be an extremely effective tool for emphasizing data. 1-2-3 makes it possible to control the color of a cell's contents as well as background.

We'll use colors to group similar types of data on your worksheet.

1. Highlight the range C8..G10.
2. Pick the *Color...* command from the Style menu.

Figure 4-19.

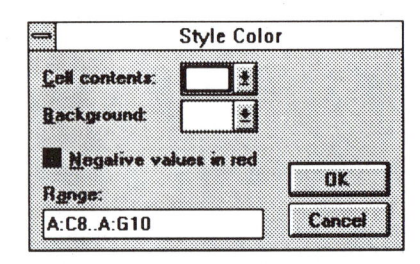

The Style Color dialog box will appear, as shown in Figure 4-19. There are two drop-down list boxes for changing the color of the *Cell contents* and *Background*. There is also a *Negative values in red* check box to display values less than zero in red.

When choosing a cell content color, you'll want to pick a color that shows up clearly against the background color.

3. Click the *Background* drop-down arrow.

A drop-down list box will appear, displaying the available color options.

4. Select the color green by clicking on it, and click *OK*.

The range will switch to a green background with black characters (black is the default cell contents color).

Let's use the same technique to color the other portions of your worksheet.

5. Select C12..G17 and change the background color to magenta (dark pink).
6. Change the background color of B6..G6 to yellow.

Figure 4-20.

You should have three different colored sections on your worksheet. You can more quickly color the remaining sections by using the *Paint* SmartIcon shown in Figure 4-20. To use the *Paint* SmartIcon, first select a cell that displays the color you want to use, and then click the icon. When the pointer changes to a paintbrush, hold down the left mouse button, and drag the paintbrush over the range you want to color.

The *Paint* SmartIcon will automatically apply the color in the original cell to the specified range. In fact, it will copy all of the style settings appearing in the original cell. For example, if you select a boldfaced cell with a yellow background, the range you paint will appear boldfaced and have a yellow background.

Let's use this technique to apply the style used in C8..G10 to another range.

7. Select the cell C8.
8. Click the *Paint* icon.

The pointer will change to a paintbrush. You are now ready to paint a range.

9. Move the paintbrush to C18 and hold down the left mouse button.
10. Drag the paintbrush to G19 and release the mouse button.

The style used in cell C8 will be applied to the specified range. We'll use this technique to paint additional data cells.

11. Select C6.
12. Click the *Paint* icon and paint B6..B19.

Look at B8 and B11—what happened to them? Their contents now appear in normal text and general format. This is because the original cell used to paint them contained these styles.

Let's return these cells to their original format but retain the yellow background.

13. Move to B8 and click the *Bold* icon.
14. Move to B11 and click the *Bold* icon.

The last range we want to color is the heading. This time, let's change the colors for both the cell contents and background colors.

15. Highlight the range C2..F4.
16. Pick the *Color...* command from the Style menu.
17. Click on the drop-down list for *Cell contents*.
18. Select the dark blue color.
19. Display the color choices for *Background* and choose cyan (bluish green). Click the *OK* button.

Wow! Colors really make a dramatic difference in the appearance of your worksheet.

Using Shading

Shading is also an effective means of accentuating data. 1-2-3 uses the default cell contents color to shade the cells in a selected range. To shade a range, you simply select the *Shading...* command from the Style menu.

Let's explore the three types of shading.

1. Select the range B11..G11.
2. Choose the *Shading...* feature from the Style menu.

Figure 4-21.

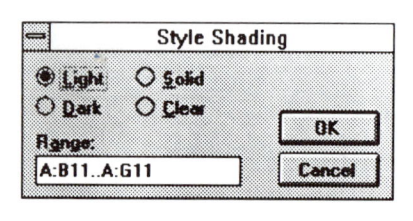

The Style Shading dialog box will appear, as portrayed in Figure 4-21. In addition to the standard *Range* text box, this dialog box displays four radio buttons. These radio buttons make it possible to choose the type of shading you want, *Light*, *Dark*, or *Solid*. You can also select the *Clear* radio button to erase shading from a range without affecting other style settings.

3. Click the *Solid* radio button and *OK*.

Solid shading will completely cover the contents of the cell. This prevents the data from being displayed. So, let's try another option.

4. Using the *Shading...* command, change the radio button to *Dark*.

This is better, but it is still difficult to read the label with the dark shading.

5. Change the shading to *Light*.

You can now see the label; however, it is still somewhat difficult to read. Let's remove the shading from the cell containing the label but leave it in the empty cells to provide a break between the sections of your worksheet.

6. Select B11.
7. Choose the *Shading...* command, pick the *Clear* radio button, and click *OK*.

Chapter 4 Enhancing a Worksheet

This will clear the shading from the cell and leave the other format settings intact.

> **NOTE**
>
> The *Name...* command from the Style menu lets you assign a name to a style. This makes it easier to apply styles to ranges. To use a style name, first highlight the range you want to change and then select the name style from the list in the Style menu. The selected range will display all the style attributes associated with that name.

8. Select the range B2..G19.
9. Use the *Page Setup...* command to change the header to **Lab 4-2**
10. Click the *Save* icon.
11. Print your worksheet.

The worksheet will print out using shades of gray to simulate colors on your screen. Since this worksheet is meant to be displayed in color, some data may be obscured by darker shades. Of course, if you have a color printer, all your data will be clearly visible in color.

12. To return 1-2-3 to its default setting, issue the *Display Options...* command from the Window menu.
13. Then select the *Grid lines* check box and click *OK*.
14. Exit 1-2-3.

LAB 4-3 USING GLOBAL FORMATS AND TITLES

In this lab, you'll explore the techniques for globally changing the format of your worksheet, freezing titles, and protecting cells. These features can be incorporated into any worksheet, regardless of its size. However, global commands are most effective when applied to a larger worksheet.

It will be easier to understand the benefits of using these commands if we first increase the size of your worksheet. Let's begin by retrieving the unformatted copy of the worksheet, BUDGET2. To increase the size of the worksheet, you will insert additional columns and copy data into them.

> • **HINT**
>
> Normally, you'll want to globally format a worksheet when you first create it. This sets the default format for the entire worksheet. If you do your global formatting later, any cells that have been previously formatted with the Range menu command will not be affected by the global formats.

1. Start Windows and open 1-2-3 for Windows.
2. Retrieve BUDGET2.WK3 from drive A and maximize your worksheet.
3. Insert three columns by selecting E1..G1 and issuing the *Insert...* command from the Worksheet menu.
4. Click the *Column* radio button and *OK*.

The three new columns will appear, but they are wider than the other data columns. Let's change the width to 8 characters.

5. Highlight the range E1..G1 and change the width to **8** characters using the *Column Width...* command from the Worksheet menu.

The columns will now be set to the proper width. Next, we'll title the new columns and then enter the necessary values and formulas.

6. Enter **Apr** in E5, **May** in F5, and **Jun** in G5.
7. Use the *Align Center* icon to center the range E5..G5.
8. Highlight the range D7..D20 and click the *Copy Cells* icon.
9. Using the pointing hand, select the range E7..G7 and click the mouse.

The new columns will contain headings and data. Let's look at how these new columns affected the Total and Average values.

10. Click on cell H8.

Notice the formula doesn't include the new columns. You'll need to complete the following instructions to update the formulas in your worksheet so that they contain the proper range references.

11. Edit H8 to read: **@SUM(B8..G8)**
12. Copy H8 to H12..H17 using the *Copy Cells* icon.
13. Copy H8 to H20 using the *Copy Cells* icon again.
14. Change the formula in H19 from **+D19** to **+G19**

Chapter 4 Enhancing a Worksheet

15. Edit I7 to read: **@AVG(B7..G7)**
16. Select I7 and click the *Copy Cells* icon.
17. Point to the range I8..I20.
18. Use the *Cut* icon to remove the contents of cells I10..I11 and I18.

Since this is no longer a quarterly budget, we need to edit the labels in cells B1 and B3 so they reflect this fact.

19. Edit B1 to read "Cash Flow Budget" by erasing "Quarterly."
20. Edit B3 to read "1993" by erasing "- First Quarter."

The visible portion of your worksheet should match the area shown in Figure 4-22.

Figure 4-22. The worksheet after several modifications.

	B	C	D	E	F	G	H	I
2	Going Native							
3	1993							
4								
5	Jan	Feb	Mar	Apr	May	Jun	Total	Average
6								
7	2000	2355	2735.86	3143.23	3577.77	4040.17	2000	2975.34
8	1445	1476.31	1508.3	1540.97	1574.36	1608.47	9153.41	1525.57
9	3445	3831.31	4244.15	4684.2	5152.13	5648.64	11153.4	4500.91
10								
11								
12	100	100.5	101.003	101.508	102.015	102.525	607.55	101.258
13	90	90.45	90.9023	91.3568	91.8135	92.2726	546.795	91.1325
14	725	728.625	732.268	735.929	739.609	743.307	4404.74	734.123
15	100	100.5	101.003	101.508	102.015	102.525	607.55	101.258
16	75	75.375	75.7519	76.1306	76.5113	76.8938	455.663	75.9438
17	1090	1095.45	1100.93	1106.43	1111.96	1117.52	6622.3	1103.72
18								
19	2355	2735.86	3143.23	3577.77	4040.17	4531.12	4531.12	3397.19
20	355	380.858	407.368	434.543	462.398	490.95	2531.12	421.853

Using Global Formats

1-2-3 initially uses the general format for all values entered in your worksheet. This is the default global setting. You can change this setting to alter all the values that currently use the global default and to control the format of future values as you enter them.

Let's change the global default setting to currency.

1. From the Worksheet menu choose the *Global Settings...* command.

The Worksheet Global Settings dialog box will open. Use the *Format* button to change the global format settings.

2. Click the *Format* button.

Figure 4–23.

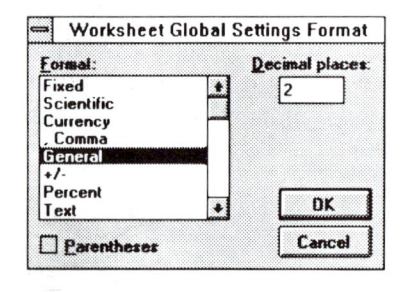

The Worksheet Global Settings Format dialog box will appear, as shown in Figure 4–23. It looks very similar to the Range Format dialog box.

3. Highlight *Currency* in the list box, change the decimals to **0** and click *OK*.
4. Then select the *OK* button in the Global Settings dialog box.

All the values on your worksheet will appear as currency without decimal points. This includes the values displayed in B22 and B23. These are the only noncurrency values in the worksheet. So we'll use the % SmartIcon to format them.

5. Choose the range B22..B23 and click the % icon.

Your worksheet will display all the values in the proper format. Any values you enter from here on out will be in the new default format of currency without decimal points.

Freezing Columns and Rows

With the addition of the three new columns, the entire worksheet is no longer visible on the screen. This is a problem when titles that give meaning to your data are not on the screen. **Freezing** a title locks important labels on the screen to prevent this from happening. It is as if the rows and/or columns you have identified become "frozen" to the worksheet frame.

Let's use this technique to freeze the labels that identify the data in your worksheet.

1. Select A1.

The labels in column A identify the data contained in the rows that extend beyond the right edge of your viewing area. To freeze this column on your worksheet, you simply place the cell pointer in the first column to the right of the column you wish to freeze. Then issue the *Titles...* command from the Worksheet menu.

2. Move to B1.
3. Choose the *Titles...* command from the Worksheet menu.

Figure 4-24.

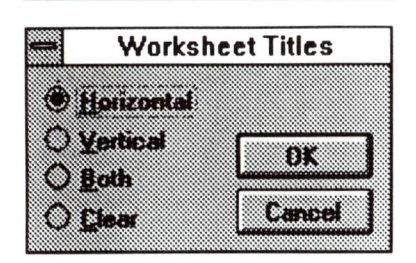

The Worksheet Titles dialog box will appear, as shown in Figure 4-24. By selecting the appropriate radio button you can freeze the titles *Horizontal* (the rows above), *Vertical* (the columns to the left), or *Both* relative to the current position of the cell pointer. The *Clear* radio button will allow you to unfreeze any titles currently frozen.

4. Pick the *Vertical* radio button and *OK*.

Although your titles in Column A are now frozen, it is not immediately apparent from viewing the worksheet. Let's scroll to the right and see what happens.

5. Click the right scroll arrow three times.

As you move to the right, data will scroll off the left side of the worksheet. The frozen titles, however, will remain locked in place. It is now quite easy to identify all the values in your worksheet.

6. Try selecting cell A1 by clicking on the worksheet letter (the A in the upper left corner of the worksheet window frame).

Because A1 is part of the frozen column, you will no longer be able to select it. The cell pointer will move to B1 instead, the closest it can get without entering the frozen column. To place the cell pointer in the frozen column, you will either need to "unlock" the column with the *Clear...* command or use the *Go To...* command.

7. Choose the *Go To...* command from the Range menu.

Figure 4-25.

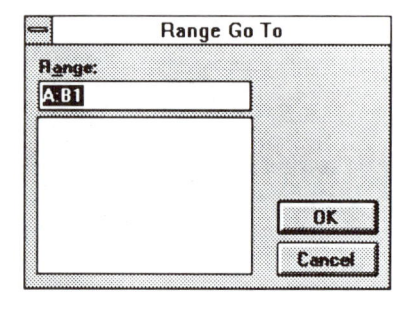

The Range Go To dialog box will open, as shown in Figure 4-25. It contains a *Range* text box that allows you to enter the address you want to move to. The empty list box is for named ranges, a topic you will explore in Lab 4-4. Because the *Range* text box is highlighted as the default, you can simply type the new address.

8. Type **A1** and select *OK*.

A temporary duplicate of the frozen column will appear, as depicted in Figure 4-26. You can edit or add data to this column as you would normally. Once this temporary column scrolls off the screen, only the frozen column will remain.

Figure 4-26. A second column A appears in the worksheet, indicating the column has been title-locked.

	A	A	B	C	D	E
1			Cash Flow Budget			
2			Going Native			
3			1993			
4						
5			Jan	Feb	Mar	Apr
6	CASH RECEIPTS	CASH RECEIPTS				
7	Opening Cash Balance	Opening Cash Balance	$2,000	$2,355	$2,736	$3,143
8	Professional Fees	Professional Fees	$1,445	$1,476	$1,508	$1,541
9	Total Cash Available	Total Cash Available	$3,445	$3,831	$4,244	$4,684
10						
11	CASH DISBURSEMENTS	CASH DISBURSEMENTS				
12	Advertising	Advertising	$100	$101	$101	$102
13	Office Supplies	Office Supplies	$90	$90	$91	$91
14	Rent	Rent	$725	$729	$732	$736
15	Phone	Phone	$100	$101	$101	$102
16	Utilities	Utilities	$75	$75	$76	$76
17	Total Cash Disbursements	Total Cash Disbursements	$1,090	$1,095	$1,101	$1,106
18						
19	Closing Cash Balance	Closing Cash Balance	$2,355	$2,736	$3,143	$3,578
20	Net Monthly Cash Flow	Net Monthly Cash Flow	$355	$381	$407	$435

9. Click to the right of the scroll box on the horizontal scroll bar.

The temporary duplicate column will scroll off the screen.

10. Click the worksheet letter to move quickly to the upper right corner of your worksheet.

The cell pointer will be located in B1 and only the frozen column remains (the temporary column is no longer there). To unfreeze this column simply choose the *Titles...* command and select the *Clear* radio button.

11. Pick *Titles...* from the Worksheet menu.
12. Select the *Clear* radio button from the Worksheet Titles dialog box.
13. Click *OK*.

Your titles will be unlocked. To test this, use the cell pointer to move to A1.

14. Move to A1.

You can now navigate within column A in a normal manner.

Protecting Cells

You may develop a worksheet that other co-workers or colleagues will use. Perhaps their use of the worksheet would only involve certain portions that are pertinent to their needs. As the manager or creator of that worksheet, you want to prevent important data from being accidentally altered.

To accomplish this you can protect your worksheet and only allow changes to unprotected areas. **Protected** ranges can't be removed or changed, while **unprotected** ranges can be edited, cleared, or replaced.

> **NOTE**
>
> Protected ranges can easily be unprotected by someone with a knowledge of 1-2-3 commands. An even more effective way to protect your worksheet is to use a password. A **password** is a code only authorized individuals can use to have access to certain files or commands. See your reference manual for further information on using a password to protect a worksheet.

To protect cells on your worksheet you must first globally protect everything. You then use the *Unprotect...* command from the Range menu to select the cells that you want to leave available for alteration. All other cells will remain protected.

1. Open the Worksheet Global Settings dialog box by using the *Global Settings...* command from the Worksheet menu.
2. Place a check in the *Protection* check box and click *OK*.

All the cells on your worksheet will be protected. Let's pick a cell and test this to see if it actually works.

3. Move to D13.

Notice that the format line will display the letters "PR" along with the (W8). You may recall that this line shows what has been altered from the default settings. PR means that this cell is protected.

4. Click the *Cut* icon.

Normally this would cause the contents of the cell to disappear. This time, however, the Edit menu drops down with the edit commands dimmed to indicate they are currently unavailable.

5. To go back to your worksheet, just click anywhere outside the menu box.

You can see that the protection does work. Let's unprotect some cells and see how we can provide access to only limited parts of your worksheet.

6. Highlight the range B12..B16.

Figure 4-27.

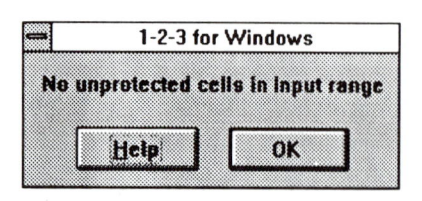

A 1-2-3 for Windows dialog box will open with a warning, as shown in Figure 4-27. This warning means you have selected a range of cells that are protected. You must select the *Unprotect...* command before selecting the range.

7. Click *OK* to close the warning dialog box.
8. From the Range menu, select *Unprotect...*.

Chapter 4   Enhancing a Worksheet

Figure 4-28.

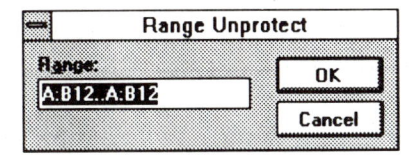

[Range Unprotect dialog box: Range: A:B12..A:B12, OK, Cancel]

This will cause the Range Unprotect dialog box to appear, as shown in Figure 4-28. You can either type the range into the text box or use the POINT mode to select the range. Let's use the POINT mode.

9. Select B12 and hold down the left mouse button.

The dialog box will vanish.

10. Drag the pointer to B16 and release the mouse button.

This will cause the dialog box to reappear with the selected range displayed in the text box.

11. Click the *OK* button.

The range is now unprotected. The format line will display the letter "U" to designate it as an unprotected cell. The color of the cell contents will change to indicate the new status. You can now alter the contents of these cells.

12. While the cell pointer is in B12, click the *Cut* icon.

The cell contents will disappear.
It is quite easy to re-protect an unprotected range. Simply select the range and issue the *Protect* command.

13. Select the *Undo* icon to recover the contents of B12.
14. Highlight the range B12..B16.
15. Choose the *Protect* command from the Range menu.

The color of the cell contents will change back to the same color as the other protected cells. Let's turn off the global cell protection and print this worksheet.

16. Use the *Global Settings...* command to turn off the *Protection* check box.
17. Select the print range A1..I23.
18. Use the *Page Setup...* command to open the Page Setup dialog box.
19. Activate the *Automatically fit to page* radio button.

When this feature is selected, 1-2-3 will reduce a worksheet that is wider than one page so it will fit on a single page. It is done by selecting a smaller font. It may not be practical in all situations. Since your worksheet is just slightly wider than what can fit on a single page, it will work very nicely in this case.

Have 1-2-3 print the grid lines and worksheet frame this time.

20. Turn on the *Show worksheet frame* and the *Show grid lines* check boxes.
21. Change the header to **Lab 4-3** and choose *OK*.
22. Save your worksheet.
23. Click the *Preview* icon.

The preview page will appear showing your worksheet with the features you selected in the Page Setup dialog box. Although it is difficult to read the values, the general appearance should resemble Figure 4–29.

Figure 4–29. The preview page shows how the selected range will appear when printed.

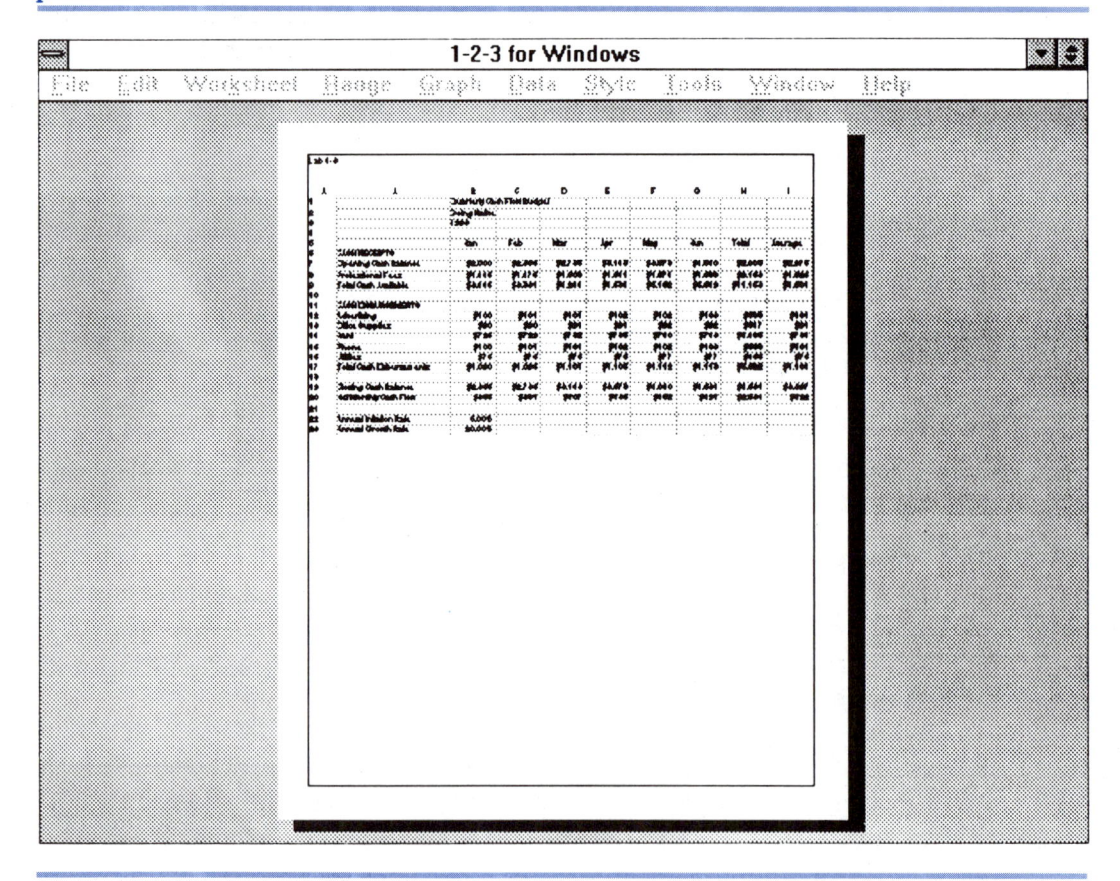

Chapter 4   Enhancing a Worksheet

24. After returning to your worksheet, use the *Print* icon to send it to the printer.
25. You may exit 1-2-3 for Windows.

LAB 4-4   NAMING CELL RANGES

Sometimes it is difficult to remember what you stored in a particular cell range, especially if the range is not visible. 1-2-3 solves this problem by letting you give cell ranges descriptive names. For example, instead of referring to a range as B6..D6, you might assign it the name "sales." The name "sales" instantly tells you what's in the cell coordinates B6..D6.

You can use range names in formulas to make them more meaningful. For instance, the formula "sales-expenses" is immediately comprehensible, while the formula "A1-A2" is not.

A range name is also easier to remember than cell addresses. By using names that indicate a place on your worksheet, you can quickly move to them. For example, if you named one area INCOME and another EXPENSES, you could move rapidly between them without remembering their exact cell addresses.

Let's retrieve the BUDGET2 worksheet from your data disk and explore the steps necessary to name a range.

1. Start Windows and launch 1-2-3 for Windows.
2. Retrieve and maximize A:\BUDGET2.WK3 from your data disk.

Creating a Range Name

You must use certain rules or conventions when naming a range. The name you choose can be up to 15 characters long. 1-2-3 does not distinguish between uppercase and lowercase letters in range names. Never start a range name with ! (exclamation mark), and never include a space, comma, semicolon, period, or any of the following characters in a range name: + * − / & > < @ # { ?

Avoid creating a range name that looks like a cell address, such as A10 or D167, or names that begin with numbers, such as 27OCT. It is also improper to use @function names or command key words as range names.

To create a named range, you must first select the range you want to name. Choosing *Range Name Create...* will open a dialog box that allows you to enter the name you want for the selected range. After the range is named, you can refer to it by using the name instead of the range address.

Figure 4-30.

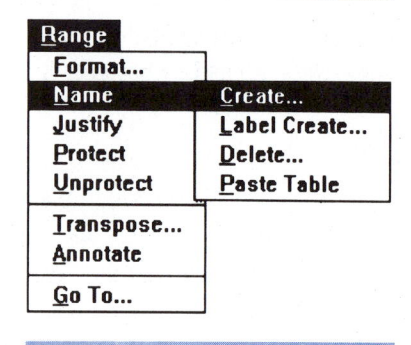

Figure 4-31.

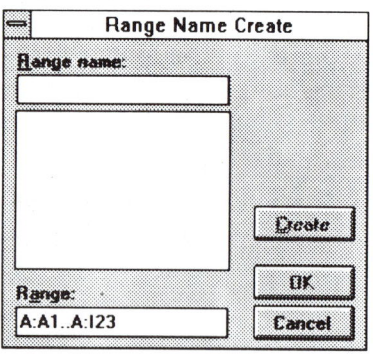

Let's create several named ranges that will allow you to take advantage of this feature.

1. Highlight the range A1..I23.
2. From the Range menu select the *Name* command.

Another menu will appear to the right of the *Name* command, as shown in Figure 4-30. The triangle (▲) appearing after a command indicates a cascading menu. A **cascading menu** is a submenu that pops out when you select a command.

3. Select *Create*....

The Range Name Create dialog box will open, as depicted in Figure 4-31. This dialog box contains the standard *Range* text box in addition to the *Range name* text box. The large empty box is a list box that will display the names of ranges after you create them. The *Create* button allows you to create a named range and remain in the dialog box to create another. You can exit the dialog box with the *Cancel* or *OK* buttons.

4. Type the name **print** and click the *Create* button.

This will create a named range called "print." The association between the name PRINT and the range A1..I23 is called a **range name definition**.

5. Select the *Range* text box and change the contents to: **B9**
6. Click in the *Range name* text box, enter the name **CashAvailable** and click the *Create* button.

This will add the name CASHAVAILABLE to the list. It's associated with the cell B9.

Let's create one more range name using the same technique.

7. Create a named range for B17 with the name: **Disbursements**. Click the *OK* button.

Each name will be added to the list, and an association between the name and the range address is established.

Using a Range Name

To use a range name, you simply use the name as you would a range address. Let's try this by examining a range that is easily changed by accident, the print range.

1. Select the range B7..G9.
2. Click the *Preview* icon.

You will only see the selected range on the preview screen. You have reset the print range. The next time you try to print your entire worksheet, you will have to select the proper print range. If you don't remember the address for the range, you will have to return to the worksheet and check it. Naming the range eliminates this wasted step.

3. Return to the worksheet and choose the *Preview...* command from the File menu.
4. Select the *Range* text box, edit it to read **print** and click the *OK* button.

This time the preview screen will display your entire worksheet.
To see how range names simplify formulas, let's replace the cell addresses in January's Closing Cash Balance formula with two of the range names we just created.

5. Select B19.
6. Type **+CashAvailable−Disbursements** and press Enter.

Notice that the contents box now displays the more descriptive range names. This is a very convenient way to create formulas. You don't have to remember cell addresses from various parts of a worksheet, just range names. By associating important values with names, you can easily reference them in calculations.

Editing a Range Name

Since a range name is simply an association between a name and an address, it can be changed easily. Issue the *Name Create...* command from the Range menu to open the Range Name Create dialog box. Highlight the name you want to edit. It will appear in the *Range name* text box, and the range address will be displayed in the *Range* text box. You can change either one by editing it and then clicking the *OK* button.

Let's change two of the range names that already exist on your worksheet.

1. Pick the *Name* and *Create...* commands from the Range menu.

This will cause the Range Name Create dialog box to open. The three range names you previously created will be visible in the list box.

2. Highlight the range name *CASHAVAILABLE*.

The range name will appear in the *Range name* text box, and its range address will occupy the *Range* text box. By clicking in the *Range name* text box, you can edit its contents.

Since spaces are not permissible in a range name, the underscore character (_) can be used where a space would normally appear. This will make the range name easier to read.

Let's try this technique.

3. Click in the right side of the *Range name* text box.
4. Insert an underscore (_) between the words "CASH" and "AVAILABLE."
5. Choose *OK*.

The new range name will be added to the list. The range address of B9 will now be linked with both the names CASH_AVAILABLE and CASHAVAILABLE. You will learn how to delete unneeded or redundant range names later in this lab.

For now, let's change your formula so it uses the clearer range name.

6. Select cell B19 and edit the formula to read:
   +CASH_AVAILABLE−DISBURSEMENTS

Deleting a Range Name

To delete a range name, issue the *Name* and *Delete...* commands from the Range menu. Then select the *Delete* button to remove the range name.

1. Choose the *Name* and *Delete...* commands from the Range menu.

Figure 4-32.

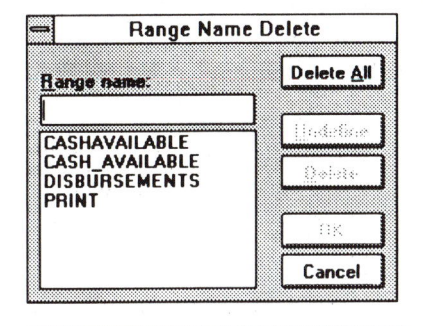

The Range Name Delete dialog box will appear, as shown in Figure 4-32. In addition to the list of range names, it contains a *Delete All*, *Delete*, and an *Undefine* button. The only button that is active when you initially open the dialog box is the *Delete All* button. The other two buttons become active after you select a range name. You will use the *Undefine* button momentarily. Let's first try the *Delete* option.

2. Highlight the range name *DISBURSEMENTS*.

The *Delete* and *Undefine* buttons will become active.

3. Click the *Delete* button.

The range name will disappear, and the range name in your formula will be converted to the actual range address. The formula will still produce an accurate result.

4. Pick *CASH_AVAILABLE* and use the *Undefine* button.

This time something quite different will happen. The range name disappears from the list, and yet the formula still contains the name. The results of the formula will show an ERRor condition.

A range name is **undefined** when it's no longer associated with a range address. This allows you to leave the name in a formula, so you can reestablish a link to a range address at a later time. To correct the error, you simply create a link to a range address with the *Name Create...* commands.

5. Choose the *Name* and *Create...* commands from the Range menu. Create the range name "CASH_AVAILABLE" with the range address B9.

The formula will remain unchanged, but the ERRor condition will disappear.

Your range names will become a permanent part of your worksheet once you save it to your disk.

6. Use the *Page Setup...* command to change the header to: **Lab 4-4**
7. Save your worksheet.
8. Select B19 and issue the *Format...* command from the Range menu.

Let's change the cell format so we can print the actual formula.

9. Choose the *Text* option and click *OK*.

Your formula should be partially visible in cell B19.

10. Set the column-width so that the entire formula is visible.
11. Print your worksheet.
12. Exit 1-2-3 for Windows without saving.

COMING ATTRACTIONS...

In the upcoming chapters, you will explore the methods for displaying your data in graphs and charts. You will also learn new techniques for manipulating information through the use of database functions. Finally, you will examine ways to automate your worksheet and utilize multiple worksheets.

KEY TERMS

Border A line that sets off data in your worksheet. It can include specific edges of cells or totally surround the data. Optional drop shadows can be added to borders for a three-dimensional effect.

Cascading menu A menu that occurs when a command on a menu invokes another menu.

Font The design or shape shared by a set of characters.

Formatting The process of changing the display characteristics of a cell or range of cells.

Freezing a title This will lock important labels on the screen to prevent them from scrolling off as you change your location on the worksheet.

Password A code only authorized individuals can use to have access to certain files or commands.

Protected ranges Ranges that can't be removed or changed.

Range name definition The association between the name of a range and its range address.

Style Changing the style allows you to add shape, size, color, and alignment to the characters in a cell.

Undefined A range name is undefined when it is no longer associated with a range address.

Unprotected ranges Ranges that can be edited, cleared, or replaced.

EXERCISES

4-1. In this exercise, you will practice formatting and hiding numeric data.

   a. Start Windows and 1-2-3 with your BUDGET2.WK3 worksheet maximized.
   b. Highlight the range B7..B20.

       c. Use the *Format...* command from the Range menu to change the range to *Scientific*.
       d. Change the same range to *,Comma* with two decimal places.
       e. Click the *Comma (0,0)* SmartIcon.

Because the ,Comma format was already in place, selecting it again removes the ,Comma format and it reverts back to the default.

       f. Pick the *Comma* icon again.

Notice the SmartIcon defaults to zero decimal places.

       g. Select the range B22..B23.
       h. Choose the *Percent* icon to remove the Percent formatting.
       i. Use the *Format...* command to change these values to Percent with zero decimal places.

The percentage will be displayed without decimal points. If you use the SmartIcon to format percent values, it will default to two decimal places.

       j. Hide the current range using the Hidden format.

Hiding the values does not affect any of the formulas that reference them. Although they don't show up on the worksheet, they can be seen in the contents box. They can also be cleared or deleted from the worksheet; they are not protected using this technique.

       k. Print the range A1..I23 using the *Automatic fit to page* feature. Change the header to **Exercise 4-1**. Do not include the grid lines or the worksheet frame.
       l. Close your worksheet without saving it.
       m. Continue with the next exercise, or quit 1-2-3 for Windows.

4–2. In this exercise, you will review the skills you learned to alter the style of the characters displayed on your worksheet.

       a. If necessary, start Windows and launch 1-2-3.
       b. Open your A:\BUDGET.WK3 worksheet.
       c. Move to C2 and change the font to Arial 24 using the *Font...* command from the Style menu.

Observe that 1-2-3 automatically adjusted the row height, but did not increase the width of the border.

    d. Select the range C6..G6 and click the *Align Left* icon.
    e. Highlight the range C3..F3 and select the *Alignment...* command from the Style menu.
    f. Check the *Align over columns* check box, and the *Even* radio button. Click the *OK* button.

The label "Going Native" will spread out in an attempt to evenly space the characters throughout the range.

    g. Clear the border around the heading by selecting the range C2..F4 and using the *Clear Special...* command from the Edit menu. The only check box you want selected is *Style*.

Unfortunately, this clears the border and all other style commands in that range.

    h. Select the range C2..F4 and add an outline border with a drop shadow, using the *Border...* option from the Style menu.
    i. Pick the *Color...* command from the Style menu, change the cell contents to red, and change the cell background to green.
    j. Click the *Paint* icon and use the paintbrush to paint B7..B23.

This will apply all the styles that were in the range C2..F4 to the range B7..B23.

    k. Clear the shading from the range C11..G11 using the *Shading...* command from the Style menu. Activate the *Clear* radio button and select *OK*.
    l. Print the range A1..I23 using the *Automatic fit to page* feature. Change the header to **Exercise 4-2**. Do not include the grid lines or the worksheet frame.
    m. Exit 1-2-3 for Windows without saving this worksheet, or close this worksheet without saving it and continue to the next exercise.

4–3. This exercise will provide an opportunity to review the material covered in Lab 4-3. We'll practice changing global formats and freezing titles.

    a. If necessary, start Windows and 1-2-3, then open and maximize the BUDGET2.WK3 worksheet.
    b. Select the *Global Settings...* command from the Worksheet menu.
    c. Click the *Format* button.

Chapter 4   *Enhancing a Worksheet*   177

    d. Choose the *,Comma* format with zero decimal places and click *OK*.
    e. Close the Worksheet Global Settings dialog box by clicking the *OK* button.
    f. Go to B6.
    g. Pick the *Titles...* option from the Worksheet menu.
    h. Select the *Both* radio button and *OK*.
    i. To confirm that the titles are frozen, use the scroll arrows. Click the right scroll arrow three times. Click the down scroll arrow three times.

In both situations, the titles above and to the left of B6 will remain frozen.

    j. Use the *Go To...* command from the Range menu to move to A1.
    k. Type the label: **Final Draft**
    l. Click the right scroll arrow three times, and the down scroll arrow seven times to remove the temporary columns and rows.
    m. Use the shortcut method of clicking the worksheet letter (the A in the upper right corner of the worksheet frame) to move the home position.
    n. Clear the frozen titles from your worksheet by selecting the *Clear* radio button in the Worksheet Titles dialog box.
    o. Move to A1 and use the *Cut* icon to remove it.
    p. Print your worksheet using the *Automatic fit to page* option with the header: **Exercise 4-3**. Don't include the worksheet frame or grid lines.
    q. Close this worksheet without saving it and continue with the final exercise, or quit 1-2-3 for Windows.

4-4. This exercise reviews the concepts and skills presented in Lab 4-4. We'll practice working with range names.

    a. Start Windows and 1-2-3 if necessary, and open your A:\BUDGET2.WK3 worksheet.
    b. After maximizing the worksheet, delete all the current range names using the *Name* and *Delete...* commands from the Range menu.
    c. Highlight the range B5..B20.
    d. Use the *Name* and *Create...* commands to create the range name: **Jan**
    e. Move the cell pointer to A1.
    f. Select the *Border...* command from the Style menu.
    g. Pick the check boxes *Outline* and *Drop Shadow*.
    h. Click in the *Range* text box, type **jan**, and then select *OK*.

i. Create the following range names for Jan values: **open_cash_bal** (range B7) and **close_cash_bal** (range B19).
  j. In B20 enter the formula: **+open_cash_bal−close_cash_bal**
  k. Print the range A1..I23 using the *Automatic fit to page* feature. Change the header to **Exercise 4-4**. Do not include the grid lines or the worksheet frame.
  l. Exit 1-2-3 without saving the worksheet.

REVIEW QUESTIONS

True or False Questions

1. T F It is not possible to format numeric values using the default Smart-Icons.

2. T F Data that are hidden can't be edited or removed from a worksheet.

3. T F Fonts only affect labels, not values.

4. T F It is possible to center align values in 1-2-3.

5. T F You can choose different line styles when surrounding a range with a border.

6. T F Only the color will be painted to the new range when using the *Paint* icon.

7. T F It isn't possible to remove shading without removing all the current styles used in a range.

8. T F Once a cell has been formatted using the *Format...* command, global formats will no longer affect it.

9. T F Protected cells will not be displayed on the worksheet.

10. T F It is possible to have more than one range name with the same range address.

Multiple Choice Questions

1. Which of the following is only available when using the *Align over columns* option?

    a. Left
    b. Center
    c. Right
    d. Even

Chapter 4 Enhancing a Worksheet **179**

2. Which are legitimate options when adding a border to a range?

    a. Adding a drop shadow of the cells
    b. Changing the line style
    c. Only using a border on certain edges
    d. All of the above

3. Which of the following commands would be used to prevent 1-2-3 from displaying the grid lines?

    a. *Global Settings...*
    b. *Display Options...*
    c. *Format...*
    d. *User Setup...*

4. What are the possible options when freezing titles?

    a. Horizontal
    b. Vertical
    c. Both
    d. All of the above

5. Which of the following keys or commands can be used to move the cell pointer into a frozen row or column?

    a. Any of the scroll arrows
    b. The mouse pointer
    c. The *Go To...* command
    d. All of the above

6. Which of the following is a legal range name?

    a. !HERE
    b. AREA 2
    c. SUM_OF_JAN
    d. @SUM

7. Which dialog box would you want open to edit a range name?

    a. Range Name Create
    b. Range Name Edit
    c. Range Name Delete
    d. Any of the above

8. Which of the following is an acceptable use of a range name?

    a. In a *Range* text box
    b. In a formula
    c. In a *Go To...* command
    d. All of the above

9. A formula will display an ERRor condition when you do what to a range name?

    a. Undefine it
    b. Delete it
    c. Edit it
    d. Move it

10. Which of the following can be accomplished using a default SmartIcon?

    a. Attributes such as bold and italics
    b. Numeric formatting
    c. Alignment of labels
    d. All of the above

CHAPTER 5

Graphing Your Data

• *Objectives*

Upon completing this chapter, you'll be able to:
1. Transform numeric data into a graph.
2. Choose from the various graph types.
3. Place your graph inside a worksheet.
4. Enhance your graph with fonts, color, and borders.
5. Move and size a graph.
6. Print your graph.

OVERVIEW

You've heard it before—a picture is worth a thousand words. If you've ever thought of a graph as "a nice extra touch," or even "a needless waste of time and energy," think again!

If the purpose of your worksheet is to increase the reader's understanding of numerical data and to provide information about trends and conditions, then adding a graph is much more than a frill. It's an integral part of the information package. A graph can enhance clarity and add power to your message.

Until now we've been working strictly with numbers. We won't deny the importance of numbers—just try sending a bunch of graphs to the IRS and see how far you get! But in most cases, your numeric data is only a means to an end. A graph can enable you to direct your reader's focus and make your points with pizzazz.

Are you trying to convince potential investors that they should invest their life savings in your dog shampooing machine? Do you need to prove to your boss that your plan isn't harebrained after all? Try a graph!

Chapter 5 *Graphing Your Data* **181**

LAB 5-1   CREATING A GRAPH

Before we begin, it's important to understand some basic terminology common to most graphs. First, we will be using the terms *graph* and *chart* interchangeably. Technically, a chart is any sort of visual aid.

Charts can include references to numeric data, such as pie charts and line graphs, or textual information, such as organizational charts and maps. **Graphs** have a narrower definition and just refer to representations of numeric data.

Figure 5-1 illustrates a graph with its components labeled. A graph usually contains a descriptive **title**. If necessary, a **subtitle** may be added to indicate the source or time period of the data. Notes can be used to describe the data further. Other common additions include data labels, legends, and grids.

Figure 5-1. A typical graph with its key components labeled.

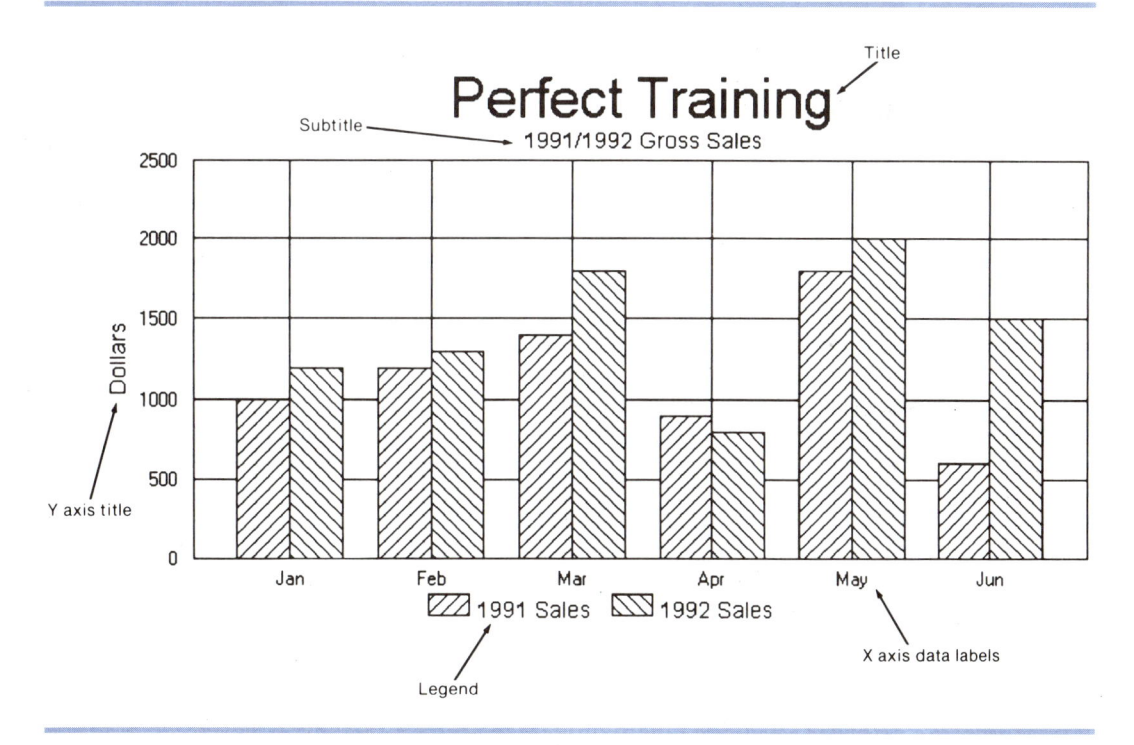

Every graph except a pie chart has an **X axis** (the horizontal plane) and at least one **Y axis** (the vertical plane).

The X axis contains **data labels** to show the reader how the data are categorized (e.g., weeks, months, products, etc). The Y axis displays the numerical increments for measuring a **data set** (i.e., a series of numbers).

Legends are keys that identify different data ranges according to their colors, patterns, or symbols. A grid is made up of horizontal and/or vertical lines corresponding to the X and/or Y axes. Grid lines can add focus to a graph, but be careful—they can also add clutter if used unwisely.

That just about covers the basics. It's time to dive in and create your first graph.

You can create a graph from an existing worksheet by selecting a data range and specifying the graph type. Table 5–1 describes the basic graph types accessible through 1-2-3's Graph window SmartIcons. Most of these graph types can be further customized by using the Chart Type menu.

Table 5–1. Graph types.

Line	A line graph emphasizes the continuity of data over time. It is especially effective for showing large sets of data, like the sales of a product over a five-year period.
Bar	A bar graph excels at comparing related data at a point in time or displaying a small amount of data over time.
Pie	A pie chart is best suited for displaying a proportional relationship between data, such as the market share of all the companies in a particular industry.
Area	A variation on the line graph, an area graph excels at showing large changes in volume over time.
HLCO	An HLCO, or High-Low-Close-Open, graph is typically used to express variations in stock or bond prices.
Mixed	A mixed graph combines both bars and lines in the same chart.

In this case, we'll start from scratch by entering data into a new worksheet and then graphing the results for maximum impact.

Going Native is about to make a presentation to John Muirwood, a very important prospective client. Rose has collected data on suggested flora and their relative costs. She has reached the conclusion that Mr. Muirwood would get the most value for his money by purchasing 15-gallon size trees. The trick is to present the data in a way that clearly demonstrates this conclusion to Mr. Muirwood.

The primary variable is the size of the plants. They come in four sizes: 1-gallon, 5-gallon, 15-gallon, and 24-inch box (in this case, a 24-inch box is approximately equal to 20 gallons).

Chapter 5   Graphing Your Data

The advantage of larger plants is an immediate landscaped appearance. But purchasing mature plants is more expensive, since the time the nursery spends cultivating them is factored into the cost. Smaller plants are cheaper, but it takes a lot longer to get a great-looking garden.

Our graph will be a straight comparison of the cost of purchasing smaller vs. larger trees. It will graphically demonstrate that the 15-gallon size is the best value.

Okay, let's go.

1. Start Windows and launch 1-2-3 for Windows.
2. Maximize the worksheet.
3. In cell A1, enter: **Presentation for John Muirwood**
4. In cell A2, enter: **Cost of Landscaping**
5. In cell A5, enter: **'1 gallon**

Don't forget that apostrophe to let 1-2-3 know that this is a label and not a value.

6. In cell B5, enter: **5**
7. Move to cell A6 and enter: **'5 gallon**
8. In cell B6, enter: **16**
9. Move to cell A7 and enter: **'15 gallon**
10. In cell B7, enter: **40**
11. Move to cell A8 and enter: **'24" box**
12. In cell B8, enter: **250**

Just so we know we're working with dollar figures when we look at the worksheet later, let's format the numbers as currency.

13. Select the range B5..B8.
14. Click on the currency $ SmartIcon.

Your worksheet should now resemble the one shown in Figure 5-2.

We know you're getting impatient and want to get your graph on the screen as soon as possible. This is it. Pay attention. You're about to see your first 1-2-3 for Windows graph.

15. Highlight the range A5..B8.
16. Choose the *New...* command from the Graph menu.

Figure 5-2. The worksheet after entering the data to be graphed.

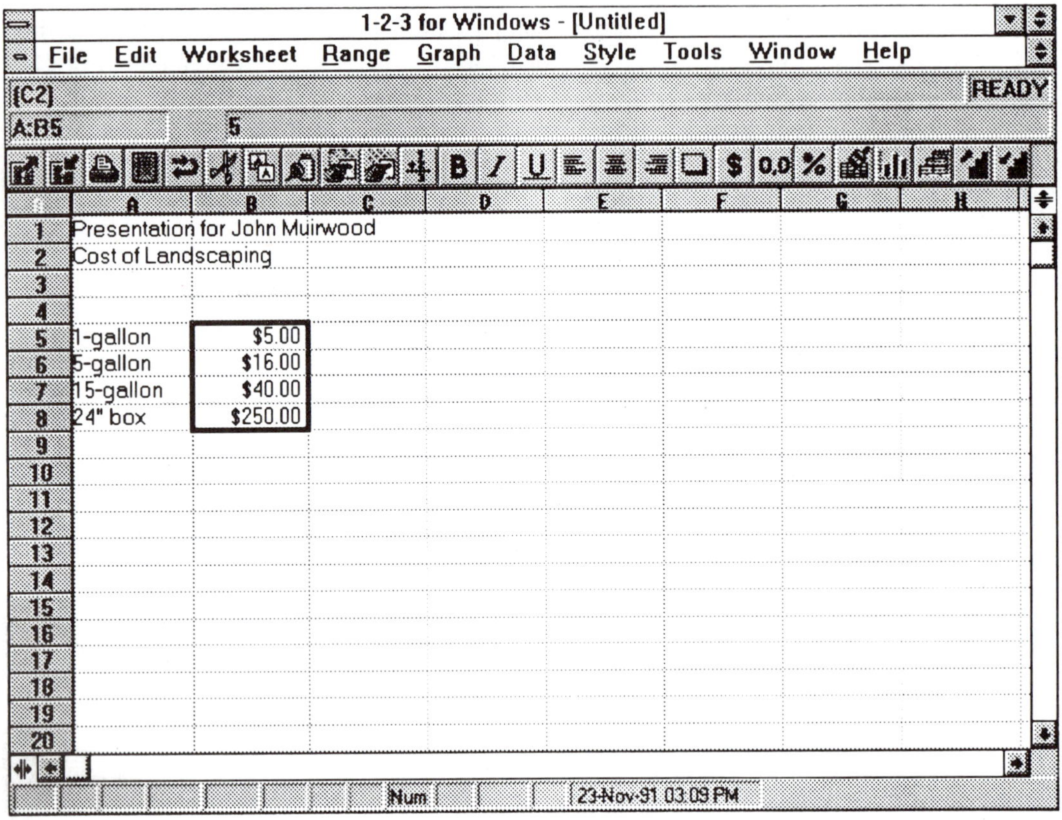

Figure 5-3.

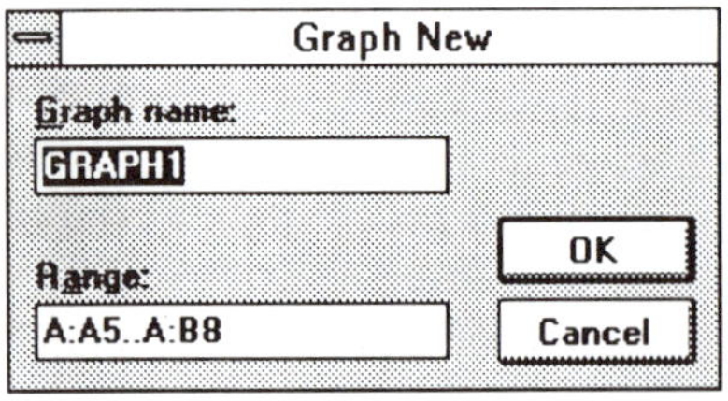

The Graph New dialog box will appear as shown in Figure 5-3, with the text in the Graph Name text box selected. GRAPH1 is the default name (which means that will be the name of your graph unless you tell 1-2-3 something else). We'll use a more descriptive name.

17. Type **tree size** and click on *OK*.

Almost instantly, a graph will appear in a window, as shown in Figure 5-4. The title bar of the graph window displays the graph's title. A graph window can be moved, resized, or reduced to an icon just like any other window.

Well, that didn't take too long, did it? You've just created your first graph, and we're very proud of you. Hang on, though. The fun is just beginning.

Figure 5-4. A line graph.

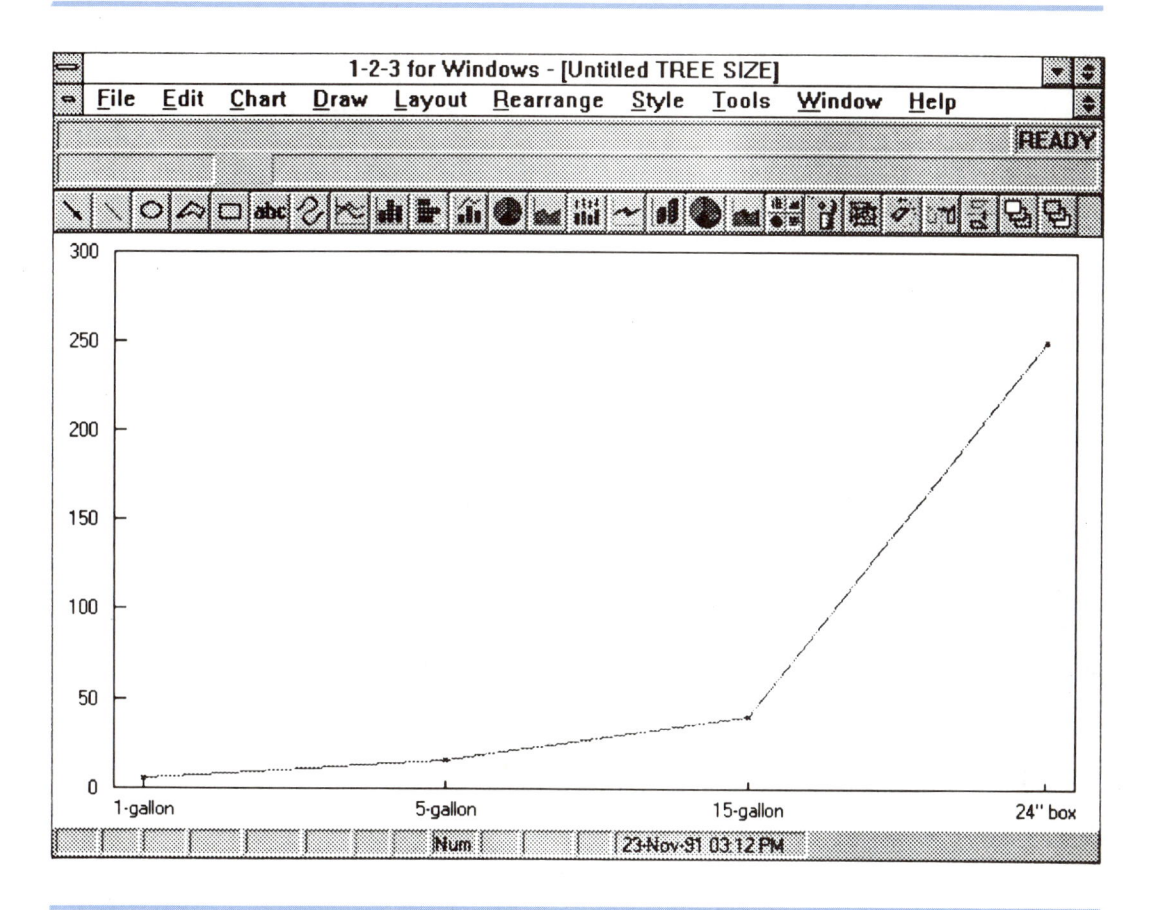

The graph you just created is a simple line graph, which is 1-2-3's default graph style. At this point, the graph doesn't contain any embellishments such as titles, notes, or legends. All we've got is some raw data and a generic graph that really doesn't convey much of a message. Let's see what we can do to spiff it up.

We'll start with the graph style. The default line graph mistakenly gives the impression that a continuous relationship exists between the size and the price of trees. From the look of this graph, it appears that the client could choose a range of tree sizes (e.g., 2 gallons, 3 gallons, etc.).

The line graph fails to emphasize the four possible choices and the price trade-offs. We want to show that each size is a separate item, that the 15-gallon size isn't *that* much more expensive than the 5-gallon size, and that it costs a lot less than the 24" box.

Selecting a Different Graph Type

We've discussed the various graph types. It's time to see just how easy it is to change a 1-2-3 graph from one type to another.

In Table 5-1, we told you that a pie chart is good for showing which items are largest or smallest. Let's see if a pie chart might be more to our liking.

1. Click on the *Pie Chart* SmartIcon, shown in Figure 5-5. (Don't forget that you can always point to a SmartIcon and click on the right mouse button to get a description of the icon's function.)

Figure 5-5. The Chart Icon Palette.

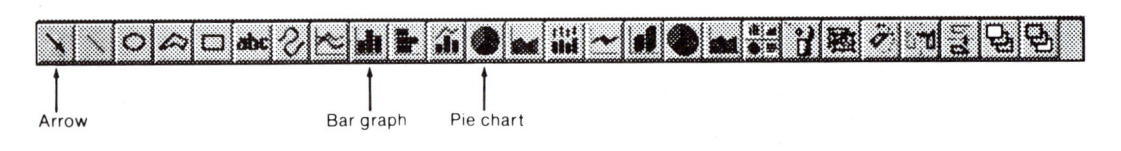

↑ Arrow   ↑ Bar graph   ↑ Pie chart

Zap! It's a pie chart, as shown in Figure 5-6. All the standard graph types are accessible with a single click on the SmartIcon palette.

This pie chart looks great, but does it really show what we want? It looks as though there's a proportional relationship between the various tree sizes. Since we're not trying to show which is the largest or smallest, maybe a pie chart isn't the way to go. (Gee, all this pie talk is making us hungry.)

Since it's so easy to try different graph styles, we'll just change this into a bar graph to see if that does the trick.

2. Click on the *Bar Graph* SmartIcon, as shown in Figure 5-5.

I think we've got it. The bar graph in Figure 5-7 clearly expresses the relationship between tree size and price. But it's still just a bunch of bars. Until we add some descriptive text, we can't use it to convince anyone of anything.

Adding a Title to a Graph

1-2-3 allows us to add up to two titles to our graphs: a main title and a subtitle.

Let's add a title to describe the purpose of the chart.

1. Choose *Headings...* from the Chart menu.

Figure 5-6. A pie chart.

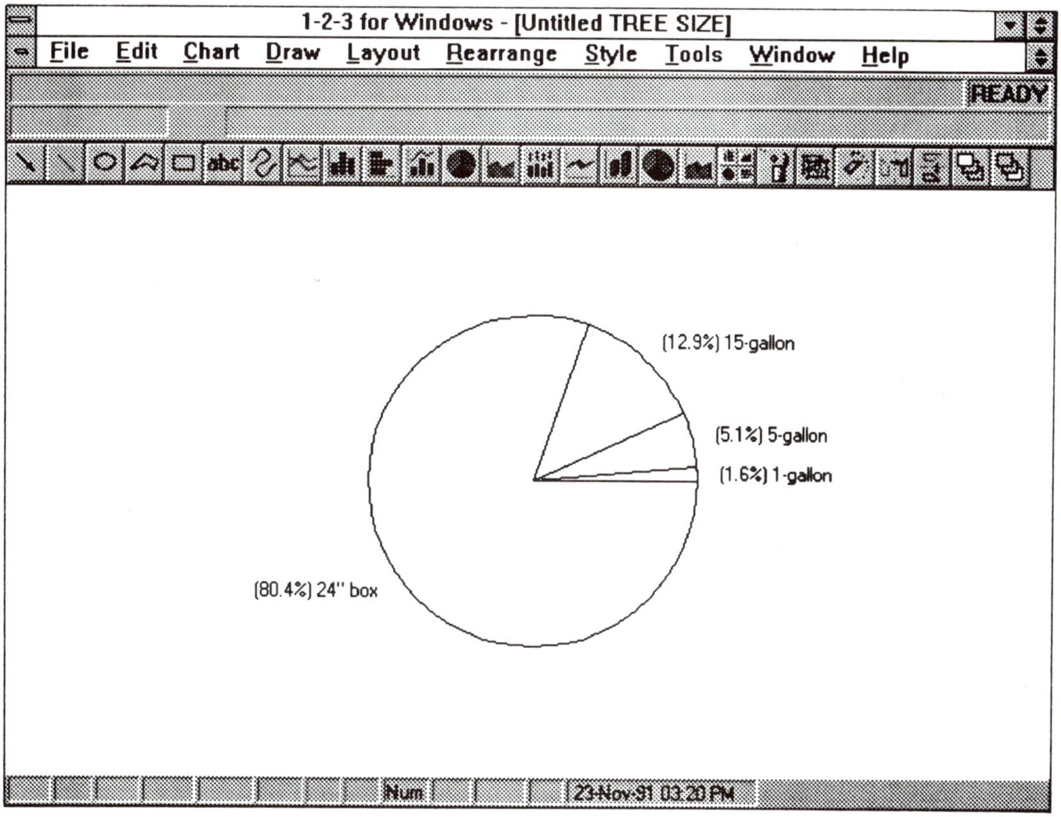
1-2-3 for Windows - [Untitled TREE SIZE]
File Edit Chart Draw Layout Rearrange Style Tools Window Help
READY
(12.9%) 15-gallon
(5.1%) 5-gallon
(1.6%) 1-gallon
(80.4%) 24" box
Num
23-Nov-91 03:20 PM

The Chart Headings dialog box will appear, as depicted in Figure 5-8, with the insertion point in the *Title* text box.

2. Type **Tree Size Cost Comparison** and press the Tab key.
3. In the Subtitle text box, type: **Based on Fall 1992 Costs**
4. We won't add any Notes right now, so just click on *OK* (or press the Enter key).

Your graph will change to display the title and subtitle, as illustrated in Figure 5-9.

Adding Labels

The graph is starting to make more sense, but labels on the X (horizontal) axis and Y (vertical) axis would make the picture even clearer.

Figure 5-7. A bar chart.

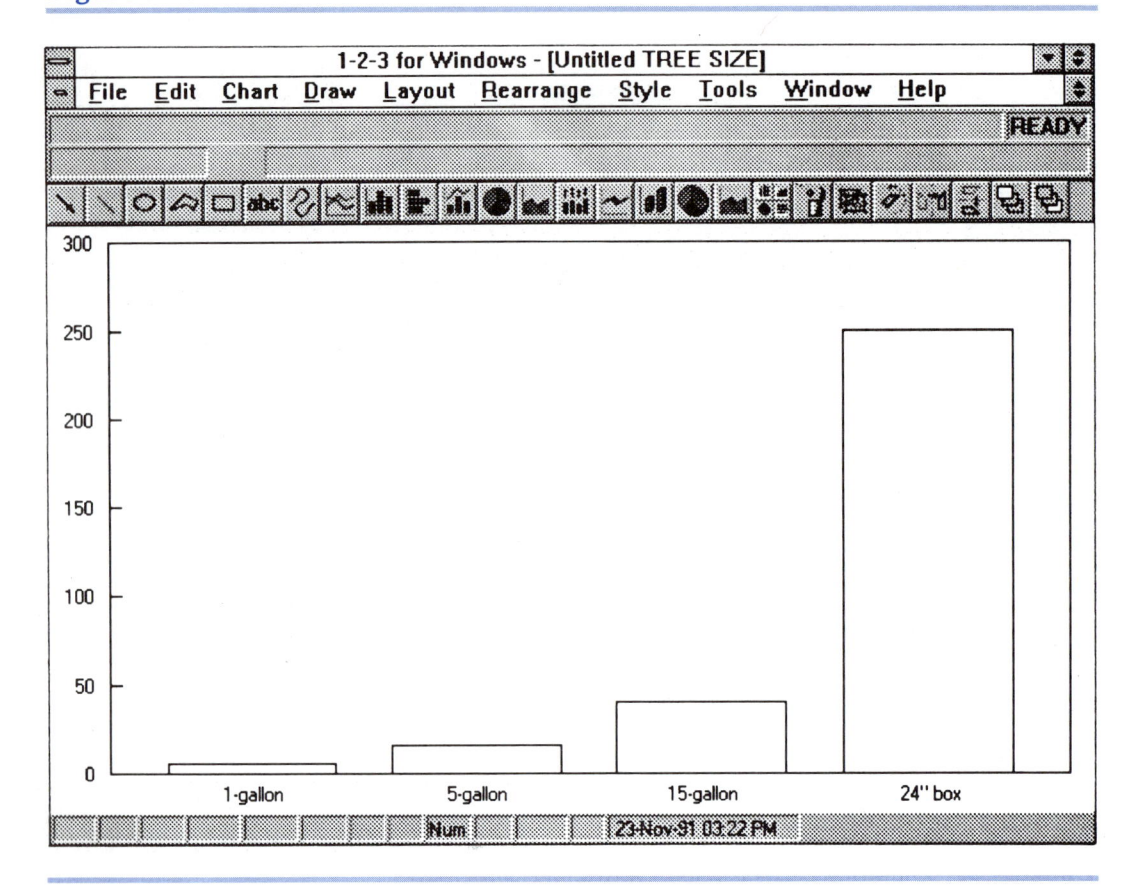

Figure 5-8. The Chart Headings dialog box enables you to title your graph.

Figure 5-9. The graph now displays a title and subtitle.

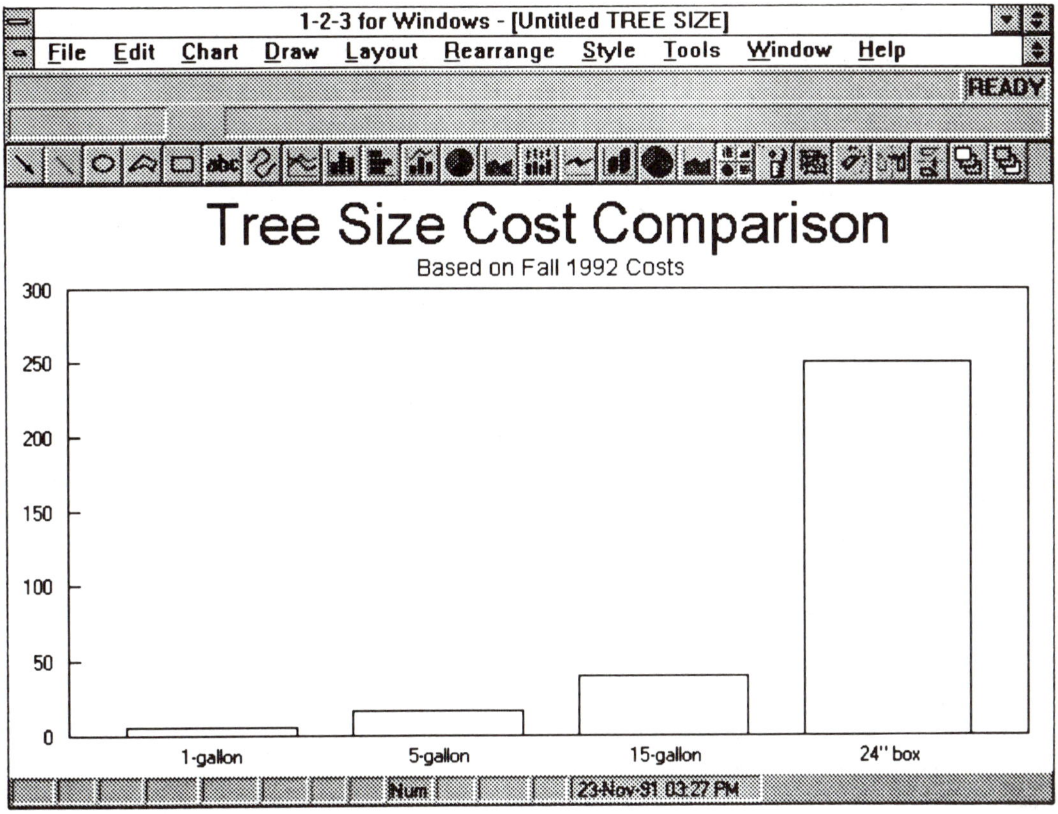
1-2-3 for Windows - [Untitled TREE SIZE]
File Edit Chart Draw Layout Rearrange Style Tools Window Help
READY
Tree Size Cost Comparison
Based on Fall 1992 Costs
300
250
200
150
100
50
0
1-gallon
5-gallon
15-gallon
24" box
Num
23-Nov-91 03:27 PM

First we'll label the X axis "Tree Sizes."

1. Select *Axis* from the Chart menu and click on *X....*

The Chart Axis X dialog box will appear, as shown in Figure 5-10. It provides options to scale, change the units of measure, and select the type of scaling for the X axis. This dialog box also contains buttons leading to other formatting features and options.

2. To create an X axis title, click on the *Options* button.

The Chart Axis X Options dialog box will appear, as portrayed in Figure 5-11. The only option we want to use at this time is the *Axis Title*. The insertion point is already there, just waiting for your input.

Figure 5–10.
The Chart Axis X dialog box provides a variety of options for formatting the X axis.

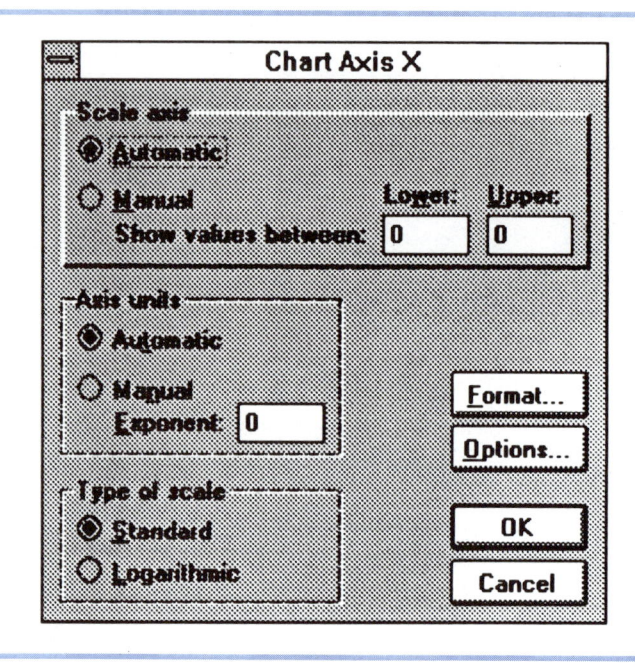

Figure 5–11.
The Chart Axis X Options dialog box makes it possible to title the X axis.

3. Type **Tree Sizes** and click on *OK*.
4. Click on *OK* once again to close the dialog box.

   Now we'll give the Y axis a label. How about "Dollars per Tree"?

5. Choose *Axis* from the Chart menu, and this time click on *Y*....

Chapter 5   Graphing Your Data   **191**

The Chart Axis Y dialog box will materialize. It looks almost identical to the Chart Axis X dialog box. The only difference it that this dialog box formats the Y axis.

6. Click on the *Options* button.

The Chart Axis Y Options dialog box will appear. It bears a remarkable similarity to the Chart Axis X Options dialog box.

7. Type **Dollars per Tree** and click on *OK*.
8. Click *OK* to close the Chart Axis Y dialog box and return to the graph.

At this point, your graph should match the one pictured in Figure 5-12.

Figure 5-12. The graph now displays titles for both the X and Y axes.

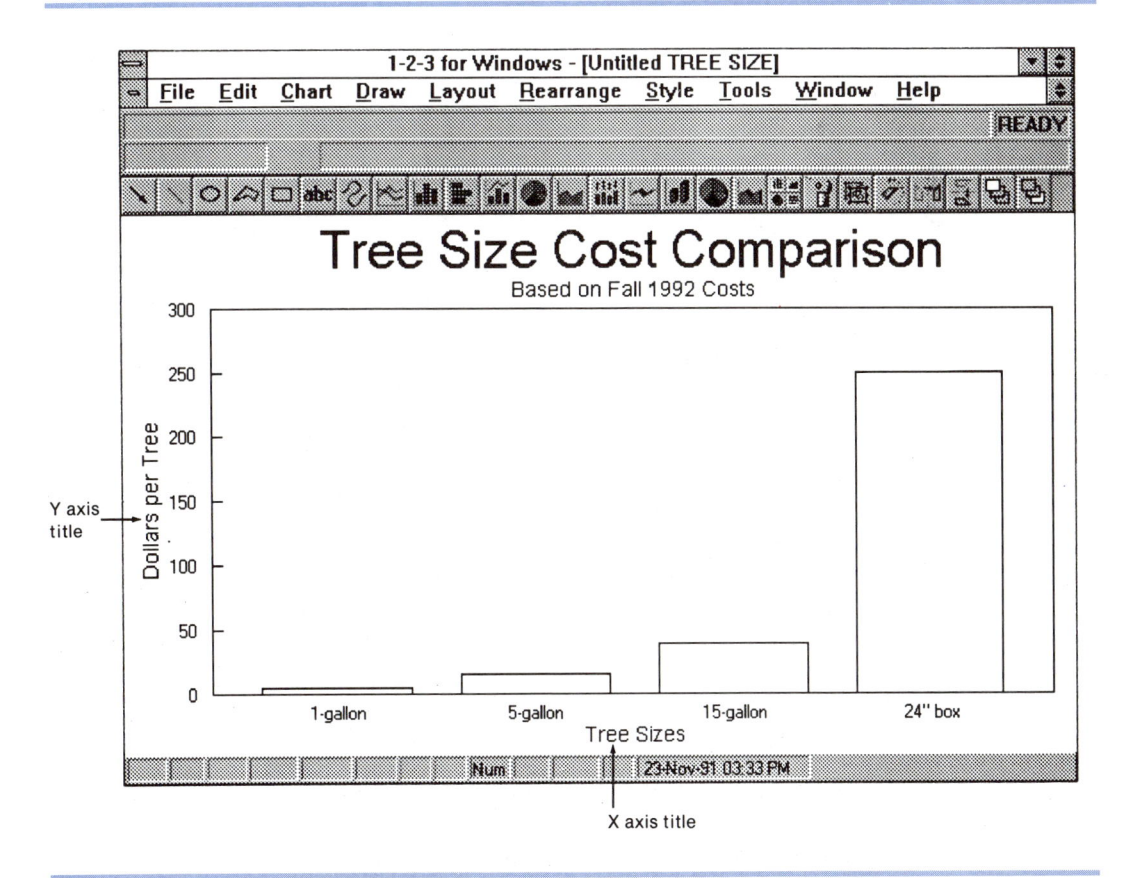

Formatting a Graph

1-2-3 gives us a variety of ways to format the graph. Many of the options are the same as for formatting a range in a worksheet.

The numbers on the Y axis are dollar amounts, so let's format them as currency, just as we've done with some of our numbers in the 1-2-3 worksheets.

1. Select the *Axis* command from the Chart menu and click on *Y*....
2. Click the *Format* button.

Figure 5–13.

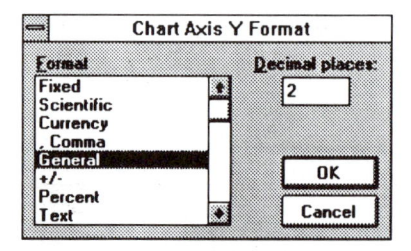

The Chart Axis Y Format dialog box will appear as shown in Figure 5–13.

3. Click on *Currency* and then press the Tab key to select the *Decimal places* text box.
4. Type 0 and then click on *OK*.
5. Click on *OK* once more to clear the dialog box.

Let's add this graph to the worksheet and print it. Before we can do that, we have to close the graph window.

6. Choose *Close* from the File menu to return to the worksheet.

Placing a Graph in a Worksheet

To place a graph in a worksheet, simply select the range of cells where you want to place the graph, and then issue the *Add to Sheet...* command from the Graph menu.

> ● **HINT**
>
> Choosing a range of cells for your graph requires more planning than you might expect. Your graph proportions can change depending on the dimensions allotted in the worksheet. For example, if you don't select a wide enough range, you could end up with a tall, skinny graph that doesn't properly convey your message. You might want to experiment with several ranges before deciding on the best choice.

1. Select the range D5..G13.
2. Click on *Add to Sheet...* from the Graph menu.

Figure 5–14.

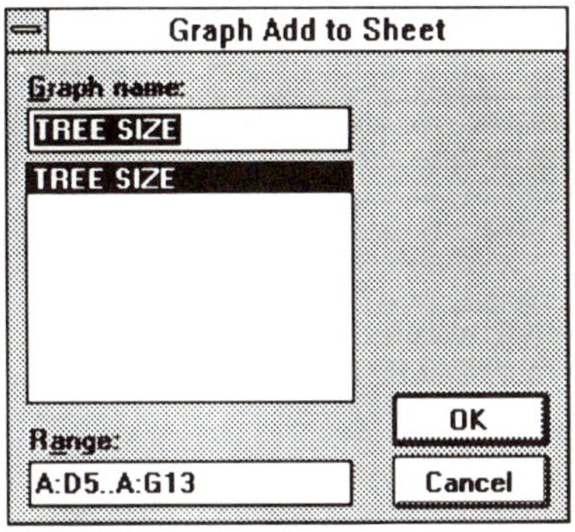
Graph Add to Sheet
Graph name:
TREE SIZE
TREE SIZE
OK
Range:
A:D5..A:G13
Cancel

The Graph Add to Sheet dialog box will appear, as portrayed in Figure 5–14.

3. There is only one graph name listed, so click on *OK*.

The graph will be placed on the worksheet alongside the data, as shown in Figure 5–15.

We certainly hope you appreciate how great it is to be able to work with graphs and data on the screen at the same time. In previous versions of Lotus 1-2-3, you had to switch back and forth between the graph and the worksheet data. Having both on the worksheet at once makes analysis and presentation of your work much easier.

Figure 5–15. A graph placed on the worksheet alongside its data.

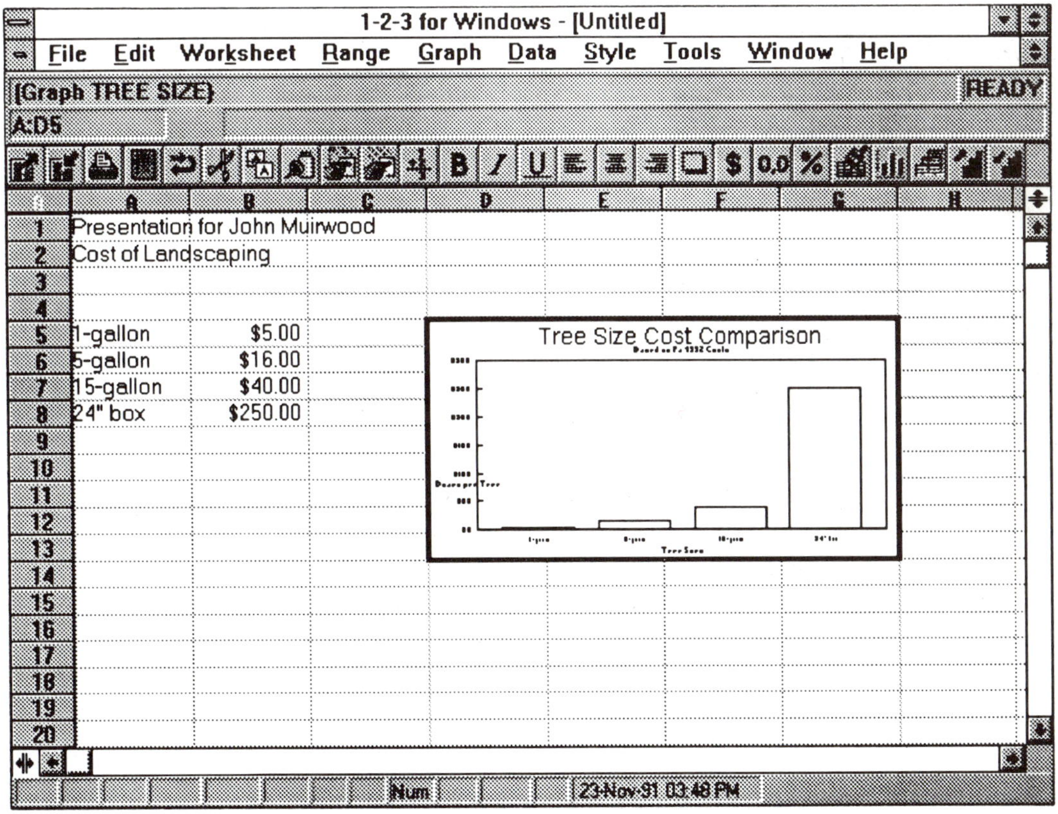
1-2-3 for Windows - [Untitled]
File Edit Worksheet Range Graph Data Style Tools Window Help
[Graph TREE SIZE]
READY
A:D5
Presentation for John Muirwood
Cost of Landscaping
1-gallon $5.00
5-gallon $16.00
15-gallon $40.00
24" box $250.00
Tree Size Cost Comparison
Num
23-Nov-91 03:48 PM

Updating a Graph

As spiffy as it is having the graph on the worksheet, you ain't seen nothin' yet. You've just placed a picture of the graph in the middle of your worksheet, but this is no ordinary picture. A 1-2-3 graph, wherever it is placed, is a live, dynamic representation of your data. Change the data and the graph will change, right before your eyes! If you don't believe us, try it out for yourself.

Rose has been shopping around to find the latest prices on the different sized trees. She found a special sale on the 15-gallon size, which makes her recommendation even stronger. Let's change the amounts and see what happens to the graph.

1. Enter **8.5** in cell B5.
2. Enter **17.5** in cell B6.
3. Enter **28** in cell B7.
4. Enter **283** in cell B8.

Did you notice the bars change as you entered the numbers? This is cool stuff. Before we print this worksheet/graph, we'd better save it.

5. Select the range to print: A1..G13.
6. Create a header with the title **Lab 5-1** and a footer with your name, followed by the label: **1-2-3 for Windows**
7. Select *Save As...* from the File menu and type: **A:\MUIRWOOD**. Click on *OK*.
8. Click on the *Print* SmartIcon.
9. Close the file, exit 1-2-3 if you're not continuing right now, and get ready for more fun with graphs.

LAB 5-2 ENHANCING A GRAPH

Now that you've had some experience with simple graphing, we can really go to town with graph enhancements.

Rose was originally planning to use eucalyptus trees for Mr. Muirwood, and she based her estimates on that assumption. But then she discovered that acacias are a bit less expensive than eucalyptus right now.

Adding Another Data Range

The costs we placed in column B were our first data range. Frequently you'll want to compare two sets of information. Using additional data ranges gives us the ability to do so.

Chapter 5 *Graphing Your Data*

Adding the prices for acacias as a second *data range* will not only make the cost comparison clear, it will also draw attention to the fact that Rose has been working hard to get the best deal for her client.

1. If necessary, start Windows and launch 1-2-3 for Windows.
2. Maximize the worksheet.
3. Open the file A:\MUIRWOOD.

First we'll title the two data ranges in the worksheet.

4. In cell B4, enter: **Eucalyptus**
5. In cell C4, enter: **Acacia**

Now we'll enter the dollar amounts for the various sized acacias.

6. Enter the following numbers in the range C5 through C8:

   9

   24

   32.5

   340

Let's format the range as currency so that it matches the eucalyptus range.

7. Select the range C5..C8 and then click on the currency $ SmartIcon.

Why didn't the graph change? We just added a bunch of new data. What gives? Well, when we created the graph we told 1-2-3 what range to use. To add a new data range to an existing graph, we need to go back to the graph window and let 1-2-3 know what we want to do. You can easily move from the graph on your worksheet to the graph window by double-clicking anywhere inside the worksheet graph area.

8. Double-click anywhere on the graph in the worksheet

The graph window will appear so that we can edit our graph.

9. Choose *Ranges...* from the Chart menu.

The Chart Ranges dialog box will appear, as shown in Figure 5–16.

10. Click in the *B Data ranges* text box and type: **C5..C8**. Click on *OK*.

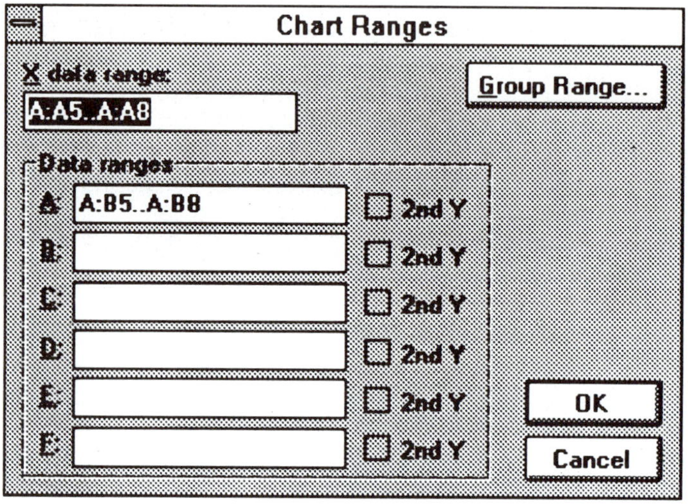

Figure 5-16.
The Chart Ranges dialog box enables you to specify different ranges to graph.

The graph will change to reflect the new data, as illustrated in Figure 5-17.

● **HINT**

If the data for the graph is contained in a contiguous range, it's easier to use the Group Range method to select the range for the graph. This can save a lot of time if you have several data ranges to enter. In this case, we could have simply entered one data range in the Group Range dialog box, selected from the Chart Ranges dialog box, and entered A5..C8 as the range.

The default orientation for Group Ranges is Columnwise, which means that the data are arranged vertically. Since our data are oriented Columnwise, we can just accept the default. If the data were oriented in Rowwise (horizontal) fashion, we would click on the Rowwise radio button to let 1-2-3 know how to interpret the data.

Creating a Legend

Instantly, we have a comparison between the two types of trees. But now we've got another problem. We got two sets of bars, and we don't

Chapter 5 Graphing Your Data

Figure 5-17. The two sets of values graphed on the spreadsheet.

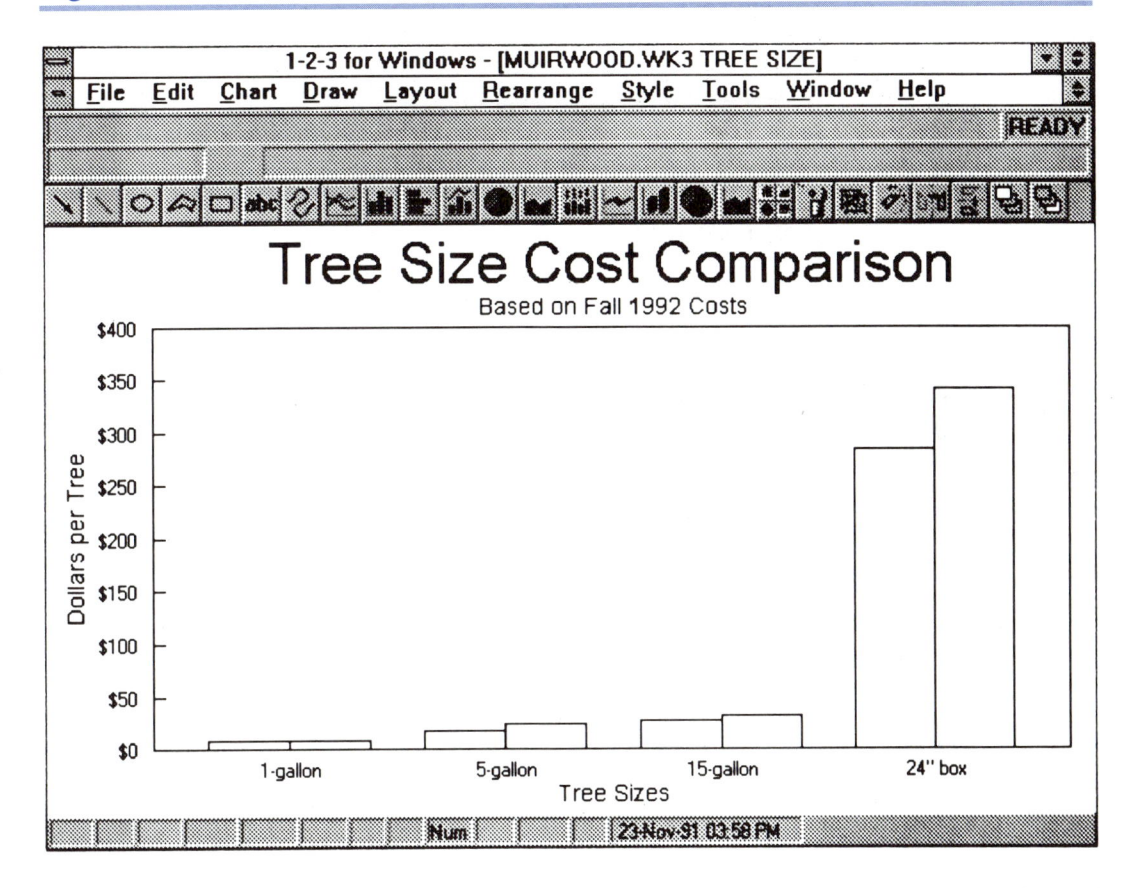

know which bar represents which tree. What we need is a legend to identify the two groups.

1. Select *Legend...* from the Chart menu.

The Chart Legend dialog box will appear, as depicted in Figure 5-18. Here's a great opportunity to try out the Group Range technique we discussed in the last Hint box. You *did* read the Hint box, didn't you? Of course you did.

We've already typed the names of the two trees in the worksheet once, so why should we have to retype them here? You know the answer: We don't.

2. Click on *Group Range....*

Figure 5-18. The Chart Legend dialog box provides text boxes to create names for your different data sets.

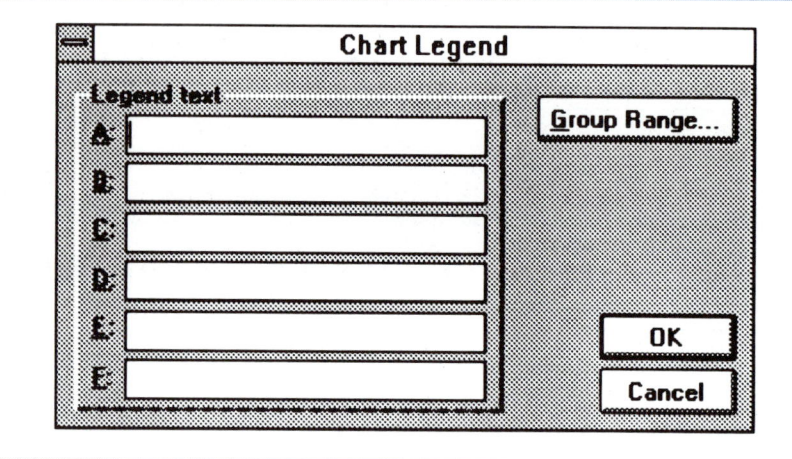

Figure 5-19.

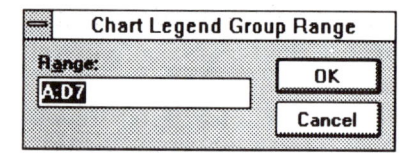

The Chart Legend Group Range dialog box will materialize as seen in Figure 5-19, with the Range text box displaying the address of the cell you pointed to the last time you were in the worksheet.

Since the names of our data sets are in cells B4 and C4, all we need to do is specify these in a range.

3. Type **B4..C4** and click on *OK*.

The text from cells B4 and C4 will appear as a legend at the bottom of the graph.

4. Click on *OK* to clear the dialog box.

Adding Text and Arrows to Your Graph

Now anyone can see that the 15-gallon size trees are clearly the best value, but suppose that Mr. Muirwood still doesn't get the point. Of course Wild Rose will point it out to him, but the graph has to function as a "leave behind" sales tool, in case Mr. Muirwood doesn't make a decision on the spot.

Rose wants to make sure that Mr. Muirwood can't miss the point. To this end, we'll draw an arrow that points toward the 15-gallon bars.

1. Click on the *Arrow* SmartIcon (refer back to Figure 5-5 if necessary).

Chapter 5 Graphing Your Data

The pointer will change to a crosshair, and the Control Panel will prompt you to "Move to the first point." The numbers below the prompt are your pointer coordinates. The first number is the horizontal position, and the second number is the vertical position.

2. Move the mouse until the numbers read approximately 2250, 2450. Click and release the mouse button to anchor the starting position for the arrow.
3. Move the mouse down and to the right, until the numbers are approximately 2600, 2860.

Notice that the line will stretch as you move the mouse.

4. Double-click to complete the arrow.

Well, that was easy, but Mr. Muirwood's pretty dense. Without some explanation, he might wonder why there's an arrow in the middle of the graph. Since we went to all this fuss to point out the 15-gallon bars, let's label the arrow so that there's no room for misunderstanding.

5. Select *Text...* from the Draw menu.

The Draw Text dialog box will appear on your screen, as depicted in Figure 5-20. This dialog box holds a *New text* text box. The text you type in this box can be placed anywhere on your chart.

Figure 5-20. The Draw Text dialog box.

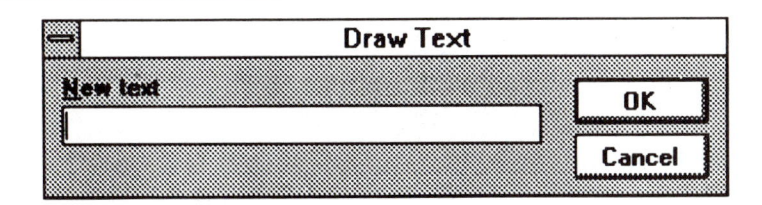

6. Type **Best Value** and click on *OK*.

A dotted outline of a box with crosshairs inside will appear.

7. Move the mouse until the box is positioned just over the end of the arrow.

The numbers in the Control Panel should read approximately 2200, 2200.

8. Click the mouse to drop the text into place.

   Notice that the text is still selected. You could perform another operation on it at this point if you wanted to (such as moving or deleting).

9. Click anywhere on the chart to complete the operation.

Adding a Three-Dimensional Effect

You can emphasize the data in a graph by adding a three-dimensional effect. This creates the appearance of depth.

Let's add another (better?) dimension to our graph by choosing the 3D Bar graph type.

1. Choose *Type...* from the Chart menu.

   The Chart Type dialog box will appear, as shown in Figure 5-21. Before we select our new chart type, let's take this opportunity to look at pictures of the various chart types you can choose from. If you click on a radio button in the Types section of the dialog box, you can see a graphic representation of the chart type. This makes it possible to preview several chart styles before making your selection.

Figure 5-21. The Chart Type dialog box allows you to choose the type and orientation of a chart.

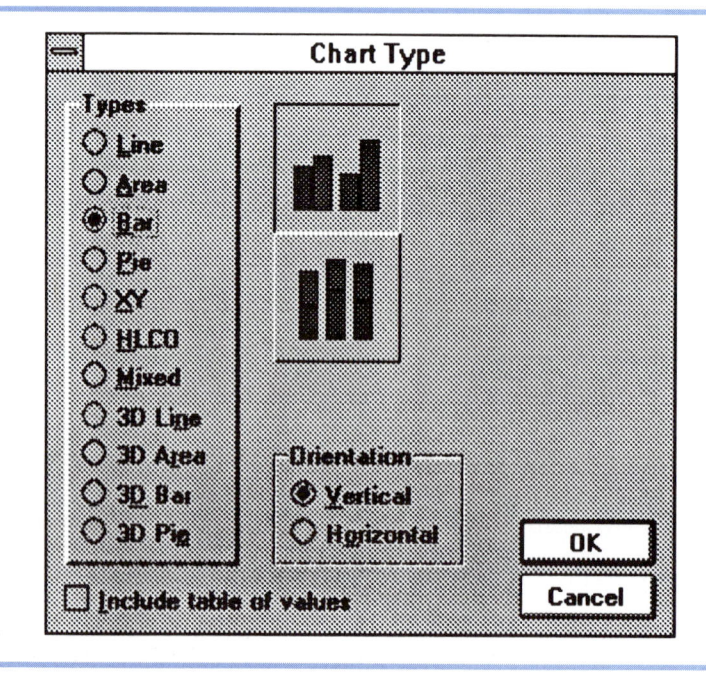

Chapter 5 Graphing Your Data

2. Click on a few of the buttons in the Types section.

Take a moment to check out some of the different styles. When you're done, move to the *3D Bar* radio button.

3. Click on the *3D Bar* radio button.
4. The standard 3D Bar is the default, so just click on *OK*.

Wow! Cool looking graph! Your graph should match the one pictured in Figure 5-22. If Muirwood doesn't get the point now, we give up.

Figure 5-22. The graph now displays data using a three-dimensional effect.

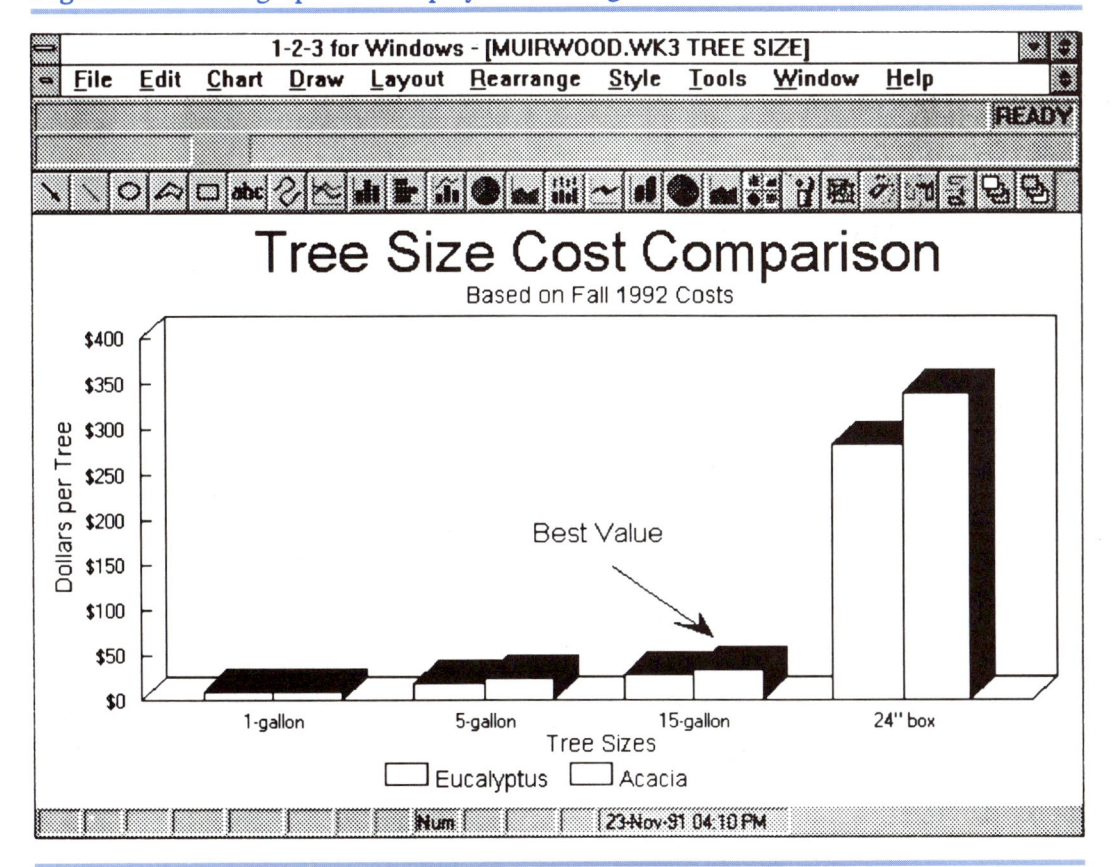

Selecting Graph Patterns

Before we end this lab, we're going to print the worksheet. This brings up a possible problem. The way the bars look now, you can easily tell the difference between the eucalyptus and acacia bars by their color. However, unless you are using a color printer, you're going to end up with a bunch of solid black bars, and the legend won't help you since it will also be printed in black.

Of course 1-2-3 wouldn't leave us in the lurch here. We can use patterns (called hatching in 1-2-3 lingo) to help us differentiate between the bars.

1. Select *Colors...* from the Chart, Options menu.

The Chart Options Colors dialog box will appear as pictured in Figure 5–23. It lets you alter the colors used to display the elements in your chart. Let's use this dialog box to make the A and B Data range colors black.

Figure 5–23. The Chart Options Colors dialog box lets you alter the colors used to display the elements in your chart.

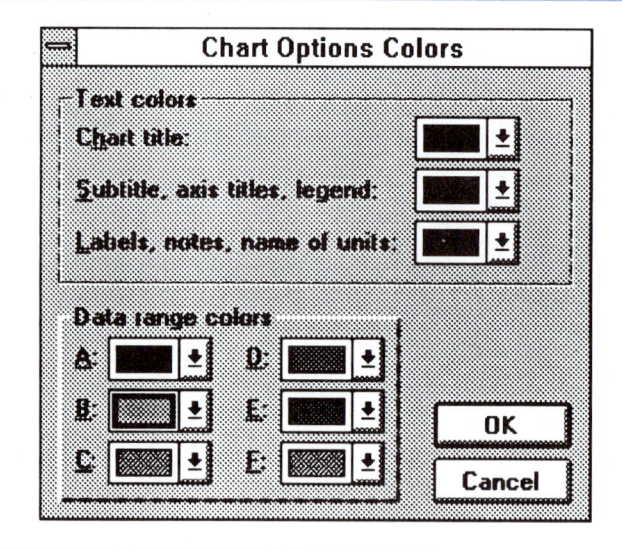

2. Click on the down arrow next to the A Data range color, and then click on the black box.
3. Click on the down arrow next to the B Data range color, and then click on the black box.
4. Click on *OK*.

We know the graph looks worse right now, but be patient. We're not through yet.

5. Choose *Hatches...* from the Chart, Options menu.

Chapter 5 Graphing Your Data

The Chart Options Hatches dialog box will appear, as pictured in Figure 5-24. This is where we'll change from solid black to patterns, and we'll distinguish between the A and B ranges by selecting different patterns.

Figure 5-24. The Chart Options Hatches dialog box.

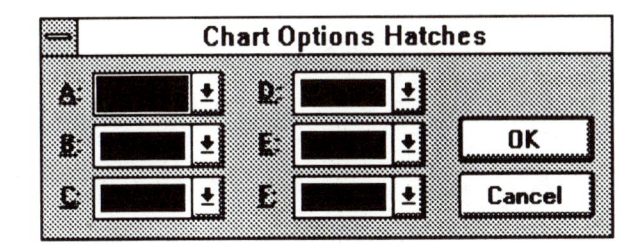

6. Click on the down arrow next to the A box and then click on the third pattern down (the one with diagonal lines slanting toward the right at the top).
7. Click on the down arrow next to the B box and then click on the fourth pattern down (the one with diagonal lines slanting toward the left at the top).
8. Click on *OK*.

Now we've got something to compare. Let's get back to the worksheet.

9. Click on *Close* from the File menu.

Sizing a Graph

Wow again! All the changes we just made are reflected in the graph. You may have noticed that when we printed the worksheet in the last lab, the graph was too small. Let's do something about that right now.

1. Select the range D5 through G13.
2. Choose *Cut* from the Edit menu.

Oh no—it's gone! Hey, guys, don't panic. We'll get the graph back, bigger and better than ever.

3. Scroll the worksheet down so rows 9 through 28 are visible, and select the range A10 through H27.
4. Select *Paste* from the Edit menu.

There you have it, as shown in Figure 5-25, a graph Wild Rose can be proud to present. Now let's print it. Yes, of course we're going to save it first. We're proud of you for remembering.

Figure 5-25. The completed chart.

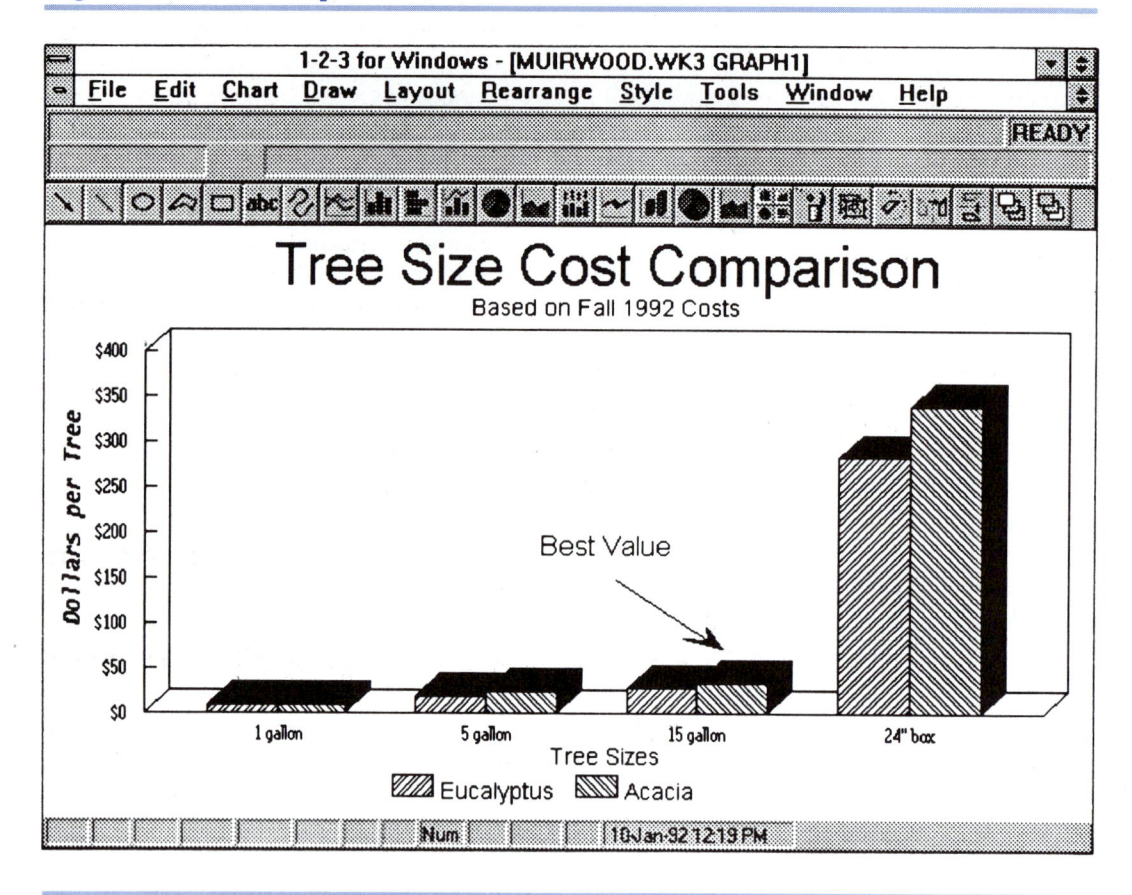

5. Select A1 through H27, change the header to **Lab 5-2**, and save the worksheet.
6. Print the worksheet.
7. Exit 1-2-3 if you'll be leaving us now.

COMING ATTRACTIONS...

In this chapter, you learned to create, enhance, and print graphs to give visual impact to your numbers.

Chapter 5 *Graphing Your Data* **205**

In the next chapter, you'll learn to take advantage of 1-2-3's powerful database capabilities to sort and select information on your worksheet.

KEY TERMS

Chart Visual display of numeric data, including pie charts, line graphs, and textual information such as organizational charts and maps.

Data labels Indicators to show the reader how data are categorized in a chart (e.g., weeks, months, products, etc.).

Data set A series of numbers.

Graph Visual representation of numeric data.

Graph title A text line at the top of a graph describing its purpose.

Graph subtitle A text line often used to indicate the source or time period of the data in a graph.

Legends Keys that identify different data ranges according to their colors, patterns, or symbols.

X axis The horizontal border line in a graph that shows how data are categorized.

Y axis The vertical border line in a graph that displays numerical increments for measuring data sets.

EXERCISES

5-1. The following exercise will give you the chance to practice material you learned in Lab 5-1.

   a. Start Windows and launch 1-2-3 for Windows if it is not already running.

We'll create a home budget and graph the numbers.

   b. In cell A1 enter: **My Budget**

We'll enter our categories in A3 through A5.

   c. In A3, enter: **Rent**
   d. In A4, enter: **Food**
   e. In A5, enter: **Other Stuff**

Now we'll put month headings in B2 through D2.

   f. In B2, enter: **Jan**
   g. In C2, enter: **Feb**
   h. In D2, enter: **Mar**

Next we'll enter some completely realistic budget numbers.

    i. In B3, enter: **65000**

It's just a modest little mansion.

    j. In B4, enter: **8800**

We think we'll be hungry!

    k. In B5, enter: **350**
    l. In C3, enter: **72000**

We're expecting a small rent increase.

    m. In C4, enter: **9000**
    n. In C5, enter: **370**
    o. In D3, enter: **72000**
    p. In D4, enter: **8750**
    q. In D5, enter: **1024**

The budget is now ready to be graphed, and we're in a hurry, so let's use the most automated method possible. Since the data are in adjacent cells, we can simply select the range to graph.

    r. Select the range B2 through D5.
    s. Click on the *Create a New Graph* SmartIcon. It's the one that looks like a bar graph. (If you have trouble finding it, use the right mouse button to scan the SmartIcons.)

Well, we have a default line chart, but it looks pretty worthless. Let's convert it to a bar graph.

    t. Click on the *Bar Graph* SmartIcon. Again, use the right mouse button if you have trouble finding it.

Something's wrong here! The problem is, 1-2-3 assumes that the data in the selected range are oriented columnwise. But these data aren't. They're rowwise, so we need to let 1-2-3 know.

    u. Choose *Ranges...* from the Chart menu and then click on the *Group Range* button.

Chapter 5   Graphing Your Data

Figure 5-26.

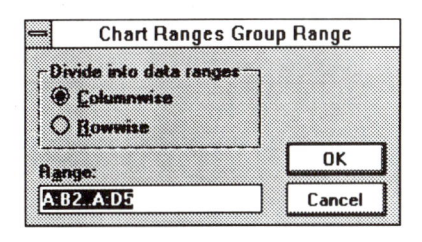

You'll see the Chart Ranges Group Range dialog box, as shown in Figure 5-26, with the *Columnwise* radio button selected

v. Click in the *Rowwise* radio button and click *OK*. Click *OK* again to close the dialog box.

That's better. Let's add a title so we'll know what this graph is all about.

w. Choose *Headings...* from the Chart menu.
x. Enter **My Budget** in the Title text box and then click on *OK*.
y. To change the colors of the bars in your graph, choose the *Colors...* command from the Chart Options menu and select the *Colors* option. When the dialog box appears, use the drop-down menu in the Data range colors area to select the color yellow for data set A. Then click *OK*.
z. Click on *Close* from the File menu.
aa. Select the range A7..F20.
ab. Choose *Add to Sheet* from the Graph menu and double-click on GRAPH1.
ac. Select the range A1..F20.
ad. Create a header with the title **Exercise 5-1** and a footer with your name, followed by the label: **1-2-3 for Windows**
ae. Save the file as **A:\EXER5-1**
af. Print the worksheet, and exit 1-2-3 if you've had enough for now.

5-2. The following exercise will give you the chance to practice material you learned in Lab 5-2.

We're going to enhance the graph you created in Exercise 5-1, so make sure you have that file available on your disk. If you haven't completed the last exercise, you'll need to do so before starting this one.

a. Start Windows and launch 1-2-3 for Windows if it is not already running.
b. Open the file A:\EXER5-1.

This graph is a reasonable representation of our three-category budget. But there is another form of bar graph that, in addition to showing us the three categories, shows us the total spent in each month. Let's move into the Graph window so we can change the graph type.

      c. Double-click anywhere in the graph that's on the worksheet.
      d. Select *Type...* from the Chart menu.
      e. Double-click on the Stacked Bar picture in the Chart Type dialog box.

There, now we can see how the total month's expenses compare to each other. Let's create a legend so we'll know what each part of the bar represents.

      f. Select *Legend...* from the Chart menu.
      g. In the A: text box, enter: **Rent**
      h. In the B: text box, enter: **Food**
      i. In the C: text box, enter: **Other Stuff**
      j. Click on *OK* to add the legend to the graph and close the dialog box.

That helps clarify the graph. Let's draw attention to the first month where we had a rent increase, February.

      k. Click on the *Ellipse* SmartIcon, the one that looks like an oval.
      l. Move the crosshairs so they are just above the left corner of the middle bar.
      m. Press and hold the left mouse button and drag the mouse down and to the right, until the crosshairs are just below the bottom right corner. Release the mouse button.

Let's include some text inside the oval we've drawn.

      n. Click on the *Text* SmartIcon, the one with *abc* in it.
      o. Type **Rent increase starts here**, and click on *OK*.
      p. Move the outline of the box so it's vertically and horizontally centered over the middle bar, and click the mouse to drop the text onto the graph.

Wait a minute. This text is too wide to fit inside the oval. But we have the solution. We'll rotate the text!

      q. Click on the *Rotate* SmartIcon, the fifth icon from the right. Use the right mouse button if you have trouble finding the correct SmartIcon.

Since the text we just entered is still selected, we can simply move the mouse to rotate it.

Chapter 5   Graphing Your Data

- **r.** Move the crosshairs so they are at the right side of the box that is outlining the text, and then move the crosshairs up until they are just under the top of the oval.
- **s.** Click the mouse to drop the text into its new position.
- **t.** Select *Close* from the Edit menu to return to the worksheet.
- **u.** Select the range A1..F20.
- **v.** Change the header to: **Exercise 5-2**
- **w.** Save the file as **A:\EXER5-2**
- **x.** Print the selected range.
- **y.** Exit 1-2-3 if you're not continuing right now.

REVIEW QUESTIONS

True or False Questions

1. T F   A chart represents only numerical data.
2. T F   The X axis of a graph displays the data labels that show how data are categorized.
3. T F   A pie chart is best suited for showing a relationship between items.
4. T F   The *New...* command in the Graph menu lets you create a graph from data in your worksheet.
5. T F   Clicking the *Bar Graph* SmartIcon changes the graph type to a double stacked bar.
6. T F   The *Add to Sheet...* command in the Graph menu places a graph in your worksheet.
7. T F   The Chart Headings dialog box lets you change the relationship between the X axis and the Y axis.
8. T F   You can add an arrow to a graph with the *Arrow* SmartIcon.
9. T F   To emphasize your data, you should use the 3-D effect on almost every graph.
10. T F   The Chart Type dialog box lets you preview various chart types.

Multiple Choice Questions

1. Which chart type is well suited for showing changes over time?
   - a. Line
   - b. Bar
   - c. Pie
   - d. All of the above

2. The Y axis of a graph
   a. Displays the numerical increments for measuring a series of numbers
   b. Shows the labels for categorizing data
   c. Is the horizontal plane of a graph
   d. a and c
   e. None of the above

3. To label the Y axis of a graph, start by issuing the command
   a. *Axis* from the Chart menu
   b. *Options* from the Graph menu
   c. *Label* from the Chart menu
   d. None of the above

4. To place a graph in a worksheet,
   a. Double-click on it
   b. Click on the *Add to Sheet...* command from the Chart menu
   c. Click on the *Add to Sheet...* command from the Edit menu
   d. None of the above

5. If you change the data in a worksheet associated with the values in a graph
   a. Nothing happens to the graph
   b. The graph changes to reflect the alterations
   c. The graph will change to reflect the alterations after you click on the *Recalculate* button
   d. None of the above

6. To add a second data range to your graph,
   a. Type the data in your worksheet
   b. Double-click on the graph
   c. Issue the *Ranges...* command from the Chart menu, update the *B Data* ranges text box, and click *OK*
   d. a and b
   e. a, b, and c

7. Which is NOT an option you can add to a graph?
   a. Arrow
   b. 3-D effect
   c. Legend
   d. Flashing bars or lines

8. The *Colors...* command in the Chart Options menu lets you adjust the
   a. Patterns in a graph
   b. Colors in a graph
   c. Size of a graph
   d. a and b

9. To resize a graph,
   a. Drag one of its borders in the desired direction
   b. Double-click on the graph and use the mouse to reshape it
   c. Cut and paste it
   d. None of the above

10. A chart is a visual representation of
    a. Numeric data
    b. Textual information
    c. Organizational charts
    d. Maps
    e. All of the above

CHAPTER 6

Database Applications

• *Objectives*

Upon completing this chapter, you'll be able to:
1. **Create and sort a 1-2-3 database.**
2. **Search a database.**
3. **Extract and delete information from a database.**

OVERVIEW

This chapter will explore 1-2-3 for Windows' database facility. You'll learn to create, edit, sort, and search a 1-2-3 database. In addition, you'll discover how to extract and delete information from a database.

DATABASE BASICS

Databases are all around us. Telephone books and encyclopedias are databases, which simply means they are made up of groups of organized data entries. A **database** is really just a collection of related information. A computerized database is much easier to manipulate than a printed database, since the data can be arranged and rearranged to suit your needs. Computerized data can be searched, sorted, extracted, and deleted. 1-2-3 even includes a large set of statistical @functions designed specifically for use with databases.

Before you create your first 1-2-3 database, it's important to understand some basic terminology common to all computer databases. Let's use the telephone book example to examine the various components of a database. This is a particularly apt example because the information in a telephone book is organized in the same fashion as a 1-2-3 database.

Each line in the directory is called a record. A **record** contains the entire set of information for each telephone customer. Within each record, there are several pieces of information that are always found in the same order, from record to record. From left to right, these items are: last name, first name, address, and phone number. Each of these items is called a **field**.

In 1-2-3, just as in the phone directory, each record occupies a single row and each field a single cell. There is one additional rule for 1-2-3 databases. Since 1-2-3 needs a way to differentiate one field from another, the first row of every 1-2-3 database must consist of field names.

LAB 6-1 CREATING, EDITING, AND SORTING A DATABASE

Going Native has been advertising in 20 different area newspapers on an experimental basis. Rose wants to determine the relative effectiveness of each paper so that she can allot her resources in the most productive manner. As part of this process, Going Native has been tallying the number of responses they are getting from each ad.

Right now, all Rose has is a bunch of unrelated data. She knows how much she's spending on each ad, and she knows how many responses she's gotten. Let's create a database to organize the information and clarify the relationships.

Entering Records in a Database

1. Start Windows and launch 1-2-3 if it is not already running.
2. In Cell A1, enter: **Advertising Log**
3. Starting in Cell A3, enter the information shown in Table 6–1.
4. Widen column A so the entire name of each newspaper fits in the column.

Since one of our goals is to be able to evaluate the cost effectiveness of each paper, we need to determine the cost of each response. To do this, we'll add a fourth field that automatically gives us that calculation.

The cost of the ad divided by the number of responses will give us the cost per response.

5. In cell D3, enter: **Cost per Response**
6. In cell D4, enter the formula **+C4/B4** and press the Enter key.
7. Copy the formula down through cell D23.
8. Format the range D4..D23 as fixed with two decimal places.

Table 6-1. Advertising log data.

	A	B	C
3	Newspaper	Responses	Cost per Ad
4	Cheney Tribune	1	35
5	Spokane Gazette	3	112
6	Newport News	6	60
7	Wenatchee Herald	4	125
8	Sandpoint Star	3	28
9	Newport Gazette	2	47
10	Pullman Enquirer	2	25
11	Cheney Gazette	1	28
12	Pullman Mirror	2	72
13	Freeman Free Press	1	15
14	Marshall Chronicle	1	26
15	Valleyford Journal	2	18
16	Clayton Star	3	38
17	Rathdrum Daily	2	22
18	Green Bluff Voice	1	28
19	Davenport Daily News	4	18
20	Spokane Sun	5	145
21	Spokane Times	7	175
22	Boise Bugle	2	78
23	Fairfield Fish Wrap	1	33

Now that we've entered all that data, let's save the worksheet. You'll really be glad we did if you make any mistakes during the next few steps.

9. Save this worksheet with the name **A:\ADCOSTS**

Sorting a Database

Rose wants to scan this list to find newspapers in particular towns. Right now, that's pretty difficult since the newspaper names aren't arranged in alphabetical order. Never fear! To 1-2-3, this is just a simple **sorting** task.

Before we can perform a sort, we need to define a range. This is where most sorting disasters begin. (We don't mean to scare you; we know *you* would never make the kind of mistakes we're talking about.)

Most 1-2-3 beginners (we don't mean you) would select just the column to be sorted; in this case, A4..A23. Sorting just that range would put the newspapers in alphabetical order, but would leave the rest of the information where it is. Each newspaper would be matched up with the wrong Responses, Cost per Ad, and Cost per Response fields. (And the someone who would do this might even forget to save the worksheet before sorting!)

1. Select the range A4..D23.

Wait a minute. Why aren't we including the first row of the database, row 3? Well, if we did, it would be sorted alphabetically with the rest of the data. Since we want the field names to remain at the top of the database, we won't include them in the sort.

2. Click on the Data menu.

The Data menu will appear as shown in Figure 6-1.

Figure 6-1. The drop-down Data menu.

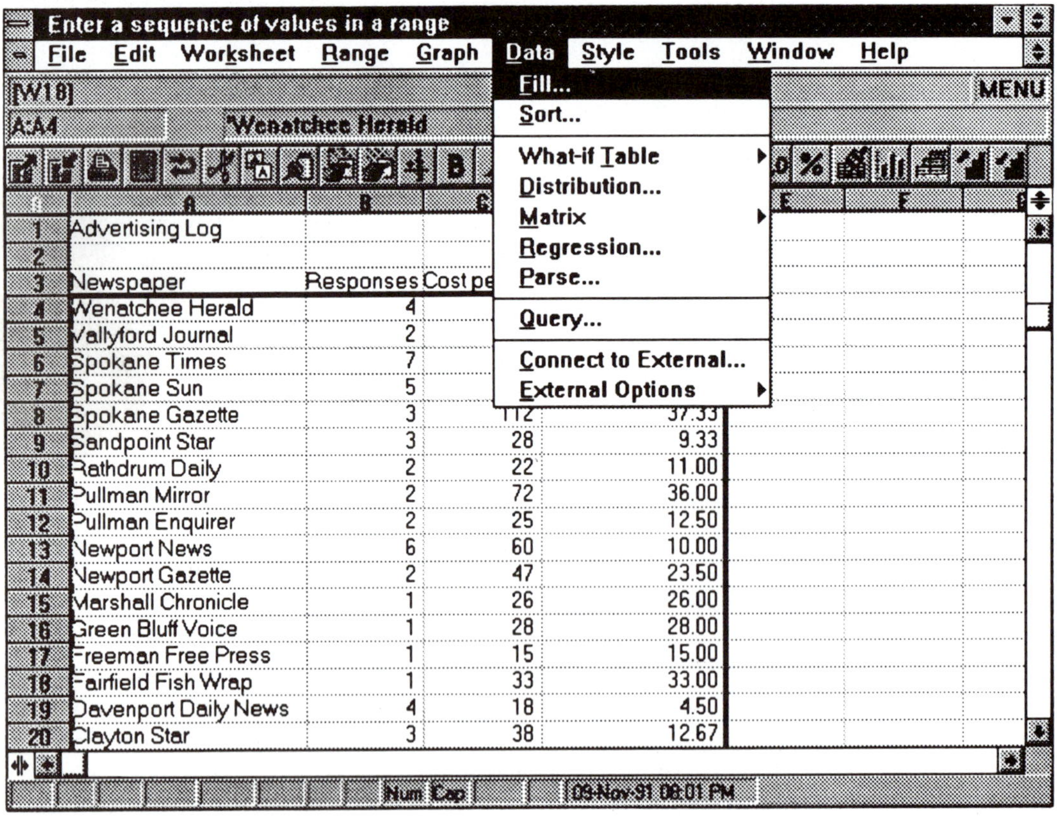

3. Select *Sort*....

The Data Sort dialog box will appear, as depicted in Figure 6-2. The range in the *Data Range* text box makes sense. But what's this stuff about Primary key and Secondary key? Don't worry. It'll make sense in a little while.

Figure 6-2. The Data Sort dialog box lets you rearrange the information in a database.

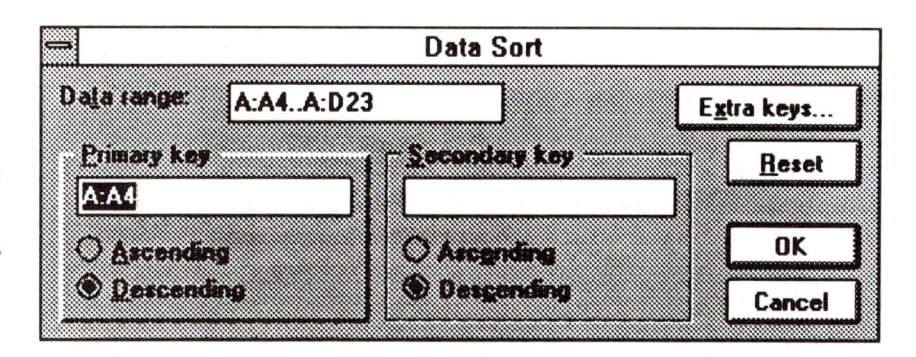

Remember our telephone directory analogy? Get ready. We're going to use it again. The **primary sort key** in the phone book is the last name field. The last names are sorted in ascending alphabetical order. See, that makes sense. So what's the secondary key, you ask?

Suppose there is more than one person with the same last name. We need a way to perform a *secondary* sort on the first name. That way, all the Smiths would be grouped together, with Al Smith first, followed by Amy Smith, and then Bill Smith.

We'll be working with secondary sort keys soon. For now, let's get this information sorted by city using just the primary sort key. The primary sort key already appears as A4. We want to use the entire column as the primary sort key, so don't we need to inform 1-2-3 of our intention? Nope.

All 1-2-3 needs to know about a sort key is what column to work with. We can tell 1-2-3 that the sort key is any cell in column A.

There's one more change to make before we do the sort. We need to tell 1-2-3 that we want the information sorted in **ascending** order instead of the default **descending** order. This will sort the newspaper names A to Z. Ascending order will be more useful in this case than descending, which would sort the names Z to A.

4. Click in the *Ascending* radio button.

All right, enough talk—let's get this information sorted.

5. Click on the *OK* button.

We love this sorting stuff. It seems like magic, doesn't it? The first portion of your worksheet should look like Figure 6–3.

Figure 6–3. The database has been sorted in ascending order.

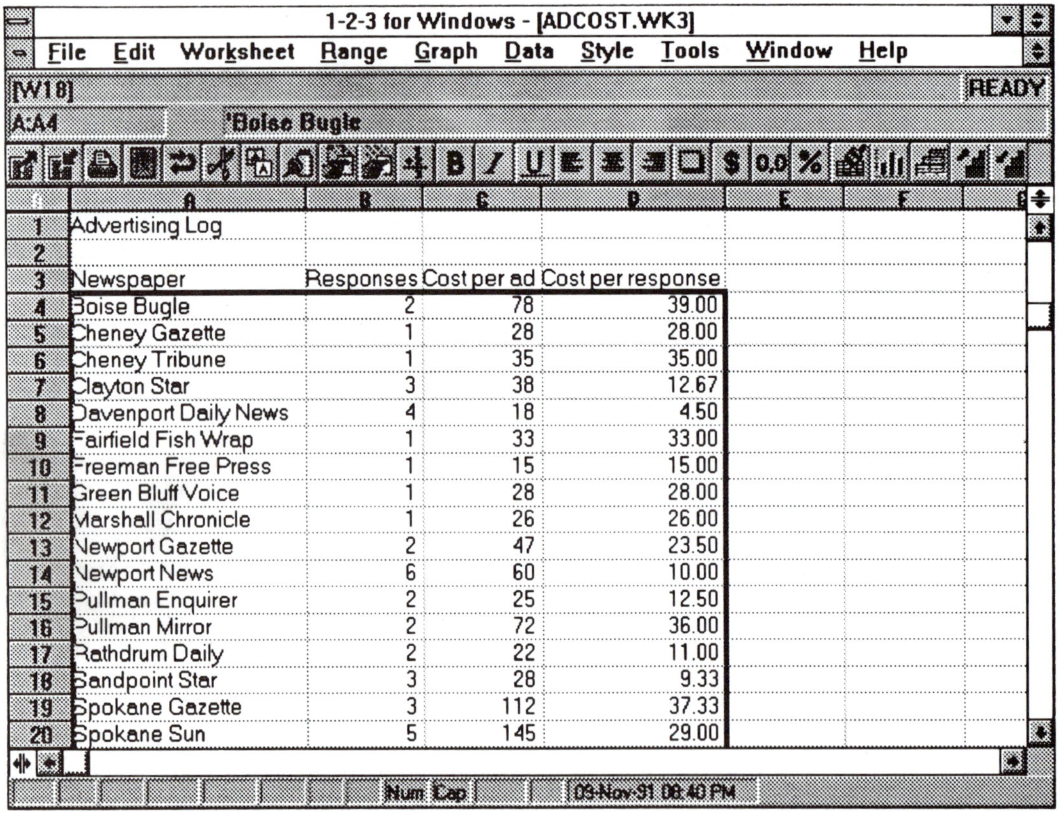

```
1-2-3 for Windows - [ADCOST.WK3]
File  Edit  Worksheet  Range  Graph  Data  Style  Tools  Window  Help
[W18]                                                         READY
A:A4          'Boise Bugle
```

	A	B	C	D
1	Advertising Log			
2				
3	Newspaper	Responses	Cost per ad	Cost per response
4	Boise Bugle	2	78	39.00
5	Cheney Gazette	1	28	28.00
6	Cheney Tribune	1	35	35.00
7	Clayton Star	3	38	12.67
8	Davenport Daily News	4	18	4.50
9	Fairfield Fish Wrap	1	33	33.00
10	Freeman Free Press	1	15	15.00
11	Green Bluff Voice	1	28	28.00
12	Marshall Chronicle	1	26	26.00
13	Newport Gazette	2	47	23.50
14	Newport News	6	60	10.00
15	Pullman Enquirer	2	25	12.50
16	Pullman Mirror	2	72	36.00
17	Rathdrum Daily	2	22	11.00
18	Sandpoint Star	3	28	9.33
19	Spokane Gazette	3	112	37.33
20	Spokane Sun	5	145	29.00

Num Cap   09-Nov-91 06:40 PM

Sorting the database by newspaper name helps Rose to find the particular paper she's looking for, but it doesn't bring the information we need into focus. To do that, let's try sorting on another primary key, the Responses field. A4..D23 should still be selected.

6. Select *Sort...* from the Data menu.
7. Type **B4** in the Primary key text box.

We could leave the *Ascending* radio button checked, but that would give us the responses sorted from fewest to most. Wouldn't it be better if the papers giving us the best response were at the top of the list? Of course it would.

8. Click in the *Descending* radio button.
9. Click on *OK*.

The newspapers should now be sorted from best to worst response.

Using Two Sort Keys

Great. This is getting more useful by the minute. We could organize the data even further by using a **secondary sort key**. Let's sort the newspapers by city within each response number.

1. Select *Sort...* from the Data menu.
2. Click in the *Secondary key* text box and enter: **A4**
3. Click in the *Ascending* radio button under the *Secondary key* text box.
4. Click on *OK*.

Notice that six papers gave us two responses each, and each of them is sorted in ascending alphabetical order. Pretty nifty!

• HINT

You can see how easily you can sort data using different sort criteria. Your data don't have to be organized in database fashion to use 1-2-3's Sort feature. You can use it with any of your worksheet data.

You can also use more than two sort keys. The *Extra keys* button in the Data Sort dialog box lets you assign additional sort keys as "tie-breakers." Using the phone book as an example again, if there were five Bill Smiths, it would help to have a third sort key (say, the middle initial).

Let's print the worksheet before leaving this lab.

5. Select the range A1..D23.
6. Create a header with the title **Lab 6-1** and a footer with your name, followed by the label: **1-2-3 for Windows**

7. Save your worksheet again, retaining the same file name.
8. Print the worksheet.
9. Exit 1-2-3 if you're not moving on to Lab 6-2 right away.

LAB 6-2 SEARCHING A DATABASE

Searching a database? Why? We can easily see every record of our database by simply scrolling up and down a few rows on our worksheet. That's true. But what if we were tracking responses for 200 (or 2,000) newspapers, instead of just 20? With large databases, you need a way to find specific records or portions of records.

The first two terms you'll need to understand before we query the database are input range and criteria range.

Query is just computer lingo that means searching a database to find data matching a specified set of criteria.

The **input range** is the range that contains the database. We've already set up the input range just by creating the database. The input range for a query is just like the Data range used in a sort.

The **criteria range** is the range that lists the information you want to find.

Creating a Criteria Range

As we just said, we don't need to do anything further to set up the input range, so the next step is defining the criteria range. This is the area where we'll specify what information we are looking for.

The criteria range is simply a range of cells, consisting of at least two rows. The first row must contain some or all of the field names used in the database. The field names must be entered *exactly* as they were in the database. The second row is left blank until you enter the search criteria. If your search criteria are complex, you may require more than one row below the field names.

All this different terminology may sound confusing if you are new to databases. Don't worry. Everything will become clear as we work through the lab.

Let's create the criteria range. We could type in the field names, but that would be a lot of work and could also cause problems if we mistyped anything. Instead, let's copy the field names to the beginning of our criteria range.

1. Start 1-2-3 if it's not already running.
2. Open the file A:\ADCOST.

We'll create a criteria range below the list of newspapers.

● **HINT**

While the criteria range can be placed anywhere on the worksheet, placing it directly below the database makes it easier to visualize the relationship between the database and the criteria range.

The downside to this positioning is that, when you want to add records to the database, you'll have to insert extra blank rows. You could consider placing the criteria range above the database to avoid this problem.

3. Select the range A3..D3.
4. Choose *Quick Copy...* from the Edit menu.
5. In the *To* text box, enter **A25** and click on *OK*.
6. Select cell A26.

The bottom of the database and the criteria range will look like Figure 6-4.

● **HINT**

Using the copy method for placing the field names in the criteria range not only ensures field name accuracy, but also maintains the same field order. The order of the fields in the criteria range doesn't have to match the order of the fields in the database, but keeping the same order will make working with the criteria range easier.

Now we're ready to enter the search criteria in the rows below the criteria range. If we want to search for a particular newspaper, we only need one row below the field names in the criteria range.

Let's say Rose wants to find the record for the Boise Bugle newspaper. All we need in the criteria range is the name of the newspaper we're searching for under the Newspaper field name.

7. Type **Boise Bugle** and click the confirm check box or press Enter.

NOTE

1-2-3 criteria are not case sensitive. It wouldn't matter if we entered Boise Bugle, BOISE BUGLE, or bOiSe bUgLe.

8. Choose *Query...* from the Data menu.

Figure 6-4. The criteria range lets you specify the items to search for in your database.

	A	B	C	D
8	Wenatchee Herald	4	125	31.25
9	Clayton Star	3	38	12.67
10	Sandpoint Star	3	28	9.33
11	Spokane Gazette	3	112	37.33
12	Boise Bugle	2	78	39.00
13	Newport Gazette	2	47	23.50
14	Pullman Enquirer	2	25	12.50
15	Pullman Mirror	2	72	36.00
16	Rathdrum Daily	2	22	11.00
17	Vallyford Journal	2	18	9.00
18	Cheney Gazette	1	28	28.00
19	Cheney Tribune	1	35	35.00
20	Fairfield Fish Wrap	1	33	33.00
21	Freeman Free Press	1	15	15.00
22	Green Bluff Voice	1	28	28.00
23	Marshall Chronicle	1	26	26.00
24				
25	Newspaper	Responses	Cost per ad	Cost per response
26				

Criteria range

Figure 6-5.

Data Query dialog box with:
- Input range: A:A26
- Criteria range: A:A26
- Output range: A:A26
- Extract unique only checkbox
- Buttons: Find, Delete, Extract, Modify..., Reset, Cancel

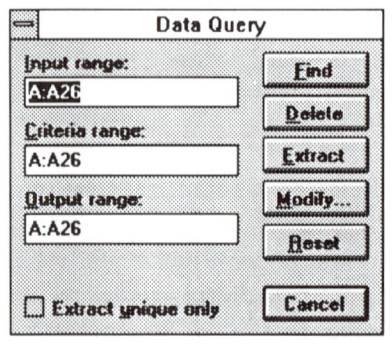

The Data Query dialog box will appear, as shown in Figure 6-5. In addition to Finding records, the Data Query dialog box includes options to Delete and Extract records. This dialog box also allows you to eliminate duplicate records (by using the *Extract Unique Only* check box) and modify groups of records.

9. Enter **A3..D23** in the *Input range* text box.
10. Enter **A25..D26** in the *Criteria range* text box.
11. Click on the *Find* button to initiate the query.

The entire record for the Boise Bugle will be selected. Once the record is found, we might want to view the contents of the various fields (cells). If more than one record matches our search criteria, we need a way to move between the located records. Table 6-2 shows the keystrokes that can be used to move through and edit the selected records.

Table 6-2. Data Query Find keystrokes.

Up and down arrows	Move to the previous or next selected record.
Left and right arrows	Move between fields in the selected record (contents visible in Control Panel).
Enter or Esc	Returns you to the Data Query dialog box.
F2 (Edit key)	Allows editing of the current field.
Home or End	Moves to the first or last matching record.
F7 (Query)	Ends the query operation and returns you to the READY mode.

Let's take a look at the contents of the various fields. We know you can see all of them on the screen right now, but play along, and use your imagination. Pretend there are 20 fields, and you *can't* see them all.

12. Alternately press the right and left arrow keys.

You won't see anything happening in the selected area, but the contents of the current field will become visible in the Control Panel.

We're ready to move on to other search criteria, so let's get out of this Data Query operation.

13. Press the F7 (Query) key to end the query operation.

The Data Query dialog box will reappear. Since *Cancel* is the default option, all you need to do to end the operation is press the Enter key (or click on Cancel if you prefer).

14. Press the Enter key to close the dialog box.

Finding Records with Wildcards

It's easy to find a record when we know the full name of the newspaper. But suppose we only remember that a newspaper name starts with Spokane. Or what if we want to find *all* the newspapers starting with Spokane, not just a particular one? No problem. 1-2-3 allows us to use *wildcards* to take the place of unknown or multiple search criteria. There are three **wildcard** characters that can be used in the search criteria: *, ?, and ~ .

> **NOTE**
>
> The * wildcard is used to represent any number of characters, including none. The * wildcard can only be used at the end of a search criteria. The ? wildcard takes the place of any single character and can be used anywhere in the search criteria. The ~ wildcard is the "not" wildcard. The ~ is used to find records that do *not* match the text following the ~ wildcard. The ~ wildcard is used at the beginning of the search criteria, but it can also be mixed with the * and ? wildcards.
>
> All three of these wildcards can only be used in label (text) fields. Wildcards cannot be used with values.

Well, getting back to our search for newspapers starting with Spokane....

1. Enter **Spokane*** in cell A26.

Remember the F7 Query key we used to end our last query? It's also a great shortcut for repeating the Data Query Find command. If you're using the same criteria range, changing only the search criteria, F7 is the way to go. Let's try it.

2. Press the F7 key to find the Spokane papers.

The Data Query dialog box didn't appear this time. When you press F7, 1-2-3 assumes that you want to repeat the last used search criteria and immediately issues the *Find* command.

The record for the Spokane Times is selected, since it's the first record containing Spokane in the Newspaper field. With a wildcard search, all of the records containing the search criteria are included, and you can move between them using the up and down arrow keys. Let's find the rest of the Spokane papers.

3. Press the down arrow key to see the next matching record.
4. Press the down arrow key once again to move to the last record.
5. Press the down arrow key again.

Hey, it beeped at you! It's just 1-2-3's not-so-subtle way of telling you that there are no more matching records.

6. Press F7 to end the query.

Why didn't the Data Query dialog box appear like it did the last time we ended a query? Well, we told you that 1-2-3 assumes you don't want to change the criteria range when you use the F7 shortcut to initiate a query. It also assumes that you're not going to change the criteria range when you're finished, so it ends the query without stopping at the dialog box for more input.

Let's try the ? wildcard. Rose wants to find the Spokane Gazette record, but she's forgotten whether it's Ga*z*ette or Ga*s*ette.

7. In cell A26, enter **Spokane Ga?ette** and then press the F7 key.

The Spokane Gazette is selected even though we weren't sure of the correct spelling.

8. Press the F7 key to end the query.

Now Rose wants to find all the records that do *not* contain papers starting with Spokane. No problem. We'll combine the ~ (not) wildcard with the * wildcard.

9. Enter ~**Spokane*** in cell A26, and then press the F7 key to activate the Find operation.
10. Use the down arrow key to move through the selections until the computer beeps to let you know you're done.

Notice that the query finds all the records except those that start with Spokane.

11. Press the F7 key to end the query.

Suppose we want to find all the records with papers from Pullman *or* Cheney. Here is where we need to use more than one row in the criteria range.

12. In cell A26, enter: **Pullman***
13. In cell A27, enter: **Cheney***

We can't just press the F7 key at this point, because the criteria range has changed. We need to let 1-2-3 know about the change.

14. Select *Query...* from the Data menu.
15. Edit the *Criteria range* text box to read: **A25..D27**
16. Click on the *Find* button.

17. Use the down arrow key to view all of the Pullman and Cheney newspapers.
18. Press the F7 key to end the query.

Searching a Database for Values

The wildcard characters discussed above only work when searching text (label) fields. If you're searching for values, simply enter the value you're searching for exactly as it appears in the database.

But what if you want to search for a range of values? 1-2-3 gives us logical operators to help us find specific groups of values, as shown in Table 6–3. **Logical operators** are symbols that evaluate conditions and make comparisons between values.

Table 6–3. Logical operators.

>	Greater than
<	Less than
<>	Not equal to
=	Equal to
<=	Less than or equal to
>=	Greater than or equal to
#NOT#	Meets neither search criterion
#AND#	Meets both search criteria
#OR#	Meets either search criterion

NOTE

If you are entering search criteria with one of the logical operators, be sure to start with a label prefix such as '. This will ensure that 1-2-3 will correctly identify the search entry.

Rose wants to know which newspapers gave her more than two responses. Using the logical operators, it's a simple matter to find the answer.

1. In cell B26, enter an apostrophe, the "greater than" operator, and the number: '>2
2. Erase the range A26..A27.

A26 and A27 need to be erased because we don't want Pullman and Cheney to be part of the new search criteria. We don't need to reduce the size of the criteria range, since we're not adding anything to it. It doesn't matter if the criteria range contains extra fields.

3. Press the F7 key, and the proper records will be selected.

Use the arrow keys to move through the selections.

4. Press the F7 key again to end the query.

We've seen how we can search for records that meet either of two criteria by placing criteria labels on two rows. When we searched for records containing Pullman or Cheney, we had to enter Pullman and Cheney in two separate cells.

But how about a search to locate all of the records in a particular range? For example, Rose wants to find out which newspapers got more than two responses, but less than six.

In this case, we enter the two conditions on the same row, separated by the logical AND operator.

The only new trick here is that we have to reference the first record of the field that we're searching—in this case, the Responses field, which is in column B. Follow along and you'll see what we mean.

5. Clear the contents of cell B26.
6. In cell B26, enter: **+B4>2#AND#+B4<6**

The formula breaks down as follows:

+B4	Enters cell B4 as a value. B4, being the first cell in the Responses field, is used to represent the entire field.
>2	Greater than 2.
#AND#	The logical operator for AND. The number signs act as markers, or **delimiters**, to show the beginning and end of the operator.
+B4	Again enter cell B4 as a value. We're comparing two values in the same field.
<6	Less than 6.

This search string tells 1-2-3 to find all records in the database, starting with cell B4, that have values greater than 2 and less than 6 in column B.

The formula will appear in the Control Panel, but the value in cell B26 will appear as zero. Don't worry about the zero—the search will work just fine.

• HINT

You have the option of using field names instead of cell references in formulas with logical operators. In the above example, the formula would look like this:

+RESPONSES>2#AND#+RESPONSES<6.

If you use field names without having assigned them as range names, you will end up with an ERR in the criteria range. This doesn't affect the query, but if it bothers you, you can use the Range Format Text command to display the formula criteria.

---

7. Press the F7 key.
8. Browse through the selected records with the up and down arrow keys.
9. Press F7 to end the query.

We'll print this worksheet and then move on to the next lab, which covers extractions and deletions. Sounds painful, but it really isn't. It doesn't involve going to the dentist (unless you bite off more than you can chew).

10. Select the range A1..D26.
11. Change the header to: **Lab 6-2**
12. Save the worksheet.
13. Print the range.
14. Exit 1-2-3 if you're too scared about that extraction stuff to go on to Lab 6-3 right away.

LAB 6-3 EXTRACTING AND DELETING RECORDS

Extracting Records from the Database

Searching for and finding records using search criteria is quite useful, but sometimes you'll need to use the found records in some way other than just viewing them. Perhaps you want to print just the specified records, or produce a graph, or perform some other analysis that uses only specific records from your database.

We've created a database and defined it for 1-2-3 as the input range. We've defined a criteria range where we can enter search criteria. To extract records from the database, we need to define a place for the records to go. We do this in 1-2-3 by defining an **output range**.

Like the criteria range, the output range can be placed anywhere on the worksheet. For visual clarity, we prefer to place the output range below the database and below the criteria range.

1. Start Windows and launch 1-2-3 if it's not already running.
2. Open the file A:\ADCOST.
3. Select the range A25..D25.
4. Choose *Quick Copy...* from the Edit menu.
5. In the *To* text box, enter **A29** and click on *OK*.

Copying the field names to the output range is the safest way to ensure accuracy, just as for the criteria range. In the criteria range, it's okay to use all the field names, even if they're not all included in the search criteria.

It's important to be more selective when defining the output range. The fields that you use in the output range will be the only ones extracted from the database. It's possible, for example, to build a new table that contains just the newspaper name and the cost per ad. If those are the only two fields you want to extract, simply create an output range that includes only those two fields.

We only need to identify one row (the row containing the field names) as the output range. If only one row is defined, 1-2-3 will use as many rows as necessary below the field names for the extracted records.

If you define a predetermined number of rows, your ability to perform queries will be limited. For example, if you defined the output range to include 10 rows, no more than 10 records could be extracted, even if the query finds more than that number of records.

⊘ HAZARD

If a single row output range is defined, all the data below the output range will be deleted with every Data Query Extract. Even if the results of the extraction would only bring in 10 fields, and you have data 20 rows below your single row output range, the data will be destroyed.

The solution is simple. Don't put data below single row output ranges, or don't use single row output ranges. We know you're saying to yourselves, "Gee, like, that was *so* obvious." Sorry about that, but it's our job to point out the obvious.

Now we're ready to extract some records. Data extraction requires the same skills you learned when we searched for records in the last lab.

We enter our search criteria in the criteria range. The only difference between the Data Query Find and the Data Query Extract operations is how 1-2-3 presents you with the results of the query.

With the Find operation, 1-2-3 simply shows you the records in the database and allows you to move through them using the arrow keys. With Extract, 1-2-3 places the results of the query in the output range.

Rose wants to extract records for newspapers with cost per response less than $15 and responses greater than 1.

6. In cell B26, enter: '>1
7. In cell D26, enter: '<15
8. Select *Query...* from the Data menu.

Our old friend, the Data Query dialog box, will once again appear.

9. In the *Output range* text box, enter: **A29..D29**

We're only defining one row for the output range so that 1-2-3 can use as many rows as it needs for the extraction.

10. Click on the *Extract* button.
11. Click on the *Cancel* button to close the Data Query dialog box.

If you've done everything correctly (and we know you have), your screen should look like Figure 6-6. Let's try one more extraction so you can see that there's no need to erase the data in the output range prior to doing an extraction.

Now Rose wants to extract a list of the newspapers starting with Spokane. Hey, this'll be a snap. We've done it before using the *Find* command.

12. Erase the data in cells B26 and D26.
13. In cell A26, enter: **Spokane***
14. Select *Query...* from the Data menu and click on the *Extract* button in the Data Query dialog box.
15. Click on *Cancel* to close the dialog box.

All right! We've got a list that contains only the Spokane newspapers, and the previous data in the output range are gone.

Chapter 6   Database Applications

Figure 6-6. The output range shows the extracted record.

	A	B	C	D	E	F
21	Freeman Free Press	1	15	15.00		
22	Green Bluff Voice	1	28	28.00		
23	Marshall Chronicle	1	26	26.00		
24						
25	Newspaper	Responses	Cost per ad	Cost per response		
26		>1		<15		
27						
28						
29	Newspaper	Responses	Cost per ad	Cost per response		
30	Newport News	6	60	10.00		
31	Davenport Daily News	4	18	4.50		
32	Clayton Star	3	38	12.67		
33	Sandpoint Star	3	28	9.33		
34	Pullman Enquirer	2	25	12.50		
35	Rathdrum Daily	2	22	11.00		
36	Vallyford Journal	2	18	9.00		
37						
38						
39						
40						

Rows 29–36 are the Output range.

Deleting Records from the Database

Records often need to be deleted from a database. Of course, we could go into the database and delete individual rows. But if we wanted to delete a group of records that matched certain search criteria, using 1-2-3's Data Query Delete command would be the most efficient method.

Deleting groups of records in a database is just like searching for records, except that, instead of selecting records that match the search criteria, 1-2-3 deletes them.

Now that Rose has the Spokane newspapers on a separate part of the worksheet, she no longer wants them as a part of the main database. Okay, they're history.

• HINT

Prior to deleting records from a database, it's a very good idea to save the worksheet. If you've entered the search criteria incorrectly, you could delete more or different records than you intended. If you save the worksheet just before the deletion, the original worksheet can be retrieved if something goes wrong.

We'll follow our own advice.

1. Save the worksheet.

Since we want to delete the Spokane newspapers, there's no need to alter the search criteria, which are already set as Spokane*.

2. Select *Query...* from the Data menu.
3. Click on the *Delete* button.

Figure 6-7.

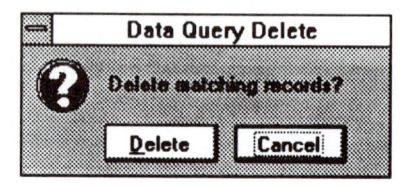

The Data Query Delete dialog box will appear, as depicted in Figure 6-7. Before the data are deleted, 1-2-3 asks you to confirm that you really do want to delete them.

4. Click on the *Delete* button in the Data Query Delete dialog box.
5. Click on the *Cancel* button to clear the Data Query dialog box.

Explore the database, and you'll notice that not only were the records with Spokane newspapers deleted, but the rows themselves are gone. What a clever program!

6. Select the range A1..D32.
7. Change the header to read: **Lab 6-3**
8. Save the worksheet.

We know, we know. You just saved it before deleting the Spokane records. We want to save it again, now that it is in the form we want.

9. Print the range.
10. Exit 1-2-3 if you're not going on to the next chapter now.

COMING ATTRACTIONS...

In this chapter, you learned to create, sort, search, extract, and delete records from a 1-2-3 database.

In the next chapter, you'll learn to take advantage of 1-2-3's incredible macro facility to automate all your repetitive tasks. You're gonna love it!

KEY TERMS

Ascending Sort Data are arranged from smallest to largest (e.g., A to Z; 1 to 100; etc.).

Criteria range The range that lists the information you want to find or extract.

Database An electronic collection of related information, organized in 1-2-3 as a table of rows and columns.

Delimiters Number signs (#) that act as markers to show the beginning and end of an operator (e.g., #AND#).

Descending Sort Data are arranged from largest to smallest (e.g., Z to A; 100 to 1; etc.).

Fields The individual cells in a database.

Input range The range that contains the database.

Logical operators Symbols that evaluate conditions and make comparisons between values.

Output range The area (in a worksheet) specified to contain records extracted from a database.

Primary sort key The field (column) that controls how data are sorted.

Query Searching a database to find data that match a specified set of criteria.

Records The rows of related items in a 1-2-3 database.

Secondary sort key The field (column) that provides a second level of organization during a sort.

Sorting The process of rearranging the information in a database.

Wildcards Special characters used in searching a database to take the place of unknown or multiple search criteria.

EXERCISES

6-1. The following exercise will give you the chance to practice material you learned in Lab 6–1.

    a. Start Windows and start 1-2-3 if it's not running.

Let's create a small client database with three fields, including the client name, phone number, and favorite food. This is good "inside" information to know around holiday gift-giving time.

    b. In cell A1, enter: **Client List**
    c. In cell A3, enter: **NAME**
    d. In cell B3, enter: **PHONE**
    e. In cell C3, enter: **FOOD**
    f. Starting in cell A4, enter the field entries shown in Table 6–4.

Don't forget to use label prefixes for the phone numbers!

Table 6-4.

	A	B	C
4	Sprat, Jack	323-4567	Bran Flakes
5	Sanders, Colonel	568-9689	Fried Chicken
6	McCartney, Paul	234-7865	Hot Wings
7	Pooh, Winnie	774-9000	Honey
8	Reagan, Ron	444-7895	Jelly Bellies
9	McDonald, Ron	889-2626	Big Macs
10	Mom	656-7767	Apple Pie

Okay, technically Mom isn't a client, but we do need to keep track of these things.

    g. Widen column A so all the labels are visible.

We'll sort the database, using the first field as our primary sort key.

    h. Select the range A4..C10.
    i. Choose *Sort...* from the Data menu.

Column A is selected as the Primary key, which will sort the database by the last names of our clients (except Mom). If we clicked on *OK* now, the database would be sorted in descending alphabetical order (Z through A). That's not what we want.

    j. Click in the *Ascending* radio button in the Primary key area of the dialog box.
    k. Click on *OK*.

Let's save and print this worksheet.

    l. Select the range A1..C10.
    m. Create a header with the title **Exercise 6-1** and a footer with your name, followed by the label: **1-2-3 for Windows**
    n. Save the worksheet as **A:\EXER6-1**
    o. Print the selected range.
    p. Exit 1-2-3 if you've had enough exercise for now.

6-2. The following exercise will give you the chance to practice material you learned in Lab 6-2.

You'll need the worksheet we created in the last exercise in order to proceed with this exercise.

  a. Start Windows and start 1-2-3 if it's not running.
  b. Open the file A:\EXER6-1.

We want to be able to find specific records in this huge database, so we'll create a criteria range.

  c. Select the range A3..C3.
  d. Choose *Quick Copy...* from the Edit menu.
  e. In the *To* text box, enter **A12** and click on *OK*.

We'll search for the record that matches a phone number that was left on a phone message for us. We can't read the name because of the horrible handwriting, and we don't recognize the number.

  f. In cell B13, enter: **'656-7767**
  g. Select the range A3..C10.
  h. Select *Query...* from the Data menu.
  i. In the *Criteria range* text box, enter **A12..C13** and click on the *Find* button.

Since we started with the input range selected, it's still selected. But look whose name is in the Contents box of the Control Panel. It's Mom! We'd better return that call right away.

  j. Select the range A1..C13.
  k. Change the header to: **Exercise 6-2**
  l. Save the worksheet, using the name **A:\EXER6-2**
  m. Print the selected range of the worksheet.
  n. Exit 1-2-3 if you've done enough of this excruciating work (or if you need to call your mom).

6-3. The following exercise will give you a chance to practice material you learned in Lab 6-3. You'll need the worksheet we created in the last exercise in order to proceed with this exercise.

  a. Start Windows and start 1-2-3 if it's not running.
  b. Open the file A:\EXER6-2.

Let's extract the record that matches that no longer mysterious phone number. First, we'll define an output range below the criteria range.

    c. Select the range A12..C12.
    d. Choose *Quick Copy...* from the Edit menu.
    e. In the *To* text box, enter **A15** and click on *OK*.

The search criteria are already selected, so we just need to tell 1-2-3 to go ahead with the extraction.

    f. Select *Query...* from the Data menu.

The input and output ranges remain from our previous queries. All we need to do is enter the output range.

    g. In the output range text box, enter **A15..C15** and click on the *Extract* button.

Great! Now we'll be able to call Mom more often and bring her that apple pie she loves.

    h. Click on the *Cancel* button to clear the dialog box.
    i. Select the range A1..C16.
    j. Change the header to: **Exercise 6-3**
    k. Save the worksheet.
    l. Print the worksheet.
    m. Exit 1-2-3 and Windows, if you're leaving us for now.

REVIEW QUESTIONS

True or False Questions

1. **T**   **F**   A database is an electronic collection of related information.

2. **T**   **F**   Records are the columns in a 1-2-3 database.

3. **T**   **F**   Fields are the columns in a 1-2-3 database.

4. **T**   **F**   The criteria range specifies what to search for in a database.

5. **T**   **F**   A query searches a database for data matching a specified set of criteria.

6. **T**   **F**   A secondary sort key organizes the information in relation to the fundamental sort key.

Chapter 6 Database Applications **235**

7. **T F**   Wildcards let you use partial criteria to search your database.
8. **T F**   Extracting information permanently removes it from a database.
9. **T F**   Deleting information permanently erases it from a database.
10. **T F**   You edit a 1-2-3 database in much the same way that you edit data in any 1-2-3 worksheet.

Multiple Choice Questions

1. A 1-2-3 database lets you
   a. Organize information
   b. Sort information
   c. Find information
   d. Extract information
   e. All of the above

2. Which command lets you organize information in a 1-2-3 database?
   a. *Arrange...*
   b. *Descending*
   c. *Find*
   d. *Sort...*
   e. None of the above

3. Which command allows you to locate information in a 1-2-3 database?
   a. *Arrange...*
   b. *Descending*
   c. *Find*
   d. *Sort...*
   e. None of the above

4. To extract information from a database, you must first define a
   a. Criteria range
   b. Input range
   c. Output range
   d. All of the above
   e. None of the above

5. Which search criteria below is invalid?
   a. Spokane*
   b. S?o?a?e
   c. *Spokane
   d. ~pokane

6. If you wanted to locate all the numbers above 10 and below 100, which of these search criteria would accomplish the task?
   a. +B4>10#AND#B4<100
   b. +B4<10#AND#B4>100
   c. +B4>10#OR#B4<100
   d. +B4<10#OR#B4<100
   e. None of the above

7. The *Query...* command in the Data menu
   a. Deletes information from a database
   b. Extracts information from a database
   c. Finds information in a database
   d. a and c
   e. None of the above

All of the above

8. A record in a 1-2-3 database occupies
   - a. A row
   - b. A column
   - c. a and b
   - d. None of the above

9. To ensure field name accuracy in the output range, you should
   - a. Copy the desired field names into the output range
   - b. Move the desired field names into the output range
   - c. Type the desired field names into the output range
   - d. None of the above

10. The most advantageous place to locate a criteria range is
    - a. Below the database
    - b. Above the database
    - c. Right of the database
    - d. Left of the database
    - e. None of the above

CHAPTER 7

Creating a Macro

• *Objectives*

Upon completing this chapter, you'll be able to:
1. **Create macros to automate tasks.**
2. **Assign a macro to a SmartIcon.**
3. **Pause a macro so data can be entered.**

OVERVIEW

In this lab, you'll discover how to automate many of the repetitive tasks normally associated with building a worksheet. This will involve learning to plan, write, and document a macro.

WHAT ARE MACROS?

Macro is just a fancy word for a type of shortcut. With a macro, you can give a name to a series of actions and then play back the entire sequence with just a couple of keystrokes or mouse clicks.

1-2-3's SmartIcons act like macros. Each SmartIcon represents several 1-2-3 commands or actions. For example, when you click on the *Bold* SmartIcon, it's just as if you had chosen *Font* from the Style menu and then clicked on *Bold* in the Style Font dialog box.

The Macro feature allows you to create your own shortcuts. If you find yourself changing column widths all the time, put the commands into a macro. Do you use the same formula on a regular basis? Put it into a macro.

A macro is just a set of commands and/or text stored as labels in consecutive cells in a single column. You name your macro by assigning a range name to the cells in which the commands are stored. Once you've named the range, you can run the macro by using the range name.

> We'll explore some simple macros in this lab to give you a taste of the power of macros. But we don't want to leave you with the impression that this is all macros can do. 1-2-3 for Windows contains an amazingly versatile set of macro commands that allow you to customize 1-2-3 in every conceivable way.
>
> You can create custom menu choices for specific groups of tasks. Macros can make "smart" decisions based on your responses to various prompts. You could even create an automated invoice system where the cursor pauses at the correct places to allow you to enter the information for quantity, part number, description, price, etc., and then automatically calculates totals.
>
> We won't be delving into the advanced macro commands in this book, but we encourage you to experiment with them after mastering the basics.
>
> You don't need to be a programmer to take advantage of lots of incredible possibilities. With your manual, a little exploration, and some patience, you'll have 1-2-3 doing your bidding in no time.

LAB 7-1 WRITING A SIMPLE MACRO

Writing a simple macro can be broken down into six steps:

- Planning
- Entering the commands and keystrokes
- Naming the macro
- Saving the macro
- Testing the macro, and fixing it if necessary
- Documenting the macro

We'll explore each of these steps.

Planning a Macro

Planning is an important part of writing a macro. Since a macro is literally a set of 1-2-3 actions or commands, it helps to plot out the steps before you begin. Knowing what actions need to be performed lets you minimize mistakes.

Chapter 7 Creating a Macro   **239**

> **NOTE**
>
> For the sake of consistency, we've been using the mouse almost exclusively so far. But do you remember us telling you that there are keyboard alternatives for most of the mouse actions? In some cases, the keystrokes can even be faster than using the mouse.
>
> Well, mouse clicks can't be directly stored in macros, so we'll be discussing and using keyboard alternatives during this chapter. All of the 1-2-3 menus can be accessed through the keyboard by holding down the Alt key and tapping the underlined letter. For example, you can access the File menu by pressing Alt+F because the F is underlined.

Our first macro will widen a column to 20. The only way to be sure about what needs to go into the macro is to perform the sequence. Let's see what steps go into widening a column. This will also give you a chance to practice using the keyboard.

1. Start Windows and launch 1-2-3 for Windows.
2. Maximize the worksheet.
3. Make sure that cell A1 is highlighted.
4. Choose the Worksheet menu by holding down the Alt key and tapping the letter **k**.
5. Select *Column Width...* by pressing the letter **c**.

The Worksheet Column Width dialog box will appear.

6. Type **20** in the *Set width to* text box.
7. Hit the Enter key to accept the command and close the dialog box.

In most cases, hitting the Enter key is just like clicking on *OK* in a dialog box.

What did we just do? Glad you asked. We used a series of keystrokes that resulted in an action being performed. We pressed the following sequence of keys: Alt-k-c-20-Enter. Now that we've planned it out, all we have to do is translate the steps into a macro.

Let's reset Column A to its default width before proceeding.

8. Select *Column Width...* from the Worksheet menu.
9. Type **9** in the *Set width to* text box.
10. Press the Enter key to accept the value.

Entering Commands and Keystrokes in a Macro

Entering the commands and keystrokes necessary to carry out a particular function is much like entering any other data in a worksheet. You simply move to a cell and type in the data.

1. Move to cell B1.
2. Type the following exactly as shown: **{Alt}kc20~** and press the Enter key.

Your screen should look like the one pictured in Figure 7-1.

Figure 7-1. A column-widening macro.

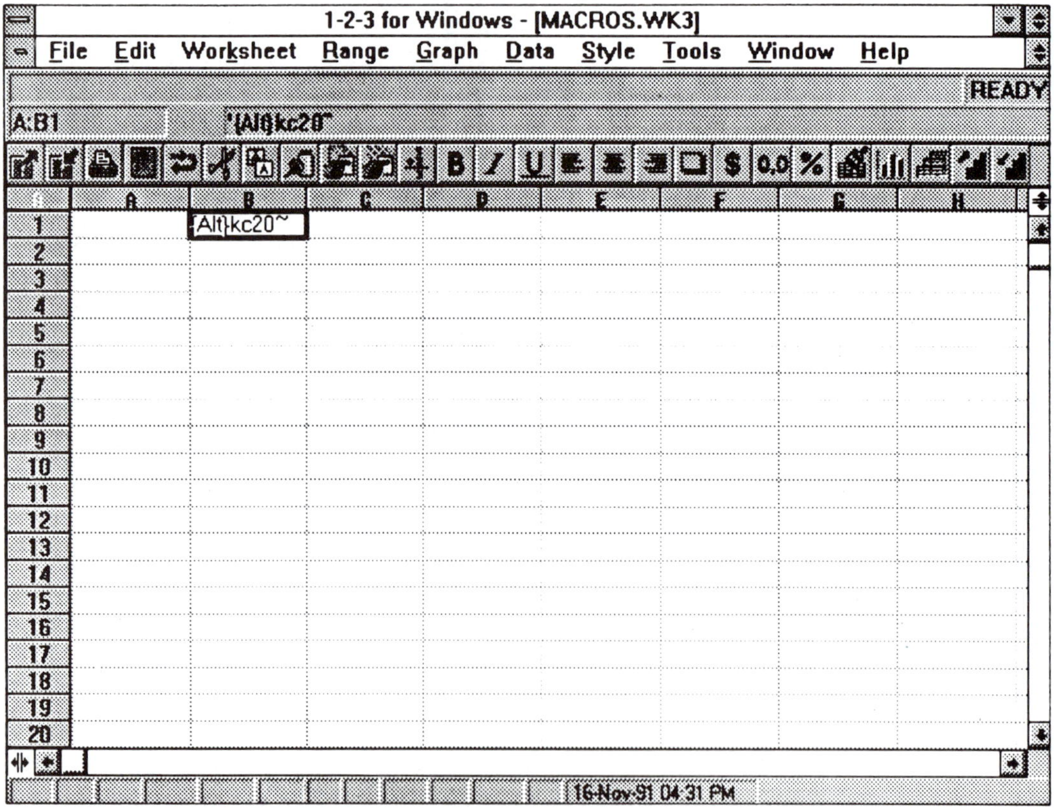

The sequence you just typed will appear as a label in cell A:B1. But what is it? Looks like a bunch of hieroglyphics. Well, don't panic, it'll all be clear in a moment. Let's break it down step by step.

Chapter 7 Creating a Macro **241**

The curly brackets tell 1-2-3 that whatever is between them is a **macro command** and not ordinary text. {Alt} is the macro command for pressing the Alt key.

The next two letters are the letters you pressed to select the Worksheet menu and Column Width dialog box.

The number 20 is the value you entered in the *Set width to* text box.

Okay, now for the weird one. The squiggly doohickey at the end is called a **tilde**, and in macros it represents the Enter key. When you run this macro, 1-2-3 will look at the tilde and say, "Yup, there's a tilde—it must be time to press the Enter key."

⊘ HAZARD

Don't forget those tildes! That's probably the most common mistake that people make when writing macros. If you've got a macro that's not working properly, check to make sure you have tildes in all the right places.

Notice that the entire sequence was entered without any spaces. Macros play back whatever's in them literally. If there's a space between commands or characters, 1-2-3 will act as if the space bar had been pressed. Depending on what's happening at the time, this could have an adverse effect on your macro.

That's all there is to entering data for a macro. You just type in the keystrokes literally, making sure that keystroke commands (like the Alt key) are enclosed in curly brackets. Table 7-1 lists some common keystroke commands and their corresponding macro symbols. Since we haven't been using keystrokes much in this book, the table also tells you what action each key performs.

● HINT

There's a shortcut for entering repetitive cursor movement commands. Instead of entering the command several times in a row, you can enter the command once, followed by the number of repetitions you want. For example, if you want to enter a macro command to move down four cells, you can type {D 4} instead of {D}{D}{D}{D}. Just make sure the number is inside the curly braces.

You've just written a macro, but 1-2-3 won't be able to run it until you give it a name.

Table 7-1. Keystroke commands and common macro commands.

1-2-3 Keystroke	Action	Macro Commands
Cursor Movement Keys		
Home	Moves cursor to the first cell in the current worksheet.	{home}
PgUp	Moves cursor up one screen.	{pgup}
PgDn	Moves cursor down one screen.	{pgdn}
Ctrl-right arrow or Tab	Moves cursor to the right one screen.	{bigright}
Ctrl-left arrow or Tab	Moves cursor to the left one screen.	{backtab} or {bigleft}
Up arrow	Moves cursor up one row.	{u} or {up}
Down arrow	Moves cursor down one row.	{d} or {down}
Left arrow	Moves cursor left one cell.	{l} or {left}
Right arrow	Moves cursor right one cell.	{r} or {right}
Function Keys		
F1	Activates on-screen Help feature.	{help}
F2	Puts 1-2-3 in EDIT mode so you can edit cell entries.	{edit}
F4	In READY mode, anchors the cell pointer so you can specify a range.	{abs}
F5	Moves cursor to a specified cell.	{goto}
F9	Updates all formulas in your worksheet.	{calc}

Naming a Macro

You must name a macro before you can run (invoke) it. Naming a macro consists of assigning a range name to the first cell of the macro. You use exactly the same process you used before to assign range names. The only difference is that, in a macro, you don't have to include all of the macro cells in your range.

When 1-2-3 runs a macro, it looks at the information in the first cell assigned to the macro and continues reading down cell by cell until it comes to an empty cell. Because of this, the range name for a macro only needs to include the first cell.

There are two ways to name macros.

The first is to use a backslash (\) followed by any letter of the alphabet. Macros named with a backslash can be run by holding down the Ctrl key and pressing the appropriate key. For example, if you named your macro "\c," you would play it back by pressing Ctrl+C.

With this method, it helps to use a letter that reminds you of the macro's function. For example, calling our column-widening macro \c would help us remember that it has something to do with columns.

The other option for naming macros is to use a descriptive name of up to 15 characters. Does that sound familiar? Well, it should. Since a **macro name** is really just a range name, the same naming rules apply. For example, a macro that inserts the current date into your worksheet could be named "date."

Macros with descriptive names are played back differently than backslash macros. To play a named macro, you choose *Macro, Run* from the Tools menu (or you can use the Alt+F3 function key, which is actually a shortcut to the *Run* command).

NOTE

The decision to give a macro a descriptive name or a backslash name should be determined by two factors: the macro's complexity and the frequency with which you plan to use it. If it's a macro you'll use a lot, or one that doesn't perform a whole lot of actions, a backslash name is the clear choice. That way, you'll be able to play it back quickly by pressing the Ctrl key and one letter. If the macro is complex *and* won't be used often, a descriptive name would be the best way to go. The more steps involved in the macro, the more sense it makes to use a descriptive name.

Okay, we're done talking for now. Let's give this macro a name. Since the macro only saves us six keystrokes, a descriptive name wouldn't make much sense. How about calling it "\c"? That will put it just a Ctrl key away, and the "c" makes it easy for us to remember what the macro does.

1. Make sure your cursor is in cell B1 (where you entered the macro data).
2. Choose *Name* from the Range menu.
3. Select *Create*.

The Range Name Create dialog box will appear.

4. Type **\c** in the *Range Name* text box and click on *OK* (or press the Enter key) to accept the name and close the dialog box.

Saving a Macro

You should always protect your worksheet by saving it before testing a macro. Since a macro can radically change the appearance and contents of a worksheet, it can potentially cause serious damage (e.g., erasing data).

1. Issue the *Save As...* command from the File menu.
2. Name the worksheet **A:\MACROS** and click *OK*.

Testing a Macro

That's all you have to do. The macro includes all the necessary data, and it has a name. Okay, okay, we know you're getting impatient. It's time to see if this baby flies.

1. Move your cursor to cell C1.
2. Hold down the Ctrl key and tap **c**.

Wow! Column C's getting bigger right before our eyes. Okay, we know it's not *that* great, but it does give you a glimpse of what's possible with macros. This one only saved us a few keystrokes, but the possibilities are just about limitless.

Well, this is great, but what happens when we retrieve this file two weeks from now and try to remember what we did? There's nothing here to tell us what the macro's called or what it does. We think a little documentation is in order.

> **NOTE**
>
> Lotus 1-2-3 provides powerful features to help you test and "debug" more complicated macros. These features include a Step mode for slowing down the execution of the macro so you can spot where a problem is occurring. Please refer to your user reference manual for information on the macro debugging capabilities of 1-2-3 for Windows.

Documenting a Macro

As you've seen, the macro is technically complete. The only purpose of documentation is to remind you of the macro's name and function.

The convention we use is to put the macro name in a label in the cell just to the left of the first macro cell. Then we include some comments describing the steps involved in the macro in the cells immediately to the right of the macro column. That way we can see what's happening at a glance without having to rely on our failing memories.

> **NOTE**
>
> Entering the macro's name as a label in the cell immediately to the left of the first macro cell also enables you to use the Range Name Label Create command to assign names to a group of macros at once. Check your 1-2-3 manual or the Help screen for instructions.

1. Move your cursor to cell A1.
2. Type **'\c** and press the Enter key.

Why do you need to type the apostrophe? If you don't, 1-2-3 will see the backslash as a label prefix. Since the backslash is the label prefix that repeats text across a cell, entering \c without the apostrophe would cause a series of c's to appear across the entire cell.

Next we'll enter a description of the macro in cell C1.

3. Enter **Widens column to 20** in cell C1.

Check to make sure your screen looks like Figure 7–2. Hey, I think we're on a roll here. Let's not stop now.

Writing a Macro to Insert the Current Date

Now that you've got the hang of it, let's add a twist. Our next macro will use an @function to insert the current date into the worksheet.

Since 1-2-3 looks at the first cell in a macro and then reads down consecutive cells in the row until it encounters a blank line, we have to make sure there's a blank row between our two macros. We'll begin this macro in cell B3.

Figure 7–2. Column C has been successfully widened by the macro.

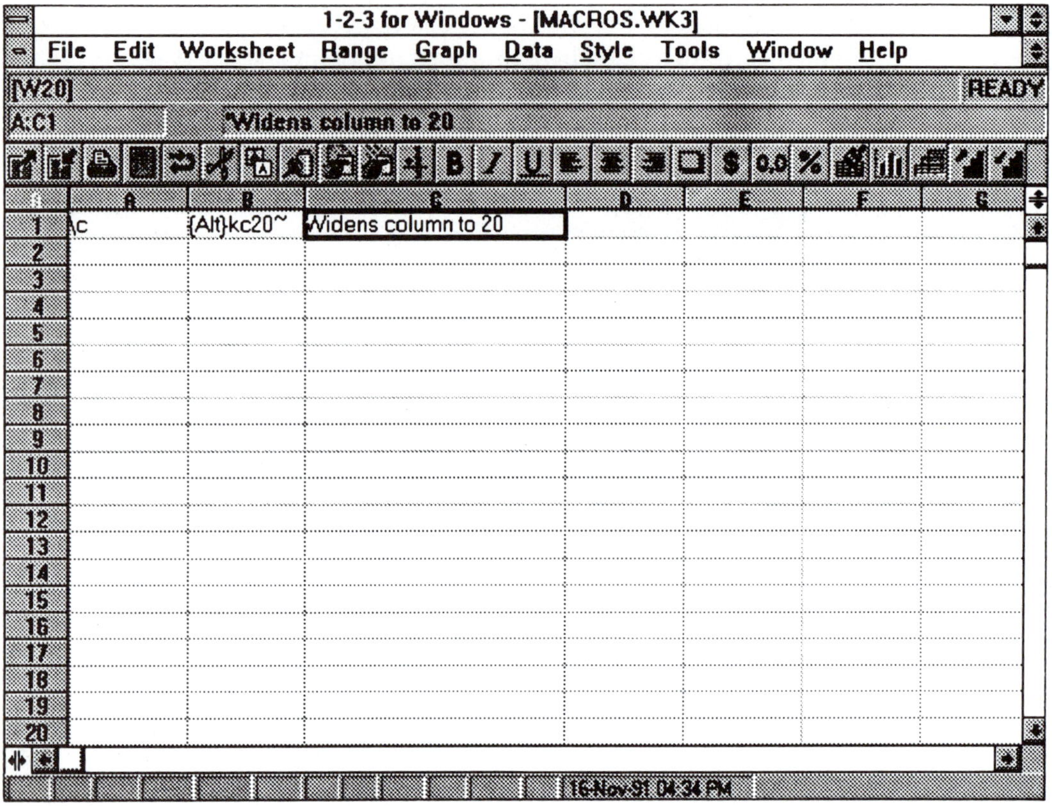

Let's go ahead and enter the macro data and the documentation all at once.

1. Starting in Cell A3, enter the information shown in Table 7–2.

Table 7–2.

	A	B	C
3	date	'@TODAY~	Date stamp macro
4		{Alt}rf4~	

Your worksheet should now resemble Figure 7–3. The @TODAY command generates a serial number that represents the current date. 1-2-3 stores dates as numbers. January 1, 1900, is number 1 and the numbering continues through December 31, 2099 (number 73050).

Figure 7-3. A macro to insert the current date in your worksheet.

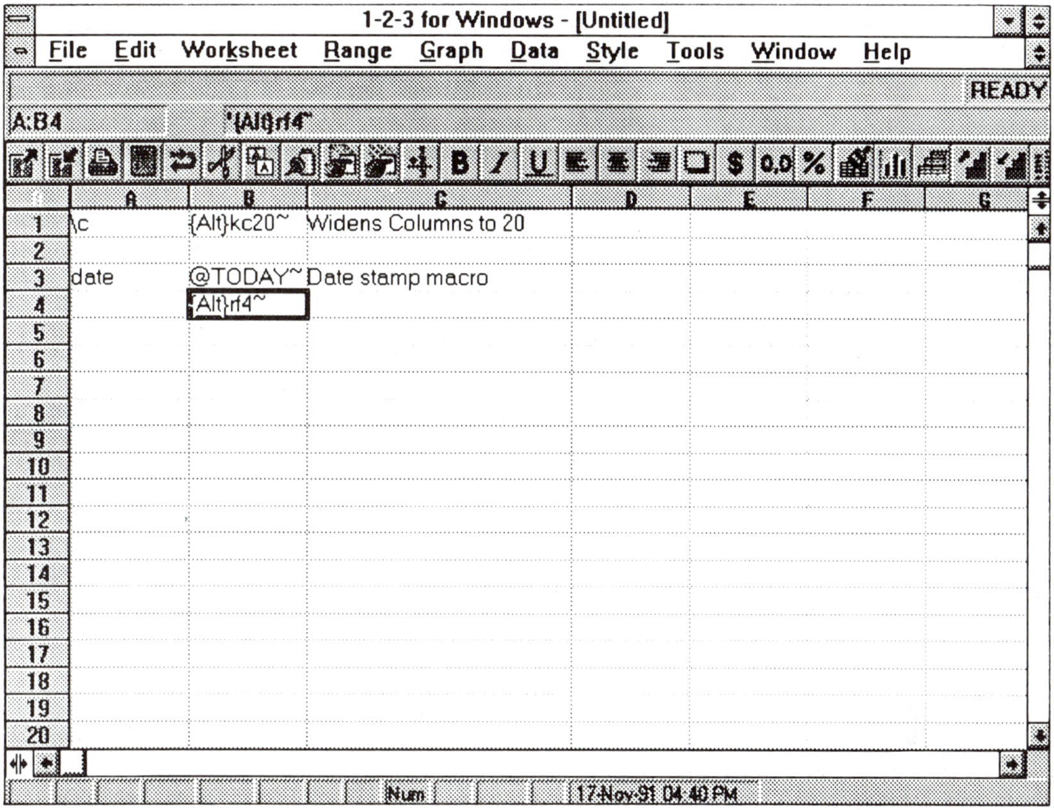

```
                      1-2-3 for Windows - [Untitled]
  File   Edit   Worksheet   Range   Graph   Data   Style   Tools   Window   Help
                                                                          READY
A:B4           '{Al0}rf4~

       A          B              C              D       E       F       G
  1   \c      {Alt}kc20~   Widens Columns to 20
  2
  3   date    @TODAY~      Date stamp macro
  4           {Alt}rf4~
  5
  ...
                            Num        17-Nov-91 04:40 PM
```

The entry in cell B4 is necessary to format the date so that it makes sense. Without a date format, November 16, 1991, would appear as 33558. Huh?

As we discussed in Chapter 4, the *Range Format* command makes it a simple matter to turn this gibberish into plain English. There are nine different date and time formats to choose from. The one we're using in this macro gives us the month, day, and year separated by forward slashes (e.g., 11/16/91).

We've entered the macro data and the documentation. All that's left to do is name it. This time we'll use a descriptive name so that you'll have a chance to use the *Run* command (Alt+F3).

2. Give cell B3 the following range name: **DATE**

Remember, the range name only needs to reference the first cell of the macro.

3. Save the worksheet to protect it using the name **A:\MACROS**

It's always a good idea to save your worksheet before you test a macro.

Figure 7-4.

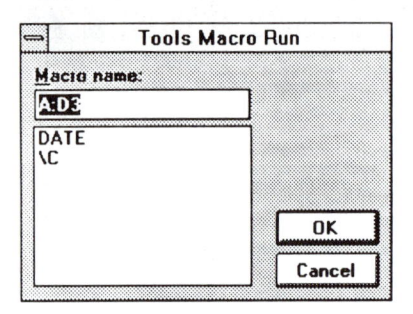

4. Select cell D3 (this is where we'll test the macro).
5. To play back the macro, press Alt+F3.

The Tools Macro Run dialog box will appear, as shown in Figure 7-4, with the *Macro name* text box selected. The dialog box contains a list of all named ranges in the current worksheet.

You can run the macro either by clicking on the range name in the list or by typing the macro name in the text box. In this case, we'll type the name.

6. Type **DATE** and press the Enter key.

The current date will appear in cell D3. Your worksheet should resemble Figure 7-5 (of course the date on your worksheet will be different).

7. Select the range A1..D4.
8. Create a header with the title **Lab 7-1** and a footer with your name, followed by the label: **1-2-3 for Windows**
9. Save the worksheet again.
10. Print the selected range.
11. Exit 1-2-3 if you're not moving right on to the next lab.

● HINT

Since macros are simply labels entered in a worksheet, you save a macro by saving the worksheet. Macros can be part of an existing worksheet, or you can have a separate worksheet specifically for macros. Placing macros in a separate worksheet lets you create a macro "library" that can be used with other worksheets. Because a macro can be run any time the worksheet containing it is open, all you need to do to have a macro library at your fingertips is to retrieve your macro file every time you begin a new worksheet. (In the next chapter, we'll show you how to work with multiple worksheets and files.)

Figure 7-5. The macro inserts the current date in the worksheet.

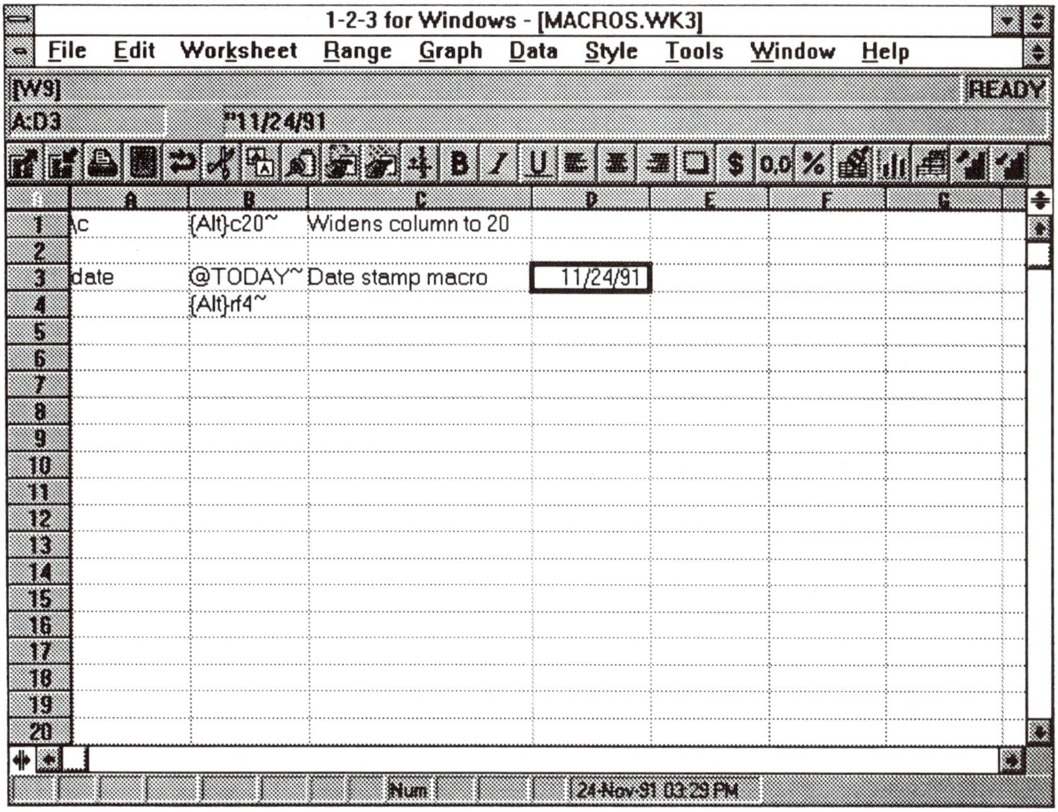

	A	B	C	D
1	\c	{Alt}c20~	Widens column to 20	
2				
3	date	@TODAY~	Date stamp macro	11/24/91
4		{Alt}rf4~		

LAB 7-2 ASSIGNING A MACRO TO A SMARTICON

At the beginning of this chapter, we said that macros act like SmartIcons. SmartIcons are 1-2-3's built-in way of automating certain tasks, and macros enable you to automate and customize the program further. Well, how about putting the two features together? We'll get so automated we can just sit back and watch 1-2-3 do its thing—it won't need us at all!

The column-widening macro you wrote in the last lab is pretty nifty, and it's also pretty easy to play back any time you want. But we can make things even easier by assigning it to a SmartIcon so that all you'll have to do to run the macro is click on an icon. Is that the height of laziness or what?

Let's do it.

1. If necessary, start Windows and launch 1-2-3 for Windows.
2. Maximize the worksheet.
3. Open the file A:\MACROS.
4. Choose *SmartIcons...* from the Tools menu.

Figure 7-6.

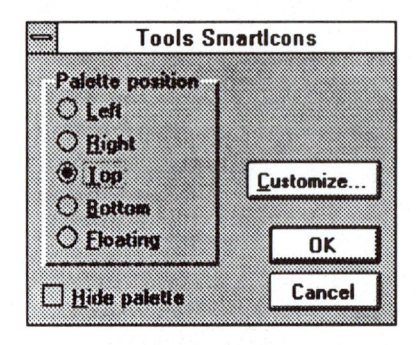

The Tools SmartIcons dialog box will appear, as shown in Figure 7-6. The Palette position box allows you to change the location of the SmartIcon palette. It can be placed on the left, right, top, or bottom of the screen. The Floating option puts the palette in a movable, sizeable window that can be dragged wherever you want. You can even choose to hide the SmartIcon palette by clicking the Hide palette check box, but *why*? The Customize option will take us to the Tools SmartIcons Customize dialog box, which is where we need to be to assign a macro to a SmartIcon.

5. Click on the *Customize...* button.

The Tools SmartIcons Customize dialog box will appear, as shown in Figure 7-7. This dialog box lets you add, delete, and move SmartIcons to suit your specific preferences. This is also the next stop on the road to adding our macro to the SmartIcon palette.

The first step is to pick one of the Custom SmartIcons for our macro. How about the one that sort of looks like a page with three columns? The whole idea here is to pick an icon that reminds us of what the macro does so it's easy to remember (we wouldn't want to have to do any actual *thinking* now, would we?). Anyway, since the macro widens a column, the picture of three columns should remind us of columns.

6. Click on the icon with the three columns of squiggly lines in the Custom SmartIcons box.

The icon will start blinking to let you know that it's been selected. Now we have to tell 1-2-3 what we want to do with this icon. To assign our macro to it, we need to click on the *Assign macro...* button.

7. Click on the *Assign macro...* button.

Figure 7-7. The dialog box lets you customize SmartIcons.

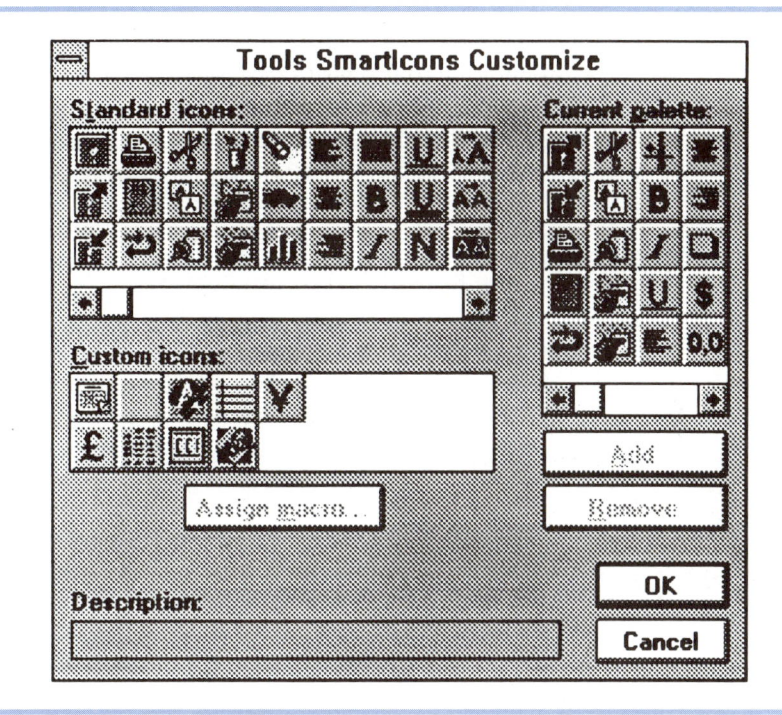

The Tools SmartIcons Customize Assign Macro dialog box (how's that for a tongue twister?) will appear, as shown in Figure 7-8, with your cursor in the *Macro* text box.

Figure 7-8. The Tools SmartIcons Customize Assign Macro dialog box provides options for assigning a macro to a SmartIcon.

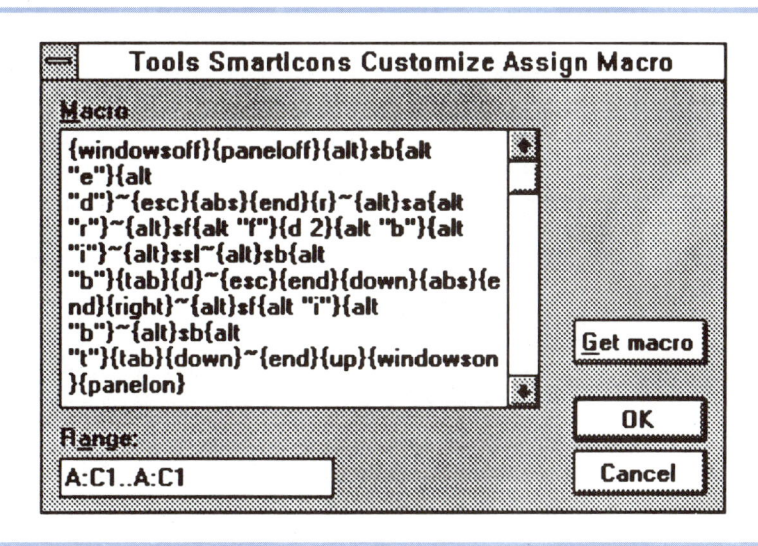

Don't worry about the data in the text box. It will disappear when we replace it with our macro data.

You could actually write your macro in this text box if you wanted to. But since we've already written the macro, all we need to do is let 1-2-3 know where we put it (by entering the macro's range in the *Range* text box). Once we've done that, we just need to tell 1-2-3 to "go fetch it."

8. Select the *Range* text box, and type: **B1**

Our macro only takes up one cell, so A:B1 is the full range address. If your macro extends beyond one cell, you have to enter the full address, not just the address for the first cell. For example, if we were assigning the DATE macro to a SmartIcon, the range address would be B3..B4.

9. Click on the *Get macro* button.

The macro in the specified range (in this case, B1) will be copied to the *Macro* text box. Your screen should now look like Figure 7-9.

10. Click on *OK* to confirm the action and return to the Tools SmartIcons Customize dialog box.

Figure 7-9. Your macro is now entered in the *Macro* text box.

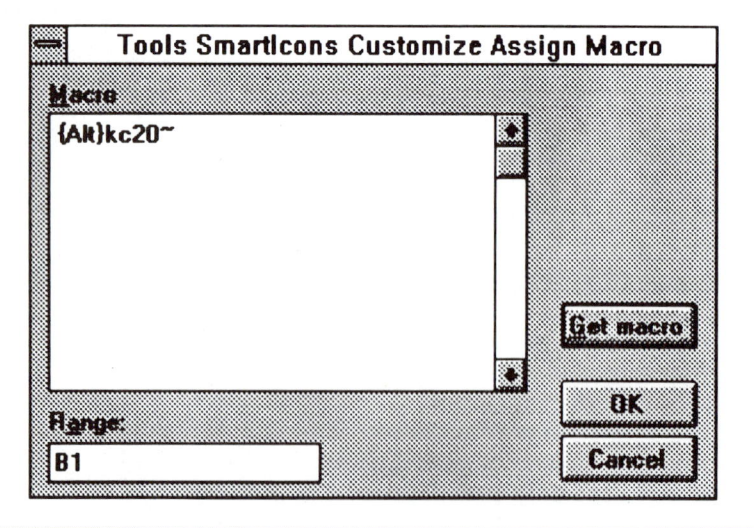

Adding an Icon to the Icon Palette

The macro is now assigned to the *Column* icon, but there's one more step. We need to add the icon to the icon palette.

1. Click on the *Column* icon in the *Custom icons* box.
2. Click on *Add*.

The *Column* icon will appear in the *Current palette* box, and your screen should look like Figure 7-10.

Figure 7-10. The *Column* icon appears in the *Current palette* box.

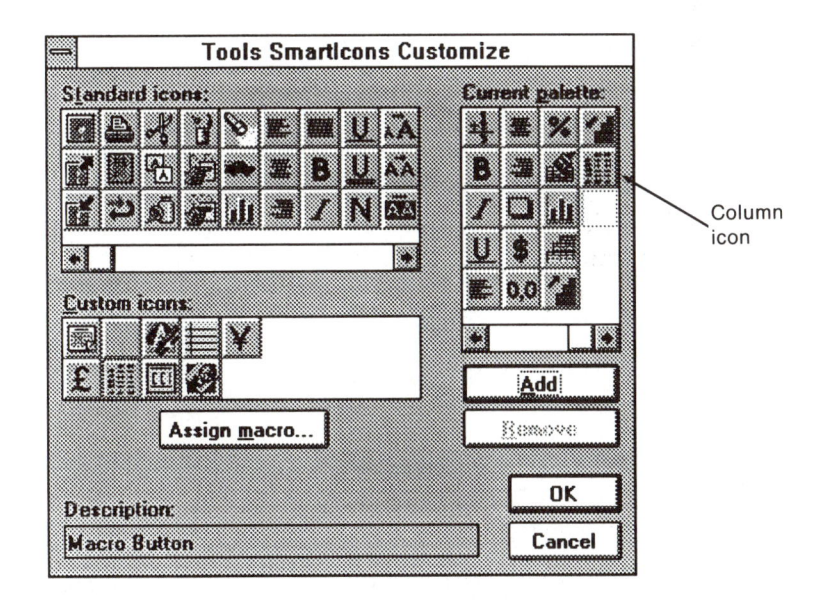

3. Click *OK* to close the Tools SmartIcons Customize dialog box.
4. Click *OK* again to close the Tools SmartIcons dialog box and return to your worksheet.

Changing the Position of the Icon Palette

Take a look at your icon palette. The *Column* icon should be there, but it's only partially visible at the right end of the palette. If we added another icon to the palette, it wouldn't show up on the screen at all.

Once you start adding icons to the palette, you have a couple of choices. You can delete an existing icon each time you add a new one, so that you always have the same number of icons. Or you can change the palette position to allow room for more icons.

For now, let's change the palette position so that all the icons are visible.

1. Select *SmartIcons* from the Tools menu.

The Palette position box in the Tools SmartIcons dialog box gives you several choices. The first four (*Left, Right, Top,* and *Bottom*) just place the palette in the indicated position on your screen. None of these choices allow you to display more icons.

The last option, *Floating,* turns the palette into a sizeable, free-floating window. With a floating palette window, you can display as many icons as you want.

2. Click on the *Floating* radio button.
3. Click *OK* to accept the selection and close the dialog box.

Your icon palette will disappear from its position under the Control Panel, and reappear as a window at the bottom of the screen.

You can move the palette anywhere on the screen by moving your pointer inside the window and dragging to a new position. You can also resize the window by grabbing any of the borders with your mouse and dragging to a new size.

Now for the big test. We've gone through a whole bunch of steps to assign our column macro to a SmartIcon. But does it work?

4. In cell D1, enter: **Going Native is expanding**

Notice that the text extends into column E. Let's widen column D to make the text fit.

5. Click on the *Column* icon.

Hey, it works! Column D is now widened to 20 characters. (Check to make sure your screen looks like Figure 7-11.)

Before we finish this lab, we'd better put the SmartIcon palette back the way we found it so the next student will be able to go through this exercise.

6. Choose *SmartIcons*... from the Tools menu.
7. Click on the *Customize*... button.

Chapter 7   Creating a Macro

Figure 7-11. Column D now appears 20 characters wide.

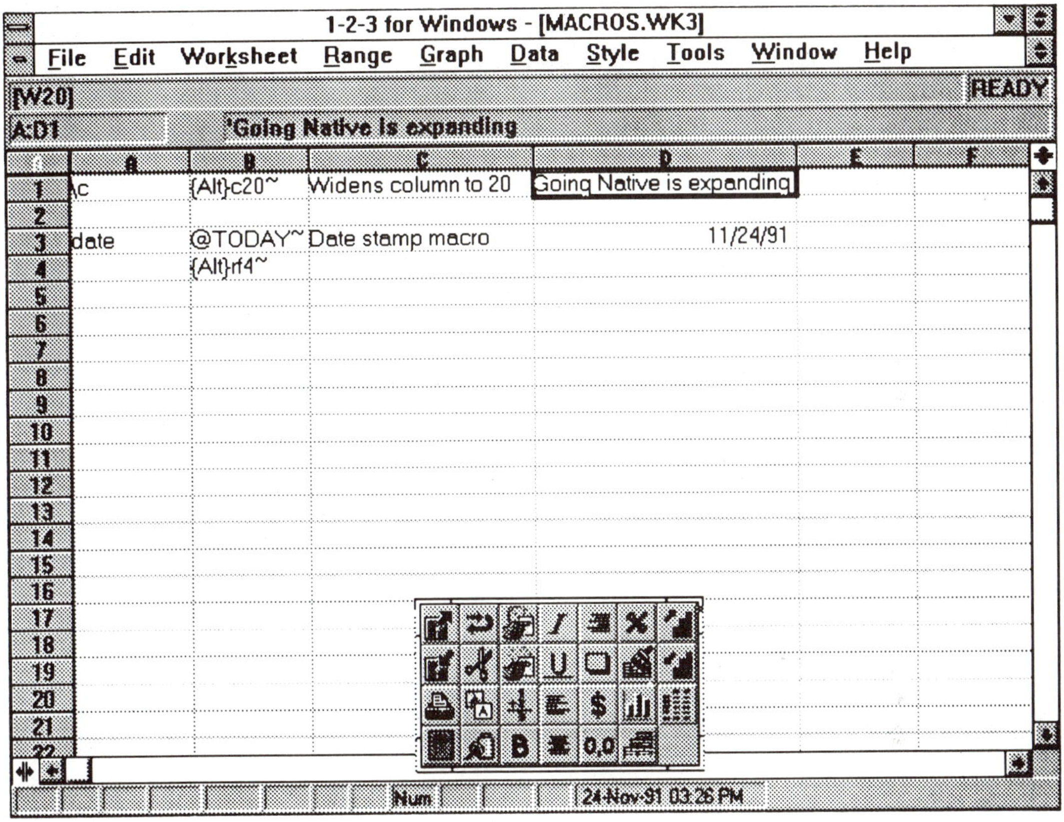

8. Click on the *Column* icon in the *Current palette* box in the Tools SmartIcons Customize dialog box.
9. Choose *Remove* to delete the icon from the current palette.
10. Click *OK* to close the dialog box.
11. Click on the *Top* radio button in the Tools SmartIcons dialog box and click *OK*.
12. Select the range A1..D4.
13. Change the header to: **Lab 7-2**
14. Save the file as **A:\MACROS**
15. Print the selected range.
16. Exit 1-2-3 if you're through for the present.

LAB 7-3   PAUSING A MACRO FOR INPUT

Well, this is all pretty terrific. But what if you wanted to widen a column to 15 instead of 20? You'd need another macro to do it. But wait—

maybe there's another way. Wouldn't it be nice to be able to insert a pause into the macro so that it would automatically activate the Column Width dialog box and then pause for you to enter a number? Of course it would. And you can. Read on.

1. Start Windows and launch 1-2-3 for Windows.
2. Maximize the worksheet.
3. Open the file A:\MACROS.
4. Highlight cell B1 (the cell that contains the data for the column-widening macro).
5. Replace the characters **20** with **{?}**

Your screen should match the one shown in Figure 7-12.

Figure 7-12. The command {?} will cause the macro to pause and prompt you for input.

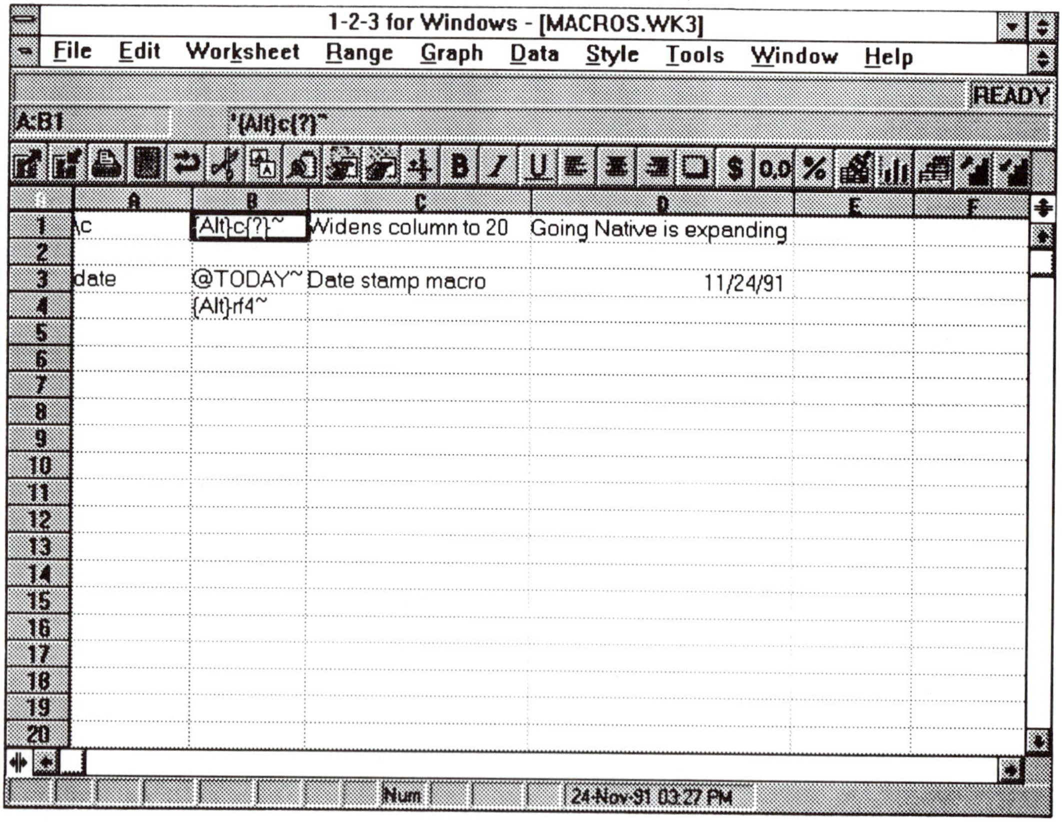

Very cryptic. A question mark in brackets? What does it do? The question mark is the macro symbol for a pause, and it's inserted in brackets to tell 1-2-3 that this is a macro command and not ordinary text.

When 1-2-3 sees {?} in a macro, it stops and says, "Wait a minute, I'm not doing another thing until you give me further instructions." While the macro is paused, you can enter data, move the cell pointer, make menu selections, or perform any other function. When you hit the Enter key, that's 1-2-3's cue that you're done with the pause and want to continue the macro.

Since we modified the macro, we should save and revise the description in column C to reflect the change.

6. Save the worksheet to protect your work.

Now let's try it out.

7. Select any cell in column E, and press Ctrl+C.

⊘ HAZARD

If you decide to stop a macro while it's running, DON'T click on *Cancel* in a dialog box or press the Escape key. Either of these actions could cause adverse, unpredictable responses.

Fortunately, 1-2-3 doesn't leave you in the lurch here. There is a safe way to stop a macro in its tracks. Just press Ctrl+Break. A dialog box will appear, asking you to confirm the action. Just click on *OK*, and you'll be out of the macro.

This is a good keystroke to remember. Particularly as you get into more complex macros, there may be times when it looks as if nothing's happening on your screen, and you can even forget that there's a macro in progress. If it seems like your screen's frozen, try pressing Ctrl+Break before you panic. (If that doesn't work, you have our permission to panic.)

The macro will select *Column Width...* from the Worksheet menu, and then pause with the Worksheet Column Width dialog box on the screen.

Since the current width selection is already highlighted, all you have to do is type in the number you want.

8. Type 15
9. Tap the Enter key.

In this case, hitting the Enter key simply causes the macro to continue. The macro goes on to the next step after the pause—the tilde. The tilde is the macro symbol for the Enter key, so the macro concludes by accepting your selection and closing the dialog box.

10. Finish up by changing the contents of cell C1 to read:
    Widen Column with Pause

And there you have it—a macro that widens a column to your specifications. This macro doesn't save us a whole lot of time, but are you beginning to see the possibilities? Almost any task that you perform in 1-2-3 can be streamlined through the use of macros.

11. Select the range A1..D4.
12. Change the header to: **Lab 7-3**
13. Save the worksheet again.
14. Print the selected range.
15. Exit 1-2-3 if you're not going right on to the exercises.

● HINT

It's possible to develop macros by recording commands and keystrokes as you perform them. 1-2-3 records all actions as they occur in the **Transcript window**, and these actions can be played back and inserted into macros without manually typing in the commands. For more information on this feature, choose *Macros* from the Help menu and click on *Using the Transcript Window*.

COMING ATTRACTIONS...

This chapter has given you the tools you need to begin wielding the power of 1-2-3 macros. Now all you need to do to become a macro expert is to experiment. Whenever you do something in 1-2-3, ask yourself whether it would make sense to turn it into a macro. (We're still trying to come up with a macro that will write our next book for us.)

Chapter 8 will put the force of 3-D into your hands. We'll show you how to work with multiple worksheets, files, and windows.

KEY TERMS

Macro A stored set of 1-2-3 actions that can be played back at any time.

Macro command A keystroke (e.g., Alt) or command (e.g., pause) surrounded by brackets { }.

Macro Name A set of characters (e.g., \c) used to invoke or start a macro running.

Tilde The character that represents the Enter key in a macro.

Transcript window 1-2-3 records all actions in this window. It can be used to collect and play back any 1-2-3 operation.

EXERCISES

7-1. This exercise provides a chance to practice the materials covered in Lab 7-1.

    a. Start Windows and 1-2-3, if necessary.

Let's write a macro that automatically changes the height of a row to 20. We'll start by planning the macro. This will involve stepping through the operation manually to see what keystrokes are needed.

    b. In a fresh worksheet, move to cell A5 and press the Alt key to activate the menu bar.
    c. To choose the drop-down Worksheet menu, press the letter **k**.
    d. Select *Row Height*...by pressing the letter **r**.
    e. Type **20** in the *Set Height to* text box.
    f. Tap the Enter key to complete the command and close the dialog box.

Now that you know the sequence of steps needed to perform the operation, we're ready to enter the keystrokes in your worksheet.

    g. Move to cell A:B1 and type: **{alt}kr20~**
    h. Name your macro **\r**
    i. Save your worksheet as **A:\EXER7-1**
    j. Test your macro on row 7 and then on row 8.
    k. Document your macro.
    l. Select the range A1..B10.
    m. Create a header with the title **Exercise 7-1** and a footer with your name, followed by the label: **1-2-3 for Windows**
    n. Save your worksheet again.
    o. Print the range.
    p. You may exit 1-2-3 and Windows.

7-2. The following instructions will give you the opportunity to review the materials presented in Lab 7-2. (You must have completed Exercise 7-1 to proceed with this exercise.)

    a. If necessary, start Windows and 1-2-3.
    b. Open the file A:\EXER7-1.

c. Change the macro so that it changes row height by 30 instead of 20 spaces.
d. Save the worksheet as **A:\EXER7-2**

We'll now create a SmartIcon to activate this macro.

e. Issue the *SmartIcons...* command from the Tools menu.
f. Click the *Customize...* button, select the icon with the three columns of squiggly lines in the *Custom* SmartIcons box, and then click the *Assign macro...* button.
g. Select the *Range* text box, type **B1**, click the *Get macro* button, and signal *OK*.
h. Click the *Column* icon in the *Custom icons* box, then select the *Add* button and *OK*.
i. Position the cell pointer in row 10 and use the new SmartIcon to increase the height of this row.
j. To remove the new SmartIcon, issue the *SmartIcon...* command from the Tools menu, select the *Customize...* button, click the *Column* icon in the *Current palette* box, and choose *Remove*.
k. Select the range A1..E12.
l. Change the header to: **Exercise 7-2**
m. Save the worksheet again.
n. Print the range.
o. You may exit 1-2-3 and Windows.

7-3. The steps in this exercise will review the concepts presented in Lab 7-3. (You must have completed Exercise 7-1 to do this exercise.)

a. If necessary, start Windows and 1-2-3.

We'll use the pause command {?} to write a macro that lets you decide how many spaces to increase the height of a row.

b. Open the file A:\EXER7-1
c. Highlight cell A:B1 (the cell that contains the data for the row height macro).
d. Replace the characters **20** with **{?}**
e. Save the worksheet as **A:\EXER7-3** to protect your work.
f. To change the height of row 15, select any cell in the row, and press Ctrl+R.
g. Then type **3** and tap the Enter key.
h. Change the documentation to reflect the new function of the macro.

i. Select the range A1..D16.
j. Change the header to: **Exercise 7-3**
k. Save the worksheet again.
l. Print the range.
m. You may exit 1-2-3 and Windows.

REVIEW QUESTIONS

True or False Questions

1. T F   A macro stores keystrokes or commands for later playback.
2. T F   A macro name is used to stop the execution of a macro.
3. T F   Planning a macro lets you minimize mistakes in writing a macro.
4. T F   A tilde tells 1-2-3 that a macro is ready to start.
5. T F   Before you can run a macro, it must be documented.
6. T F   The *Name* command from the Worksheet menu lets you name a macro.
7. T F   The macro {Alt}kr20˜ will widen a row by 20 spaces.
8. T F   You can assign a macro to a SmartIcon.
9. T F   A macro name can consist of a backslash and one of the letters of the alphabet.
10. T F You should save a macro only after testing it.

Multiple Choice Questions

1. A macro can be run (invoked) from a
   a. Descriptive name
   b. SmartIcon
   c. Backslash name
   d. All of the above

2. The steps in writing a simple macro are
   a. Planning, entering, naming, saving, testing, and documenting
   b. Planning, saving, entering, testing, documenting, and naming
   c. Planning, naming, entering, saving, testing, and documenting
   d. Planning, entering, naming, saving, testing, and recording
   e. None of the above

3. If you fail to place an apostrophe in front of the macro name \g
   a. The macro will immediately begin running
   b. The letter "g" will be repeated across the cell
   c. The macro will work improperly
   d. a and c

4. A macro can be used to
   a. Create custom menu choices
   b. Automate almost any worksheet activity
   c. Make "smart" decisions based on your responses to prompts
   d. a, b, and c
   e. None of the above

5. The macro command {D 3}
   a. Moves the cell pointer down three cells
   b. Moves the cell pointer directly to cell D3
   c. Does nothing
   d. Tells 1-2-3 the macro is finished

6. Which macro would increase the height of a row?
   a. {Alt}kr20~
   b. {Alt}kx20~
   c. {Alt}kc20~
   d. None of the above

7. Which is NOT a macro symbol standing for a 1-2-3 keystroke?
   a. {home}
   b. {pgup}
   c. {u}
   d. {o}

8. You document a macro to
   a. Protect your worksheet
   b. Provide the name and purpose of a macro
   c. Run a macro
   d. None of the above

9. You can change the position of the Icon Palette from the
   a. Tools SmartIcons dialog box
   b. Tools Palette Position dialog box
   c. *Preferences...* command in the File menu
   d. None of the above

10. Testing a simple macro involves
    a. Naming it
    b. Running it
    c. Documenting it
    d. Planning for problems
    e. None of the above

CHAPTER 8

Working with Multiple Worksheets and Files

• *Objectives*

Upon completing this chapter, you'll be able to:

1. **Create and navigate through multiple (3-D) worksheets.**
2. **Use multiple files.**
3. **Build formulas to link multiple worksheets and files.**

OVERVIEW

In this final chapter, we'll explore the power of using multiple worksheets and files to organize information and increase productivity. Using multiple worksheets and files allows you to protect and isolate separate portions of your data, and consolidate information from multiple sources.

UNDERSTANDING THREE-DIMENSIONAL WORKSHEETS

Three-dimensional worksheets is just an elaborate way of describing a feature that's really very simple and straightforward. All it means is that, with 1-2-3 for Windows, you have the ability to link multiple worksheets together in the same file.

The ability to link data across multiple worksheets opens up many interesting possibilities. For example, you could set up one worksheet to enter information, a second to perform calculations on the information, and a third to display the results of the calculations. Separating data in this fashion protects your formulas from damage during data entry or analysis.

1-2-3 also lets you link multiple worksheet files, and even retrieve multiple files into memory at the same time. Imagine that you wanted to combine information from several different worksheet files into a consolidated worksheet. Instead of performing endless cut and paste operations to move the data into a single file, you could link all the files together so that the required information simply appeared in the consolidated worksheet.

The possibilities for applying three-dimensional techniques to solve problems are almost endless. We hope the taste you get here will inspire you to explore further.

LAB 8-1 USING MULTIPLE WORKSHEETS

Rose wants to automate the check reconciliation process for Going Native. Each month, Rose receives a checking account statement from the bank that lists all checks written and deposits made and gives her an ending balance.

Of course, Rose has written checks and made deposits since the date the statement was issued. To reconcile her records with the bank statement, Rose must add the deposits made after the statement date to the ending balance shown on the statement to arrive at a new total. She must then subtract the checks written after the statement date from the new total to compute her *current* ending balance.

This figure is then compared to the ending balance in Rose's checkbook register. If they match, the reconciliation process is complete. However, when a discrepancy exists, Rose must find and correct the error(s) in her checkbook register.

Rose would like to develop a worksheet that automates as much of this process as possible. Since she plans to have her assistant enter the data, she decides to simplify the entry process by creating separate worksheets for gathering the checking account information, performing the necessary calculations, and displaying the results.

1. Start Windows and launch 1-2-3 if it is not already running.

The first worksheet we'll prepare is the input form. The input form is where Rose, or her assistant, will input (enter) the check numbers and dollar amounts as they are written. This input form will be a very simple worksheet with no formulas, since we don't want to give her sometimes clumsy assistant the opportunity to mess things up.

2. Maximize the worksheet.
3. In cell A1, enter: **Checkbook Reconciliation Input Form**

Let's make the worksheet title larger so we can easily distinguish it from the other sheets we'll be creating.

4. With the cell pointer on A1, select *Font...* from the Style menu and double-click on *Arial MT 14*.
5. In cell A4, type: **Outstanding Checks:**
6. In cell A6, enter: **Check #**
7. In cell B6, enter: **Amount**
8. In cell D4, enter: **Bank Statement Balance**

Oops! The text in column D is spilling over into column E. What to do? Hey, you know the answer to that.

9. Widen column D to 20.
10. In cell D6, enter: **Checkbook Balance**
11. In cell D8, enter: **Outstanding Deposits**

Let's format the Check # and Amount cells as right aligned.

12. Select the range A6..B6.
13. Choose *Alignment...* from the Style menu.
14. Click in the *Right* radio button in the Align label area of the Style Alignment dialog box and click *OK*.

Let's format the ranges where we'll be entering account data as currency.

15. Format the range B7..B40 as currency by clicking on the *$* SmartIcon.
16. Format the range E4..E30 as currency.

We'll add the numbers for a few of the checks, deposits, and balances so you'll be able to see how everything works.

17. In cell A7, type the check number: **112**
18. In cell B7, type the check amount: **345**
19. In cell A8, enter: **114**
20. In cell B8, enter: **23**
21. In cell A9, enter: **118**
22. In cell B9, enter: **123**
23. In cell E4, type the bank statement balance: **760**
24. In cell E6, type the checkbook balance: **2200**
25. In cell E8, type the first outstanding deposit: **456**
26. In cell E9, type the second outstanding deposit: **25**
27. In cell E10, type the final outstanding deposit: **600**

That completes the data entry for this worksheet. Your screen should now look like the one shown in Figure 8-1.

Figure 8-1. The checkbook reconciliation input form.

```
1-2-3 for Windows - [CHECKREC.WK3]
File  Edit  Worksheet  Range  Graph  Data  Style  Tools  Window  Help
                                                                    READY
A:A6           "Check #
```

	A	B	C	D	E
1	Checkbook Reconciliation Input Form				
4	Outstanding Checks:			Bank Statement Balance	$760.00
6	Check #	Amount		Checkbook Balance	$2,200.00
7	112	$345.00			
8	114	$23.00		Outstanding Deposits	$456.00
9	118	$123.00			$25.00
10					$600.00

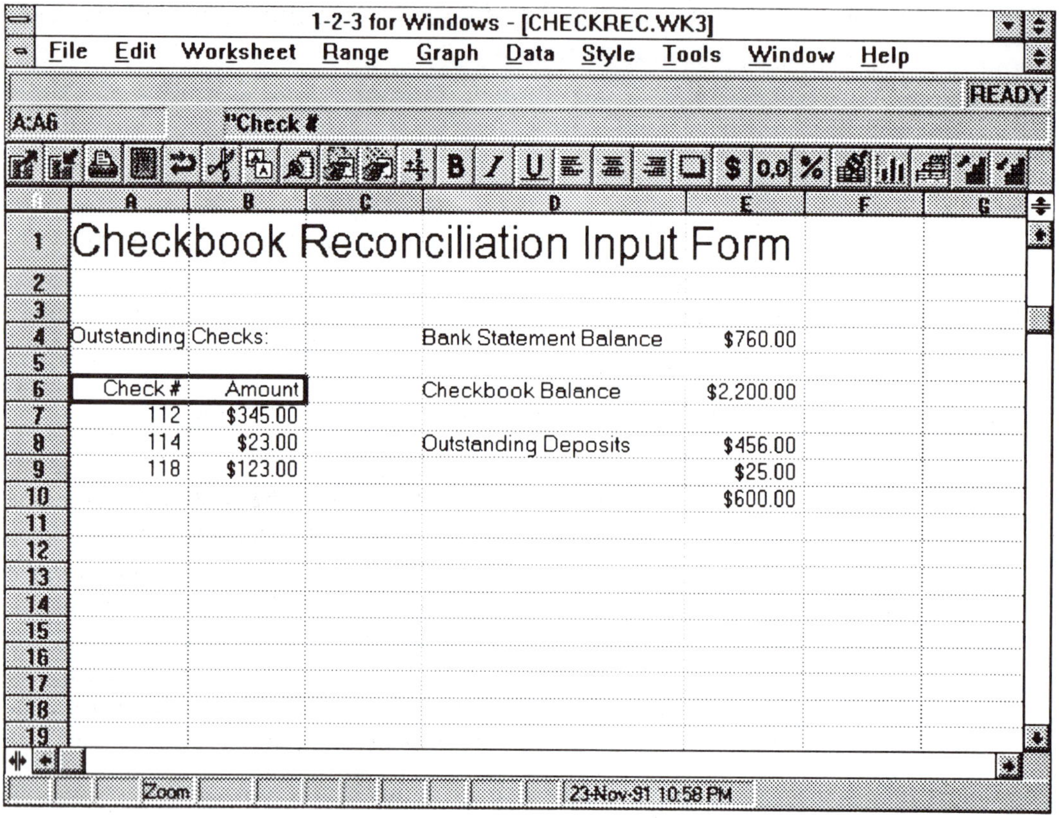

28. Save the file using the *Save As...* option from the File menu, and assign it the name **A:\CHECKREC**

Adding Worksheets

You insert an additional worksheet in a file pretty much the same way you insert a row or column. You begin by selecting the *Insert...* command from the Worksheet menu. Once the Worksheet Insert dialog box appears, as illustrated in Figure 8-2, select the *Sheet* button. Then choose where you want to place the new worksheet (before or after the current worksheet) and specify the number of worksheets you want to add (1-2-3 allows a maximum of 256 worksheets per file, but you're also limited by the amount of memory you have in your computer).

Figure 8-2.

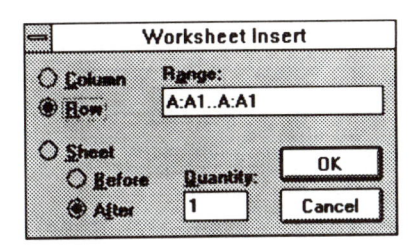

We need to insert two new worksheets into the file created earlier. One will hold the formulas for reconciling the bank statement, and the other will present the results of the computations.

1. Select the *Insert...* command from the Worksheet menu.
2. Click in the *Sheet* radio button to let 1-2-3 know that we want to insert new worksheets and not just rows or columns.
3. Enter 2 in the *Quantity* text box.

The *After* radio button is the default selection for placement of the new worksheets. Since that's what we want, we'll just leave it checked. Don't worry about the *Range* text box; you only need to specify a range if you're inserting columns or rows, not when you're inserting entire worksheets.

4. Click on *OK*.

1-2-3 presents you with a blank worksheet, the first of the two new sheets we just added. The Control Panel lets you know that this is worksheet B because the current cell address is B:A1. We can also tell we're in sheet B by looking at the letter in the upper left corner of the worksheet frame.

The first worksheet in our group isn't gone, it's just not the active worksheet right now. There are several ways of moving between multiple worksheets, which we'll explore in just a moment. But for now, we could use a change in perspective—how about you?

Gaining a New Perspective

You can view three consecutive worksheets in a file at the same time by issuing the *Split* command from the Window menu, choosing the **Perspective** check box, and clicking *OK*.

Figure 8-3.

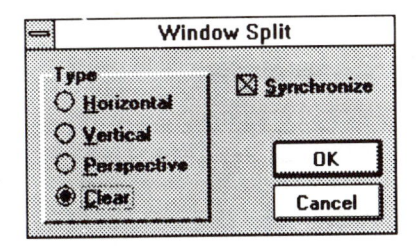

Let's use Perspective mode so that we can easily work with all three of our worksheets at once.

1. Choose *Split...* from the Window menu.

The Window Split dialog box will appear as shown in Figure 8-3.

The *Synchronize* box is already checked. This means that any scrolling operation you perform while in Perspective view will affect all of the currently visible worksheets. When Synchronize is on, you will always be able to see the same row and column area in each worksheet.

Synchronize will work fine for this lab, so just leave it checked.

NOTE

The Window Split dialog box also allows you to split individual worksheets vertically or horizontally so you can view nonadjacent segments on the screen simultaneously.

2. Click in the *Perspective* radio button and then click on *OK*.

Your screen will look like Figure 8-4, with the first worksheet, worksheet A, in front and at the bottom.

Figure 8-4. The Perspective mode arranges the open worksheets in a cascading order within the workspace.

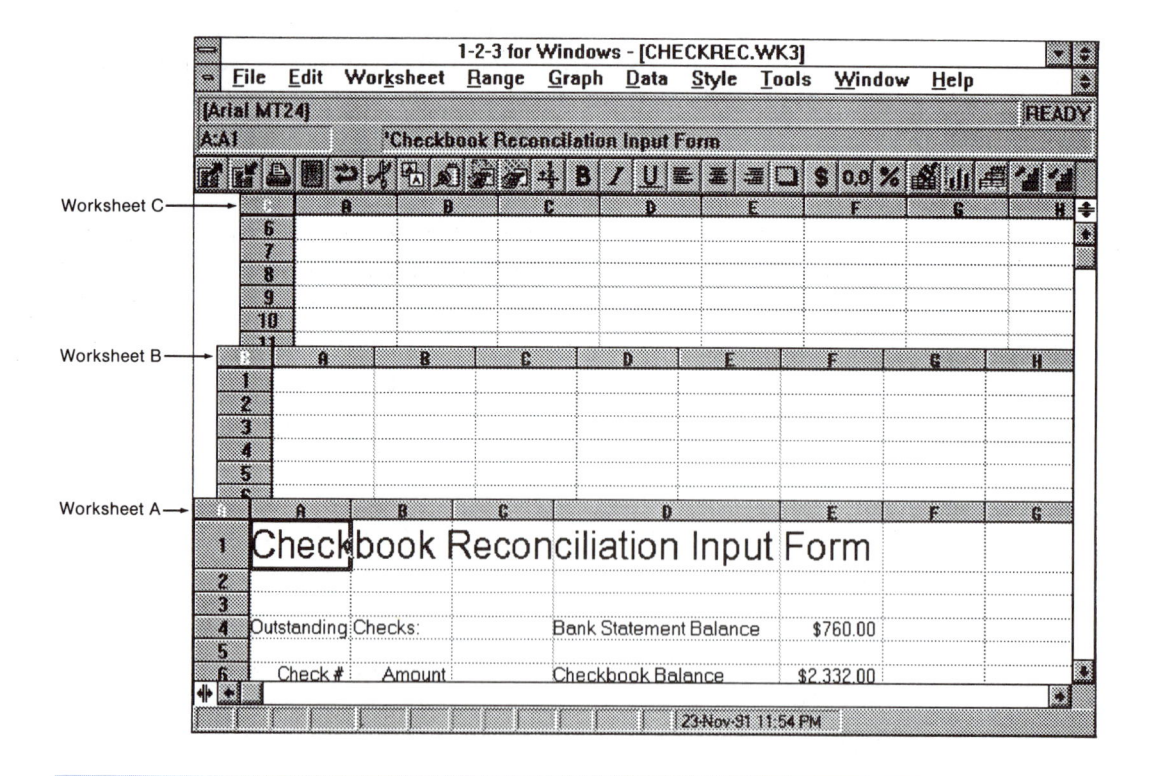

As we mentioned earlier, you can tell which worksheet you are in from the cell address in the Control Panel and the letter in the upper left corner of the worksheet frame.

Moving among Worksheets

The easiest way to navigate among worksheets while in the Perspective mode is to simply click on the worksheet you want active.

1. Click anywhere in worksheet A.
2. Make worksheet B current by clicking on it.
3. Go to worksheet C by clicking on it.
4. Click on worksheet A again to make it active.

When you move from sheet A to sheet B, you are *moving up*. Going from sheet B to sheet C is also moving up, while traveling in the opposite direction is referred to as *moving down*.

• HINT

The Perspective mode helps you visualize the direction you are moving as you go from one worksheet to the next. Understanding this concept will help you remember which SmartIcons to click, or which keys to press to move between worksheets.

There are two SmartIcons especially designed for moving between worksheets. The first is called *Next Worksheet*. It's located second from the right on the Icon Palette and looks like a staircase with an arrow pointing up. Clicking the *Next Worksheet* icon moves you up one worksheet at a time.

5. To move to worksheet B, click on the *Next Worksheet* icon.
6. To activate worksheet C, click *Next Worksheet* again.

The other SmartIcon is *Previous Worksheet*. It's the first icon from the right and also looks like a staircase, but with the arrow pointing down.

7. To move back to worksheet B, click on the *Previous Worksheet* SmartIcon.
8. Click on the *Previous Worksheet* SmartIcon again to move all the way back to worksheet A.

While the clicking method, along with the *Next Worksheet* and *Previous Worksheet* SmartIcons, is often the most efficient way of moving between the different worksheets, there are several keyboard alternatives for moving around worksheets. Table 8-1 shows some of the keystrokes you can use for worksheet navigation.

Table 8-1. Worksheet navigation keystrokes.

F6	Cycle through sheets.
Alt+F6	Maximize current sheet (**Zoom**). Press Zoom again to restore.
Ctrl+PgUp	Move up one sheet.
Ctrl+PgDn	Move down one sheet.
Ctrl+Home	Home position of first sheet.

9. Practice moving around in your worksheets using the keystrokes in Table 8-1.

NOTE

1-2-3 often refers to both worksheets and files as (window) **panes**. In fact, there is a pane function key (F6) that moves the cell pointer between windows (or panes).

Linking Worksheets with Formulas

Next, we'll create a worksheet to total the information from our input form. This will require building a formula in one worksheet that references a range in another. Sounds tricky, but with 1-2-3, it's a breeze.

Before we get to the formulas, we'll enter worksheet labels.

1. Move to worksheet B and Zoom in (Alt+F6).
2. In cell B:A1, enter **Checkbook Reconciliation Processing Form**
3. With the cell pointer on B:A1, select *Font...* from the Style menu and double-click on *Arial MT 14*.
4. Widen Column B to **20**.
5. In cell B:B4, enter: **+A:D4**

Wow! All we had to do was type a worksheet/cell address, and we duplicated the label from the first worksheet. Now that can save us some serious typing.

6. In B:B6, enter: **Total Outstanding Deposits**
7. In B:B8, type: **Subtotal**
8. In B:B10, type: **Total Outstanding Checks**
9. In B:B12, enter: **Adjusted Ending Balance**
10. In B:B14, enter: **+A:D6**
11. In B:B16, enter: **Discrepancy (if any)**

At this stage, your worksheet B should match the one shown in Figure 8–5.

Figure 8–5. Worksheet B with the labels entered for the checkbook reconciliation processing form.

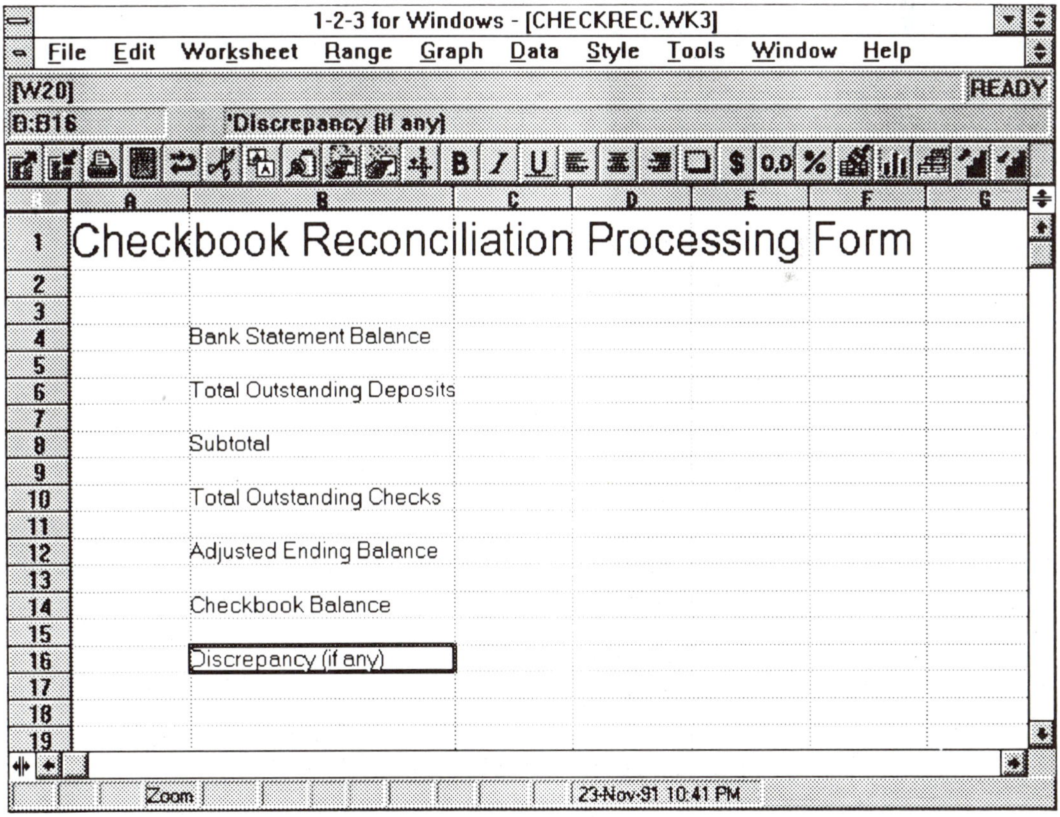

We've entered a couple of labels by typing in worksheet and cell references. But sometimes it's even easier to reference ranges in another worksheet by just pointing to them. "Okay," you're thinking, "I can't even see the other worksheet, so how can I point to it?" Oh come now.

Do you think we would have suggested pointing if you couldn't do it? Of course not.

The best way to see both worksheets at once is (you guessed it) the Perspective view we used earlier. Last time, we selected the Perspective view by choosing *Split...* from the Window menu. As usual, there's a shortcut: one of those ever-so-handy SmartIcons.

12. Click on the *Perspective view* SmartIcon, the one that looks like three worksheets, located third from the right on the Icon Palette.

Notice that the visible area is nearly the same for all three worksheets, starting with row 12 and ending with row 16 for worksheets B and C and row 18 for worksheet A.

13. Using the scroll bar or the cursor movement keys, scroll up through the worksheets until rows 4–8 are visible in all the sheets.
14. Click in cell B:C4 and type: **+**

Now we can reference a cell in worksheet A by simply pointing to it. What could be easier?

15. Click on cell A:E4.

The Contents box in the Control Panel indicates the range +A:E4..A:E4, which is where the Bank Statement Balances will be entered on our input form.

16. Press the Enter key.

The value from A:E4 will appear in cell B:C4.

Now the fun begins. We're going to place a function in worksheet B that references a range in worksheet A. We'll use the @SUM function to add up the outstanding deposits.

17. Click in B:C6 and type: **@SUM(**
18. Point at cell A:E8, hold down the left mouse button, drag the pointer down to A:E19, and release the button.
19. Finish the function by typing **)** and pressing Enter.

The sum of the values from cells A:E8 through A:E19 will appear in cell B:C6.

20. In B:C8, enter: **+C4+C6** to add the bank statement balance to the total outstanding deposits.

Now we'll add an @SUM function to total the outstanding checks. Again, we'll assume a limited number of checks will be outstanding.

Chapter 8 Working with Multiple Worksheets and Files **273**

21. Make sure that rows 7 through 10 are visible in all sheets.
22. Click in cell B:C10 and enter: **@SUM(**
23. Point to A:B7 and drag down to A:B19. Release the mouse.
24. Type **)** and press Enter.
25. Scroll down until B:C12 is visible and click on it.
26. Type **+C8+C10** and press Enter.
27. To reference the checkbook balance in worksheet A, move to B:C14, and enter: **+A:E6**
28. To compare the adjusted ending balance with the checkbook balance, move to B:C16, enter: **+C12−C14**, and press Enter.
29. To provide a better view, press Alt+F6 to zoom in on worksheet B.
30. Format the range B:C4..B:C16 as currency.

All right! That takes care of that worksheet. (Check your screen against the one displayed in Figure 8-6.) All that's left is to set up our last sheet so that Rose can quickly see just the relevant numbers.

Figure 8-6. Worksheet B with the sheet-linking formulas entered.

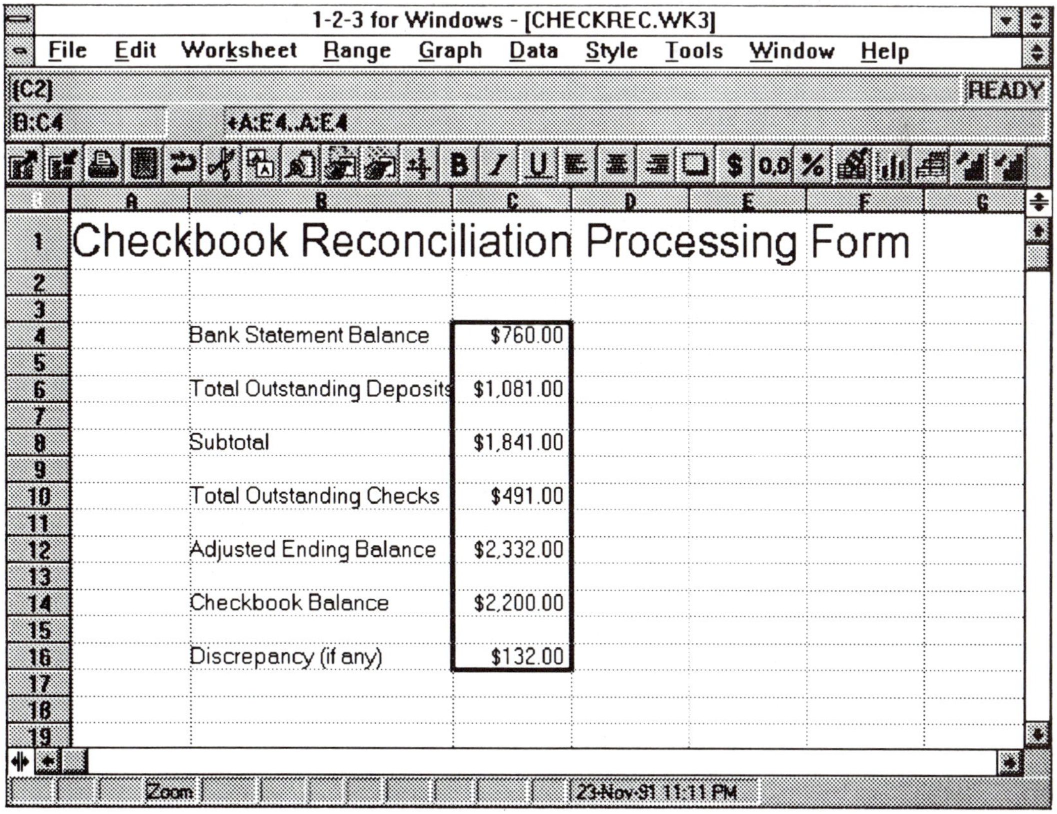

	B	C
1	Checkbook Reconciliation Processing Form	
4	Bank Statement Balance	$760.00
6	Total Outstanding Deposits	$1,081.00
8	Subtotal	$1,841.00
10	Total Outstanding Checks	$491.00
12	Adjusted Ending Balance	$2,332.00
14	Checkbook Balance	$2,200.00
16	Discrepancy (if any)	$132.00

31. Click the *Next Worksheet* icon to move to sheet C, then press the Home key to move to cell C:A1.
32. In cell C:A1, enter: **Checkbook Reconciliation Output Form**
33. With the cell pointer on C:A1, select *Font...* from the Style menu and double-click on *Arial MT 14*.
34. In cell C:B4, enter: **Adjusted Ending Balance**
35. In cell C:B6, enter: **Checkbook Balance**
36. In cell C:B8, enter: **Discrepancy (if any)**
37. Widen column B to **20**.

The following instructions will cause the totals computed in worksheet B to appear in sheet C.

38. In cell C:C4, enter: **+B:C12**
39. In cell C:C6, enter: **+B:C14**
40. In cell C:C8, enter: **+B:C16**
41. Format the range C:C4..C:C8 as currency.

Figure 8-7 shows the completed output form. As you can see, it appears that Rose has a $132 error somewhere in her checkbook register. After checking the register, she finds a subtraction error that changes the checkbook balance to $2332.

Let's correct the checkbook balance in sheet A and see if the discrepancy disappears.

42. Click the *Previous Worksheet* icon twice to go to sheet A.
43. Change the contents in cell A:E6 to **2332**
44. Select the *Perspective view* icon.
45. Scroll down to expose the discrepancy figure in sheet C.

Hurrah! The discrepancy is gone. The reconciliation process is complete.

46. Press Ctrl+Home to move to cell A:A1.

There you have it. Three worksheets, easily created and linked to each other. The screen should look like the one shown in Figure 8-8.

There is one problem with Perspective view, though. We've got all three worksheets on the screen, but we can't see a very large portion of any of them. But of course 1-2-3 gives us a neat trick that allows us to display more information on the screen at once.

47. Select *Display Options...* from the Window menu.

Figure 8-7. The finished checkbook reconciliation output form.

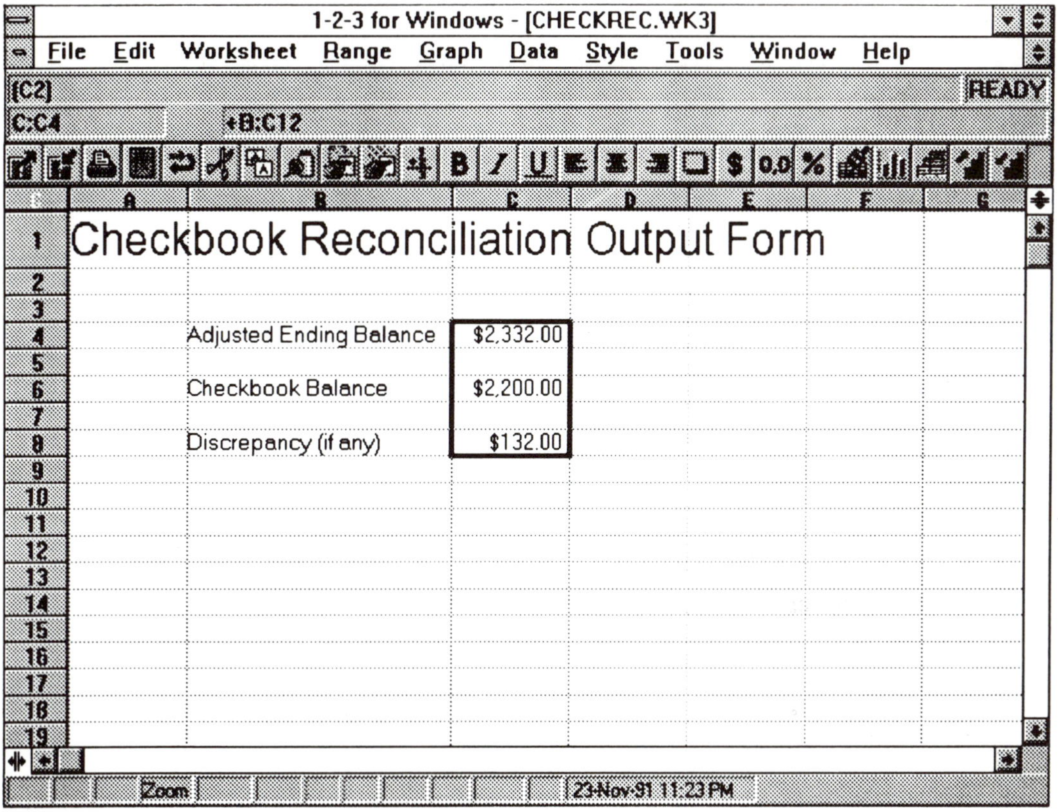

The Window Display Options dialog box will appear, as shown in Figure 8-9. By reducing the Zoom percentage, we can squeeze more information into the same amount of space.

48. Select the contents of the *Zoom* text box.
49. Type **50** to reduce the Zoom to 50% and click on *OK*.

The screen displays more rows by compressing the data, as shown in Figure 8-10. Zoom is handy when you want to get an overall view, but it's not very useful for actual data entry. Okay, there's more information on the screen, but we can't read it (or at least the old fogies who wrote this book can't read it—maybe you can). For our sake, let's return the Zoom to its original percentage.

50. Select *Display Options...* from the Window menu.
51. Select the contents of the *Zoom* text box, enter **87**, and click on *OK*.

Figure 8–8. Three worksheets linked together in Perspective mode.

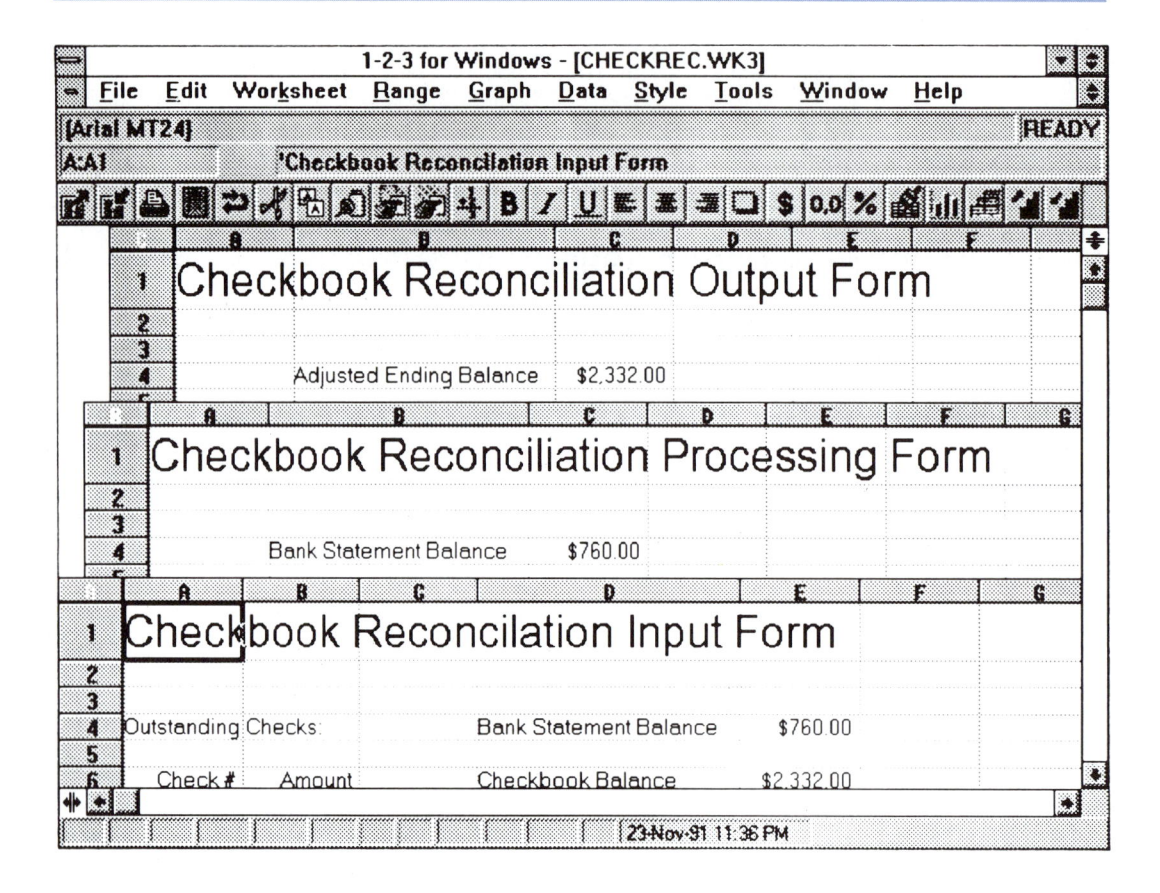

Ah, that's better.

• **HINT**

When working in Perspective view, you may find it easier to move around in the worksheets if Synchronize is turned off. This can be accomplished by choosing *Split...* from the Window menu, clicking the *Synchronize* check box so it's not checked, and then clicking *OK*.

You can now move anywhere in one of the worksheets without affecting the position of the others.

Figure 8-9.
The Window Display Options dialog box lets you zoom out to get an overview of the contents of a worksheet.

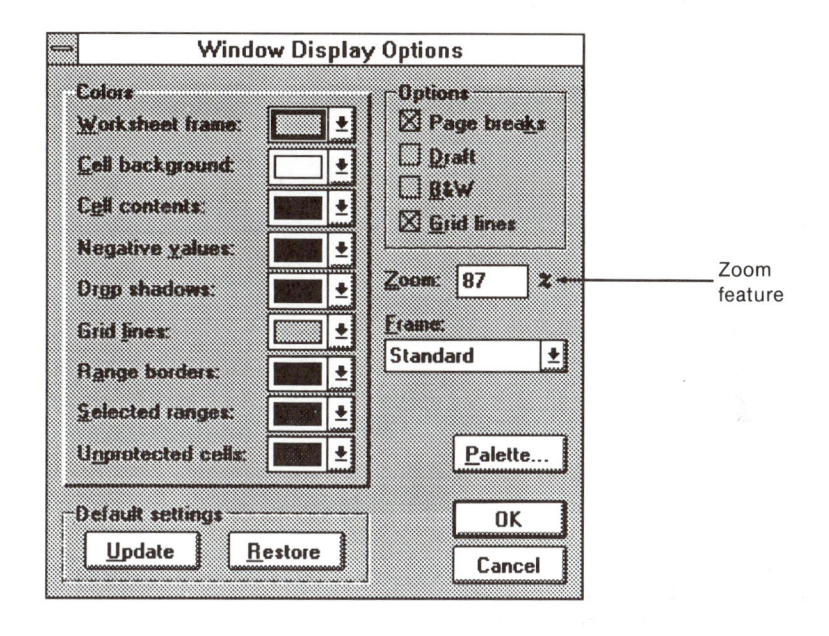

— Zoom feature

NOTE

There will be times when you are no longer in need of one or more of the multiple worksheets you've created. You can delete a worksheet from a file by moving to that sheet and selecting *Delete...* from the Worksheet menu. Click in the *Sheet* radio button and click on *OK*.

Printing a Group of Worksheets

Printing a group of worksheets is just like printing single worksheets, except that the print range encompasses all the sheets you want to print.

1. Press Ctrl+Home to move to the first cell in the first worksheet: A:A1.

Figure 8-10. Zoom displays more rows and columns in the Perspective mode.

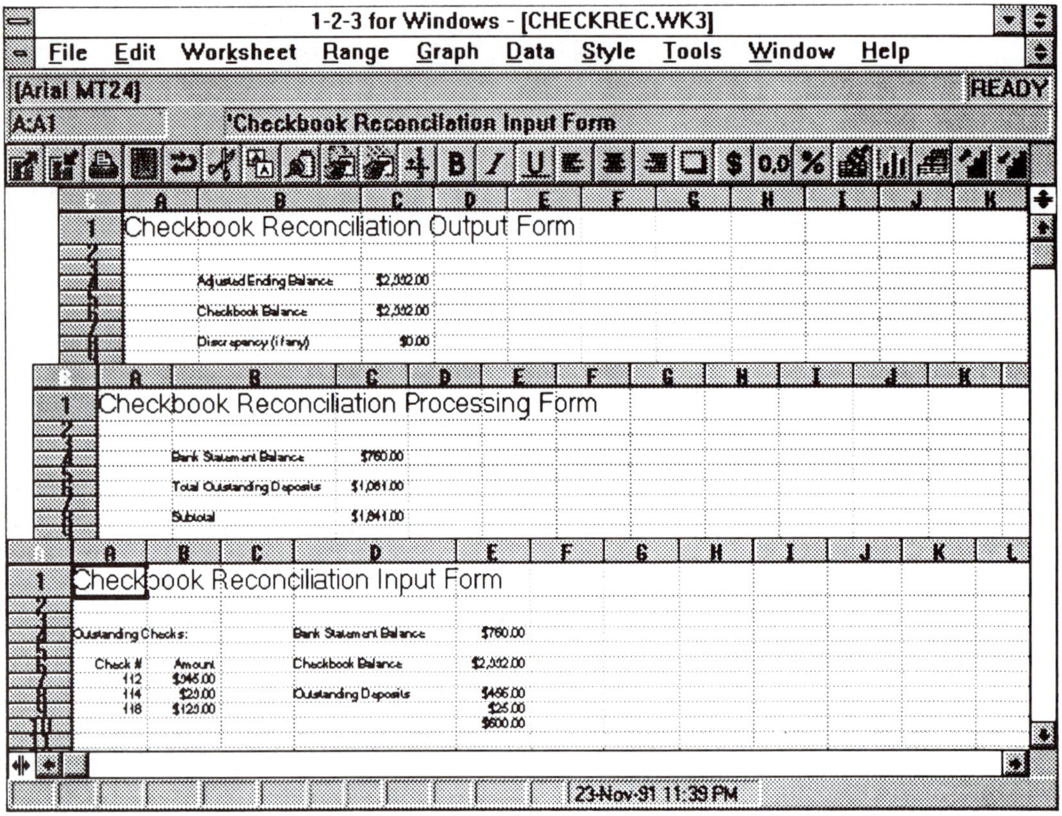

We'll use keystrokes to select the entire active range for all of the worksheets, starting with A:A1. We can't just press a period here because that would make 1-2-3 think we were about to enter a value. Fortunately, the F4 (ABS) key can be used to anchor a range at any point.

2. Press the F4 (ABS) key to anchor the range.
3. Press End and Ctrl+Home again to extend the selection to the last active cell in the worksheets.
4. Press Enter to accept the range.
5. Create a header with the title **Lab 8-1** and a footer with your name, followed by the label: **1-2-3 for Windows**
6. Save the worksheets.
7. Print the selected range.
8. Exit 1-2-3 if you're not going to proceed to the next lab.

LAB 8-2 USING MULTIPLE WORKSHEET FILES

There will be times when you'll need to consolidate information from several different worksheet files. This lab will show you how to join data from several worksheet files into a single file.

You'll learn to create **file-linking formulas** that merge the information from multiple files into one single consolidated file. You'll also discover how to "refresh" these links when changes are made to the files.

Creating the Worksheet Files

Get ready to use your imagination. Let's say that ten years have passed, and Going Native has expanded operations into two other cities. The original location and the two branches are all thriving.

In fact, things are going so well that Rose has instituted a quarterly revenue report to track the fast-paced progress of all three locations. It works like this—each location submits a separate report detailing consulting activity for the previous quarter. The information from each city is manually transferred to a consolidated revenue report that provides grand totals for the entire operation.

Rose wants to streamline the process by creating a separate file for each location and a master file to automatically consolidate all this information. Each location will send her an updated file. Information from these files will then be linked to form the consolidated report.

Let's begin by creating a **template**, which is just a blank worksheet with labels and formulas, that we can use for all three operations as well as the consolidated report form.

• HINT

Using a template to create the files you plan to link insures a uniform structure for each worksheet. As you will soon see, working with identical worksheet files greatly simplifies the process of building multifile formulas.

1. Start Windows and 1-2-3, if necessary.
2. Maximize the worksheet.
3. In cell A1, enter: **Going Native Revenue Report - Master**
4. Select *Font...* from the Style menu and double-click on *Arial MT 24*.

We'll enter month and quarter headings in cells B3 through E3 and center the text within the cells.

5. In cell B3, enter: **January**
6. In cell C3, enter: **February**
7. In cell D3, enter: **March**
8. In cell E3, enter: **Qtr. Totals**
9. Format the range B3..E3 for center alignment.

Next, we'll enter labels for the income categories in column A.

10. In cell A5, enter: **Professional Fees**
11. In cell A6, enter: **Miscellaneous Income**
12. In cell A8, enter: **Monthly Totals**
13. Widen column A so all the labels fit (18 should do it).

Since cells B5 through E8 will contain numerical data, we'll format them for currency.

14. Format the range B5..E8 as currency.

Row 8 will contain the formulas for monthly and quarterly totals.

15. In cell B8, enter the formula: **+B5+B6**
16. Copy the formula to the range C8..E8.

Column E will show the quarterly totals for each category.

17. In cell E5, enter the formula **@SUM(B5..D5)** and copy the formula down to cell E6.
18. Save the file as **A:\REVRPT**

That's the master template. We'll need to modify it just a bit, but it's got most of the formulas and formats that we'll need in each file. Your screen should look like the one pictured in Figure 8-11.

To create files for the three locations, we'll simply use the *Save As...* command to save the master file using three other names. We'll input the numbers for the three locations as we go.

19. In cell A1, edit the label to read:
    Going Native Revenue Report - Spokane
20. In B5, enter: **5600**
21. In C5, enter: **4760**

Figure 8–11. The master template.

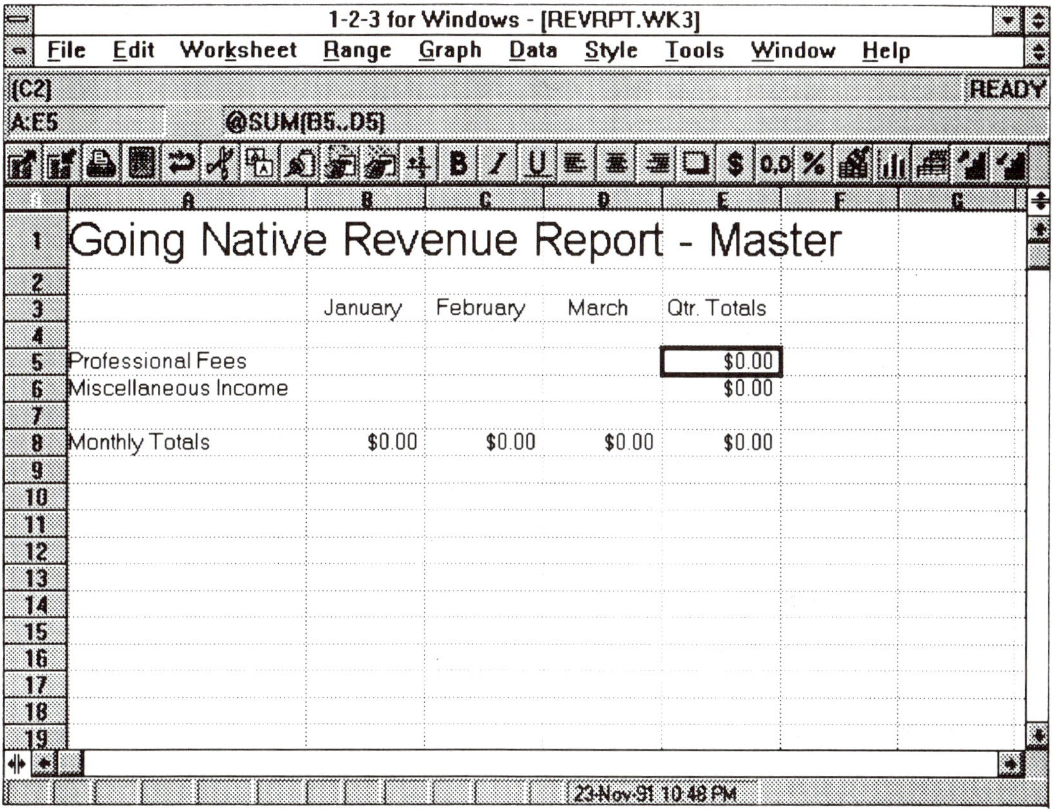
1-2-3 for Windows - [REVRPT.WK3]
File Edit Worksheet Range Graph Data Style Tools Window Help
(C2)
READY
A:E5
@SUM(B5..D5)
Going Native Revenue Report - Master
January
February
March
Qtr. Totals
Professional Fees
$0.00
Miscellaneous Income
$0.00
Monthly Totals
$0.00
$0.00
$0.00
$0.00
23-Nov-91 10:48 PM

22. In D5, enter: **6080**
23. In B6, enter: **625**
24. In C6, enter: **385**
25. In D6, enter: **740**
26. Select *Save As...* from the File menu and enter: **A\REVSPO** as the file name (for the original location in Spokane).

That gives us the first file. All we had to do was add the location-specific data to the template and save it with a different name. We just need to repeat the process two more times for the other locations.

27. Edit the label in A1 again to read:
    Going Native Revenue Report - Cheney
28. In B5, enter: **3890**
29. In C5, enter: **4620**

30. In D5, enter: **5430**
31. In B6, enter: **280**
32. In C6, enter: **575**
33. In D6, enter: **380**
34. Choose *Save As…* again and enter **A:\REVCHE** for the Cheney branch.
35. In cell A1, edit the label to read:
    Going Native Revenue Report - Coeur d'Alene
36. In B5, enter: **4840**
37. In C5, enter: **7420**
38. In D5, enter: **6100**
39. In B6, enter: **670**
40. In C6, enter: **435**
41. In D6, enter: **845**
42. Choose *Save As…* again and enter **A:\REVCDA** for the Coeur d'Alene branch.

Opening Additional Worksheet Files

All four files are now created, but only REVCDA is currently open. All four files need to be in the computer's memory if we're going to work with all of them at once.

1. Select *Open…* from the File menu and enter: **A:\REVRPT**
2. Open the file A:\REVCHE.
3. Open the file A:\REVSPO.

Whew, that was tough. Seriously, though, that's all there is to having multiple files open at the same time.

Moving among Active Files

Okay, all four files are open, but where are they? We need a way to move between them. Well, as usual, 1-2-3 gives you some options. You can move between open files just the same way you move between multiple worksheets, by using the Ctrl+PgUp and Ctrl+PgDn keystroke combinations. You can also cycle through all currently open files using Ctrl+F6.

> **NOTE**
>
> Ctrl+F6 cycles through *all* open 1-2-3 graph and transcript windows, not just worksheet files. If you have any graph or transcript windows open, Ctrl+F6 will move in sequence through those as well as any worksheets in memory.

Chapter 8 *Working with Multiple Worksheets and Files* **283**

Let's cycle through all the files just to make sure they're all there. (*We* know they're there, but we want you to see for yourself.)

1. Press Ctrl+F6 as many times as necessary to see all four files. End up with REVSPO in view.

All four files are open, and we can easily move between them and work with any one of the files. But in order to tap the full power of multiple files, we need to be able to see all of them at the same time. We can do this by using the **Tile** command from the Window menu. When you choose the Tile command, all open files become visible. The more open files you have, the smaller each tile will be.

2. Choose *Tile* from the Window menu.

Your screen should look something like Figure 8-12.

Figure 8-12. Tiling worksheet files lets you view a portion of all of them simultaneously.

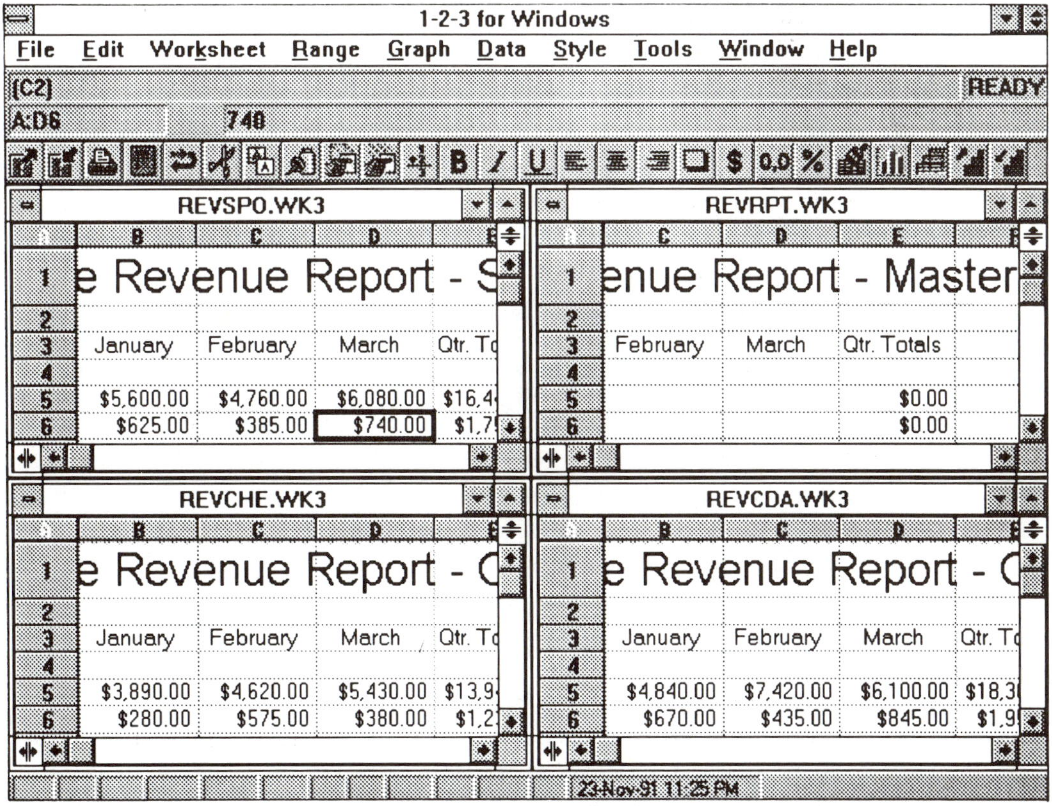

When the windows are tiled, you can still use Ctrl+PgUp, Ctrl+PgDn, and Ctrl+F6 to navigate between files. But now that they're all in view, you have yet another option. You can just click in any visible file to make it the current one.

3. Cycle through the files using any of the methods mentioned above.

Keeping the files tiled will make it easier to implement our file-linking formulas. Each file is in its own window and can be scrolled independently.

Linking Files with Formulas

Linking worksheets that are in different files is much like linking multiple worksheets within a file, except that, in addition to a range reference, a file reference is also required. A **file reference** must contain the name of the file being referenced so that 1-2-3 knows where to look. It's a good idea to include the full path (the drive and directory as well as the file name) to insure that 1-2-3 will always be able to access the reference.

A file reference begins with two "less than" symbols, "<<," and ends with a pair of "greater than" symbols, ">>." The syntax (or format) for the reference is <<drive\directory\file>>. For example, in the file reference <<C:\123W\FILE.WK3>>, C: is the drive, 123W is the directory, and FILE.WK3 is the file name.

If ranges in several files are being referenced, the amount of typing required can easily get out of hand. Since we want to avoid excessive typing at all costs, we'll use the pointing method to link our four files.

1. Click in the REVRPT window and scroll through it so that A3 through B8 are visible. Make sure that cell B5 is visible in all of the other files.

⊘ HAZARD

Make sure that the cells you will be referencing are visible before you begin a file-linking formula. You can't scroll through a file while you're in the middle of entering a formula, so if the cell you want to reference is not visible, you won't be able to point to it. You can still reference a nonvisible cell, but you'll have to type in the entire range address.

2. In cell B5 of the REVRPT file, type: **@SUM(**

Chapter 8 Working with Multiple Worksheets and Files

Since this file will be a consolidation of the figures for all three locations, we need a formula that will total the data from cell B5 in the other three files.

3. Click in B5 of the REVSPO file.

The first part of the file-linking formula is displayed in the contents box, as shown in Figure 8-13.

Figure 8-13. The contents box displays the first part of a file-linking formula.

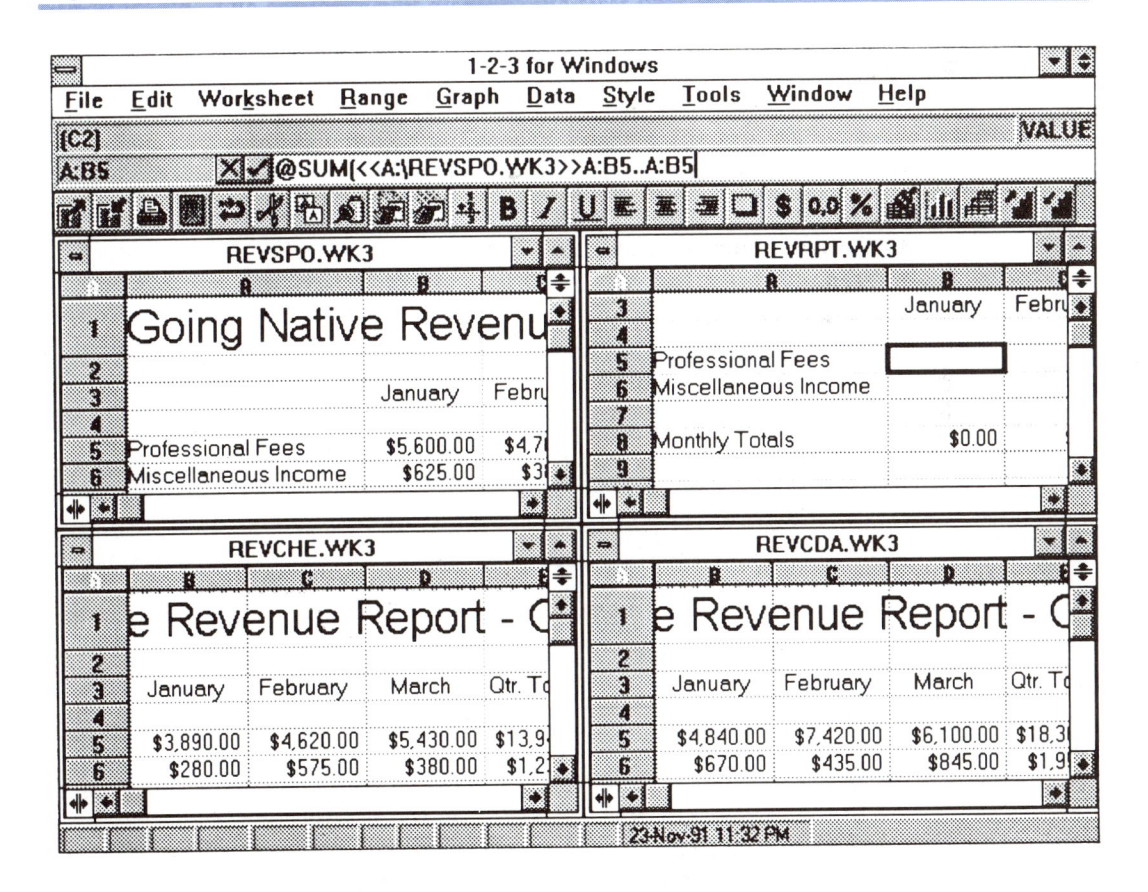

4. Press + to continue the formula, and then click in cell B5 of the REVCHE file to add it to the reference.
5. Press + and click in cell B5 of the REVCDA file.
6. Press) to end the formula, and press the Enter key.

Is that slick or what? The results of our file-linking formula are instantly calculated. And to make it even slicker, we can perform the rest of the links just by copying the formula we've already created.

7. Maximize the REVRPT file to make it easier to work with.
8. Copy the formula in cell B5 of REVRPT to cell B6.
9. Now copy the range B5..B6 to C5..D6.

Way cool! We created an instant link to three files just by copying that single original formula. Your screen should match the one portrayed in Figure 8-14.

Figure 8-14. The master worksheet before the *Update Links* command is issued.

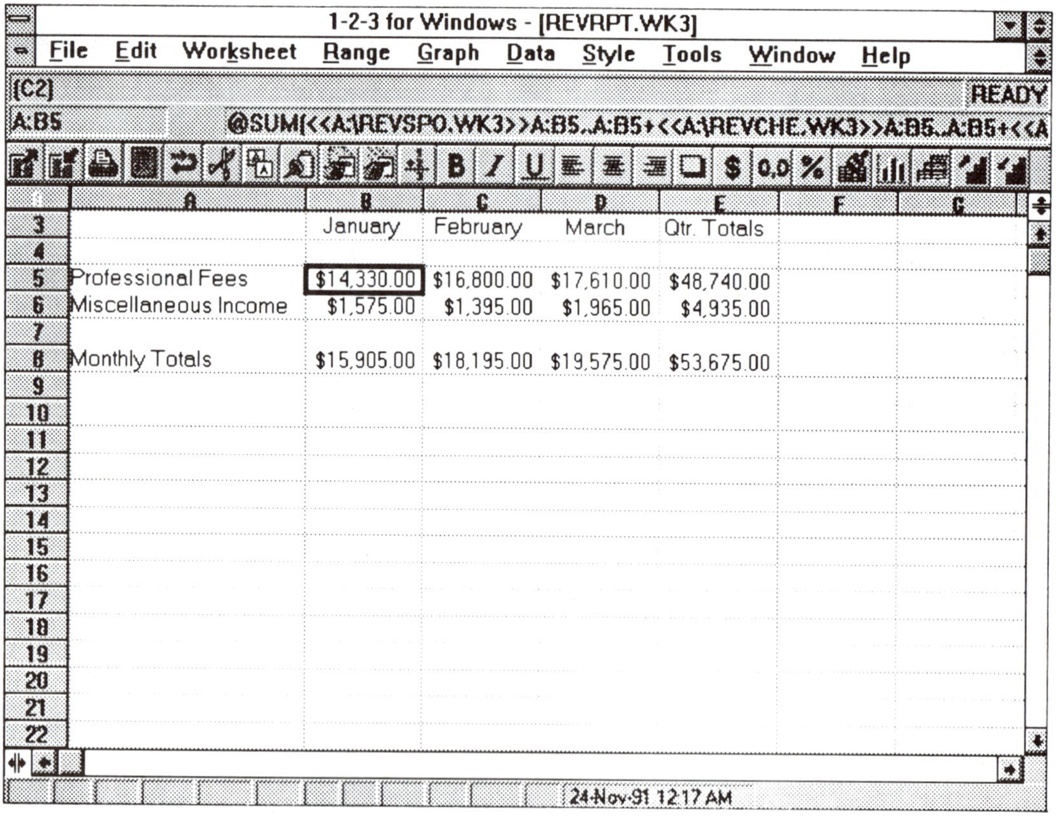

Chapter 8 Working with Multiple Worksheets and Files **287**

> • **HINT**
>
> You can also use range names as file-link references, which, if you are referencing multiple cell ranges, can help avoid linking errors. As discussed earlier in the book, it's easier to remember a range name than a cell address.

Saving Multiple Files Simultaneously

With multiple files open, it would be nice to be able to save all of them at once, instead of having to save each one individually. Hey, this is 1-2-3. No problem.

1. Select *Save As…* from the File menu.
2. Click on the *Save All* button.

The *Save All* button saves all open files that have been modified. If the files already exist on the disk, you'll be asked to confirm that you want to replace them. That's it.

3. When the dialog box appears asking what you want to do with the existing file on disk, click the *Replace* button.
4. Close REVRPT since we're through with it for now.

Recalculating Linked Formulas

As we said before, the purpose of this project is to be able to receive updated files from the three divisions and automatically link the new numbers to the master file. That works fine if all four files are in memory (open) at once.

But Rose doesn't want to have to take the time to open each of the division files just to see the new consolidated figures. And she doesn't have to. We've already created the links in the master file. All that's necessary is to open the master file and update the links.

To show you how this works, we'll change some figures in the three division files and save and close them. Then we'll open the master file and dazzle you.

1. Select the REVCDA file.
2. In B5, enter: **6820**

3. In C5, enter: **7470**
4. In D5, enter: **8350**
5. In B6, enter: **730**
6. In C6, enter: **510**
7. In D6, enter: **950**
8. Save and close the file.
9. Select the REVCHE file.
10. In B5, enter: **4210**
11. In C5, enter: **5312**
12. In D5, enter: **6160**
13. In B6, enter: **340**
14. In C6, enter: **620**
15. In D6, enter: **490**
16. Save and close the file.
17. Select the REVSPO file.
18. In B5, enter: **7590**
19. In C5, enter: **6635**
20. In D5, enter: **7120**
21. In B6, enter: **880**
22. In C6, enter: **530**
23. In D6, enter: **910**
24. Save and close the file.

All the files are now closed. Let's imagine that Rose just received the three updated files. All she needs to do, after copying them to her computer's disk, is to open the master file and update the links.

25. Open the file A:\REVRPT.

The numbers should look familiar; they haven't changed since we entered the original numbers in the three files. Pay close attention now, and you'll see the numbers updated, like magic, right before your eyes!

26. Select *Update Links* from the *Administration*, File menu.

The **Update Links** command will automatically recalculate linked formulas in all active files (all of the files currently in memory).

Your floppy disk drive will chug away for a little while before the new numbers appear. In real life, all the files would probably be copied to Rose's computer's hard disk drive, which would update the links many times faster than a floppy disk.

Figure 8-15 displays the updated worksheet. Mighty impressive! If you're not impressed yet, you've been taking the wrong class.

Figure 8–15. The worksheet displays updated figures.

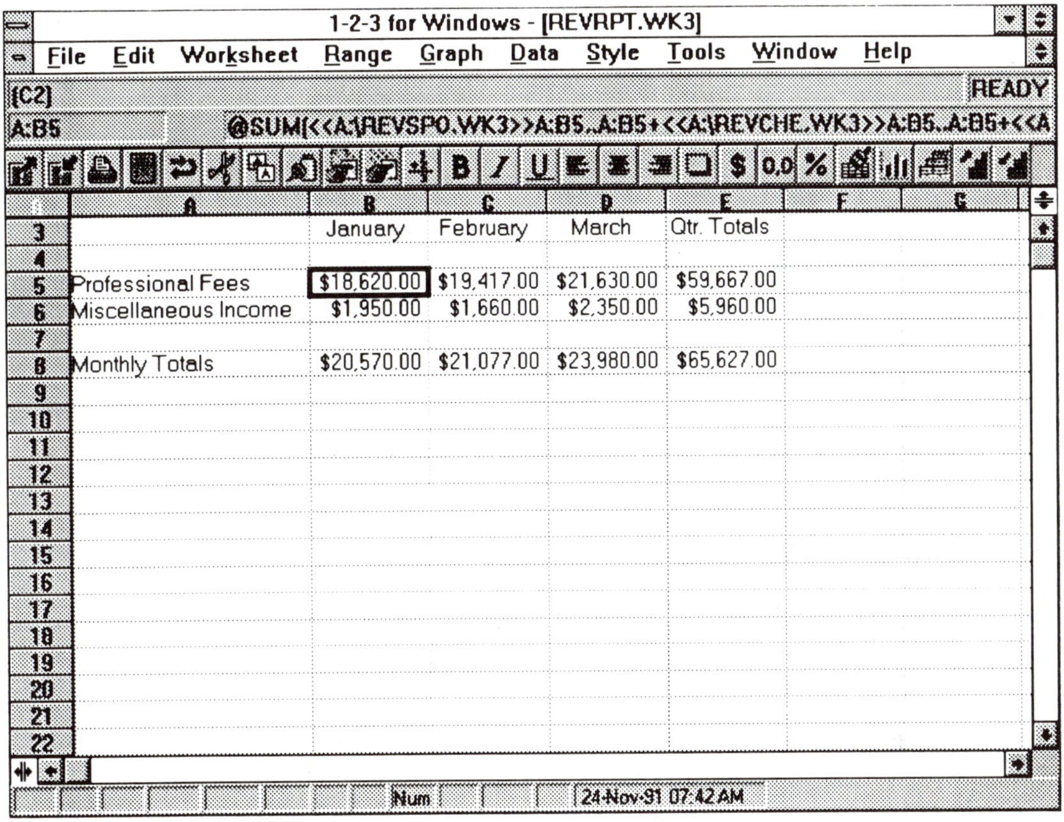
1-2-3 for Windows - [REVRPT.WK3]
File Edit Worksheet Range Graph Data Style Tools Window Help
(C2)
READY
A:B5
@SUM(<<A:\REVSPO.WK3>>A:B5..A:B5+<<A:\REVCHE.WK3>>A:B5..A:B5+<<A
January February March Qtr. Totals
Professional Fees $18,620.00 $19,417.00 $21,630.00 $59,667.00
Miscellaneous Income $1,950.00 $1,660.00 $2,350.00 $5,960.00
Monthly Totals $20,570.00 $21,077.00 $23,980.00 $65,627.00
Num
24-Nov-91 07:42 AM

27. Select the range A1..F8.
28. Change the header to: **Lab 8-2**
29. Save the file again.
30. Print the range.
31. Exit 1-2-3 for Windows.

KEY TERMS

File-linking formula A formula that references data in another file or files.

File reference A file name (which may include the full path), enclosed in << >> (double angle brackets). File references are used in formulas and commands to refer to files other than the current one.

Insert The Worksheet menu command used to insert additional rows or columns into the current worksheet, or to add additional worksheets to the current worksheet file.

Pane The 1-2-3 function key (F6) that moves the cell pointer between all windows (or panes) displayed using the Window Split dialog box. If you've used Window Split Vertical or Window Split Horizontal, F6 will move you between the two sections of the current worksheet. If you've chosen Perspective, F6 will move you sequentially through all the worksheets in the file.

Perspective The command in the Window Split dialog box that allows you to view three worksheets at the same time.

Synchronize The command in the Window Split dialog box that causes all worksheets in the file to scroll simultaneously.

Template A worksheet with preset formats, labels, and formulas that can be used to build similar worksheets quickly.

Three-dimensional worksheets The 1-2-3 feature that enables you to work with multiple worksheets in one file.

Tile The Window menu command that brings all currently open files into view, with each file taking up an equal amount of the workspace area.

Update Links The File menu command that updates linked formulas in all active files automatically.

Zoom (Alt+F6) The function key that enlarges the current pane to full size or reduces it to its original size (this key is a toggle, which means that you use the same key to enlarge *and* reduce the pane). There is also a Zoom option in the Window Display Options dialog box that allows you to specify the Zoom percentage.

EXERCISES

8–1. The following exercise will give you the chance to practice material you learned in Lab 8–1.

   a. Start Windows and launch 1-2-3 for Windows if it's not already running.

Crazy Donny's Computerama is a discount computer retailer. There are two divisions, both at the same address. One division sells computer hardware and the other sells software. Donny has been going crazy trying to come up with a way to create separate spreadsheets for the two divisions that could then be consolidated for an overall view of the company's business.

Of course, Donny wouldn't be having this problem if he had upgraded to a spreadsheet program more recent than Supercalc on an Osborne portable. Donny's accountant advised him to donate the Osborne to his favorite charity, SGCP/MD, which stands for the Support Group for CP/M Diehards.

Don upgraded to a 386 computer and bought Lotus 1-2-3 for Windows. 1-2-3's 3-D capabilities will take care of his consolidation problem nicely.

We'll create one worksheet for the software division, and then we'll duplicate its format for the hardware and consolidation worksheets.

   b. In cell A1, enter: **Crazy Donny's Computerama - Software**
   c. In B3, enter **January**, in C3 enter **February**, and in D3 enter **March**
   d. In A5, enter **IBM Compatible**, in A6 enter **Macintosh**, and in A7 enter **CP/M**

Chapter 8 Working with Multiple Worksheets and Files

      e. In cell A9, enter: **Total**
      f. Widen column A to about **13**, until the widest label fits in the column.
      g. Format the range B3..D3 for center alignment.
      h. To total software sales for the three types of computers, enter **@SUM(B5..B7)** in cell B9.
      i. Copy the formula in cell B9 to the range C9 through D9.
      j. Format the range B5..D9 as currency.

That takes care of the basic structure of our file. Now we just need to create the other two worksheets, one for the hardware division, and one to consolidate the numbers.

      k. Select *Insert...* from the Worksheet menu.
      l. Click in the *Sheet* radio button and enter **2** in the *Quantity* text box.

You already know you can move between the sheets with Ctrl+PgUp or Ctrl+PgDn, but let's get a better perspective (sorry 'bout that—we couldn't resist) on these sheets with the Perspective view.

      m. Select *Split...* from the Window menu, click in the *Perspective* radio button, and then click *OK*.

We'll copy the first worksheet, sheet A, to sheets B and C and then modify B and C to meet our needs.

      n. Select the range A:A1..A:D9.
      o. Select *Quick Copy...* from the Edit menu.
      p. In the text box, enter **B:A1..C:A1** and click *OK*.

All right! Three identical worksheets. Well, not *exactly* identical. You'll notice the column width in column A of the two new sheets didn't change. That's because column widths are not transferred when you copy a range.

    We can fix this easily using the Group mode. If you use this feature in your real worksheets, be very careful. If will instantly copy *all* formatting information in the current worksheet to all active worksheets. That's great if you want all the worksheets to be identical, but it can also be dangerous if you don't intend to make such sweeping changes.

      q. Select *Global Settings...* from the Worksheet menu, click in the *Group mode* text box, and click *OK*.

Instantly, the column widths in the two new sheets are updated to match sheet A. It's a good idea to turn off Group mode when you're through with it so you won't inadvertently wreak future havoc.

Let's zoom in on sheet C and add some numbers.

- **r.** To toggle off the Group mode, select the *Global Settings...* command from the worksheet menu, click in the *Group Mode* check box, and click *OK*.
- **s.** Click anywhere in sheet C and press the Zoom key combination, Alt+F6.
- **t.** In cell C:B5, enter:**4820**
- **u.** In cell C:C5, enter:**3270**
- **v.** In cell C:D5, enter:**4990**
- **w.** In cell C:B6, enter:**3130**
- **x.** In cell C:C6, enter:**3460**
- **y.** In cell C:D6, enter:**2210**
- **z.** In cell C:B7, enter:**0**
- **aa.** In cell C:C7, enter:**0**
- **ab.** In cell C:D7, enter:**0**

CP/M products haven't sold very well for a few years now, but Crazy Donny just can't bear to write off the leftover inventory.

- **ac.** Let's Zoom back out by pressing the Zoom key again, Alt+F6.
- **ad.** Make B the current worksheet and Zoom in on it.
- **ae.** Edit the label in B:A1 to read: **Crazy Donny's Computerama - Hardware**
- **af.** In cell B:B5, enter:**48735**
- **ag.** In cell B:C5, enter:**65420**
- **ah.** In cell B:D5, enter:**53270**
- **ai.** In cell B:B6, enter:**12130**
- **aj.** In cell B:C6, enter:**11785**
- **ak.** In cell B:D6, enter:**9480**
- **al.** In cell B:B7, enter:**0**
- **am.** In cell B:C7, enter:**0**
- **an.** In cell B:D7, enter:**0**
- **ao.** Zoom back out and click in sheet A.
- **ap.** Edit the label in A1 to read: **Crazy Donny's Computerama - Master**
- **aq.** Click in cell A:B5, which is where we'll enter a formula with a 3-D range.
- **ar.** Type:**@SUM(**

Chapter 8 Working with Multiple Worksheets and Files

- **as.** Click in B:B5 and type:+
- **at.** Click in C:B5, type**)** and press Enter.
- **au.** Copy the formula in A:B5 to the range A:B5..A:D7.

All that's left to do is save and print this stuff.

- **av.** Press Ctrl+Home to move to cell A:A1. Press F4 (ABS) to anchor the cell pointer, then press End and Ctrl+Home to select the entire group of sheets.
- **aw.** Create a header with the title **Exercise 8-1** and a footer with your name, followed by the label: **1-2-3 for Windows**
- **ax.** Select *Save As...* from the File menu, and save this file as **A:\EXER8-1**
- **ay.** Print the selected range.
- **az.** Exit 1-2-3 if you're not going on to the next exercise right now.

8-2. The following exercise will give you the chance to practice material you learned in Lab 8-2. To complete this exercise, you'll need the file A:\MACROS we created in Chapter 7.

- **a.** Start Windows and launch 1-2-3 for Windows if it's not already running.

One of the best uses of 1-2-3's multiple file capability is to be able to access your standard macros no matter what you're doing. Reading a macro file into memory makes your macros available at all times.

- **b.** Open the file A:\MACROS.

Now all of the macros in this file can be used in any other file we're working on.

- **c.** Select *New* from the File menu.
- **d.** In cell A1, type the name of this book, **Working with Lotus 1-2-3 for Windows** and press the Enter key.

Now we'll put today's date in cell B1, using the macro we created in Chapter 7.

- **e.** Click in B1 and press Alt+F3.
- **f.** In the Tools Macro Run dialog box, double-click on <<*MACROS.WK3*>>, the file name of our macro file, and then double-click on *DATE* to play the date macro.

Great, but now we can only see part of our book title. That will never do. We need to widen the column.

    g. Click anywhere in column A and press Ctrl+C to play our column width macro.

    h. In the Worksheet Column Width dialog box, enter the number you want for this column (29 should do it) and then press the Enter key.

You can see how much easier it is to access Ctrl+key macros than named macros.

    i. Select the range A1..B1.
    j. Use the header *Exercise 8-2* and a footer with your name, followed by the label: **1-2-3 for Windows**
    k. Save this file as **A:\EXER8-2**
    l. Print the selected range.
    m. Exit 1-2-3 for Windows.

REVIEW QUESTIONS

True or False Questions

1. **T F** New worksheets can be added to a file by using the *File Open* command.

2. **T F** Before inserting a new worksheet, you must specify a range.

3. **T F** You can tell which worksheet is current by looking at the cell address.

4. **T F** When Synchronize is on, any formula that you enter in the current worksheet will automatically be copied to all worksheets in the file.

5. **T F** Ctrl+Home is the keystroke combination that moves you to cell A1 of worksheet A (the cell address would be A:A1).

6. **T F** You can move between multiple files by using the scroll bar.

7. **T F** The *Tile* command brings all open files into view.

8. **T F** A file reference is the line at the top of each worksheet that displays the file name.

9. **T F** Issuing the *Tile* command makes it easier to create a formula by pointing to any cell in any open file.

10. **T F** Range names can be used as file link references.

Chapter 8 Working with Multiple Worksheets and Files

Multiple Choice Questions

1. Three-dimensional worksheets allow you to
   a. Place a 3-D border around the outside of your charts
   b. Link multiple worksheets into one file
   c. View graphs in a special 3-D mode
   d. a and c

2. The maximum number of worksheets you can have in a file is
   a. 10
   b. 2,054
   c. 256
   d. Unlimited

3. By default, where are new worksheets inserted in relation to the current worksheet?
   a. Before
   b. After
   c. Added to bottom of current worksheet
   d. None of the above

4. How do you move to the next worksheet?
   a. Ctrl+PgDn
   b. Click in the worksheet (from Perspective mode)
   c. Click on the *Next Worksheet* SmartIcon
   d. All of the above

5. The Window Split dialog box gives you options for
   a. Dividing one worksheet into two so that you end up with two separate files.
   b. Viewing two different sections of one worksheet.
   c. Placing three worksheets on the screen at one time.
   d. b and c

6. You can reference a cell in another worksheet by
   a. Entering the cell and worksheet address of the cell you're referencing in the cell where you want the reference to appear
   b. Using the Multiple Worksheet Reference dialog box
   c. Clicking on the *Cell Reference* SmartIcon
   d. None of the above

7. The best way to use a template is to
   a. Use the *Save As...* command to create new files from it
   b. Copy all of the formulas from the template to the new file
   c. Enter all of your data, and then retrieve the template into your file
   d. a or c

8. Which File menu command is used to bring additional files into memory?

   a. Retrieve
   b. Combine From
   c. Import From
   d. Open

9. A file reference must contain

   a. The file name
   b. The directory names
   c. The drive name
   d. All of the above

10. The *Update Links* command will recalculate linked formulas in

    a. All active files
    b. Just the current file
    c. All files on your hard disk
    d. All files in the current directory

INDEX

@Functions
  defined, 76
  using, 76–78
@Functions, on Help menu, 31
@STD, 77
@SUM, 76, 77
@TODAY, 246

A

About 1-2-3... command, 8, 9, 32
Absolute cell address, defined, 114
Active window, defined, 20
Address
  cell, 48
  range, 61
Address box, defined, 49
Add to Sheet... command, 192
Aligning cells, 147–149
Align Left icon, 147
Alignment... command, 148
Align Right icon, 147
Annotate... command, 38
Application icons, defined, 6
Applications window, defined, 5
Arithmetic operators, defined, 73
Arrows, adding to graph, 198–200
Ascending order, defined, 215

B

Back button, defined, 34
Bar
  menu, 12
  scroll, 13
  title, 12
Bar Graph icon, 186
Borders
  adding, 150
  defined, 80
Boxes
  address, 49
  check, 10
  contents, 49
  control-menu, 12
  dialog. *See* Dialog box
  drop-down list, 10
  list, 10
  text, 10
  maximize, 12
  minimize, 13
  split, 13
Browse button, defined, 35
Buttons
  command, 10
  radio, 10

C

Cancel button, 55
Cascade command, 18
Cascading menu, defined, 170

Cell
  aligning, 147–149
  clearing a, 100–104
  current, 49
  defined, 48
  protecting, 165–169
  selecting a, 50–51
Cell address
  absolute, 114
  defined, 48
  relative, 114
Cell contents
  cutting, 114–116
  pasting, 114–116
Cell entry, changing, 96–100
Cell pointer, defined, 49
Cell ranges, naming, 169–174
Cell referencing, 76
Cell styles, changing, 143–159
Center icon, 147
Charts
  defined, 181
  pie, 186
Check boxes, 10
Clear command, 101
Clear Special... command, 103
Clicking, defined, 5
Clipboard, defined, 93
Close command, 30
Closing a window, 29–30
Collapsing a window to an icon, 21–23

297

Color... command, 155
Colors, altering, 155–157
Colors... command, 202
Column letters, 48
Columns
   deleting, 104–108
   freezing, 162–165
   inserting, 108–113
Column width
   changing, 57–60
   defined, 58
Column Width... command, 60
Command buttons, 10
Commands
   defined, 7
   entering in a macro, 240–242
   global, 62
   macro, 241
Confirm button, 55
Contents box, defined, 49
Control-menu box, defined, 12
Control panel, defined, 49
Copy command, 38
Copying data, 118–129
Creating a new worksheet window, 18
Criteria range
   creating a, 218–221
   defined, 218
Current cell, defined, 49
Cutting cell contents, 114–116

D

Data
   copying, 118–129
   editing, 96–100
   formatting numeric, 139–142
   hiding, 142–143
Database
   basics, 211–212
   defined, 211
   deleting records from, 229–230
   entering records in, 212–213
   extracting records from, 226–229
   searching a, 218–226
   searching for values, 224–226
   sorting a, 213–217
Data labels, defined, 181
Data range, adding another, 194–196
Data set, defined, 182
Date, current, macro to insert, 245–249
Default, defined, 58
Define... command, 38
Delete... command, 104
Deleting columns and rows, 104–108
Delimiters, defined, 225
Descending order, defined, 215
Desktop, defined, 2
Dialog box
   defined, 8
   understanding, 8–10
Display options, changing, 150–158
Display Options... command, 151
Document icons, defined, 5
Document window, defined, 5
Double-clicking, defined, 5
Dragging, defined, 5
Drop-down list boxes, 10
Drop-down menu, defined, 8

E

Editing data, 96–100
Edit line, defined, 49
EDIT mode, 87, 96, 98, 100
Electronic spreadsheet, defined, 48–50
Enlarging a window, 24
Entering values, 69–73
ERROR mode, 87
Exit command, 10
Exit Windows... command, 11
Expanding an icon to a window, 23–24

F

Field, defined, 212
File, saving a worksheet, 65–67
File-linking formulas, defined, 279
File reference, defined, 284
Files, worksheet. *See* Worksheet files
FILES mode, 87
FIND mode, 87
Font... command, 144
Fonts
   changing, 143–147
   defined, 143
Footer, defined, 78
Format... command, 139
Format line, defined, 49
Formatting
   defined, 139
   a graph, 192
   numeric data, 139–142
   ranges, 138–143
Formulas
   constructing, 73–76
   defined, 73
   file-linking, 279
   linking worksheet files with, 284–287
   linking worksheets with, 270–277
   link, recalculating, 287–289
For Upgraders, on Help menu, 32
Frame, defined, 12
Freezing
   columns and rows, 162–165
   defined, 162

G

Global commands, defined, 62
Global formats, using, 162
Global Settings... command, 62
Go To... command, 163
Graph
   adding text and arrows to, 198–200
   adding three-dimensional effect to, 200–201
   adding title to, 186–187
   creating, 181–194
   defined, 181
   enhancing, 194–204
   formatting, 192
   line, 185

Index

299

placing in a worksheet, 192–193
selecting different type of, 186
selecting patterns for, 201–203
sizing, 203–204
types of, 182
updating, 194
Graphical user interface, defined, 1
Grid lines, controlling display of, 151–152
Group Range... command, 197
Group window, defined, 3

H

Hatches... command, 202
Header, defined, 78
Headings... command, 186
Height, row, 64
Help
　browsing in, 35
　defined, 30
　getting, 30–38
　going back in, 34–35
　printing, 37–38
　searching in, 35–37
　starting, 30–32
Help Index, checking, 32–34
Hiding data, 142–143
Home position, 50
How Do I?, on Help menu, 32

I

Icon Palette
　adding icon to, 253
　changing position of, 253–255
　defined, 92
Icons
　adding to Icon Palette, 253
　application, 6
　collapsing window to, 21–23
　defined, 5
　document, 5
　expanding to window, 23–24
　program item, 5

recognizing, 5–6
Index, checking Help, 32–34
Index, on Help menu, 31
Index command, 32
Input range, defined, 218
Insert... command, 108, 266
Inserting columns and rows, 108–113

K

Key
　primary sort, 215
　secondary sort, 217
Keyboard, on Help menu, 31
Keystrokes
　common, and macro symbols, 242
　entering in a macro, 240–242
　worksheet navigation, 270

L

Label
　adding, 187–191
　data, 181
　defined, 54
　entering, 54–57
LABEL mode, 55, 87
Label-prefix character, defined, 54
Legend... command, 197
Legends
　creating, 196–198
　defined, 182
Line
　edit, 49
　format, 49
Line graph, creating, 185
List boxes, 10
Logical operators, defined, 224
Lotus 1-2-3 for Windows, 1
　quitting, 10–11
　starting, 6–7

M

Macro
　assigning to SmartIcon, 249–255

defined, 237
documenting a, 244–245
entering commands and keystrokes in, 240–242
to insert current date, 245–249
naming, 242–243
pausing for input, 255–258
planning, 238–239
saving a, 244
testing a, 244
writing simple, 238–249
Macro command, defined, 241
Macro name, defined, 243
Macros, on Help menu, 31
Maximize box, defined, 12
Menu
　cascading, 170
　defined, 7
　drop-down, 8
　working with, 7–8
Menu bar, defined, 7, 12
MENU mode, 87
Microsoft Windows
　defined, 1
　ending session in, 11–12
　getting around in, 2–12
　starting, 2–3
Minimize box, defined, 13
Mode indicator, defined, 49
Move cells... command, 116
Move cells... icon, using, 116–118
Moving
　data, 113–118
　window, 25–26
Multiple files, saving simultaneously, 287
Multiple worksheet files, using, 279–289. *See also* Worksheet files
Multiple worksheets, using, 264–278

N

Name, macro, 243
Name range, creating, 169–170
New command, 18
Numeric formats, 140

O

Open... command, 67
Open... icon, 94
Opening a worksheet, 67–68
Operator
  arithmetic, 73
  defined, 73
  logical, 224
Order of precedence, overriding, 119–121
Output range, defined, 226

P

Page
  previewing, 82–84
  setting up, 79–81
Page Setup... command, 79
Panes, defined, 270
Password, defined, 165
Pasting cell contents, 114–116
Patterns, selecting for graph, 201–203
Perspective view, 267–269
  defined, 267
Pie chart, creating, 186
Pie Chart icon, 186
Point, defined, 64
Pointer
  cell, 49
  defined, 3
  shapes of, 3–4
  using, 3–5
POINT mode, 61, 87
Precedence numbers, defined, 119
Preview... command, 79
Previewing a page, 82–84
Primary sort key, defined, 215
Print... command, 79
Print icon, 95
Printing
  group of worksheets, 277–278
  Help, 37–38
  worksheet, 78–85
Print Topic command, 37
Program item icons, defined, 5
Program Manager, defined, 3
Proofing a worksheet, 129–131

Protected ranges, defined, 165
Protecting cells, 165–169

Q

Query, defined, 218
Query... command, 219
Quick Copy... command, using, 121–129
Quick Copy icon, 121

R

Radio buttons, 10
Range
  criteria. See Criteria range
  defined, 61
  input, 218
  output, 226
  selecting a, 61–64
Range address, defined, 61
Range name
  deleting, 172–174
  editing, 171–172
  formatting, 138–143
  undefined, 173
  using, 171
Range Name Create... command, 169
Range name definition, defined, 170
READY mode, 55, 61, 66, 70, 85, 87, 113
Recalculating linked formulas, 287–289
Record
  defined, 211
  deleting from database, 229–230
  entering in database, 212–213
  extracting from database, 226–229
  finding with wildcards, 221–224
Reducing a window, 24–25
Referencing, cell, 76
Relative cell address, defined, 114
Restore command, 23

Row height, defined, 64
Row Height... command, 64
Row numbers, 48
Rows
  deleting, 104–108
  freezing, 162–165
  inserting, 108–113

S

Save As... command, 65
Save Changes check box, 11
Save command, 73
Save icon, 94
Saving
  macro, 244
  worksheet file, 65–67
Scroll bars, defined, 13
Scrolling
  contents of a window, 14–16
  methods of, 16
Search button, defined, 35–37
Searching
  database, 218–226
  in Help, 35–37
Secondary sort key, defined, 217
Selecting
  cell, 50–51
  range, 61–64
  window, 20–21
Shading, using, 158–159
Shading... command, 158
Sizing
  graph, 203–204
  window, 27–29
SmartIcon... command, 96
SmartIcons
  assigning macro to, 249–255
  defined, 92
  using, 92–96
Sort... command, 215
Sorting
  database, 213–217
  defined, 213
Sort key
  primary, 215
  secondary, 217
  using two, 217–218
Split box, defined, 13

Split... command, 267
Splitting a worksheet window, 16–18
Spreadsheet, electronic, 48–50
Spreadsheet basics, 47–50
Subtitle, defined, 181
Switch To... command, 21
Synchronize command, 267

T

Template, defined, 279
Text boxes, 10
Three-dimensional effect, adding to graph, 200–201
Three-dimensional worksheets
  defined, 263
  understanding, 263–264
Tilde, defined, 241
Tile command, 18, 283
Title
  adding to a graph, 186–187
  defined, 181
Title bar, defined, 12
Titles... command, 163
Transcript window, defined, 258
Type... command, 200

U

Undefined range name, defined, 173
Undo command, 102
Undo icon, 102
Unprotect... command, 166
Unprotected ranges, defined, 165
Update Links command, 288
User Setup... command, 102

Using Help, on Help menu, 31

V

VALUE mode, 70, 74, 75, 77, 87
Values
  defined, 69
  entering, 69–73
  searching database for, 224–226

W

WAIT mode, 66, 87
"What-if?," 48
Wildcard
  defined, 221
  finding records with, 221–224
WIN, defined, 2
Window
  active, 20
  application, 5
  arranging worksheet, 18–20
  closing a, 29–30
  collapsing to an icon, 21–23
  controlling, 12–30
  creating a new worksheet, 18
  document, 5
  enlarging a, 24
  expanding an icon to a, 23–24
  group, 3
  moving a, 25–26
  recognizing elements of, 12–13
  recognizing types of, 5
  reducing a, 24–25
  scrolling contents of a, 14–16
  selecting a, 20–21

sizing a, 27–29
splitting a worksheet, 16–18
transcript, 258
Worksheet
  adding, 266–267
  defined, 7
  getting around in, 50–53
  linking with formulas, 270–277
  moving among, 269–270
  multiple, using, 264–278
  navigating in a, 51–53
  navigation keystrokes, 270
  opening a, 67–68
  placing a graph in a, 192–193
  printing a, 78–85
  printing group of, 277–278
  proofing a, 129–131
Worksheet files
  creating, 279–282
  linking with formulas, 284–287
  moving among active, 282–284
  opening additional, 282
  saving, 65–67
Worksheet frame, defined, 48
Workspace, defined, 13

X

X axis, defined, 181

Y

Y axis, defined, 181

Z

Zoom, defined, 270